Land Reform and Social Revolution in Bolivia

PRAEGER SPECIAL STUDIES IN
INTERNATIONAL ECONOMICS AND DEVELOPMENT

Land Reform and Social Revolution in Bolivia

Dwight B. Heath
Charles J. Erasmus
Hans C. Buechler

FREDERICK A. PRAEGER, Publishers
New York · Washington · London

The purpose of the Praeger Special Studies is to make specialized research monographs in U.S. and international economics and politics
available to the academic, business, and government communities. For
further information, write to the Special Projects Division, Frederick
A. Praeger, Publishers, 111 Fourth Avenue, New York, N.Y. 10003.

FREDERICK A. PRAEGER, PUBLISHERS
111 Fourth Avenue, New York, N.Y. 10003, U.S.A.
5, Cromwell Place, London S.W. 7, England

Published in the United States of America in 1969
by Frederick A. Praeger, Inc., Publishers

© 1969 by Frederick A. Praeger, Inc.

Library of Congress Catalog Card Number: 68-18916

Printed in the United States of America

CONTENTS

PART I: INTRODUCTION TO BOLIVIA AND HER LAW OF AGRARIAN REFORM

Chapter

PART V: CONCLUSIONS

LIST OF TABLES

LIST OF MAPS

Land Reform and Social Revolution in Bolivia

INTRODUCTION

—Dwight B. Heath

PLAN OF THE STUDY

This volume is a report of the first coordinated study
on land tenure in various regions of Bolivia. A brief
general introduction to Bolivia is followed by a discussion
of the background and meaning of the nation's agrarian
reform law. A brief history of the law provides context
for the first detailed paraphrase of the decree, and some
of the problems of administration are briefly outlined.
The major portion of the book includes detailed ethnographic descriptions of some important regions in Bolivia
which differ ecologically, historically, and culturally.
Although emphasizing land reform and cultural change,
these are among the most detailed and accurate studies
available for the country to date. Each section can be
profitably read alone, although the entire book is unified
in theme as well as subject matter.

The study was conducted under the auspices of the
Land Tenure Center, University of Wisconsin, in an
effort to provide basic data on patterns of land tenure and
use in key regions of Bolivia. In order to understand and
evaluate the report, it is necessary to know the background
of the research project and the purposes and methods of
the investigators.

BACKGROUND

Agrarian reform has often been cited as a major preliminary step in virtually any program of economic development for underdeveloped nations. This implies widespread

agreement that patterns of land tenure are immediately related to patterns of economic, social, and political organization, especially in areas where agriculture is the predominant occupation. Such consensus does not prevail, however,
with respect to the exact nature of this relationship, nor
the actual consequences of change in patterns of land tenure.
The most effective way of evaluating these factors is to
study changes which have come about in specific situations
where agrarian reform has been implemented.

     Bolivia provides just such a case, where agrarian re-
form was instituted in 1953 as one major plank of a political
program avowedly aimed at effecting economic development
within the context of a sweeping social revolution.

     The abundant literature by Bolivian authors on the
subject (listed in Cardozo, 1962), is predominantly theoretic
or polemic and offers little evidence on the application of
the law in the countryside. The historic and economic
background of the decree has been well summarized by the
distinguished Mexican economist Edmundo Flores (1954),
who was a United Nations advisor during the early administration of the reform. In the same paper, he briefly outlined the principal articles of the law and provided a realistic evaluation of some problems which might ensue. A
very different interpretation of the historical context of the
law was offered by Richard W. Patch (1956), who has continued to publish information on the broad impact of this
and associated reforms (in several sources, but excellently
summarized in Patch, 1960). Among the outcomes of my
anthropological research in 1956-57 were a critical summary
of successes and shortcomings of the agrarian reform
throughout Bolivia, in terms of the aims specified within
the text of the law itself (Heath, 1959a), as well as intensive
study of changes in land tenure in one area (see, e. g.
Heath, 1960a). Some of the principal problems in the
administration of the reform were incisively reviewed by
F. A. O. advisor Casto Ferragut (1963), who also offered
sound recommendations for action. Despite the value of
these individual contributions, and the mass of juridical
and philosophic studies, there was no significant body of
substantive data dealing with actual behavior and attitudes

at the local level. *

It was clear that a reexamination of the Bolivian
experience should be fruitful at the end of a decade of
agrarian reform under an administration which was proudly
both "nationalistic" and "revolutionary."** The relevance
of such a study for the problematic political and economic
situations in Bolivia is obvious, but it is also pertinent for
other Latin American countries, most of which have only
recently begun land reform or intend to do so shortly.

A research proposal was the subject of discussion at a
Land Tenure Center Seminar in November, 1962. Among
participants were Thomas Carroll and Casto Ferragut,
both of the Inter-American Development Bank, Edmundo
Flores of Princeton University, Dwight B. Heath of Brown
University, and Richard W. Patch of American Universities
Field Staff; portions of the proceedings have been published
by the Land Tenure Center (1963). The proposal was
accepted in February, and the staff were selected to do
three months' field work between June and September, 1963.
Analysis and writing were completed in April, 1964, after
which minor editorial revisions were made in all initial
drafts. Major revision of the manuscripts was completed
in July, 1964, and the work of each author reflects his

----

*An important exception to this generalization is the ex-
cellent work by William F. Carter, in several Aymara
communities on the northern altiplano (Carter 1963, 1965).
He is correct in emphasizing continuity in the indigenous
communities (a "comunidad indígena" is a corporate group
holding common title to lands since colonial times), although he also notes that "...patterns of community-wide
leadership and cooperation have actually changed,
particularly in the case of the ex-haciendas" (Carter,
1965:57).

**The political party which came to power by revolution in
1952 and dominated the government continuously until November, 1964, is the Movimiento Nacional Revolucionario
(MNR, Nationalist Revolutionary Movement). Agrarian
reform had been an important plank in their platform
since before they gained control of the government.

individual interests, field methods, and expository style,
although many of our comparisons and conclusions grew
out of mutually fruitful discussion. Revisions were introduced and the findings were updated early in 1968. *

METHODS

Anthropological techniques of direct observation, partic-
cipation, and interviewing, supplemented by documentary
research and surveys, have been used in this study. Legal
and administrative documents afforded insight into statutory
regulation, titles, taxation, and so forth. Actual patterns
of land tenure and use were discerned from observation and
sampling. Other actions, beliefs, and attitudes with regard
to economic, political, and other social relations were
observed and secured through interviews, collected in
accordance with a loose schedule designed to be flexible
enough to allow for the demographic, geographic, and
cultural diversity of the country. We hoped that such data
could be coordinated with existing cadastral surveys, but
found none available. It was obvious that rigorous random
sampling would be impossible in such a small-scale study;
so representative sampling was applied in each area where
we worked, since any systematic approach to Bolivia must
include information from regions which contrast markedly
in climate, terrain, physical and cultural ecology, history,
and customs.

The zones chosen for study were the northern altiplano
and yungas, valleys around Chuquisaca and Tarija, eastern
lowlands (or Oriente) and valleys around Cochabamba.
(See Map 1). The northern altiplano is important as an
area of dense population in which reallocation of land was
effected relatively early. The culture of Aymara-speakers
there has often been inappropriately generalized as the
"typical" Bolivian pattern, and the little data available on
pre-reform land tenure usually relates to this region. In
the yungas are people of the same cultural tradition, living
in a markedly different ecological situation, who are more

_____

*Publication of this book was supported in part by grants
from Brown University and the Institute for Cross-Cultural
Research.

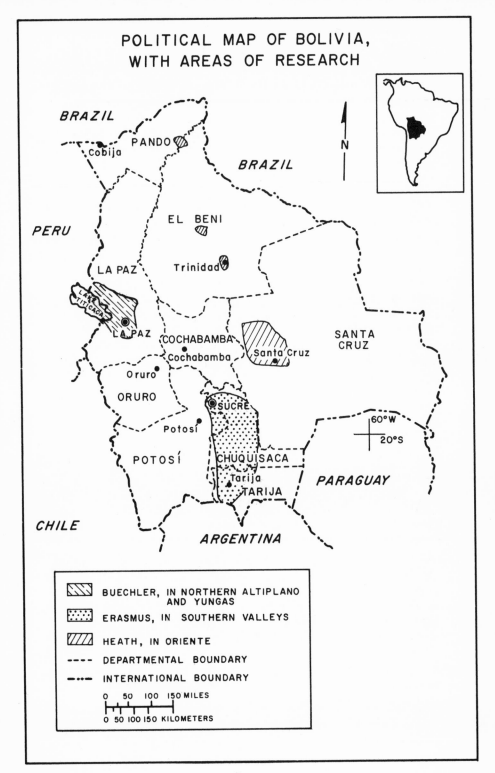

POLITICAL MAP OF BOLIVIA,
WITH AREAS OF RESEARCH

BRAZIL

PANDO

Cobija

BRAZIL

PERU

EL BENI

Trinidad

LA PAZ

LAKE TITICACA

LA PAZ

COCHABAMBA

Cochabamba

Santa Cruz

SANTA CRUZ

Oruro

ORURO

SUCRE

60°W
20°S

Potosí

POTOSÍ

CHUQUISACA

Tarija

TARIJA

PARAGUAY

CHILE

ARGENTINA

BUECHLER, IN NORTHERN ALTIPLANO AND YUNGAS
ERASMUS, IN SOUTHERN VALLEYS
HEATH, IN ORIENTE
DEPARTMENTAL BOUNDARY
INTERNATIONAL BOUNDARY

0   50   100 150 MILES

0 50 100 150 KILOMETERS

concerned with commercial agriculture than those who eke
out a meager subsistence on the altiplano. Chuquisaca and
Tarija departments in southern Bolivia had been virtually
neglected in terms of social science research, but it was
apparent that the Quechua-speakers of this area were far
less politically active and less militant about land reform
than were their relatives in Cochabamba, an area of similar
climate and terrain immediately to the north. The eastern
lowlands deserved special notice because they constitute
an enormous tropical plain, with an ecology, history, and
culture which differ markedly from the western one third
of the nation. An abundance of unused land, sparse population, and a different social order contributed to a distinctive
regional response to land reform; and the national government's concern for developing this frontier region has
markedly affected its economy. The densely populated
temperate valleys around Cochabamba are in a setting like
Chuquisaca and Tarija, but the history of the campesinos*
there has developed in a distinctive direction during the last
few decades. Militant political activism here is thought, by
some, to have been a crucial factor in the issuance of the
agrarian reform decree at the village of Ucureña, and
agitation has continued dramatically during the sweeping
social revolution.**

For the sake of clarity, we have deliberately avoided
excessive use of non-English terms. Inclusion in Webster's
Third New International Dictionary (1961) has been used as
the criterion of acceptance in common non-anthropological
usage of words that have come into English from other

---

*The term "campesino" is used here in the anthropological
sense of "peasant," a small-scale farmer who participates
marginally in a money economy. In Bolivian usage, the
word carries a special further implication; it has been
substituted for the term "indio" ("Indian") which used to
be an epithet in the pre-1952 caste-ordered feudal society.

**It is unfortunate that Jorge Dandler Hanhart was unable
to complete his report on the Cochabamba region for
inclusion in this volume (Dandler, 1967).

languages. A few Spanish and Indian words have necessarily
been retained, however, where there is no English equivalent. Such words are underscored and defined where they
first appear in the text, and in an appended Glossary.

Both land reform and social revolution are sensitive
subjects; we probably encountered no Bolivian who had not
been in some way affected by them, and the majority had
very strong feelings on both subjects. We are grateful to
our Bolivian friends who gave us their time, confidence,
and hospitality so that we could come to understand how
they felt and why. The administrative staff of the Land
Tenure Center provided support and cooperation throughout
the period of research; William C. Thiesenhusen and
Herman Felstehausen bore most of the burden, under the
direction of Dr. Raymond J. Penn. Fritz Albert of the
Department of Agricultural Journalism, University of
Wisconsin, caught on film much of the beauty of Bolivia
and warmth of her people. Members of U.S. agencies
throughout the country offered a variety of information and
assistance. Officials and employees of Bolivian agencies,
from the level of cabinet ministers to local clerks, were
interested and helpful; those of the National Agrarian Reform
Service never ceased to offer complete cooperation whenever
they were called on throughout the entire period of research.
Ing. Marcelo Peinado shared with us his understanding of
projected economic development, and the hospitality of
René Pessoa, Walter Frerking, and Pascual Amasay
deserve special mention. Manuel Carballo kindly collaborated
in describing the history of the agrarian reform decree;
several students and other friends provided valuable assistance in the preparation of the manuscript, including Helen
Erasmus, Jaime Ardiles-Arce, Richard Lange, and David
Heath.

IMPLICATIONS

Our study provides valuable information on the nature
of actual changes in land tenure in a relatively well-
documented situation of agrarian reforms. Detailed information was secured on the degree of congruity between ideal
patterns (those prescribed in the decree) and real patterns
(those actually practiced), an important consideration in
long-range planning and evaluation of any program of

social reform. Data collected systematically on the local
level also provide a basis for evaluating the conflicting
assertions of authors whose partisan writings contain
little or no empirical evidence. Furthermore, the relation
of actual change in land tenure to other aspects of culture
is often readily discernible, and here has been related to
a large body of general theory on economic development
and cultural change.

The new constitution of 1961 recognized and sanctioned
the program of sweeping agrarian reform that had been
enacted by the MNR's revolutionary government; this contrasts sharply with the virtual neglect of rural matters in
previous constitutions. * Bolivia is basically an agricultural country. Mining, more famous because it has long
been the country's major export industry, actually employs
a very small proportion of the population, only some
40,000 people. This is why a study of land tenure such as
the one undertaken here is of such importance. Another
reason for the importance of land tenure is the relationship
between land and political control. Under former regimes,
there was an almost feudal oligarchy based on restricted
landholding and limited voting privileges. Today, however,
universal suffrage has been granted, and the extensive
land reform program is well under way. The Agrarian
Reform Law of 1953 has brought radical changes in the
land tenure system, aimed at the emancipation of the
Indian and the transformation of the fundamental socio-
economic patterns which have persisted since early
colonial times. The development, content, and results of
this land reform and the associated social revolution are
the subject of this book.

---

*The military junta which came to power in November,
  1964, repealed the constitution of 1961 but pointedly
  retained the principal innovations of agrarian reform,
  nationalization of the mines, and universal suffrage.
  Their so-called Revolution of Restoration did not repudiate
  the achievements of the MNR; it is supposedly not reac-
  tionary but rather aimed at a return to the original goals
  of the 1952 revolution which had been corrupted in twelve
  years of personalistic rule by Victor Paz Estenssoro and
  his small circle of supporters. The government elected
  in 1967 represents continuity with the junta.

PART   I

INTRODUCTION TO BOLIVIA

AND

HER LAW OF AGRARIAN REFORM

CHAPTER **1** TOWARD
UNDERSTANDING
BOLIVIA

—Dwight B. Heath

Bolivia is a land of contrasts. Enormous geographical
and climatological diversity has been and remains today an
all-pervasive aspect of Bolivia's political, economic, and
cultural development. To provide a setting for our discussion of land reform, we present here a brief general introduction to the geographical, historical, and cultural context in which reform has taken place in Bolivia.*

THE PHYSICAL SETTING

With an area of approximately 424,000 square miles,
Bolivia stands fifth in size among South American republics. Although it is roughly twice the size of Texas,
Bolivia's population is probably less than 4 million,
about that of Chicago. The ecological diversity of the
country is reflected in the irregular distribution of people,
with roughly three fourths of the total population crowded
into the third of the country that lies above 4,000 feet

---

*Probably the best single source for a brief general intro-
duction to the geography, history, politics, and economy
of Bolivia is by Harold Osborne, Bolivia: A Land Divided
(third revised edition), Royal Institute of International
Affairs, London, 1964. A slightly more detailed U.S. Army
Area Handbook for Bolivia, Special Operations Research
Office, Washington, 1964, is also excellent. Demography
and rural social institutions were the focus of attention
in Olen E. Leonard's Bolivia: Land, People, and
Institutions, Scarecrow Press, Washington, 1952.

elevation, and only one fourth scattered through the lowland two thirds of the national territory.

Structurally the country can be divided into three main regions or zones: the high plateau, or altiplano, with its surrounding mountains; the valleys in the eastern slopes of the Andes; and the eastern lowlands, or Oriente. (See Map 2). These three areas are so different from each other in ecology, demography, and history that many writers say that Bolivia could justifiably be considered three countries rather than one. Subregions can be distinguished within each of the three major divisions, on the basis of differing amounts of rainfall and local topographical variations. Although the country lies entirely within the tropics, the extreme range in altitude--from about 300 feet to over 21,000 feet above sea level--produces climates ranging from the perpetual snow and bitter winds of the Andes to the moist heat of the Amazonian lowlands, with all the variations in between.

The Altiplano

The altiplano has been historically the most important of the three zones. This western part of the country has an area of about 50,000 square miles, and runs some 500 miles from Lake Titicaca on the north to the Argentine border on the south. Bounding the area on east and west are two chains of the Andes, which divide north of the Bolivian border in Peru and merge again in the southwest corner of Bolivia. The western chain, the Cordillera Occidental, lies generally along the Chilean border; the eastern chain, the Cordillera Real, runs south after out-lining Lake Titicaca. In the northern part of this range, the steep descent eastward toward the Amazonian basin is cut by distinctive rugged tropical valleys called yungas; in the southern part, the decline is more gradual and the river valleys are open and more temperate.

The high plateau formed between these two chains of mountains is only occasionally cut by deep gorges or broken by small rises. Most of it is bleak and windswept desert or grassland, with little water except in Lake

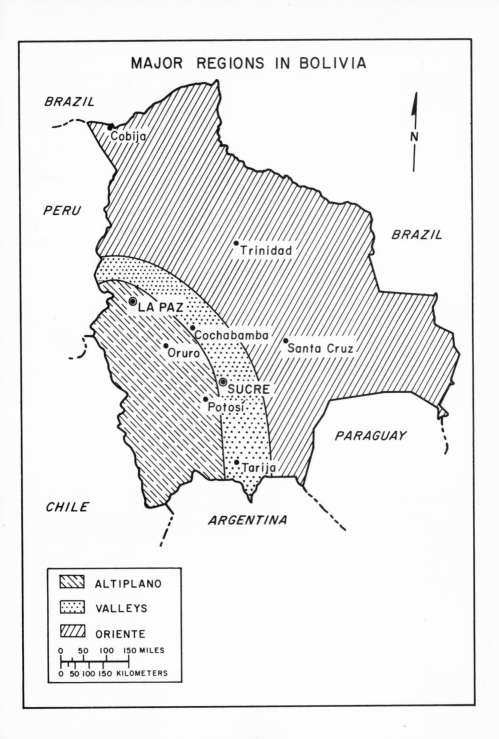

MAJOR REGIONS IN BOLIVIA

BRAZIL

Cobija

PERU

BRAZIL

Trinidad

LA PAZ

Cochabamba

Oruro

Santa Cruz

SUCRE

Potosí

PARAGUAY

Tarija

CHILE

ARGENTINA

N

ALTIPLANO

VALLEYS

ORIENTE

0   50   100   150 MILES

0   50 100 150 KILOMETERS

15

Titicaca, at 12,500 feet, the world's highest navigated lake.
The Río Desaguadero drains from Titicaca into Lake Poopó,
a shallow, highly saline body of water. Further south are
found the salares (salt pans) of Coipasa and Uyuni, remnants
of former large lakes. Rainfall decreases from north to
south and is generally sparse except in the region of Lake
Titicaca, which has a tempering influence on the climate.
Temperatures are far from tropical, averaging around 50° F,
with an overall range from $0-80^{\circ}$. In contrast to slight
seasonal variation, there is relatively great daily fluctuation
of temperature, as in other mountainous areas, with very
cold nights even in the summer.

Vegetation in the altiplano, as elsewhere, varies with
moisture, so is therefore generally sparse except in the
vicinity of Lake Titicaca, and decreases progressively
toward the south and west. A coarse bunch grass is the
most common growth and serves as food for the llama,
alpaca, and sheep and as thatch and matting for houses. On
the shores of Lake Titicaca, totora reed grows thickly; it
is also used for thatch and mats, as well as for food and in
the manufacture of small boats.

A major portion of the food plants used in the world today
are found in the Andean area, and many may have originated
there. At the time of the conquest of the area by the Spaniards, potatoes, maize, quinoa (a grain), and oca (a root
crop) were the staples. These crops persist today, with
the addition of barley and some other hardy cereals; wheat,
alfalfa, beans and other vegetables are cultivated to some
extent around Lakes Titicaca and Poopó. Horses, cattle,
hogs, and donkeys may be found, but climate and elevation
favor sheep, llama, and alpaca. Farming is generally on a
family subsistence level, but there is some surplus for
urban areas.

The altiplano has been the focus of Bolivian life since
long before the time of the Inca. Relatively barren agriculturally, this region contains some of the richest and most
diversified mineral deposits in the world. Even before the
rise of the Inca Empire, Bolivia's mineral wealth was known
and exploited. The Spaniards on their arrival were, however,
interested only in the precious metals. Most important of
these was silver, and the name of the city of Potosí in the
southern altiplano became legendary throughout the world

because of its great wealth. *

It is little wonder that Bolivia has been dependent on
mineral wealth throughout her history. Tin deposits found
in many places along the Cordillera Real have been the
mainstay of the Bolivian economy since the latter half of
the nineteenth century. Until the 1952 revolution, three tin
companies dominated the national economy. In the late
1940's minerals accounted for 98 per cent of Bolivia's exports, and nearly 75 per cent of that total was tin. However,
in spite of the wealth of mineral resources, there had been
a virtual lack of industrialization, with raw materials being
exported and most manufactures bought from abroad. Because of this economic system dominated by mining, the
western area was more developed while the eastern valleys
and lowlands remained neglected, particularly with regard
to transportation, and foodstuffs had to be imported from
abroad to the markets in the west, while immense potentially productive areas in the east lay unexploited. This
problem will be considered more fully in our discussion of
the aims and accomplishments of the 1952 revolution and
subsequent land reform.

The Valleys

A distinctive feature of Bolivia is that part which is
known by the Aymara Indian name, yungas. The yungas is
a region on the eastern slopes of the Andes, comprising
steep-sided valleys separated by sharp parallel spurs running out from the main ranges. Rainfall is heavy in the
subtropical yungas in contrast with the altiplano, and the
natural vegetation is that of the montane rain forest. There
are many trees useful for timber, and cinchona bark, from
which quinine is extracted, is occasionally an important
uncultivated export. Coffee is a major cash crop, but the
real economic mainstay of the yungas is coca. The leaves

----

*The fabulous story of Potosí, once the richest city of the
  world but now a depressed mining town, is vividly re-
  counted in Bartolomé Arzáns de Orsúa y Vela's Historia
  de la Villa Imperial de Potosí (3 volumes, edited by
  Lewis Hanke and Gunnar Mendoza), Brown University
  Press, Providence, 1964.

of this plant, from which cocaine is derived, are dried and
chewed, often with lime to heighten the effects, by the Indians of the highlands. Known and used since Inca times, coca
chewing is a ritual indulgence which seems to alleviate hunger, cold, pain, and fatigue; there is little support for widespread allegations that coca is physically or morally dam-
aging.

Many other plants, both native and introduced, grow in
this region, including grapes, figs, peaches, all types of
citrus fruits, pineapple, bananas, and so forth. Root crops
such as sweet potato, manioc, and peanuts are also cultivated, along with tobacco, coffee, and sugar cane.

The major area of valleys contains fertile, well-watered
basins with a somewhat lower rainfall than the more northern
yungas. Most notable of these valleys is that surrounding
Bolivia's second largest city, Cochabamba. The basins of
Sucre and Tarija are similar but smaller. At elevations
ranging between 5,000 and 8,000 feet, both climate and
vegetation are Mediterranean. Cultivated crops include
wheat, barley, alfalfa, and many fruits such as peaches,
apricots, and pears. Fairly good soils and a somewhat
lower rainfall combine to produce stable conditions, allowing
more diversified agriculture than in the northern valleys.
Population density is high, however, and pressure on the
land has led to fractionation of agricultural units into tiny
parcels called minifundios.

The Oriente

East of the Andean foothills sprawls an enormous plain,
the eastern lowlands, or Oriente. This is a vast and sparsely
populated region, an underdeveloped frontier area to which
little attention has been paid throughout Bolivian history.

In spite of a fairly uniform flatness of terrain, the Oriente
is not an ecologically uniform region. As in the west, rainfall
decreases from north to south, creating three general subregions: the dense tropical forest of the Amazon River basin,
a large natural pasture in the center, and open savanna and
thorn-forest to the south. Within the Oriente much local
transport is conducted by rivers, but there is as yet no
year-round connection between the various riverine systems
and the single all-weather road that leads to the highlands.

The Oriente has long been believed to be enormously rich
in both quantity and variety of natural resources. However,
it is only recently that Bolivians have begun to develop any
specific plans for "opening up" this frontier area. For example, Bolivia has some of the best forest resources in the
world, and an astonishing variety of woods and medicinal
plants are found in profusion in the lowlands. Lumbering
is a growing activity, although it is immensely expensive
to ship lumber to the highlands by airplane.

Transportation problems also hamper the development
of agriculture here. Of an area of some 190 million acres,
it is estimated that only 140,000 are under cultivation, most
of which is in the vicinity of the city of Santa Cruz. To be
sure, not all of the available land is suitable for cultivation.
Heavy rainfall produces extensive flooding each year in the
north and causes a considerable loss in the cattle which are
raised in this area of ample pasturelands. For lack of other
means of transport, meat is often flown to market areas in
the highlands to the west.

Recent agricultural expansion in Bolivia has focused on
the Santa Cruz region, which is presently the only portion of
the eastern lowlands with any appreciable concentration of
population. Although over half the land is covered by forests
which must be cleared before cultivation can begin, the subtropical climate and relatively good soils make this area of
great apparent agricultural potential. The new highway from
Cochabamba in the west and the Brazilian-built railroad to
the east have already played an important role in the development of Santa Cruz as a food-producing center. South of
Santa Cruz, the climate becomes increasingly arid, with
dry scrub and grassland the predominant vegetation. In this
region (the Chaco), newly exploited oil fields offer the tantalizing prospect of a significant new source of wealth for the
nation. *

It has been suggested by several authors that purely
physical factors in the environment have tended to override

*It seems doubtful that petroleum reserves will live up to
  the extravagant hopes that prompted large-scale exploration of the Santa Cruz area during the late 1950's.

the human elements in Bolivia's history. Historically, topography and climate have been important determinants of settlement, land use, and ethnic diversity and division; recently, they continue to present considerable handicaps in the modern development of Bolivia as a nation. But even with the above geographical background in mind, Bolivia's history and present situation cannot be understood without consideration of the social setting.

THE SOCIAL SETTING

At the time of the Spanish Conquest, early in the sixteenth century, the people of highland Bolivia shared a widespread general Andean culture complex.* Although most of the area was under Inca domination, the influence of pre-Inca cultures had not been obliterated. One of the most impressive remains of the earlier cultures can still be seen at Tiahuanaco, south of Lake Titicaca. The Inca succeeded in establishing a considerable degree of linguistic and cultural uniformity in their empire through mandatory instruction in Quechua, the imposition of a state religion, and the forced migration and dispersion of various alien groups. Of all the tribes who came under Inca domination, only the Aymara today retain their native language; even until the revolution of 1952, many of the Aymara remained remarkably isolated from intrusive cultural influences. They lived either as tenant farmers (colonos) on large agricultural estates, or as members in the few free communities (comunidades indígenas)which had managed to resist White encroachment, usually because of isolation and undesirability of the

---

*An excellent popular account of Bolivia's prehistory is available in Wendell C. Bennett and Junius B. Bird's Andean Culture History (second revised edition), Natural History Press, Garden City, N. Y., 1960. For the dedicated student, there is no better starting point for a study of the several societies and cultures from prehistoric times to the present than Julian H. Steward (ed.), Handbook of South American Indians, Bureau of American Ethnology Bulletin 143, Washington, 1946-50; Volume 1 (The Marginal Tribes) and Volume 3 (The Tropical Forest Tribes) deal with the eastern lowlands, whereas Volume 2 (The Andean Civilizations) treats the altiplano and valleys areas.

land. Most sociologists have looked to the ayllu, a group of
related families who jointly hold land, as an important ancient basis for cooperativism, but this has usually been a
presumption not based on systematic analysis of the historical evidence or contemporary patterns. Anthropologists
who have recently done intensive research in indigenous
communities demonstrate convincingly that neither the
comunidad nor the ayllu is a truly communal organization.

While the descendants of the Aymara are today concentrated in the northern altiplano, Quechua-speakers have a
much wider distribution. As among the Aymara, there is a
great degree of variation among small local groups of
Quechuas; this is reflected especially in distinctive regional
variations in costume and dialect. While the Quechua language
was imposed on many divergent peoples, these groups still
maintained separate social identities, both under Inca domination and thereafter. Some other factors responsible for
their localism include the social isolation and relative im-
mobility of the groups during both the colonial and the republican periods. Although some Quechua remain isolated and
even hostile to outside influences, many developed friendly
relations with their Mestizo and White neighbors. This is
particularly true in the Cochabamba region where the groups
lived in close proximity and shared roughly the same level
of subsistence. In other parts of the highlands, Indians were
commonly exploited as an almost subhuman caste.

In pre-Conquest times, the eastern lowlands was an area
of great linguistic and cultural diversity, and it remains so
today. Although the Inca never succeeded in incorporating
any of the lowland Indian groups into their empire, there
was considerable trade between them. Spanish control in
this area was accomplished by both religious and secular
means. The Jesuits were quite successful in establishing
missions both among nomadic and more sedentary groups.
The system which developed was that of a virtual theocracy,
although there were a few secular population centers from
which military forces were sent out against surrounding
Indian tribes. Among the many advantages for the Indian
groups which chose to settle on the missions were the
cultural elaborations offered by the missionaries, such
as steel tools, songs, dances, new kinds of clothing, and
new crops and farming techniques which raised the level

of subsistence. By royal decree, mission territories were
forbidden to the Spanish military and civil settlers. However,
with the expulsion of the Jesuits from the New World in 1767,
the Indians of the lowlands who had come under White domination became subject to many of the same pressures that the
highlanders suffered. An unknown number of groups have
managed to survive by retreating to the deeper recesses of
the tropical forests, however, and are only now being absorbed
as the frontiers of White settlement are steadily extended.

Many of the former tribal peoples in the lowlands have been
assimilated into a racially mixed lower class which, around
Santa Cruz, is a distinctive and self-conscious group known as
the Camba. Before the revolution of 1952, these people were
for the most part tenant laborers and subsistence farmers on
the large landholdings or in the deeper regions of the forest.
Although few Indian cultural elements remain, the Camba feel
themselves to be a distinct group, set off from the highland
Mestizos and Indians, who are grouped under the single,
somewhat derogatory term "kolla." Relationships between
the Camba and their White and Mestizo neighbors have been
relatively good. Because of labor shortages, tenants and
workers in the lowlands have occupied a much better position
vis-a-vis the landlords than they did in the highlands, where
pressure for land heightened problems even more.

So far we have been speaking of Bolivia's history largely
on a local level. Let us look now at the development of
Bolivia as a nation.

THE HISTORICAL SETTING

The Inca were conquered in 1532 by a small group of
Spanish adventurers under the leadership of Francisco Pizarro
and Diego de Almagro. * Within six years, Pizarro had
invaded the altiplano and founded the city of La Plata, today
known as Sucre, the official capital of the nation. The

---

* Historical sources have been incisively discussed by Charles
W. Arnade, "The Historiography of Colonial and Modern
Bolivia," Hispanic American Historical Review, vol. 42,
no. 3, pp. 333-84, 1962.

Spanish economy was based on the extraction of metals, with silver predominating. The mita (labor conscription) was adapted, possibly from a similar institution developed by the Inca, as a means for producing manpower for the mines and for some other purposes.

During the early colonial period, the basic means for effecting Spanish control was the encomienda, a royal grant giving to an individual settler both tribute collection rights and certain claims on the labor of a specific group of Indians. The encomendero was not to live among the Indians, but he was to be responsible for their spiritual well-being. The history of Spanish colonization and settlement in the New World was permeated by two parallel aims: the acquisition of wealth and prestige, and the gaining of souls for Catholicism. Although there was sometimes conflict between the civil and the religious authorities, those two aims were often incorporated in a single individual, whether priest or adventurer.

After the beginning of the seventeenth century, the encomienda was increasingly displaced by a series of Spanish officers, known as corregidores. With the encroachment of colonial authority, Indian headmen lost most of their power, and Indian societies which had once been strictly stratified became reduced almost to the position of a subordinate caste. Few Indians had direct dealings with the Spaniards; the social pattern set by the Spanish rulers has continued to dominate Bolivian life until very recent times. On top of the scale, of course, were the White conquerors and rulers who took most of the income. For example, in 1950, over 90 per cent of the land was included in 4.5 per cent of the landholdings; that is, less than 5 per cent of the people owned nearly all of the arable land.

A few Spanish settlers married European women, but there were not many available, so the majority of the conquistadors married Indians. The Mestizo children born of these marriages occupied an intermediate position in the society, depending on the degree of wealth attained and other factors. Bolivia's "racial" composition today is popularly estimated at 15 per cent White, 35 per cent Mestizo, and 50 per cent Indian. However, the criteria used in defining these groups are fluid, making such classifications extremely questionable. Although divisions are phrased in racial terms,

the distinguishing criteria often are actually social and cultural. The dominant, Spanish-speaking group is thus termed
White (blanco), in spite of the fact that most members of the
group have some Indian ancestry. An Indian (or campesino)
is usually defined as one who wears indigenous dress and
speaks a native language; an Indian may "become" a Mestizo
(or, sometimes, cholo) simply by learning Spanish and abandoning his Indian social identity, no matter the color of his
skin.

The eighteenth century was a period of great unrest among
various Indian groups. While Bolivia contributed extensively
to the opulence of Spain, the large majority of both Mestizos
and Indians led lives of bitter poverty and suppression. The
end of the eighteenth century saw a series of fruitless insur-
rections in both Peru and Bolivia (then "Upper Peru"). Under
a series of leaders, each assuming the title of Tupac Amaru,
the highland Indians revolted sporadically in an attempt to
correct injustices and to achieve acceptance in the dominant
society. These outbreaks lacked coordination and were more
along the order of local uprisings; the local atomization of
communities did not make for organized military strategy or
action.

The War of Independence* apparently did not actively involve or greatly affect the Indians, and their status generally
remained virtually unchanged until the 1952 revolution. The
period following independence which was achieved in 1825,
was a turbulent one, with a series of inept and often dictatorial presidents. Mining continued to bring tremendous wealth
to the rulers, while the rest of the economy lay in virtual
stagnation. The constant political strife of the period can be
interpreted as an unorthodox but effective mechanism for the
redistribution of power among a closed elite, with essential
socio-economic stability being maintained in spite of an out-
ward appearance of turmoil.

Mining interests led to the disastrous War of the Pacific with
Chile in 1879-83. The Atacama Desert and Pacific Coast
regions had become coveted territories because of such re-

---

*The background and outcomes of the War of Independence
 are analyzed by Charles W. Arnade, The Emergence of
 the Republic of Bolivia, University of Florida Press,
 Gainesville, 1957.

sources as guano and nitrates, and several Chilean enterprises had begun to exploit the tremendous deposits. When
Bolivia imposed higher charges to increase its share of the
revenue, Chile seized the Bolivian ports, and Bolivia was
totally unprepared for the war that followed. The final results of the clash left Bolivia completely landlocked. Since
that time, one of the recurrent nationalistic themes has been
the quest of a corridor to the Pacific. Though unable to attain
this,   Bolivia does, however, enjoy the use of Arica and
Antofagasta in Chile, and Mollendo in Peru, as free ports.

War broke out again in 1928, this time with Paraguay in a
dispute over an undeveloped region in the Chaco. The discovery of oil has often been cited as a reason for the mutually
debilitating Chaco War which raged from 1932 to 1935; Bolivia's superior numbers and supposedly superior training were
soon canceled out by several factors, including inept leadership, conflict between civil and military officials, and the
excessively high rate of non-battle casualties, from disease
as well as from wounds. Bolivia's defeat was conceded in
1935 under an armistice arranged by a commission of neutral nations.

The Chaco War is seen by Bolivians themselves as a
turning point in their history and indeed its effects were
both immediate and far-reaching. First of all, the loss of
manpower and wealth were enormous. More important ,
however, were the social consequences of that war. For
the first time, the inadequacies of Bolivia's traditional
system were revealed to large numbers of people. In addition, many Indians saw other parts of the country for the
first time and became aware both of the meaning of the Bolivian nation as an entity and of the existence of other groups
of people within the country. Many of the veterans of the
Chaco War banded together in associations which sought not
only redress of their specific grievances, but also changes
on the national level.

World War II helped to alleviate the financial situation
somewhat because of the increased demands for tin and
copper, but after the war the process of spiraling inflation
continued unchecked. It was a period of ideological ferment,
and several new political parties emerged. These included
the Revolutionary Workers Party (Partido Obrero Revolucionario , POR), which adhered to Trotskyite principles, and

the Party of the Revolutionary Left (Partido de la Izquierda Revolucionario, PIR), which was Marxist in orientation. The party which proved to be the most viable was the Nationalist Revolutionary Movement (Movimiento Nacionalista Revolucionario, MNR). * In brief, the MNR emerged as a loose coalition of diverse political views, and it retains a wide range of outlooks, although its strongest support comes from the organized miners and other labor unions, including peasant syndicates (sindicatos campesinos) in some agricultural areas.

In the mid-1940's, MNR leader Victor Paz Estenssoro served as Minister of Finance in the cabinet of Gualberto Villarroel. When that government fell to revolution, Paz went into exile in Argentinia. Most Bolivians were surprised when, still in exile, he gained a plurality in the presidential elections of 1951, but the decision went to Congress since he did not have a true majority of the votes. A military junta intervened, until the MNR finally came to power in a bloody revolution April 9-11, 1952.

The accession to power of this party did not represent, as had many of Bolivia's previous revolutions, a mere changing of the palace guard, and transfer of political incumbency from one clique to another. The revolution of 1952 was the basis of a profound social revolution. It almost completely destroyed the power of the former elite and resulted in immediate and profound modifications of political life and government policy which have subsequently been codified in constitutional changes.

---

*Recent political and historical developments have been periodically analyzed by Richard W. Patch, "Bolivia: U. S. Assistance in a Revolutionary Setting;" in Richard N. Adams, et al. , Social Change in Latin America Today, Council on Foreign Relations by Harper and Brothers, New York, 1960; and in occasional Reports, American Universities Field Staff, New York. A sympathetic account of the MNR party is provided by Robert N. Alexander, The Bolivian National Revolution, Rutgers University Press, New Brunswick, 1958; an impassioned critique of its abuses comes from a former foreign minister, Alberto Ostría Gutiérrez, A People Crucified: The Tragedy of Bolivia, Devon-Adair, New York, 1958.

Bolivia today functions under a republican system with a bicameral legislature; the executive remains the strongest branch of the government, both constitutionally and in practice. The form of local government continues much the same as before, although the focus of actual power has been greatly altered. The country is divided into nine departments (analogous to states in the United States), and these are in turn subdivided into provinces (roughly comparable to counties). The official capital of the country is Sucre, but the Supreme Court is the only governmental body located there. La Paz is the actual working capital, as well as the business and commercial center of the nation.

The platform of the MNR was concerned not only with changes in the political and governmental realms; it was also committed to a sweeping program of economic and social reform which included nationalization of the major mining companies, universal suffrage, and the introduction of many changes in social and labor legislation, including one of the most comprehensive land reforms ever enacted. The word "indio" (literally, "Indian," but with deprecatory connotations) was struck from the language, and the more affectively neutral "campesino" ("peasant," or "rural dweller") was substituted. Among campesinos, there is an incipient feeling of identity with the party and the nation, although local factionalism will probably remain for some time.

The agrarian reform brought radical changes in the land tenure system, aimed at liberating the campesinos and transforming fundamental social and economic patterns that had persisted since early colonial times.* The development,

---

*Bolivia's economic situation has improved only slightly in recent years, despite the well-reasoned recommendations of the "Keenleyside Report," officially titled Report of the United Nations Mission of Technical Assistance to Bolivia, U.N. Technical Assistance Administration, 1951. Cornelius H. Zondag made a realistic appraisal more recently in The Bolivian Economy, 1952-65, Frederick A. Praeger, New York, 1966.
The MNR was proud of its accomplishments, as illustrated in Bolivia: 10 Años de Revolución, Dirección Nacional de Informaciones, La Paz, 1962, but the MNR regime was

content, and results of this land reform and the associated
social revolution are the subject of the following chapters.

---

overthrown late in 1964. The revolutionary military junta
and its elected successors have not yet promulgated any
systematic statement of progress or prospects (cf. Heath,
1967).

CHAPTER **2** BOLIVIA'S
LAW OF
AGRARIAN REFORM

—— Dwight B. Heath,
with the assistance
of Manuel Carballo

The purpose of our research was to investigate patterns of land tenure and use, dealing both with actual
behavior and with beliefs and attitudes. A critical event
which affected many aspects of our subject matter was
the enactment, just a decade earlier, of an agrarian
reform law. In many respects, this seems to have been
a fundamental basis of the sweeping revolution which has
substantially changed the political, economic, and social
organization of the nation. Each of the following three
sections deals with the specifics of land reform and social
revolution in a particular area of Bolivia. In this chapter,
I offer a brief summary of the political and historical
background of land tenure in Bolivia and reconstruct the
complex of factors involved in the movement toward land
reform. Furthermore, rather than once more merely
summarize some of the principal specifications of the law,
Appendix A is an annotated paraphrase of each article of
the decree, for the benefit of students who may have difficulty finding or interpreting the entire original document.
And, finally, I have attempted to describe the administrative structure and some of the problems involved in enforcing the law.

HISTORY OF LAND TENURE IN BOLIVIA

A brief summary history of predominant land tenure patterns provides a context for understanding pressures which eventually led to the enactment of one of the most comprehensive agrarian reform laws in world history.

Almost every work on agrarian reform written in Bolivia* is prefaced by a brief supposed history of land tenure patterns from the pre-Columbian period to 1952. These summaries are generally literary and highly imaginative rather than well-documented, and the"precendents" for the reform are ranged from the Inca ayllu, romantically but inappropriately characterized as an ideal communal system, through evolutionistic schemes of Morgan, Engels, Marx, Mao, and other historical-materialists. A few refer to the vaguely analogous Mexican experience; but more often a combination of Marxism, traditionalism, and Indian nationalism is evoked to "prove" that the kin-based collectivistic community is "the natural" landholding entity in Bolivia. The conquest and the colonial period are considered catastrophes which resulted in alienation of the land and disruption of the communities; there is considerable truth to this, although the legal and extra-legal processes involved were far more complex and varied than is suggested.

Bolivian land tenure patterns are the outcome of fusion of aboriginal and Spanish colonial patterns. Regional variations in historical perspectives are considerable, but our discussion here deals primarily with the densely populated

---

*It is unfortunate that the overwhelming bulk of what has been written about Bolivia's agrarian reform consists of little more than polemics, pro and con. The excellent exceptions to this rule (by Flores, 1954; Ferragut, 1963; Heath, 1959a, 1963; Land Tenure Center, 1963) have already been discussed in the Introduction. Checklists by Cardozo (1962) and Heath (1966d) indicate the range of literature available; the most meaningful items have been annotated and appear in Carroll's bibliography on land tenure in Latin America (1965).

altiplano and valleys, since other areas were virtually
ignored in preparation of the land reform decree.

It is difficult to reconstruct with any degree of confidence the patterns which prevailed before the imposition
of the Inca Empire, and our information on that period is
based on a wide variety of post-conquest sources, which
are uneven and of diverse types. Recent anthropological
and historical investigation does not support the popular
belief that a strictly communal economy prevailed in the
local kin-based community. * It appears rather that only
limited portions of land were held in common by the community, serving, in effect, as a tax-producing reserve,
while the bulk of the land within any community was divided into specific plots and allotted to families, with
provision for familial work, inheritance of land, and
other non-communal features similar to those in the contemporary altiplano described below by Buechler (cf.
Ford, 1962; Moore, 1958).

European colonial patterns were superimposed on this
indigenous base, as the Spaniards assumed administration
of the empire. ** It seems doubtful that a change of personnel within the bureaucracy had any great effect on local
agriculturalists, and the difference between specifications
of the Laws of the Indies and actual practices at the local
level suggests that there was considerable continuity in
terms of patterns of land tenure and use throughout the
pre-Columbian and colonial periods. Those which had belonged to the local Indian communities were often confirmed
to them by royal patent (forming autonomous "indigenous

---

*The historical derivation of the fallacy of assuming that
Andrean Indians share a communal temperament is discussed by Adams (1962), and individualism among the
contemporary Aymara is documented in detail by
Carter (1963, 1965).

**The nature of sixteenth and seventeenth century Euro-
pean patterns of land tenure and their impact on Spanish
colonies in the New World have been well described by
Weeks (1947a, b) and Ots Capdequi (1959).

communities," "comunidades indígenas") but in practice
were often alienated from them by individual Spanish
settlers using illegal or extralegal means.

The Spanish Crown sought to reward individual conquistadors for new discoveries and other services. A few such
rewards took the form of actual land-grants (repartimientos);
more common were grants of labor, called encomiendas. *
The encomienda was a distinctive institution whereby the
beneficiary (encomendero) was given official authority to
utilize the labor of a named group of Indians, in exchange
for assuming responsibility for their indoctrination in the
Christian faith, and collecting royal taxes. The encomendero was explicitly forbidden to take land, which was
confirmed to the Indians. Reciprocal rights, duties, obligations, and responsibilities were spelled out in considerable detail, limiting the time, frequency, and ways in which
Indian labor could be used, as well as specifying the kinds
of other social relations which should prevail between an
encomendero and his native charges.

Two main streams of sentiment motivated the spread
of the Spanish Empire throughout the New World. The
religious zeal which had culminated in the expulsion of
the Moors from Spain found a new outlet in the conversion
of this vast newly conquered population, once the Indians
were recognized as human beings in a Papal Bull of 1537.
The economic motivation of individuals who came as soldiers of fortune, seeking to establish their wealth and
power in the relatively open society of the frontier often
conflicted with these official idealistic motives, and the
feudal system of Europe was effectively transplanted,
with Indians as serfs to the new self-styled gentry.

The Catholic Church became a significant force in
parts of the New World and enjoyed not only exemption

---

*The important distinction between the institutions of
 repartimiento and encomienda has been well delineated
 by Kirkpatrick (1939, 1942).

from taxes but in some regions, a considerable degree
of political autonomy as well. Scattered Indians were
often brought together in new settlements (reducciones,
analogous to reservations in North America), where they
were under clerical control. Enormous tracts of land and
other kinds of wealth eventually became concentrated in
the hands of the priesthood, one among many reasons why
the Crown saw the Jesuits as a threat and expelled them in
1767. Other orders continue to hold land even today, but
their regulation by successive governments has become
increasingly restrictive.

Elaborate laws were promulgated to protect the rights
and property of Indians, but they were seldom strictly
enforced. Private control of land by Spaniards and their
descendants became a widespread pattern, and customary
domination became accepted as ownership in many regions.

The gradual integration of Spaniards with local people
led to the emergence of a new ethnic group, the Mestizos.*
Culturally and racially disinherited in the elaborate dual
social system of the colonial administration, they came to
predominate in economic manipulation. They eventually
led the movement for independence from Spain and dominated the political realm as well. The emergence of the
Republic of Bolivia, as characterized by Arnade (1957),
was in large part the result of Mestizo agitation for the
abolition of laws which gave Indians preferential treatment.
The new nation, founded August 6, 1825, did little to modify
the agrarian structure inherited from the colonial period.
The Mestizos were able to reinforce their economic
dominance, and maintained immense landholdings utilizing
the unpaid labor of Indian serfs who no longer enjoyed even
the appeal to protective legislation. Mining remained the
principal source of cash income and foreign exchange,
although the vast majority of the population was still
engaged in labor-intensive agriculture. Farming was
primarily for subsistence rather than commerce, even on

----

*The beginnings of mestization have been analyzed by Mar-
shall (1939), and Wolf's incisive characterization of the
role of Mestizos in the development of Middle America
is generally applicable to Bolivia as well (1959: 233-56).

the vast landholdings called latifundia. Often these latifundia
were owned by absentee landlords who lived in cities and
left the administration to resident foremen (mayordomos).
The Indian families whose ancestors were traditionally associated with a piece of land became bound to the landlord
to the extent that they were often treated as part of the
realty. A sporadic succession of abortive Indian uprisings
(which had begun in the colonial period) demonstrated the
dissatisfaction of the servile caste, but also proved their
helplessness.

The republican governments, instead of restoring land
to the Indians , often usurped their land and even legalized
its alienation, which had been illegal throughout the colonial
period. For example, the notorious President Melgarejo
incurred such immense debts that he was chary of imposing
further taxes and tariffs. Instead, he turned for new revenue
to the lands of the Indian masses, whom he claimed to protect. He decreed that all communal lands should be put on
the market, to benefit the State. To be sure, Indians were
allowed to purchase their own lands, but few understood,
and fewer had any money. That which was not bought by
Indians within sixty days was auctioned to the highest
bidder, with payment to the State. In this way, the national
coffers were partially replenished ; landlords gained
control over vast areas, and the Indians were dispossessed.

As the Indians lost their land, it became progressively
concentrated in the hands of an urban oligarchy. The
immense size of some individual landholdings is revealed
in Table 1 and the degree of concentration is even more
striking when one considers that some landowners held as
many as six or eight large units.

The agricultural census of 1950, the only one of its
kind ever taken in Bolivia, was also cited in the Preamble
to the agrarian reform decree (Bolivia, 1953):

> ... according to data collected in the 1950 Census,
> 90 per cent of the private agrarian property in the
> nation is held by only about 4. 5 per cent of the total
> rural landholders... demonstrating to what degree
> the land has become concentrated in a few hands.

Table 1

SIZE, AREA, AND PERCENTAGE OF AREA OF
AGRICULTURAL HOLDINGS* IN BOLIVIA, 1950

Size of Units	Area	Per cent of Total Area	Per cent of Total Units
Less than one hectare	10,879.81	0.03	28.65
1 - 3 hectares	31,961.59	0.10	20.99
3 - 5	31,036.47	0.10	9.63
5 - 10	59,085.95	0.18	10.18
10 - 20	76,958.91	0.24	6.81
20 - 35	85,763.66	0.26	3.98
35 - 50	56,651.25	0.17	1.61
50 - 75	717,711.33	0.33	2.18
75 - 100	75,465.95	0.23	1.04
100 - 200	295,114.43	0.90	2.59
200 - 500	756,072.84	2.31	2.89
500 - 1,000	1,049,332.11	3.20	1.78
1,000 - 2,500	3,290,879.41	10.05	2.48
2,500 - 5,000	5,433,896.71	16.59	2.15
5,000 - 10,000	5,146,334.58	15.71	0.92
10,000 plus	16,233,954.41	49.57	0.71
No information	8,750.07	0.03	1.41
TOTAL	32,749,849.50	100.00	100.00

*By units
Source: Bolivia, Ministerio de Hacienda, Censo
Agropecuario: 1950, La Paz, 1950, mimeographed, p. 1.

Other problems among the motivating considerations for
enactment of such a law were likewise mentioned in the
Preamble, as follows:

   ... By archaic systems employed in its exploitation
forms of servitude in labor, rural property has not
completed its social function but rather has been

converted into an obstacle to the progress of the
nation.

... as a result of the unequal distribution of land
and the defective system of exploitation which
characterizes it, Bolivia has very little agricultural production even for the satisfaction of internal requirements, for which the State budgets
approximately 35 per cent of its cash reserves
which should be invested for other urgent necessities.

The historical background of some of these problems is also
discussed:

... in spite of the material and spiritual protection
of the Laws of the Indies in Colonial times,   the
indigenous race were unjustly deprived of property
and submitted to free and personal service by imposition of semi-feudal system with the Spanish land-
grants, creating for the first time a problem of the
Indian and the land, not as a racial or pedagogical
problem but rather a social and economic one.
(Bolivia, 1953).

Among Latin American countries, as in all underdeveloped
nations, statistics are incomplete at best, and may be worse
than worthless if distorted to make a favorable impression.
From estimates provided by the United Nations we also get
an overwhelming impression of need: Bolivia has the smallest
proportion of agricultural crop land to total area (i.e. , 0.3 per
cent) in all Latin America; this totaled (in 1950) only 0.2 acres
per person, because of the extremely high density of population in the agricultural regions.

In such a situation, protest must focus on the source of
power of the controlling oligarchy. For this reason, land reform became a rallying point for those who would effect a
social revolution.

MOVEMENT TOWARD AGRARIAN REFORM*

An accurate history of the Bolivian agrarian reform has

---

*The following discussion follows closely the excellent un-yet to be written. This is probably less due to the fact that so little time has passed since the signing of the decree at Ucureña than to the bulk of conflicting evidence which is available.

On the central question concerning the actual origins of the reform in Bolivia, two contradictory positions have been put forward. Former President Victor Paz Estenssoro said categorically, "The agrarian reform was imposed from above,"* and almost every high MNR official vigorously supported this view.

One of the most widely read North American students of Bolivia, however, has suggested that the reform was a result of a grass roots movement and that the promulgation of the law in 1953 was only a feeble gesture of self-defense to demonstrate to militant campesinos that the incumbent regime was really on their side, after they themselves had taken the initiative in expropriating and reallocating large landholdings. According to Patch (1961:119), armed peasants "... finding themselves for the first time in a position of power, embarked on a program of total land redistribution from below. It was their demand and their power which soon forced the government to recognize the serious nature of the problem and to appoint an Agrarian Reform Council." The same forces were stressed in Patch's doctoral dissertation, where he stated that, "Pressure from the indigenous population became effective in forcing the government to issue an agrarian reform decree" (Patch, 1956:51). It is doubtful that anyone in Bolivia agrees with this view, or anyone else who has first-hand acquaintance with the situation there. As is so often the case under such circumstances, the truth appears to lie somewhere between these contrasting positions.

The groundwork for the Bolivian agrarian reform was laid by excess population, concentrated in some of the most

----

published study by Manuel Carballo (1963). Mr. Carballo did documentary and field research in Bolivia during the summer of 1962, under the auspices of the Henry L. and Grace Doherty Charitable Foundation.

*Personal interview, President Victor Paz Estenssoro with   Carballo, August 18, 1962, La Paz.

agriculturally overworked regions of the country, creating
a desperate situation in which the land was divided and subdivided until entire peasant families were forced to scratch
out a living from plots which often totaled less than a hectare. The widespread institution of the latifundium, and the
inevitably concomitant minifundium, resulted in backward
technology, isolation of the agricultural sector from the
market economy, and a labor relationship between feudal
landlord and peasant which was based less on wages than
on traditional obligations and service.

The Indians, who composed by far the greatest part of
the rural population, were relegated to a virtual serf-like
caste. Educational facilities were almost non-existent.
The term "indio," was used as an epithet and the "White"
citizens of Bolivia reserved the national term "boliviano"
strictly for themselves. There was some justification for
the latter, since the Indian had no vote and no voice in
government.

The agrarian reform law as we know it is a pioneering
piece of legislation, but it is not the initial effort by Bolivians in that direction. Bolivia's Constitution of 1938 declared the abolition of slavery, and asserted that no one
might be required to give personal service without just
payment and without his complete consent. This was disregarded, however, and serfdom of the Indians persisted
throughout most of the highlands.

This inequality together with some vaguely progressive
sentiment stemming from disillusionment with the failure
of the old order in the Chaco War, spawned a new political
party, the MNR, in the early 1940's. According to Patch:

> The whole proposition of agrarian reform
> posed serious questions for the MNR as a
> political party. The party arose as a collec-
> tion of groups which united for a variety of
> purposes, and their amalgamation did not
> mean a unity of goals or ideology. The original
> farmers [sic: presumably "formers"] of the MNR
> were the "intellectuals," as they are called in
> Bolivia: persons such as Victor Paz Estens-
> soro, who had been a professor of economics
> at the University of San Andres in La Paz; Walter

Guevara Arze, Foreign Minister until February, 1956,
who has a deep committment [sic] to many of the
ideals expressed by his cousin, José Antonio Arze,
and who has always taken a position of moderate,
evolutionary socialism, and has been intensely
suspicious of the use of force, of dramatic mani-
festations, and of extremes in general.   (1956:60-1)

And yet it was precisely these two "moderate intellectuals"
who, nearly a decade earlier, as MNR-affiliated congressmen, had jointly submitted a "Proposal for Constitutional
Reforms of the Agrarian and Campesino Legal System
(Régimen)." Five of the articles dealt with agricultural
labor relations, underscoring the obligation of landlords
to provide medical care and schooling for campesinos,
and assuring campesinos the right to organize syndicates
for collective bargaining, and so forth.   The other six
dealt with land tenure: two articles defined public and
private rural property; another asserted that communal
and small properties were inalienable; another affirmed
"squatter's rights" on private and state lands.   Two of the
articles dealt specifically with the matter of land reallocation, in a manner similar to that of the law that was eventually enacted in 1953 when Paz had become President and
Guevara was Foreign Minister:

Article: For purposes of the agrarian and campesino
           legal system (régimen), the property of
           individuals or corporate entities (personas
           jurídicas o naturales) is classified according
           to its territorial extension as latifundio and
           pequeña propiedad. The conditions and maxi-
           mum area of the area of the pequeña propiedad
           are [to be] determined by law, taking into
           account the different regions of the nation.
           Rural property which is unproductive through
           the owner's neglect may be expropriated by
           the State in order to intensify its exploitation.

Article: The campesinos resident in a place who lack
           land or do not have enough for their needs
           have a right to be given land in the same
           region. For this purpose, expropriation of
           necessary land, with just indemnization, is
           a necessity and public utility ... (Paz and

Guevara, August 25, 1944).

This document contradicts the theory widely accepted
in the United States, that

> ... the MNR had no commitment concerning land re-
> form. There had been little mention of agrarian reform
> either during the period of power under Villarroel
> (1943-46), or during the elections of 1951. It now re-
> mains to examine how pressure from the indigenous
> population became effective in forcing the Government
> to issue an agrarian reform decree, a program which
> has since become a major plank of the MNR platform.
> (Patch, 1956:51; emphasis added).

Critics of the MNR rightfully claim that many of the
party's pronouncements on agrarian reform have been
post facto. But even they recognize that the party's
strong stand became public record when discussions of
the proposal were included as the core of a book published
long before the MNR came to power. In an ambitious
review of agrarian reforms around the world and an impassioned plea for one in his own country, Sanjines cited
this proposal as a promising example of what might be done
and provided a more detailed outline (ideario) for complete
agrarian legislation (Sanjines, 1945:213-28; 327-43).

During the following year, President Herzog's
chargé d' affaires to Peru published a pamphlet in which
he suggested a novel kind of reform (Saavedra, 1946).
He would have had property remain in the hands of present
owner, but with the patrón and his peons sharing all production. Despite his relative generosity toward Indians,
Saavedra shared the prejudiced stereotypes of his class
and held that they must be treated as minors, with government agents to oversee their welfare under the guardian-
ship of the White patrones. A variety of other proposals
for agrarian reform are also of historical interest but
had little effect on the law as it was eventually enacted.

We are indebted to Patch for a detailed analysis of a
very different approach to agrarian reform which was at
that time being tried in another part of the country by José
Rojas, who eventually became head of the National Agrarian
Reform Council (Conseio Nacional de Reforma Agraria,

CNRA). In the province of Jordan (formerly Cliza), within
the Department of Cochabamba, the peasants had engaged
in a running controversy with the lessee of the lands of the
Sisters of Santa Clara, which included most of the province.
In 1936, the peasants organized a syndicate in order to pool
their funds and bargain with the landowner, asking that the
land be leased directly to them. This decidedly sophisticated approach was certainly not a normal peasant reaction;
it was in large part the work of Eduardo Arze Loureiro, self-
appointed legal counsel of the peasants.* The syndicate later
became one of the major foci of the reform under the leadership of Rojas.

On May 15, 1945, the labor-oriented approach of the MNR
to agrarian problems was articulated by three decrees of the
government of Major Gualberto Villarroel. The MNR played
a significant although not a dominant role in the administration, with Paz as Minister of Economy. The decrees were
contradictory and ambiguous. They first abolished pongueaje,
the generic name for the services rendered by the colono
to the landholder. A second decree permitted the continu-
ance of these services, if the peasant were paid. Finally,
a third decree named four days as the weekly maximum
that a colono should have to work without pay for the patrón,
apparently contradicting the other decrees.

Villarroel was hanged from a lamppost shortly thereafter, and these decrees were a dead letter until subsequently
reiterated by Paz's government from the time of his accession until the signing of the agrarian reform decree.

The value of the decrees was more psychological than
practical, and newspapers around the country felt obliged
to run editorials carefully explaining them to bewildered
landholders (e.g., El País, July 2, 1952). In effect, they
challenged the traditional quasi-feudal relationship on
which the latifundia rested, and replaced it with a wage-
contract relationship. The peasants began to realize that
the government was capable of intervening on their behalf
as well as on that of the landholders. Furthermore, the
position of Villarroel and the MNR was only one of those

*Personal interview, Ambassador Hernán Siles Zuazo with
    Carballo, August 27, 1962, Montevideo. Patch agrees with
    this view (1956: 53-54).

advocated by a number of the new parties of the Chaco War
generation. In fact, the MNR position was conservative
as compared to the program of the Marxist Party of the
Revolutionary Left (PIR), and the Trotskyite Revolutionary
Labor Party (POR).

One mark of the new strength and confidence that the
peasants derived from the relatively liberal political climate created by the Villarroel-MNR government was the
strengthening of the nascent peasant organization. A so-
called   tactical high command of the Indian peasants was
created and installed in La Paz to serve primarily as a
lobby. For the first time in decades, several rallies were
held with the active participation of as many as 45,000
Indian peasants.

In short, the philosophy of the MNR began to lay the
essential groundwork for an approach to agrarian reform,
and its actions during the ill-fated Villarroel regime
provided a stimulus to which the peasants began to respond.
But Villarroel fell, and not until 1952 was the MNR to
resume power.

The victory of the MNR during April 9-11, 1952, provided the final catalyst for agrarian reform. Preoccupied
with the problems of the consolidation of power and with
the economically and psychologically critical nationalization of the major tin mines, the government moved slowly
in laying the groundwork for land reform, however. With
the passing of the Universal Suffrage Act (DS 03128, of
July 21, 1952), the MNR had placed its political future
in the hands of the campesino majority.

Almost immediately after taking power, Paz created
the Ministry of Rural Affairs (Ministerio de Asuntos
Campesinos, MAC) and placed it, significantly, in the
hands of Nufio Chávez Órtiz, a long-time advocate of land
reform. It was from this ministry that labor organizers,
labeled "agitators from La Paz" by the conservative press,
were sent out to organize the Indians, now called campesinos, into syndicates. According to Paz, representatives
of various political parties, including PIR and POR as
well as MNR, were also agitating, organizing, and
uniting the campesinos. Only the Cochabamba area
had any degree of self-organization; most of the organiza-

tion in other parts of the nation took its shape from the
agents of MAC. *

Most of those areas not approached by representatives from the ministry were organized by the political
parties. The POR, which controlled several industrial
and railroad unions in the valleys area, organized several
syndicates in the countryside, but was soon replaced by the
MNR. The MNR in the field was spearheaded by the left
sector of the party. There are several reasons for this.
First, it is important to note that many of the miners
and mine union leaders were only part-time miners, and
were essentially campesinos in outlook. Most of them
hoped eventually to return to their homes and families
in farming villages. Second, the Bolivian Labor Federation (Central Obrera Boliviana, COB) was controlled by
Lechín and the left-wing of the MNR. At times allied
with the POR, this was the organization that had had the
greatest interest in unionizing the countryside. As a
result, the role of the miner-campesinos was crucial,
and they were used freely by the MAC, since they represented the perfect link between the syndically oriented
leaders of the left-wing of the MNR and the campesinos.
Their imprint is clear in the organizational structure
adopted in the countryside. ** As a result of their influence, Bolivian campesinos rapidly formed syndicates in
order to bargain with landowners. The idea of the sit-
down strike (brazos caidos) was quickly adopted by the
campesinos.

While the government acted, sporadic revolts began
in Cochabamba. Early in July, in the isolated town of
Independencia some peasants began their own personal

---

*Personal interview, President Paz with Carballo, August
  18, 1962, La Paz.

**Personal interviews: Vice President Juan Lechín with
  Carballo, August 13, 1962, La Paz; Minister of Rural
  Affairs Dr. Roberto Jordan Pando with Carballo, August
  9, 1962, La Paz. These MNR leaders, spokesmen for
  the divergent miner and campesino interest groups
  respectively, agreed on the importance of the role played
  by the miners.

agrarian reform, and owners of the hacienda "El Convento," confronted by a sit-down strike, blamed "communist agitators from La Paz" (El País, July 29, 1952). Their success, according to Sucre's La Prensa (August 1, 1952) was not accidental; the idea had been spread by "agitators" sent from La Paz by the "victors of the April revolution." It is clear, on the basis of such statements by supporters and opponents of MNR alike, that the government was far from inactive in the countryside.*

Not only were the campesinos of the valleys area refusing to work, but they were rapidly being organized into syndicates. Even in the isolated Chapare region, Demetrio Pereira had early formed a syndicate(El País, August 3, 1952). Single units on haciendas were welded into larger units; by late September, the 211 syndicates which had been formed met in Sipe-Sipe, outside Cochabamba, to create a departmental federation (Federación de Sindicatos Campesinos). The secretary general of the organization was Sinforoso Rivas, who, following the pattern laid down by Chávez, declared: "our best intention is to cooperate with the landlords, as long as they comply with the legal formalities ... " (quoted in El País, October 5, 1952).

On the other side of the Cochabamba Valley, an older center of campesino power was also in action. The syndicate formed in Ucureña in 1936 was remobilized in 1947, after a period of inaction. Its leader, José Rojas, was strongly influenced by the PIR position on agrarian reform and had little to do with the MNR organizational effort of 1949. With the rise of the MNR-organized Sipe-Sipe group, two centers of power developed in the valley, and the result was conflict.

Late in 1952, as the resolution of power in the valley approached, the national government announced that it would attack the problem of agrarian reform during the

---

*Even Patch noted that "Beginning in 1949 members of the MNR began working in the rural areas, attempting to identify themselves with the campesinos and to enlist their support against the vested power groups" (1956:56).

new year. But when government spokesman Attorney
General Rafael Gómez Reyes was quoted as saying that
the government was busy enough with the problem of the
tin mines, which had just been nationalized, Rojas united
the twenty-four syndicates under his control into the
Central Sindical del Valle, based at Ucureña (El País,
November 7, 1952). At this time Rojas controlled only
the area to the east and southeast of Cochabamba. One
indication of this is that, when the town of Coloni was
raided for arms on the next day, probably under Rojas'
direction, the Sipe-Sipe group, which had just moved its
headquarters into Cochabamba, condemned the assault
(El País, November 8 and 16, 1952).

Rojas, sensing the challenge, rallied his forces at a
huge demonstration in Tarata, then at Ucureña. Over
6,000 armed campesinos gathered to prepare an assault
on the town of Cliza, both to get arms and to frighten the
landholders still living there. Before attacking, Rojas
told assembled listeners that, "...confronted with the
impossibility of supporting further the abuses and mal-
treatment of the landholders, the workers have decided
to take justice into their own hands" (quoted in El País,
November 19, 1952). However, the subprefect heard of
Rojas's intention and skillfully intervened, convincing
him to refrain from attacking.

Sinforoso Rivas, head of the Sipe-Sipe group, realized
that Rojas's insistent demands that the land be turned over
to the campesinos immediately seriously undermined his
position. He planned a rally in Cochabamba's municipal
stadium. On December 22, over 12,000 campesinos
turned out to hear their leaders proclaim that the Indians
"were no longer disposed to live in slavery, like sheep
with bowed heads."

Lechín and Chávez had been the leaders of the left-wing
sector of the MNR almost from the beginning. Those
members of the MNR who had been members of the Marxist
PIR and the Trotskyite POR rallied around them; as head
of the Miners' Federation and the COB, Lechín was a
natural symbol and rallying point for workers within the
MNR, while Chávez had long been an outspoken advocate
of land reform to grant small parcels to individual campesinos. Clearly, Lechín and Chávez were the two men

best qualified to bring the PIR-influenced José Rojas into
the MNR. There is circumstantial, but convincing, evidence
that they did just that; and if this hypothesis be accepted,
the conflict over the resolution of power in the valley is more
easily understood. Rivas represented the "go slowly" position of the center and right of the MNR; the government had
officially recognized him as a bargaining agent for the
peasants (El País, November 12, 1952). Rojas, on the
other hand, better represented the viewpoint of the left-wing
sector and they backed him. The result was that the various
sectors of the MNR were working at cross-purposes.

Shortly after the December meeting cited above, a
sudden coup temporarily unseated Rivas, and the power of
the right-wing in the MNR dwindled. Following the abortive
revolt in early January, Rivas was accused of mismanagement of funds and ousted from command of the Sipe-Sipe
group. Shortly thereafter, in what seemed to be an attempt
at revenge on the part of the right-wing sector of the MNR
which controlled the prefectural government, Rojas was
arrested. When a mob of campesinos marched into the city
demanding his release, he was soon freed and his victory
was complete. Significantly, the departmental COB, controlled by Lechín, joined the chorus demanding Rojas's
release.

Unrest was by no means limited to the Cochabamba
area. With a few dramatic local exceptions, however,
the people on the altiplano seemed generally more
resigned to waiting for the government to promulgate
the reform. Sit-down strikes did occur, just as in the
valleys, but a different spirit was reflected in the offer
by campesinos of Potosí and Chuquisaca, in August, 1952,
to purchase at the 1945 tax-assessed value, any land the
government might expropriate (El País, August 14, 1952).
In comparison, Rojas was well on his way to clearing his
entire province of landholders by this time.

The government took tentative steps to placate any
unrest in the altiplano. In mid-October citing "public
utility," the government expropriated two haciendas in
Nor Chichas (Potosí), and turned the lands over to the
colonos. The lands of former President Montes, around
Lake Titicaca, had already been expropriated.

In Omasuyos province (La Paz), an ex-shoemaker,
Toribio Salas, was effectively organizing campesinos
in the countryside.   On the first anniversary of the
revolution, two regiments of armed campesinos consisting
of 15,000 men from Los Andes province and 18,000 from
Omasuyos were reviewed by President Paz, (El Diario,
April 10, 1953). Little has been written about this period
on the altiplano and further research is needed. However,
some guidelines may be given here. Within five months
to a year after the April revolution most of the haciendas
had been organized into syndicates. A few of these groups
reacted violently and drove the landholders off the land.

In the early stages, the campesinos were organized
by middle-class White and Mestizo students, lawyers,
and other urban-dwellers sent by the MAC, and sometimes
by the local comandos of the MNR. Later, campesinos
took their own lead, although a few, like Toribio Salas,
were active from the beginning.

In the Potosí area, some land was taken over violently
and no attempt has yet been made to secure legal titles
through CNRA.* In the Sucre (Chuquisaca) area, the
opposite extremes held true. Little had been done by the
time the reform was decreed, and when the reform was
executed in the area, it generally followed the dictates
of the decree. Indeed, as is indicated in Erasmus's
chapters below, there was no agrarian reform at all in
some areas until the 1960's. On the whole, the campesinos
organized and waited.

Areas of sparse population, such as La Paz north of
Lake Titicaca, Beni, Pando, and Santa Cruz, hardly knew
the demand for agrarian reform until it was instilled from
above. In these areas there was not the hectic syndicalization
that followed the April revolution elsewhere.

As suggested earlier, there is no clear-cut answer to
the question: "Who made the Bolivian agrarian reform?"
It seems that the MNR was both a creator and a creation

---

*Personal interview, President of CNRA, Dr. Angel Gemio
Erqueta with Carballi, August 13, 1962, La Paz.

of the ideological ferment of the post-Chaco War era.
The MNR early proposed a reform of the traditional
agrarian labor relationship that would have had profound
repercussions. If the latifundia had been compelled to
pay for the labor on which they depended, they would
have been shattered; it is generally agreed that one of the
most basic economic underpinnings of the hacienda
system is intensive use of cheap labor to the exclusion
of modern technology (Flores, 1961:275-76). It is by no
means certain that the destruction of the latifundia was
the intended result, although the persecution of the MNR
following the fall of Villarroel indicates the reaction of
the tin and landholding oligarchy to these early proposals.

Ucureña was certainly a rallying point and a source
of inspiration for the peasants. But it is also clear that
the middle-class intellectuals who later came to be the
mainstay of the MNR, played a major role there, qualifying the validity of the "grass roots" theory. Because of
the crucial participation of MNR politicians Arze, Chávez,
and Lechín, it is apparent that even in the case of Ucureña
there was appreciable intrusive manipulation from above.
To be sure, their efforts might have been fruitless without the support of José Rojas and Toribio Salas, as well as
the underlying discontent of their peasant followers.
Nonetheless, at the very least, Lechín and Chávez were
catalytic agents bringing urban ideas of reform to the
countryside.

A strong counter-force existed in the Sipe-Sipe
syndicates, in direct opposition to Rojas's power in
Ucureña, which certainly were not organized by representatives from Ucureña. The contemporary conservative press, and Sinforoso Rivas himself, have both
claimed that the organizers of Sipe-Sipe came from
La Paz and from the "conservative" sectors of the MNR
that controlled the department capital of Cochabamba.

The early development of syndicalism in the Cochabamba Valley is important, but it is clear that events
in the rest of the nation were by no means reenactments
of those around Cochabamba. In sum, while assessing
the sources of the reform in Bolivia one cannot ignore
the promulgation of a fairly detailed proposal for agrarian
reform in 1944 by Paz and Guevara as spokesmen of the

MNR. Nevertheless, the peasant upheavals in Cochabamba
and northern Potosí undoubtedly prompted the government
to move more swiftly on the issue, to reckon more earnestly
with the countryside, and to recognize that the MNR would be
bound by its promises. Furthermore, the lands that the
peasants confiscated by force of arms served notice to the
landholders that the revolution was real and indicated to the
government that campesino opinion strongly favored total
abolition of the latifundium, rather than less drastic
revision of labor relations and only partial reallocation of
land. The Bolivian agrarian reform was the result of many
subtle, interlocking forces; to assert that it originated only
"from above," or "from below" would be to ignore the fact
that revolutions without leaders are merely aimless mobs
and leaders without followers are impotent.

With this context in mind, we can better understand
the specifications of the law itself.

THE DECREE AND ITS SPECIFICATIONS

It is clear that Bolivia's agrarian reform law was a product of social protest; but it involved partisan politics as
well as a reaction to grass roots agitation. It is also
clear that the specific conditions of the law represented a
number of compromises -- between economic feasibility
and political expediency; among the various interests and
conditions in Bolivia's enormously diverse regions; among
conflicting partisan ideologies within the loose coalition
which constituted the MNR; and so forth. Nevertheless,
this, like any other law, was conceived and shaped at the
top of the political hierarchy rather than at the bottom.

A special Agrarian Reform Commission was formed
by presidential decree   (DS 03301, January 20, 1953) to
study "the agrarian and campesino problem in its economic,
social, juridical, technical, and educational aspects,"
in order to "propose to the Government those means·
appropriate to an adequate solution in the national interest."
The membership was: President ex officio, Dr. Hernán
Siles Zuazo, Vice President of the nation; Vice Presidents ex officio, Drs. Arturo Urquidi and Alcibiades
Velarde Cronembold, representatives of the President
of the Republic; Drs. Raimundo Grigoriu and Ernesto

Ayala Mercado, representatives of the Ministry of Rural
Affairs; Dr. José Flores Moncayo and Prof. Eduardo Arze
Loureiro, representatives of the Ministry of Agriculture;
Dr. Hugo López Avila, representative of COB, the labor
federation; Dr. Federico Álvarez Plata, representative
of the Federation of Campesinos; Sr. Zenon Barrientos
Mamani, representative of the Agricultural Bank; Ing.
Oscar Alborta Velasco, representative of the small- and
medium-scale rural landholders; Secretary general, Dr.
Julio Alberto d'Avis, and Executive secretary, Dr. Mario
Rolón Anaya. Among United Nations personnel who served
as advisors were Drs. Carter F. Goodrich and Edmundo
Flores; they as well as many of the Bolivian members have
written incisive evaluations of various aspects of the reform.

The members were named to the Commission on March
20, 1953, and delivered their voluminous report to the
President on July 28, 1953. Reports of individual sub-
commissions (dealing respectively with historical, political, legal, economic, and administrative aspects of the
projected reform), together with the draft of the decree,
were published in a special issue of Revista Jurídica (1953).
These documents offer an invaluable insight into the thinking of the architects of the reform. Considerable controversy
followed, of course; and a number of compromises are reflected in the law as it was eventually promulgated.

Even the most insightful and incisive discussions of the
agrarian reform law published heretofore have been partial,
emphasizing those sections that raise current or political
problems of interpretation or administration. For this
reason we present, as Appendix A, the first fairly complete paraphrase of the entire decree in English. The
partial annotation also given with the decree provides
explanatory background material on some of the problems
described in the area studies.

ADMINISTRATION OF THE LAW

To administer such a complex law, which potentially
could affect virtually every piece of land in the nation,
would be a formidable task even under ideal conditions.
But conditions in Bolivia have been far from ideal. In
order to appreciate the difficulty of implementing the

agrarian reform, one must consider the administrative
organization and established procedures, as well as relevant physical and social factors.

The Physical and Social Context

The great size and marked physical diversity of
Bolivia have already been characterized. The natural
features that make it a nation of awesome beauty also
pose immense problems in terms of transportation and
communication. The rugged Andes are an imposing
barrier between the densely populated highlands and the
virtually unsettled tropical lowlands of the east. Most of
the nation remains unmapped and natural obstacles combine with sheer distance to make overland travel difficult
in many areas. Lack of transportation is at once a symptom and a cause of economic underdevelopment; so too is
the country's notorious shortage of capital. It is a harsh
fact of life that, although Bolivia cannot progress without
more and better roads, she cannot well afford to build
them either; it is difficult enough to maintain the few well-
developed routes that have been established.

Social obstacles are no less important than physical
ones. At the time of the reform, Bolivia lacked even the
most basic agronomic data on production, soil types, and
so forth. There was no cadastral survey; land registration and taxation were virtually unknown; in brief, there
was no systematic substantive knowledge of the existing
agricultural systems on which to base realistic plans or
hopes for a new system.

The agrarian reform was intended especially to
benefit the campesinos, who constitute at least three
fourths of Bolivia's population. But, at the time of its
enactment, fewer than one third of them knew Spanish,
and fewer yet were literate. After generations as the
subservient group in a quasi-feudal society, they lacked
not only formal education, but also a rudimentary understanding of legal and political processes. They were
unaccustomed to making decisions and working without
direction. It has been a difficult but rewarding task to
comply with Article 144, incorporating campesinos into
the juridico-legal system of the nation.

The beneficiaries of the reform had to be educated to
profit from it and to accept the responsibilities it posed.
At the same time, those who stood to lose most by its
implementation were precisely those who had formerly
enjoyed a virtual monopoly of political, economic, and
legal activities at the national and local levels. The conditions of the reform, in brief, were in general contrary to
the vested interests of the few who had enjoyed virtual
dominance within the old social order. Those who administered the law were "bucking the system," and it was a firmly
entrenched system.

Problems arose not only with claimants and defendents,
but also with those who mediated between them. Administration of such a complex and revolutionary law would require the services of large numbers of technical and professional people, who are scarce in any underdeveloped
country. In a revolutionary country, where the reform
supported the uneducated masses in opposition to the tiny
schooled elite, skilled personnel were even more difficult
to enlist. Galloping inflation, low salaries, and extreme
political pressures drove many of Bolivia's few technically
qualified people to leave the country, and those who remained were rarely in sympathy with the reform.

Considering the enormous physical and social obstacles
to agrarian reform in Bolivia in the early 1950's, it is
amazing that so much has been accomplished. A brief
characterization of the administrative organization indicates
some of the problems which were built into the law itself,
as well as the means by which land reform has, despite
all these problems, become an important reality to most
Bolivians and laid the groundwork for social revolution.

Organization and Procedures

The specifications of the agrarian reform decree are
multifarious and complex. There was no pre-existing organization that could readily be adapted to the difficult job
of administering the law, so the National Agrarian Reform
Service(SNRA) was established for that purpose. Autonomous within the Ministry of Rural Affairs (MAC), it comprises local and mobile judges throughout the nation (often
at the provincial level), a director for each department,
a small staff in La Paz including legal, technical, and

administrative specialists, and the National Agrarian Reform Council (CNRA), a small group of specialists who review and pass judgment on each claim for land.

The complex and time-consuming steps in processing claims under the law must be described in detail to be believed. Action may be initiated by an individual or a corporate entity, and consists in the filing of a claim (demanda) with the local agrarian judge. Such a claim may be for expropriation (afectación) of someone else's land, for dotation (dotación) of unused public lands, or for confirmation (consolidación; or inafectabilidad) of one's own property. The claim becomes the basis for proliferation of a dossier (expediente), comprising all documents relevant to the claim; such a dossier may total hundreds of pages as a claim drags on for years. The judge arranges a hearing (audiencia), to be attended by the claimant(s), proprietor (if he is not the claimant), owners of adjacent properties, and the local SNRA topographer. During the hearings claims and counterclaims are aired and the topographer prepares a sketch-map and initiates his report (informe), which includes an inventory of land use, livestock, production-data, capital goods, and so forth. The proprietor is encouraged to submit deeds, tax receipts, and other relevant documents in his defense, and these become part of the dossier. On the basis of this initial hearing, the judge renders an interim judgment (sentencia) which is binding until the case is reviewed by CNRA. In the judgment, he specifies whether the case is in order (procediente), what portion(s) of the land should be retained by the proprietor, what should go to the claimant(s) (demandante)(s), and so forth. After the topographer has completed his report and detailed map of the property as a whole, and of component plots, the entire dossier is forwarded to CNRA in La Paz. There it is reviewed by a technical and/or legal board if unusual problems are involved, and their interpretations and recommendations are appended. Eventually, the entire dossier is reviewed by one of the committees (salas) of CNRA, which summarizes the salient points of the case and states its judgment in a recommendation (auto de vista). A similar review and judgment takes place within MAC, before the dossier is passed on to the President of the Republic. Here again, the entire case is reviewed and the final judgment (resolución suprema) signed by the President contains a summary of the basis for his decision. These several reviews of the case are by no

means perfunctory, and previous judgments are often
countermanded rather than given "rubber-stamp approval."
The dossier then retraces its earlier route, and must be
endorsed by the Minister of Rural Affairs and the president of CNRA. CNRA prepares titles to whatever individual plots are reallocated or confirmed, and forwards
them through the same channels for the Minister's and
the President's signatures; the titles are then forwarded
to the beneficiaries (beneficiados) through the departmental
and local agrarian judges. Completed dossiers are supposed to be filed in the archive of CNRA, but may find
their way back to the departmental or local office of SNRA;
officials at all levels claim to be at a loss to explain the
basis for differential treatment of them.

Considering the complexity of the process and the
extreme centralization of authority, it is little wonder
that the simplest claim for confirmation requires at least
two years, and that some cases have dragged on over a
decade. Nearly 20 per cent of the dossiers which were
initiated have disappeared; one might expect even a higher
rate of attrition since the defendent in the majority of
cases would profit if a dossier were destroyed or "mis-
placed." Opportunities for graft (coima) and the exploitation of personal favoritism (personalismo) are rife; and
members of this research team were frankly surprised
that there was not more evidence of such abuses.

The poverty of SNRA is manifest on every hand. The
1962 annual report of the President of CNRA noted that the
organization had only one chair for every seven employees,
one typewriter for every 160, and so forth. In an administrative organization where even the field workers produce
only data, such a shortage of basic equipment is an immense handicap. The pattern of shortage at the central
office is exaggerated in outlying offices. For example,
there is no provision for office space in all of Beni, the
largest department in the country. In Riberalta, space was
lent by the local office of MNR; in Trinidad and Santa Ana,
the judges used their own homes. The Riberalta office
which has jurisdiction over an area of about the size of
New England, compiled the following complete inventory on
June 3, 1963: one table, one paper-punch, one rubber seal,
one bottle of stamp-pad ink, three boxes for files, two
loose-leaf notebooks, one register of correspondence, and

one register of accounts. They had a few chairs on loan;
a wooden crate contained seven books from the judge's
personal collection (there is no copy of the text of the law);
bats and ants were ruining the archives piled in a corner;
and yet this was among the more productive judgeships
which I visited.

One former employee lamented the shortcomings of
CNRA, and traced the deterioration of the organization
to false economy. According to him, all agrarian judges
were lawyers in the period before December, 1956, and
they lived well on salaries of $80 to $120 monthly, among
the highest in the government service. But with economic
stabilization, salaries were lowered to $50, so that "most
lawyers returned to private practice just in order to earn
enough for their families to eat; and people got the job who
had no understanding of the law or of legal affais in general."
He went on to link incompetence with graft:

> These new know-nothing judges are worse than
> merely ignorant. They are dishonest as well, and
> make a living from the poor campesinos who have
> nothing. To supplement their small pay, they charge
> the campesinos for every sheet of paper they write
> — and there are plenty. Some of them even foment
> litigation, in order to have more paper to put in the
> dossier, at so much per page. For this reason the
> agrarian reform is a failure. Let's say, for example,
> that the judge charges some $40 to $50 for the orig-
> inal claim — you know as well as I that he should
> charge nothing, but the campesinos are unaware...
> Yes, it varies depending on the size of the plot, but
> let's say, for an average, about that much. Then
> he asks more for each other paper he prepares, up
> to $100 for the judgment. And finally, after six or
> eight years, the campesino finds himself with title
> to a plot for which he paid up to $400, but which is
> only worth $80 to $100... So what has happened? We
> have a situation where the campesinos are no longer
> subordinated in a half-human state by the landlords
> (patrones de la tierra) but they continue subordinated,
> now by the political bosses (patrones del gobierno).
> The politicians have made themselves bosses and
> continue the abuses which they attribute to the rosca.

His severe criticism seems appropriate only to some
of the judges; others are truly dedicated men who have
devoted much of their time, effort, and money to their
tasks. An example of individual initiative on the part of
an agrarian judge in supplementing his salary is the list
of "honoraria" prominently posted in one of the principal
judgeships in Santa Cruz: Bs. 30,000 ($US 2.50) per
campesino named as beneficiary; 70,000 ($5.85) per
proprietor named as defendent; 10,000 ($.85) per page of
testimony; 10,000 per page of notarized copies (e.g., tax
receipts, old titles, inventories of machinery, etc.);
50,000 ($4.25) for the topographer's report (listing area,
number of livestock, land use, boundaries, etc.); and
50,000 for the certificate of judgment, which is valid until
reviewed by SNRA. The judge's federal salary is supposed
to cover all his services, so that only the mapping and
costs of the initial hearing should be borne by the claimant.

The attitudes of judges to their jobs are immensely
variable: one felt obliged to stay aloof from any active
role in party politics; another was simultaneously secretary to the local office of MNR, and secretary general
of the regional federation of campesino syndicates. In like
manner, vastly differing views concerning the obligation
to notify the defendent of claims against him were apparent.
A judge in Beni, for example, had frequent dealings with
the firm of Suárez Hnos., whose representative consistently declined to accept any notes served on him or the
corporation. Even after dozens of such refusals, however,
the judge continued to deliver each warrant in person, in
the company of two witnesses, all of whom signed a statement listing time and place of attempted delivery, which
was filed with the dossier. Contrast this with the attitude
of a judge in Santa Cruz who never bothers to notify
challenged landowners except by posting a proclamation
on the door of his office, reasoning that "If one has
interest, he knows. If he doesn't know, it doesn't matter
to him."

Not all dossiers are initiated by campesino claimants.
A considerable number are filed by landlords who want
to secure clear title together with a ruling that their land
is secure and unencumberable (inafectable), and many
of these are successful, especially if claims are supported
with ample documentation indicating original purchase of

land, tax receipts, detailed inventories of livestock and machinery, records of land use and production, and so forth. Sometimes a landlord can even present such a strong case in defense against a claim that he gets a ruling of inaffectability without having taken the initiative.

The virtual absence of records is an obstacle to effective administration. Because each judge takes with him the documents which he has processed, there is no accumulation of a continuous archive even at the local level. The difficulties which this produces are obvious and will surely be compounded as time passes.

Another problem of administration is reflected in the well-founded joke that some topographers seem never to leave their offices, and "make their maps purely from imagination, with no relation to the actual situation."

That upper echelon reviews of expedientes are not mere "rubber-stamp" formalities is tellingly illustrated by one case, (7814-A), which also indicates confusion at the highest level of administration. A property of 1,704 hectares with three salaried laborers, 97 cattle, 14 horses, and some light machinery with 39 hectares producing good yields of diversified crops, was owned by two brothers who had regularly paid their taxes. The local judge's judgment of inaffectability was approved by CNRA's recommendation but disapproved by the President's final judgment, which specified that 240 hectares should be divided equally among "the eight campesinos, whose situations had been ignored by the initial judgment and its review by CNRA." The owners did not risk an appeal, but promptly sold the property, informing the purchasers of the CNRA's approval of inaffectability but cannily making no mention of the subsequent reversal. The new owners are still unaware of the final ruling, but the agrarian judge says he would be willing to endorse and forward an appeal, pointing out the President's misunderstanding, and that a supplementary final judgment could countermand this inappropriate one.

In another instance nearby, a petition for an area of 2,500 hectares claimed by a syndicate of sixty campesinos was approved at all stages until it was noted in CNRA's recommendation that the land had already been allotted by CBF to other campesinos.

By contrast, a confusion of names went unmentioned in
successive reviews of a dossier (2675) initiated by Juan
Roas Carballo and concluded two years later in his favor,
although the topographer's notes were filed in support of
the claim by one José Roas Bauim, and all successive
entries were in that name. It is conceivable that this was
a single Indian who changed his name, but, if so, one might
have expected a notation to that effect; as it is, there is no
indication that these were not different people; yet the technical review, CNRA recommendation, and Presidential
final judgment made no reference to the apparent discon-
tinuity.

Concerning titles to land, Bolivian law is inconsistent.
According to the agrarian reform, titles issued by SNRA
are the only ones which are legally recognized, and older
titles are invalid. However, a mortgage cannot be issued
on any other than a deed which lists at least the last thirty
years of ownership, and SNRA titles are worthless as collateral even for short-term loans.

According to one cosmopolitan observer, "The key to
Bolivia's agrarian reform is that it was gradual, and not
violent. Contrast it with Mexico, with twenty years of
chaos and a million lives lost." In relative terms, he is
correct, for even the severest critics of the Bolivian
reform count no more than three years of chaos or more
than a few thousand deaths. Still, it was a violent act in
its impact no less than a virtual reorganization of the
national social structure.

Flagrant violation of generally accepted juridical practice serves to illustrate some of the problems caused by
aggressive partisanship. In one dossier, the name of the
landlord was incorrectly listed; he had subsequently asked
that the claim be dismissed because it referred to a different defendent. A prominent lawyer, strong-man leader of
a dissident local faction of MNR, appended instructions to
the judge to "Go ahead with the expropriation; the fine
points can be arranged later," and the judge felt obliged
to do so for his own safety, although it offended him to
violate the law.

Even the people who are actively engaged in agrarian
reform are not yet satisfied, however. They consistently

speak of "two stages," the first, distribution of the land,
is virtually completed in most areas. "The second stage,"
according to one agrarian judge, "consists in providing
campesinos with the means for the development of the land.
Land alone is not enough, and without means such as
credit, tools, agricultural extension, and so forth, there
is no real reform and the term has lost its meaning."
His opinion is shared by members of SNRA at every level
throughout the country, and by government and labor
leaders as well as by the campesinos themselves. One
of the reasons for this shortcoming was pinpointed
by a Bolivian economist who noted that "The agrarian
reform law is an excellent instrument, as a law. But the
discrepancy between theory and practice is enormous ....
The root of the problem is that it was drafted by theoreti-
cians who had no familiarity with the realities of rural life."

In summary, it is remarkable to what degree many of
those who administer the law have succeeded in reconciling
the ambiguous specifications of the decree with the realities
of rural life. They have done so in the face of impressive
odds, contributing to social revolution at the grass roots
level.

PART II

LAND REFORM AND SOCIAL REVOLUTION

IN SOUTHERN BOLIVIA:

THE VALLEYS OF CHUQUISACA AND TARIJA

CHAPTER **3** THE
CHUQUISACA—TARIJA
AREA

—Charles J. Erasmus

TOPOGRAPHY AND POPULATION

The single most outstanding characteristic of
Chuquisaca and Tarija for the traveler on his first visit
is the extreme ruggedness of the terrain. Relatively
broad expanses of flat land such as one encounters on
the altiplano of La Paz or in the valley of Cochabamba
are seldom found, and then only if one leaves the better
traveled "highways." The pampas of Culpina and
Ingahuasi in Nor Cinti comprise one of the few continuous
highland plains in Chuquisaca. South of Monteagudo,
as one leaves the highlands and goes toward the Chaco,
the terrain becomes less broken and relatively flat
areas consequently more common. The city of Tarija
is in a broad valley which appears flat from the escarpment above, but on arriving in the valley one finds the
landscape broken by the severe effects of centuries of
erosion. Mostly semi-arid, the southern part of Bolivia
has been overgrazed by goats and sheep with disastrous
results.

The nature of the terrain obviously impedes transportation, and roadbuilding is a difficult and extremely
costly undertaking in this area. Even in a passenger car
it is difficult to average more than thirty kilometers
(about twenty miles) per hour, for one seldom gets
out of second gear. Average truck speeds would be well
under thirty kilometers. Because of low octane gas and

the practice of overloading, trucks frequently blow head
gaskets on the steep grades. Most truckers carry spare
gaskets, but when they don't, a shipment of fish or oranges
from the lowlands (adentro) may be a total loss. The steep-
ness and the poor condition of the roads (none is paved anywhere in Chuquisaca or Tarija) are hard on both cars and
trucks, and every driver who is not himself a mechanic must
carry one with him. With their crude and limited equipment
some of these chofer-mecánicos show considerable resource-
fulness and ingenuity.

A glance at the map of southern Bolivia (Map 3) will help
the reader gain some idea of the distances involved in traveling about the area. The trip from Sucre to Monteagudo, which
is approximately 200 miles, takes a good twelve hours even
in a fast vehicle with a light load. The same distance to
Camargo takes an hour or two less because of better road
conditions. The 116 miles from Camargo to Tarija takes
another five hours. In traveling about the area, the author
covered some 4,000 miles in about 200 hours of driving,
which had to be done mainly in the daytime to avoid night
hazards on dangerous mountain switchbacks. Obviously, a
great deal of field time was consumed simply in getting from
place to place.

Table 2 gives the population and altitude of the more
important towns visited in the area. As one can see from
the figures, most of the towns are small. The population
figure for even the largest town, Sucre, is only approximate.
In the Almanaque Mundial for 1963, it is listed as having a
population of 60,000; most Sucrenos doubt the accuracy of
this figure and put the population at about 45,000. It is the
impression of most people in the Chuquisaca and Tarija area
that town populations have been fairly stable for many years.
This is not an area of rapid urbanization. The one center of
population that is very slowly expanding is Sucre. Within the
past twenty years the urban limits have moved out to include
the houses of some farmers on the outskirts. But compared
to the urbanization taking place in other countries of Latin
America, Sucre and Tarija are stagnant communities.

The total population of the department of Chuquisaca is
about 325,000 and of Tarija about 145,000. Since most of
the inhabitants of the smaller towns are farmers, the population of these two departments is obviously more than 80 per
cent "rural" or agricultural.

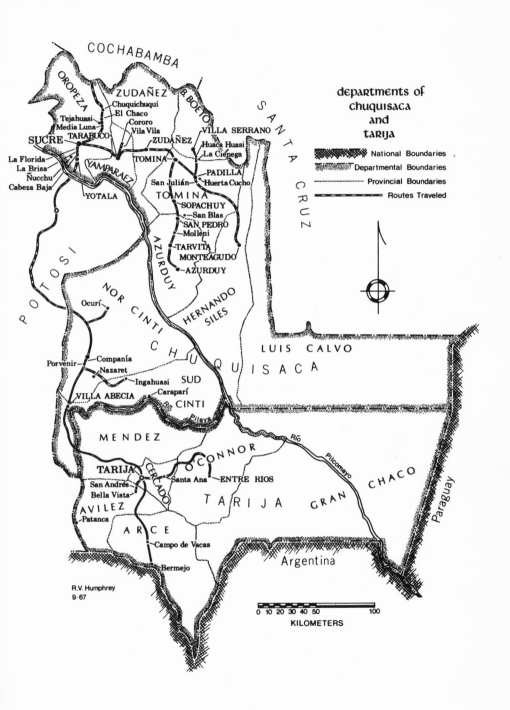

departments of
chuquisaca
and
tarija

▨▨▨	National Boundaries
▨▨▨	Departmental Boundaries
············	Provincial Boundaries
▤▤▤	Routes Traveled

COCHABAMBA

OROPEZA

ZUDAÑEZ
Chuquichuqui
El Chaco
Cororo
Vila Vila

B. BOETO

VILLA SERRANO

S A N T A

C R U Z

Tejahuasi
Media Luna
SUCRE   TARABUCO   ZUDAÑEZ
La Florida   Huaca Huasi
La Brisa   La Ciénega
Ñucchu   YAMPARAEZ   TOMINA
Cabeza Baja   PADILLA
         YOTALA   San Julián   Huerta Cucho
                   TOMINA
                   SOPACHUY
                   —San Blas
                   SAN PEDRO
                   Molleni
         A   TARVITA
         Z   MONTEAGUDO
         U   AZURDUY
         R
         D
POTOSI   U   NOR   HERNANDO
         Y   CINTI   SILES

Ocurí   LUIS CALVO
            C H U Q U I S A C A
Porvenir—Compañía
          Nazaret
          Ingahuasi   SUD
VILLA ABECIA   Caraparí   CINTI
              Río
              Pilaya

MENDEZ   Río
                          Pilcomayo
TARIJA   O'CONNOR   C H A C O
CERCADO Santa Ana ENTRE RIOS
San Andrés   G R A N
Bella Vista   T A R I J A   CHACO
AVILEZ
Patanca   A R C E
          Campo de Vacas   Paraguay
          Bermejo   Argentina

R.V. Humphrey
9-67

0 10 20 30 40 50   100
KILOMETERS

65

Table 2

POPULATION AND ALTITUDE OF SOME MAJOR TOWNS IN SOUTHERN BOLIVIA

Town	Population	Altitude*
Sucre	50,000	8,860
Yotala	3,000	8,200
Chuquichuqui	500	5,250
Tarabuco	4,500	12,000
Zudañez	3,000	8,200
Padilla	5,000	6,890
Villa Serrano	3,000	8,530
Monteagudo	2,500	4,100
Camargo	3,500	7,870
Villa Abecia	2,000	7,540
Tarija	25,000	6,000
Bermejo	3,500	3,000

*In feet.

The altitudes in Table 2 show the mountainous nature of the region. To the west the two departments border on Potosí where altitudes are highest. Eastward both departments slope drastically toward Santa Cruz and Paraguay where they eventually drop well below 1,000 feet.

CROPS

The highland zone of both departments is somewhat arid in appearance. This impression is enhanced by the quantity of cactus and thorn forest vegetation so reminiscent, to this writer, of northwestern Mexico. Yet, as in northwestern Mexico, much of the farming is temporal (dry)--dependent on rainfall rather than irrigation. Dry farming seems most successfully practiced in the higher altitudes in northern Chuquisaca and in the lower altitudes of eastern Chuquisaca and southern Tarija. Western Tarija and the western margins of Nor and Sud Cinti seem the most arid of all. Along most of the road from Villa Abecia to Tarija one sees very little human habitation, and what there is is mainly dedicated to the raising of sheep and goats. For example, Patanca in western Avilez (Tarija) was an hacienda of yerbajeros, meaning that the colonos (serfs) of the hacienda had only pasture lands and lived by raising goats and sheep of which they annually paid a percentage to the landowner. Their cereals and potatoes were obtained by bartering livestock in the lower area to the east.

The river valleys of highland Chuquisaca are undoubtedly the most productive regions, per hectare if not necessarily per man-day of labor. In the bottom of the valleys, land has been rescued from the rivers by building stone embankments to channel the water around the fields. Small irrigation canals, sometimes cut in solid rock, are used to irrigate the orchards and vegetable gardens on these canyon bottoms. Oranges, tangerines, cherimoyas, and avocados are very common and of excellent quality. Considerable labor, however, must be invested in the "defenses" against rivers which only too often break through the embankments and wash away orchards on which farmers have labored for a lifetime.

Irrigation is by no means restricted to river valleys. Throughout Chuquisaca and Tarija the peasants and former hacendados have constructed irrigation canals wherever possible. Most rivers and many springs have some water throughout the year and it is carefully led through canals and crude aqueducts to moisten as much soil as possible. No water supply is neglected in the highlands if there is any feasible means of exploiting it for irrigation. One

Table 3

MAJOR CROPS GROWN AT PLACES VISITED
IN SOUTHERN BOLIVIA

	Maize	Potatoes	Wheat	Barley	Peanuts	Chili peppers	Manioc	Rice	Vegetables	Sugar cane	Fruit
Chuquichuqui	X	X							X	X	X
Tejahuasi	X	X			X				X	X	X
Media Luna	X	X							X		X
El Chaco	X	X							X		X
Ñucchu	X	X	X	X					X		X
Cabeza Baja	X	X	X	X					X		X
La Brisa	X	X							X		X
Cororo	X	X	X	X							
Vila Vila	X	X	X	X							
Azurduy	X	X	X	X							
San Julian	X	X			X	X					
La Ciénaga	X	X	X		X	X					
Huaca-Huasi	X	X			X	X					
Monteagudo	X				X	X	X	X		X	
Camargo	X	X							X		X
Ingahuasi	X	X	X	X							
Patanca		X	X	X							
Santa Ana	X		X		X						
Bella Vista	X	X									
Campo de Vacas	X	X			X		X		X	X	X
Bermejo	X				X		X	X	X	X	X
Entre Ríos	X	X			X	X		X			

of the features of Chuquisaca and Tarija agriculture most
surprising to this observer was the amount of irrigation
practiced. Diversionary dikes are built out into the rivers
to deflect water into ditch canals. After every heavy rain
the rivers rise and destroy the dikes, which must be re-
built. Fortunately the soils in most of the highland areas
are sufficiently impermeable that water loss in the canals
is surprisingly slight. Before the reform these irrigation
systems were constructed and maintained by individual
haciendas or farmers. I encountered no intercommunity
irrigation networks. Today these simple irrigation systems
are being maintained by the peasant syndicates on those
haciendas which have been expropriated as latifundios.

Table 3 shows the major agricultural products at the
various places visited in Chuquisaca and Tarija. (All of
these towns or haciendas are located on the accompanying
map.) The most widely planted crop is maize, which is
absent only at Patanca, where it is said to be too high for
maize to produce well. The popularity of maize reflects
the strong orientation toward subsistence farming encountered everywhere in the area. A family can always eat
maize, and if it does well enough to produce a surplus
some can be sold to buy clothes and other household necessities. It is grown at all altitudes: as high as 12,000 feet
around Tarabuco and below 3,000 feet south of Monteagudo
and eastern Tarija. Production per acre is much higher at
the lower altitudes.

Potatoes are almost as ubiquitous as maize, but whereas
corn tends to inc rease in importance at lower altitudes,
potatoes increase in importance at higher altitudes. Many
places at 7,000 feet or less which grow some potatoes
must nevertheless import more to meet their needs, and
usually corn is the commodity exchanged. In areas as low
as Monteagudo and Bermejo potatoes may not be grown at
all. At Bermejo a few f armers were planting a variety
known as the "Argentine potato," which has a higher water
content than highland potatoes.

Wheat and barley are much more restricted in their
distribution than corn and potatoes. They are grown predominantly at higher altitudes, usually above 8,000 feet.
Peanuts are generally grown below 8,000 feet. They are

fairly common throughout the area. Ají (chili pepper) seems
to do best between 4,000 and 7,000 feet and much of that
consumed in Chuquisaca is grown in the provinces of Tomina
and Hernando Siles (around Padilla and Monteagudo).   In
Tarija the province of O'Connor is said to produce the most
ají.

Like maize, wheat is an important food staple and surpluses can be traded for lowland products. Barley is
predominantly a commercial crop purchased by Bolivian
brewers, particularly those in La Paz. Peanuts are quite
important in the diet of farm families that grow them,
as well as in nearby areas where they are purchased or
obtained by barter. In all the towns and cities roasted
peanuts are sold by street vendors, and in the country
unroasted peanuts are ground on a stone mortar to make
a thick, white paste which is combined with potatoes and
meat to make the all-important midday soup. Ají is
decidedly a commercial crop since its chief use is as a
condiment and most families cannot consume more than
25 pounds annually. It finds its way to the major cities, and
much of that grown in Chuquisaca is transported to Potosí
and La Paz.

Rice is a lowland crop planted in areas of abundant
rainfall. In the early 1960's it seemed to have a promising
future in the province of Hernando Siles around Monteagudo,
but Santa Cruz captured the limited internal market and
very little rice is now being commercially planted near
Monteagudo. It is grown for home consumption and the
very limited market at Monteagudo.

Manioc is another lowland crop, and again it is planted
primarily for the subsistence of the farm family.   Manioc
around Monteagudo and Bermejo will last as long as two
years in the ground after it ripens. It is an ideal tropical
subsistence plant since it presents no storage problem.
A housewife simply goes to the garden and pulls up what
she needs before preparing dinner. But manioc is doomed
as a commercial crop where there are no processing plants
to make it into flour. Once out of the ground it begins to rot
within 48 hours.

Sugar cane is common everywhere below 5,000 feet
although it is not an important commercial crop. Campe-

sinos plant a little cane to make a guarapo (fermented cane juice) and to chew the cane stalks. Near towns or cities some peasants sell cane in limited quantities much as they sell onions and cabbage. Along the Río Chico north of Sucre (around Chuquichuqui, Tejahuasi, etc.) sugar cane was an important crop before the agrarian reform. Several haciendas distilled alcohol from cane juice and sold it in Sucre, Potosí and La Paz. This industry has since disappeared in the Rio Chico. The Bolivian government is presently negotiating with Japan to build a sugar refinery at Bermejo. In anticipation, many colonists have moved into the Bermejo area to homestead twenty to twenty-five-acre plots of government lands. Around Monteagudo and Bermejo many peasants already have homemade sugar presses operated with animal traction that produce a crude form of brown sugar (dried molasses) sold in rectangular cakes (chancaca). Mixed with peanuts in smaller quantities it is sold as a candy known as empanizado. In both areas it is common to see peasant men and women who have lost fingers, hands, and parts of arms in their homemade sugar presses (trapiches).

Vegetables and fruits are grown predominantly in the irrigated lands at the bottom of the canyons or valleys. In such areas as the Río Chico (Chuquichuqui, Tejahuasi, Media Luna, El Chaco), the region between Sucre and Yotala (La Brisa, Cabeza Baja, Ñucchu) and Cinti (Camargo, Companía, Porvenir), the valleys are so narrow and steep-sided, with such pitifully narrow strips of irrigated land along the margins of the rivers running through them, that the word "canyon" could seem to fit them most accurately. It is in these canyons that the rock walls must be built and maintained to protect the fields from the occasional ravages of rivers which, during most of the year, are gentle meandering streams. Two or three times a year after heavy rains they grow into raging torrents which subside after 48 to 72 hours. These rivers are very much like the "intermittent streams" of the American Southwest except that they seldom run completely dry and thereby make possible year-around irrigation on the canyon bottoms.

In the Río Chico area, campesinos with irrigated bottomlands grow tomatoes, onions, cabbage, beets, cucumbers and sweet potatoes for the Sucre market. This valley lies at about 5,000 feet, and also produces

oranges, cherimoyas, and avocados. Since the principal
highway between Cochabamba and Sucre passes through
this canyon, these fruits and vegetables are only two hours
from Sucre by truck.

The canyon between Yotala and Sucre lies at about
8,000 feet, and there peach trees replace the citrus of the
lower valleys. Many of the same vegetables are grown with
the addition of peas, lima beans, and carrots.

The Cinti canyon.(Camargo) is too far from any major
city to be a profitable source of vegetables; it specializes
in grapes and peaches. Even these it produces in such
abundance that inundates the market. Grapes and peaches
ripen about the same time in the Cinti canyon (February) and
during that time about eight trucks a day leave Camargo
with peaches and grapes for Sucre, Potosí, Oruro, and
La Paz. Eight trucks a day cannot account for more than
3 to 5 per cent of the production around Camargo. Some of
the grapes are made into wine, but Bolivians are not wine
drinkers and the market (only in La Paz) is extremely small.
Most of the grapes are pressed and distilled into an alcoholic
beverage called singani, a close relative of Peruvian pisco.
This crude brandy has a fairly constant and dependable
market throughout Bolivia and is the main support of the
Cinti canyon vineyards.

Cinti peaches do not fare as well as the grapes. No
beverage is made from them and there is no market large
enough to absorb them. Some are dried for sale; but unfortunately peaches ripen during the rainy season in Cinti and
it is almost impossible to complete the drying process
before a rain ruins the harvest. By some estimates 80
per cent of Cinti peaches rot each year.

The Cinti canyon is a microcosm of the production and
marketing problems of southern Bolivia. The agricultural
year 1962-63 was an extremely favorable one for this area.
There were few frosts, little hail damage, and rains were
plentiful and timely. Harvests were abundant everywhere.
As a consequence, the price of maize in Monteagudo was too
low to pay the truck freight to ship it north; it was being fed
to pigs in the hope of breaking even on the price of lard.
Ají in that area was selling at its lowest price in five years.
The market for rice was so poor that it was being abandoned.

Around Azurduy, where the road had not yet arrived at the
time of the author's visit and where animal transport greatly
raised freight costs, potatoes, wheat and corn surpluses
were all spoiling. Maize surpluses were spoiling around
Entre Ríos and as far east as the province of Gran Chaco
in Tarija. Around Padilla many peasants were making
chicha for sale from their surplus maize in the hope of
salvaging something from it. Even in Cinti, landowners
with distilleries were having a hard time selling their
singani, and the peasants who had sold them grapes earlier
in the year had not yet been paid off in August. The subject
of production will be discussed later. It should be pointed
out here, however, that a major criticism of the agrarian
reform in Bolivia —perhaps the major criticism among
former landowners and many members of the urban middle
class—is that agricultural production has fallen as a result
of this reform. How important can such an accusation be
in a country which cannot absorb its own agricultural products in a good year? Farm products cannot properly be
discussed apart from farmer incentives. What production
incentives will farmers have if their best efforts in a good
year are not rewarded? Where will they obtain the funds
to buy the durable goods which will further expand their consumption needs and their expectations and thereby prod them
on to even higher production goals?

THE PEOPLE

One of the most impressive aspects of the Bolivian
agrarian reform for this writer was the intentional avoidance of the word "indio" among most of the population.
Mere avoidance of the word would not in itself be important
were it not for the tremendous social implications of the
phenomenon as well as the correlative modifications of
inter-class behavior which have apparently accompanied it.
In most of Latin America the word "Indian" is in common
use and generally has a strong deprecatory connotation.
More often than not, it is a term of social rather than ethnic
or cultural relevance and is used to place an individual or
family in the lowest social stratum. For this very reason
the founders of the Bolivian reform decided to outlaw the
word and substitute the more inclusive term for all the
peasantry—"campesino." It is said that the Indian population now resents the word "indio" since they have been

taught that it refers to an "inferior race." When I first
arrived in Chuquisaca it was pointed out to me on two or
three occasions by government officials that the word
"indio" was no longer used. Instead they often spoke of
"campesinos who speak Quechua." Later, as I came to
know these same individuals better, they relaxed and used
the term "indio" in conversation with me when it was
necessary to be precise, as in speaking of "the Indians
around Tarabuco." There was never, however, anything
demeaning in their manner or meaning when they employed
this designation. In direct address, government officials
call all campesinos "compañeros" (partners, or comrades).
Nowhere in Latin America has this observer seen government personnel treat rural and Indian peoples with such
patent equality as they do in Chuquisaca and Tarija (and
presumably in the rest of Bolivia as well).

Regarding the accuracy of the official attitude that
Quechua-speaking campesinos would now resent the appel-
lation "indio," I am not so sure. On at least one occasion
I heard a landowner of the upper class refer to his work-
men as "indios" in their presence. They were anything but
offended and showed genuine affection for this elderly gentle-
man whom they knew well and from whom they expected no
harm. From the lips of someone else the word might well
have stirred resentment, but I suspect these campesinos
would have been too polite to show it. As many persons,
including ex-landlords, often told me during my stay, the
rural people of Chuquisaca and Tarija are not rebelde —
rebellious. They are an even-tempered, passive people
who are not easily provoked to violence. Had it been up to
the people of this area to bring about a revolution, I believe
it safe to say that it would never have taken place. Chuquisaca and Tarija have benefited from changes instigated in
Cochabamba, La Paz and Potosí; they have followed the
lead of peoples elsewhere. There are very few "angry men"
in this part of Bolivia.

Perhaps the group which today comes closest to har-
boring "angry men" is that which since the reform has
suffered the greatest relative deprivation— the landowning
families of the upper and middle classes. These people in
private conversation with the author did not hesitate to use
the word "indio," and it was truly a term of opprobrium as
they employed it. According to them, the Indian is lazy;

the Indian will never change; the Indian must be treated
like a child; the Indian only looks forward to his fiestas
and chicha (corn beer); in reference to a certain congressman from Chuquisaca who was once an hacienda serf: "He
is just an Indian; he cannot even sign his name!" We shall
return to the subject of class relations when we discuss the
nature of the new power structure.

Culturally, ethnically and socially there is ample
justification for eliminating the designation "indio." In
almost every sense the term defies definition if it is used
to specify some particular component of the population. The
gradient between the "azules" or "good, blue-blooded families" of Sucre, and most aboriginal-appearing peoples of
the countryside, is a gradual one. Even these class or
ethnic extremes are not mutually exclusive. Among Quechua-
speaking campesinos who might be designated "indios" by
some "azules," one encounters individuals with blue or
light green eyes. And among the "good" families and professional people of Sucre one not infrequently encounters an
individual who could pass as "indio" if dressed in campesino
garb. Many Quechua-speaking campesinos would definitely
rank as Mestizos if they lived in Mexico, for example,
where they would in all probability be Spanish-speakers.
The term "indio" seems to be used most often to designate
a social group which adheres most closely to local custom
in its wearing apparel. For instance, the Quechua-speaking
campesinos around Tarabuco who still wear braids and a
distinctive leather headdress (montera) copied after the
Spanish helmet are most likely to be referred to as "indios"
without provoking any objections.

Quechua predominates as the language of the countryside in the northernmost third of the area and Spanish in
the south. The province of Oropeza is predominantly a
Quechua-speaking area except for the city of Sucre. Even
in Sucre, however, most of the older people seem to be
bilingual including the upper class. I did not meet any
native Bolivian landowners who could not carry on a conversation in Quechua with their laborers. It is my impression that the use of Spanish is becoming more common
among the campesinos bordering the roads to Potosí and
Cochabamba. While most of the old people are still monolingual Quechua-speakers, many children and young adults
who have been affected by the post-reform rural education

program in these areas are now bilingual.

Yamparaez and Zudañez are still predominantly Quechua-speaking provinces. In Yamparaez there is even some resistance on the part of the parents to the schooling of their children. At two haciendas visited near Tarabuco the federal school teachers had been withdrawn as punishment for poor attendance.

The southern part of Boeto is predominantly bilingual or Spanish-speaking. Tomina and Azurduy are both provinces with Quechua- and Spanish-speakers. Along the road from Sucre to Monteagudo the town of Tomina is recognized as marking the transition from Quechua to Spanish (see Map 3). However, on the road from Tomina to Azurduy, through the southern part of Tomina province and the western part of Azurduy province, there are many communities in which Quechua predominates; this is true of both San Blas and Molleni, for example. From the town of Azurduy eastward, Spanish predominates. Hernando Siles and Luis Calvo are both primarily Spanish-speaking provinces. Only the so-called "cambas" of these provinces still speak an Indian tongue, in this case Guaraní.

The word "camba" has a much more restricted meaning in the provinces of Hernando Siles and Luis Calvo than it does in the department of Santa Cruz where it is normally used, according to Heath, to refer to the Mestizo peasant population. In the former case, "camba" refers specifically to Guaraní-speaking "campesinos" or "indios" who are also frequently referred to as "los paganos" or heathen. Cambas around Monteagudo today are predominantly bilingual and are in great demand as farm laborers. They are considered more industrious than the Spanish-speaking campesinos.

Along the road south from Sucre to Tarija, Quechua gives way to Spanish not long after entering the province of Nor Cinti. Away from the road toward the east, however, Quechua is still said to predominate, particularly in northeastern Nor Cinti. In the comunidad indígena of Ocurí the majority of older people still speak only Quechua, but most of the younger men can now communicate in Spanish. In the mountains east of Camargo and in eastern

Sud Cinti there are many bilingual but few monolingual
Quechua-speakers. Those who are monolingual are Spanish-
speaking, and many family heads at Ingahuasi claimed
that their children were unable to converse in Quechua.

The department of Tarija is considered a Spanish-
speaking area. Along the border with Potosí in Avilez there
are some bilinguals (Quechua and Spanish), and in the province of O'Connor there are still small groups of "Chirihuano"
Indians who are said to speak an aboriginal language which
is neither Quechua nor Guaraní.* These tiny bands are
apparently quite autonomous, settling in semi-permanent
"ranchos" wherever they feel inclined. Landowners let them
remain because they are glad to have them available as a
potential source of wage labor when they need extra hands
during seasons of peak labor load.

Throughout the Chuquisaca-Tarija area annual religious
fiestas for community patron saints as well as other church
and household images is an important form of consumption
and community activity. In Latin America this form of consumption tends to be associated with a primarily subsistence-
oriented economy and we shall discuss this phenomenon as
an important form of consumption in this area in a later
section.

Reciprocal labor, also to be discussed more fully later,
is another institution generally associated with a subsistence-oriented economy. There are two varieties — the
simple exchange form and the festive work bee. In most of
Latin America they have been replaced or are being replaced by wage labor as cropping patterns become more
market-oriented. The strong survival of these institutions
in this region is again an important symptom of the static
nature of the rural economy.

Both ceremonial consumption and festive work parties

---

*Editor's note: These are presumably remnants of the
Chiriguano, a tribe who have occupied parts of southeastern Bolivia since late in the fifteenth century, and
who are culturally, linguistically, and historically related
to the Guarani. — DBH

serve a useful function in providing community gatherings
and dances at which young people can meet eligible mates.
The custom of "trial" marriage (a pruebas in Spanish, and
sirivinaco in Quechua) seems to be general in the Quechua-
speaking regions of northern Chuquisaca. At Tejahuasi,
Ñucchu and Vila Vila, groups of informants claimed that
marriage a pruebas was customary. Couples were said to
live together two or three years before formally getting
married, by which time most have one or more children.
Some of these couples never marry though such cases are
said to be exceptional.

    Of the 34 conjugal unions in the community of ex-colonos
at the ex-hacienda Ñucchu, all had lived together before
legalizing their union. The "trial" period ranged from one
to six years and averaged three. Actually, this can hardly
be considered a "trial" in the literal sense since separations
are very rare once the couple takes up residence together.
Spouses tend to come from the same community or from one
very nearby and women are more likely to change their community of residence at marriage than are men. Of the six
wives from other haciendas, five were from communities
within a radius of three kilometers. Of the six husbands
from other haciendas, half were from communities closer
than three kilometers.

    In the Spanish-speaking areas there seems to be greater
self-consciousness about forming free unions prior to marriage. Of seventeen married couples at Porvenir (near
Camargo), only six had lived together before marriage, and
the other eleven did not take up co-residence until after the
wedding ceremony. Many girls are already pregnant, however, at the time of the wedding. Around Tarija and Bermejo
informants claimed that most couples live together two or
three years before getting married, but no statistics were
gathered. Except at Porvenir, where only one spouse
among seventeen pairs had been previously married, no
figures were gathered on divorce. Everywhere informants
claimed it was very rare. Casual observation suggests
that divorce increases among lower-class families in the
cities, but again no quantitative data were gathered.

POLITICAL STRUCTURE

Bolivia is divided into departamentos, somewhat equivalent to our states. Chuquisaca and Tarija are the two most
southeastern departments, bordering on Argentina and Paraguay. The capital of Tarija is the city of the same name;
Sucre is the capital of Chuquisaca. Internally each department is divided into provincias, of which there are ten in
Chuquisaca and six in Tarija. Each province is further divided into cantones, the smallest political unit.

The maximum authority in each department and the
direct representative of the executive power there is the
prefecto, an appointee of the President and Minister of
Government. He is supposed to make sure that all state
offices — police, schools, mail, etc. — are being efficiently and honestly operated. From his annual budget,
which derives in part from the central government and in
part from internal taxes (on land, liquor, tobacco, etc.)
he spends such money as he can on public works including
roads, schools, water distribution systems, etc.

The representative of the prefecto in the capital of each
province is the subprefecto, who is appointed by the prefecto
with the approval of the Minister of Government. His actual
duties are few and his salary is only part-time. There is
no legislative body in the departmental government.

Each city and town has a municipal alcalde also appointed
by the Minister of Government. He operates with tax funds
from various sources including the predial urbano (taxes on
dwellings and furniture), water and light, city import taxes
and municipal licenses.(All professionals such as lawyers,
doctors, dentists, etc. , are licensed.) The alcalde sees to
the maintenance of city streets and the proper operation of
such public services as water and light. Alcaldes , prefectos
and subprefectos have indefinite tenure. They are changed
when it seems politically expedient, sometimes when popular
opinion is strongly opposed to the incumbent.

The principal authority in each canton is the corregidor.
He is selected by the prefecto from a list of three persons
recommended by the subprefecto. The corregidor acts as a
kind of local constable and minor judge.

A major duty of the subprefecto is to see that all of his
corregidores properly organize and administer prestación
vial, the labor tax of four days which every campesino man
between 18 and 60 years of age must spend each year on the
construction or maintenance of roads. This labor tax is
still being paid nearly everywhere in the area except Monteagudo and Camargo. In these two places wages are sufficiently
high and work sufficiently plentiful that most men prefer to
pay the monetary tax of Bs. 10,000 (about $ US 0.85) instead
of the four days of labor. Also in each canton is an appointed
official of the registro civil who records all births, deaths
and marriages. The juez parroquial (Chuquisaca) or juez
político (Tarija) is often a kind of errand boy of the corregidor,
who also draws up and records contracts (loans, sales, etc.)
and initiates indictments in case of local crimes.

Extremely important in the political life of Chuquisaca are
the comandos. These are political directors of the MNR party.
The jefe de comando of each department resides in the department capital. Under him are the provincial jefes de comando
— or more simply "comandos" — residing in each capital of
province. All these individuals are actually under the control
of the Minister of Government and wield considerable influence.
The chief comando for Chuquisaca, Germán Gutiérrez, is also
a Chuquisaca congressman and politically was probably the
most powerful man in the department when I was there. In
August of 1963 he managed to have the prefect of Chuquisaca,
an army colonel, removed from office and replaced by a
friend. Although formerly a leftist himself, Gutiérrez became more conservative as part of the bargain to remove the
prefect. (This power hierarchy may vary from department to
department. In Tarija the prefect, due to his friendship with
the president, is probably more powerful than the chief
comando.) In doing so he drew upon himself the wrath of
Manuel Nava, head of the Federación de Campesinos and a
leftist congressman, who until now has controlled the rural
votes in Chuquisaca. Nava has sworn he will turn the rural
votes away from Gutiérrez in the next elections; but the
latter is a very able politician, and most observers felt the
outcome of the looming political battle between Gutiérrez
and Nava was still unpredictable at the time I left. Nava's
principal objection to Gutiérrez's change of prefects is his
strong suspicion that Gutiérrez and his friend will work together to take graft from department funds. "And the more
stealing there is, the less there will be for el pueblo (the
people)," he said.

Provincial comandos are also powerful in the same sense that they can greatly influence appointments of local officials and can even effect their removal from office. During my visit to Azurduy with an official party which included the prefect and the chief of comandos, the alcalde of Azurduy was abruptly replaced at a political meeting called by the comando chief. The complaints against the incumbent alcalde had been made by the provincial comando.

At election time the comandos work through the syndicate leaders to turn out the rural population to vote for the MNR. While all the other departmental and provincial offices are traditional and existed before 1952, the comandos were a creation of the MNR regime. They were extremely important to the survival of the party, and it is therefore not surprising that they should have had considerable political power.

In each provincial capital and each departmental capital there is a Recaudador de la Dirección General de la Renta and a Recaudador de Impuestos Departamentales. The first is tax collector for the central government and the second for the department. Subprefects are supposed to supervise tax collection in their provinces but have no direct control over the collection or spending of tax money. To supervise and watch the collection of central government taxes there is also in each province a Controlor de Rentas Nacionales. Like the recaudador he is appointed by the Ministro de Hacienda (treasury). One of his duties is to review and sign every payroll in the province every month.

In each department there is a Comando Departamental de Policías (police force), which is under the Dirección Nacional de Policía, an agency of the Ministry of Government. Each province has its Comanzona (Comandante de Zona Policial), a police chief with three or four carabineros or policemen under his command. Supposedly under the supervision of the subprefect, the Comanzona usually acts quite independently of that authority.

All provinces have a juez instructor, a local judge who handles minor court cases and initiates judicial proceedings for severe crimes and expensive lawsuits. The latter cases

are then transferred to the nearest juez de partido, who has
offices only in the major centers of population.

The Servicio de Extensión Agrícola, a subdivision of the
Ministry of Agriculture, has offices in the capital of every
Chuquisaca province except the Cintis. This extension service used to operate directly under Point Four auspices, but
has recently been placed under the Bolivian ministry of agriculture, with its U. S. vehicles and the two remaining U. S.
technicians. Throughout Chuquisaca and Tarija I queried
campesinos and large landowners concerning their opinions
of the extension service. Without exception their response
was highly negative. The agents are accused of knowing
and doing nothing. "All they do is ride around in their jeeps
using up gasoline." There was no animosity against the extension personnel, who were generally considered likable
enough. The primary objection was that they were completely
incompetent to deal with the problems the farmers came to
them about. As for the U. S. technicians formerly associated
with the servicio: "They always stayed in La Paz."

The Banco Agrícola, which is a government lending
agency for farmers, has offices in the capital of each department and occasionally in a provincial capital if it is considered exceptionally important for some reason. Nor Cinti
with its rich grape harvests and relatively dependable market for singani has a special branch office all its own in
Camargo.

The Inspector de Trabajo Agrario mediates between rural
laborers and landowners. He sees that wages conform to the
minimums set by law and reviews and signs all work contracts
between landowners and campesino syndicates. He also must
attend to all complaints made to him by either farm laborers
or landowners. The campesino syndicates usually bring
complaints that the landowners do not pay as agreed in their
contracts. (Often this is because they cannot sell their crops
or they are in debt and have no cash to pay back wages.)
Landowners bring complaints of damage to crops caused by
syndicates' failure to furnish the labor they have agreed to
supply. The inspector, for lack of transportation and time,
usually sends the syndicate delegate back with a letter to the
landowner, and the landowner back with a letter to the head
of the syndicate; in each case affairs continue much as they

were.   The agrarian work inspector is appointed by the
Minister of Rural Affairs.

Also under the Ministerio de Asuntos Campesinos is the
office of the National Agrarian Reform Service, which has a
regional chief in the capital of each department and subsidiary offices in the capitals of the provinces.   In the Sucre
office there are four agrarian judges (jueces agrarios).   Two
of them are fijos — permanently stationed in Sucre.   These
two judges, one of whom is a woman, divide the province of
Oropeza and a part of the department of Potosí, which for
administrative convenience has been placed under the jurisdiction of the Chuquisaca office.   Also attached to the Sucre
office are two móviles — mobile judges, who may be sent
for brief periods anywhere in the department the jefe (chief)
decides.   In addition to the judges, the Sucre office has a
Jefe de la Sección Técnica — a head surveyor with two assistants.   With the exception of Belisario Boeto and Luis
Calvo, all the provinces have resident agrarian judges
stationed in the capital.   One juez agrario stationed in
Padilla handles both Tomina and Belisario Boeto, and the
judge in Monteagudo both Hernando Siles and Luis Calvo.
Each judge has a secretario, a man who serves as an
assistant and keeps a record of proceedings at audiencias,
meetings of campesinos formed to discuss expropriation.

Chuquisaca was unusual at the time in having a high
number of well-educated agrarian judges.   The chief judge,
Enrique Arancibia, lacked only his thesis to obtain a law
degree.   The four judges attached to the Sucre office were
all licensed lawyers.   The judges in Tarabuco, Zudañez,
Padilla, Camargo and Villa Abecia were all young men
with advanced university training who lacked only a few
requirements to obtain degrees.   Only in Azurduy and
Monteagudo were the judges purely political appointees
with little formal education.

Although the organization of the agrarian reform service in Tarija seems much the same as in Chuquisaca, the
judges did not appear to have the educational background
of those in the latter department.   For example, at Entre
Ríos in the province of O'Connor the agrarian judge was a
peasant who wore sandals.   Unfortunately I was unable to
do much work with the agrarian reform personnel in Tarija
because shortly before my arrival there the prefect, a
leftist, had managed to bring pressure through the central

government in La Paz to have the departmental head removed
from office. The director's office was under lock and key and
the staff somewhat in turmoil while awaiting the appointment
of a new head. This upset reflected a political change taking
place in Bolivia toward the end of my stay. Pressure was
being brought against all extreme leftists within the MNR
party.

FIELD METHODS

The writer arrived in Bolivia June 23, 1963. After making
official calls in La Paz and visiting Dwight Heath briefly in
Santa Cruz, work began in Chuquisaca July 3, and continued
there until September 6. Of this time four days were spent
attending a staff meeting in La Paz and six days were lost
due to illness. Thirty-nine days including travel were spent
outside of Sucre interviewing peasants and about two weeks
were spent in Sucre working.

Because of the small amount of time and the rather large
area to be covered, it was impossible to carry out the complete plan for field work. The first stage of the work, according to my original plan, was to collect a variety of data on
many subjects from widely separated points in the Chuquisaca-
Tarija area. Although I carried a list of topics for investigation no questionnaire was used. The interviews were guided
but not structured toward a schedule. By keeping interviews
open at this stage it was hoped that greater flexibility would
result and that new and unexpected material would continually
be added. Uniformity in the data was therefore sacrificed,
for the same questions were not always asked at each place
visited.

To save the time necessary to cross-check informants,
group interviews were used as much as possible. On entering a new province, the local agrarian judge was usually
contacted and arrangements made to meet with a council of
peasant family heads at two or three haciendas. This procedure was not predetermined or developed out of expediency.
After my first accidental experience with this method at
Tejahuasi early in the study, I discovered that the peasants
of this region (both Quechua- and Spanish-speakers) were
quite willing to talk and in group situations entered into
lively discussions. While a few individuals always tend to

dominate such sessions, I found that even the relatively quiet ones would voice strenuous objections if they felt someone was giving erroneous information. By using this procedure I got disagreement and corrections among my informants in the very process of gathering fresh information in a new zone. The obvious drawback to the group interviews is that they were sometimes attended by the agrarian judge or the leaders of the local syndicate. Campesino attitudes toward the syndicates had to be investigated individually, a problem I intended to concentrate upon in more detail in the second stage of the investigation.

The purpose of the first-stage survey was to throw out a net to see what variety of problems would be pulled in. On the basis of this information, more exhaustive field schedules were to be prepared which would result in comparative, quantitative data from selected points strategically located throughout the area. Unfortunately the second stage was never reached; I completely misjudged the travel time necessary to work extensively in this region. An area of 200 miles on a map looks like a morning's ride, but in Chuquisaca it may take ten to twelve hours of hard driving.

CHAPTER 4   FARM LABOR
BEFORE THE REFORM

—Charles J. Erasmus

To reconstruct in some measure the obligations of the peons on the pre-1952 haciendas of southern Bolivia, data were gathered from former arrenderos at thirty different places in Chuquisaca and Tarija. The results are condensed in Table 4. Unfortunately there is a very disproportionately high number of latifundios on this list, which means the sample may be skewed in the direction of those work situations in which the feudal obligations were most severe. However, the few cases of medianas and pequeñas on our list do not appear to have been too different in their work obligations from the latifundios in the same vicinity.

TYPES OF PATRÓN-PEON RELATIONS

In Chuquisaca and Tarija an hacienda peon was generally known by the name of arrendero although the word colono was used synonymously. Arrendero, however, was the more common term, and today people usually speak of "ex-arrenderos" rather than "ex-colonos." The word probably comes from the very "arrendar"--to rent or lease. A glance at Table 4 will show that at most of the haciendas in the sample, arrenderos paid rent in money for the parcel of hacienda land they were allowed to cultivate for themselves. But whether or not they paid rent in money they were known by the same term--arrenderos (not arrendatarios).

Table 4

LABOR OBLIGATIONS ON PRE-1952 HACIENDAS IN SOUTHERN BOLIVIA

Place	Money Rent	% of Crops	% of Livestock	Field Labor	Domestic Labor - Men	Domestic Labor - Women	Animal Care	Transport	Spinning	Weaving	Musqueo	Firewood	Arrendero Paid for Agricultural Labor	Men	Women	Latifundio	Mediana	Pequeña
Chuquichuqui		x	x	x	x		x	x	?	?	?	x		180		x		
Media Luna				x	x		?	x				?		168		x		
El Chaco				x	x		?					?		162		x		
Tejahuasi	x			x	x		?	x	?	?	?	x	x	188			x	
La Florida			x	x	x	?	x	x	?	?	?	?		113			x	
La Brisa	x			x	x	?	x				x		x	180	24			x
Cabeza Baja	x			x	x	?	x	x			x			109	24	x		
Ñucchu	x		x	x	x	x	x	x			x			125	28	x		
Cororo	x		x	x	x	x	?	x	?	?x	x			193	7	x		
Vila Vila			x	x	?	x	?	x	?	?x	x			98	84	x		
San Blas	x	x	x	x	?	?	x	x	x	x	x			85	14	x		
Molleni	x	x	x	x	x	x	x	x	x		x	x		121	62	x		
Azurduy Vicinity	x	x	x	x				x						175				
Canton Fernandez	x			x			?							104				
Huerta Cucho	x	x	x	x			?	x						175			x	
San Julián	x	x	x					x			x	x		5		x		
La Ciénaga	x	x						x			x	x		42	5	x		
Monteagudo Vic.	x			x										6				
Compañía				x	x								x	350			x	
Estancias-Camargo		x		x	?	?	?		?	?	?x			186		x		
Nazaret		x		x	x						x			156		x		
Cocha Loma	x	x		x	x	x	?		x	x	xx		x	70	38			
Caraparí		x	x	x	?	?	?	x			x			90			X	
Ingahuasi	x		x	x			?	x		?	x		x	180			X	
Patanca			x	x			?		x	x	?x			30			X	
Santa Ana	x			x			?	?			?x		x	51			X	
Bella Vista	x	x		x	x	?	x				xx			214	24		X	
San Andrés	x	x	x	x	x	?					?x			199	17	x		
Nogalito	x	x	x	x				x			x			30				
Entre Ríos	x		x	x				x			x			38				

87

Informants had great difficulty in recalling the rental sum paid because the currency had inflated so much since 1952, but figures between 35 and 50 bolivianos were mentioned most commonly. In terms of the wage-rate of that time, these rental fees equaled the value of wages for 50 to 100 days of labor per year. In some cases where rents were charged, the rental fee was cancelled by the arrendero's labor on the hacienda at so much per work-day. In most cases it apparently was not cancelled out by labor and the labor obligations were demanded in addition to the rent. At three of the places on the list the rent was usually paid in kind: at Molleni, three calves (or their money equivalent) were charged; at Carapari, three cargas (420 pounds) of maize; and at Cocha Loma, five cargas (700 pounds) of maize. In all three of these cases these payments were fixed amounts--not percentages of the arrendero's production. Percentage payments were a completely distinct obligation in addition to the fixed rental payment.

The hacienda land lent to an arrendero to work for himself was known in Chuquisaca and Tarija as an arriendo. Usually an arriendo included both pasture and cultivated land. An alleged advantage of such a system was that it allowed the arrendero to clear and plant new parcels of land within his arriendo as old plots became exhausted. In practice, however, most arrenderos planted all the cultivable lands within their arriendos year after year. On haciendas where arrenderos were given both pasture and cultivable lands, extensive pasture lands were also held by the hacienda. Arrenderos had use rights to this pasture too as long as they paid the yerbaje fee--usually a certain annual percentage of their livestock.

On haciendas where arrenderos were lent parcels of cultivable land and all pastures were used by the arrenderos and hacienda in common, the arrenderos' holdings were also known technically as arriendos but were more commonly referred to simply as parcelas. Arriendos combining both pasture and agricultural land were most common on haciendas with a large amount of temporal-- land without irrigation. Haciendas with huertas--irrigated land in canyon bottoms--usually lent small parcels to their arrenderos and held the pastures in common.

Parcelas with common pastures seem to have been
more general in the lowlands (i. e. , southward from
Monteagudo and eastward from Entre Ríos) than in the
highlands, due to different pasturing procedures. In the
lowlands, livestock have tended in the past to be more
important than agriculture and were left to forage at will.
Heavy fences are constructed around agricultural fields.
In the highlands, however, a child or a woman is usually
with the livestock to keep the animals out of the fields. The
pasture in the arriendo is used when the livestock are not
taken to the common pasture of the hacienda. Only after
harvest are animals allowed to roam at will. At this
season the entire hacienda is virtually one big pasture.

Arriendos, whether simple parcelas or units with both
pasture and cultivable land, were quite variable in size even
on the same hacienda. Although on some haciendas a distinction was made between arriendos and medio-arriendos
(half-arriendos), the latter were not necessarily just half
the size of the former. When ex-arrenderos are shown
maps of their haciendas and asked how the inequality of
arriendo sizes came to be, most are as puzzled as the
investigator. However, a few informants in widely
separated haciendas claimed to have the explanation. Some
of the arrenderos who were able to ingratiate themselves
with the patrón were made work foremen or mayordomos
and given larger arriendos. Also, any peon who gained a
reputation as a hard worker was likely to get a larger piece
of land if he asked for it. In this way, over time, arriendos
grew very unequal in size. It is debatable whether subdivision of arriendos through inheritance would have had
this effect. Ex-arrenderos claim that sons of arrenderos
who were good workers could petition the patrón for
separate arriendos and usually got them. It would be helpful to work intensively with elderly informants on several
widely separated haciendas to reconstruct the inheritance
of arriendos for at least two generations. In this study
fragmentation of holdings through inheritance was worked
out only with one informant, a Quechua originario near
Tarabuco. In that area originarios are campesinos with
small holdings to which they have titles that have been
handed down over three or four generations. Among these
individuals, fragmentation has been proceeding rapidly,
for there was no one to give them more land. However,

some heirs to these fragmented holdings preferred to give
their share to a sibling and become arrenderos on nearby
haciendas.

On those haciendas where a distinction was made
between arrenderos and half-arrenderos, the latter theoretically had just half the labor obligations of the former. If
rent was paid on the half-arriendo, it was half that for a
full one. But if percentages of harvests or livestock increments were paid, they were the same percentages for either
type.

Much more common than half-arrenderos were the
arrimantes. Arrimantes, it might be said, were the
arrenderos of arrenderos. A so-called arrendero mayor,
a peon who had obtained generous holdings from his patrón,
could, with the latter's permission, loan parts of his
holdings to an arrimante. His reason for doing so was to
get help in sharing the burden of rent and labor obligations.
The arrimante, in return for his parcel of cultivable land
within the arrendero's arriendo, would help the latter pay
his annual monetary rent. Where the semanería (one week
of service every month or in rotation) or the quincena (15
days a month) were obligatory, for example, the arrimantes
might fulfill the semanería or quincena obligations for the
arrendero or rotate with him. Again, however, if it was
the practice on an hacienda to pay percentages of harvests
and livestock increments, the arrimante had to pay the
same percentages to the patrón as the arrendero paid. On
haciendas where the arrenderos were required to bring the
hacendado a certain amount of firewood each year or prepare
a certain amount of chicha, the arrimante would share
these burdens equally with him.

In some cases arrenderos were as abusive to their
arrimantes as the hacendados were to their arrenderos.
For example, some arrenderos not only made their
arrimantes fulfill most of their labor obligations to the
patrón but insisted that they put in free labor on their
arriendo plots as well. Thus in some cases the arrimante
was in the unenviable position of having to fulfill free labor
obligations to both the patrón and the arrendero. Such
cases seem to have occurred only in highland areas where

the farm population is most dense (i. e., the Quechua areas
in northern Chuquisaca).

In addition to arrenderos and arrimantes some
haciendas also had yerbajeros (also called herbajeros).
These individuals had only pasture rights for which they
paid in money or kind and sometimes with labor. The same
man might be an arrendero on one hacienda and yerbajero
on a neighboring one. Usually the yerbajero paid 10 per
cent of his livestock increment each year (diezmo). Near
Azurduy I talked to a yerbajero who paid an annual fee of
two arrobas (50 pounds) of cheese. At Molleni a yerbajero
paid two calves annually, 12 1/2 pounds of cheese, one of
every five lambs, and loaned the patrón a milk cow for one
month a year. He also had to give labor: fifteen days of
cacha (transporting hacienda products by mule and burro)
and four days cutting and carrying firewood.

Hacienda Patanca, on the Tarija border with Potosí,
lies in a very inclement environment suitable only for
pasturing sheep and goats. Although each yerbajero kept
a very small garden plot, it was not large enough to be
considered an arriendo. These families lived almost
entirely from their livestock, which they traded in the
valleys for wheat and maize. They had to pay the hacendado
a head tax of 50 cents for each animal (Bs. 2 each for
cattle), and to give him one out of every ten new lambs and
kids each year. In addition they supplied one month's free
labor to the patrón. Since there was no work to be done at
Patanca, the owner made them work the thirty days on
farm lands he owned at lower altitudes or on the farms of
friends and relatives who paid him for this labor. Eight
days a year were also spent by each Patanca yerbajero
cutting and transporting firewood for the patrón.

In the grape-producing valleys of the Cintis a distinction was made between two kinds of farm laborers: the
peones efectivos and the arrenderos. The latter in this
instance had much in common with the Patanca yerbajeros.
Owners of vineyards in the Cinti canyon loaned small plots
of huerta (irrigated canyon bottom) land (usually much less
than an hectare) to their permanent laborers, called peónes
efectivos. These individuals worked around the hacienda
house without remuneration on Sundays, but were paid for
all work during the week. Most weeks they worked the

entire six days. Each hacienda had a store where the peón
efectivo could obtain whatever he wanted in the way of food
and clothes on credit. His weekly wages went to pay off his
debt at the store. On his parcela he grew such food staples
as maize and potatoes and some fruit. Usually he did not
devote his parcela to grapes although he might have a few
vines for household consumption. Sometimes the patrón
would let a peón efectivo plant maize between the rows of
grape vines on hacienda land. This was no great concession
since most haciendas made a practice of planting maize,
potatoes, and vegetables between their grapevines and still
do so. Although he received a wage for every week day he
worked, the peón efectivo was not at liberty to choose his
work days. He was obligated to work whenever the patrón
requested his services, or he could lose his parcela.

The peones efectivos were quite insufficient, however,
to meet the labor needs of the vineyards, for a hectare of
vineyard required about 1,200 man-days of work annually
(see Table 5). The number of peones efectivos necessary
to meet the labor needs of the hacienda would have
required so many perquisite parcelas that there would have
been no land left for the vineyards. The solution arrived
at by most of the larger winegrowers (about ten hectares
and above) was to buy an estancia. An estancia was an
hacienda in the higher altitudes around the Cinti canyon
usually acquired for the purpose of obtaining arrenderos.
The owner customarily divided the entire estancia into
arriendos without leaving any lands to be worked for the
hacienda. Instead, therefore, of working land for the
patrón on the estancia, arrenderos worked as needed on his
vineyards in the Cinti.

Usually an arriendo in an estancia included both
agricultural land and pasture with additional hacienda
pasture used in common by all the arrenderos. Hacienda
Nazaret (between Camargo and Ingahuasi) was an exception. This estancia had a high altitude canyon running
through it in which the arrenderos had irrigated parcelas.
All the non-cultivated land was a common pasture.

Arrenderos at Nazaret were obliged to work ninety
days a year in the owner's vineyards in the Cinti. They
were not paid for this, but only housed and fed while there.

Table 5

MAN-DAYS OF LABOR IN SINGANI PRODUCTION*

Farm Operation	Number of Men	Number of Women	Number of Days	Total Work Days
Hoe cultivation	10		4	40
Hoeing clods	10		3	30
Tying up plants	5	5	24	240
Pruning	30		1	30
Tying up new branches	8		15	120
Spraying	3		7	21
Second pruning	10		3	30
Weeding	10		3	30
Harvesting				38
Processing				
Extracting juice	10		1	10
Fermentation	1		12	12
Pruning shade trees	1			10
Irrigation				360
Replacing dead plants and old posts, etc.				200
Total labor (man-days per year)				1,171

* per hectare

Before the highway was built between Sucre and Tarija,
Nazaret arrenderos transported their patrón's singani
their own mules and burros as far as the city of Potosí.
They also had to cut firewood and transport it to the Cinti
hacienda, where it was used in distilling singani. Each year
they were required to cut and transport a certain number of
posts used to support the grape vines. None of these labor
obligations was remunerated by the hacienda. In addition,
the arrenderos usually paid the diezmo, one out of every ten
lambs and kids born each year. In the case of other
estancias, owners were paying wages to the arrenderos
(prior to the reform) for the time they spent in the vineyards.
This wage was usually fixed at half the wage of a peón
efectivo.

Apparently the system of estancias was not restricted
to the wine-growing areas of Nor and Sud Cinti. Hacendados
growing sugar cane (to be distilled to make alcohol) along
the Pilcomayo River also had estancias in the higher valleys
to secure their labor force. Cocha Loma was such an
estancia and its arrenderos worked on the Pilcomayo sugar
cane hacienda known as El Verano, which was owned by the
same patrón. El Verano had no resident peons, only a
mayordomo; the entire work force came from Cocha Loma.

Most of the estancias have been declared latifundios and
totally expropriated. Since the owners did not work any of
the land and held them only to obtain a free labor supply,
they were declared "feudal" in their method of exploitation
and therefore eligible for total expropriation, regardless of
size.

PAYMENTS—CATASTRO AND DIEZMO

The obligation of paying the hacienda a percentage of
the harvest grown on the arriendo, called the catastro, was
not as common as paying a money rent and only half as
common as the diezmo for livestock. As we have seen, however, paying a money rent did not obviate the catastro, for
both payments were obligatory in some cases. The catastro
percentage was quite variable: 10 per cent at Chuquichuqui,
Huerta Cucho and Carapari, one in six at San Blas, 20 per
cent at San Julián, and a full 50 per cent at Molleni and

La Ciénaga. The catastro was often highest on haciendas
where the patrón did not work any of the land himself; labor
obligations on such an hacienda were lower, and the
catastro was the patrón's major source of income. At
Chuquichuqui and Huerta Cucho this was not the case. The
catastro there was a sort of rent paid in kind, since no
monetary rent was paid there. At Carapari the catastro was
another burden in addition to rent and a sizeable labor obligation. It was in anger against the catastro that the
arrenderos of Carapari murdered their patrón shortly before
the reform--an incident we shall discuss later. At San Blas
and particularly San Julián and La Ciénaga the labor obligations were not great and the catastro was the major source
of income for the owners. In these cases the arrenderos
were for all practical purposes little different from sharecroppers. Molleni was the most abusive case of catastro
since the additional obligations were so heavy there.

The livestock diezmo was the most widespread payment
made by arrenderos, and it was for use of pasture, not
agricultural land. The most common payment was 10 per
cent of the annual increment, from which the name "diezmo."
This 10 per cent of the annual increment was charged at
Chuquichuqui, La Florida, Ñucchu, Cororo, Vila Vila, San
Blas, Azurduy, Huerta Cucho, San Julián, Nazaret,
Carapari, Ingahuasi, Bella Vista, San Andrés, and
Nogalito. At Molleni the arrenderos were charged 20 per
cent of the annual increment of lambs and calves. At La
Ciénaga they were charged one of every five calves and
one of every seven lambs. While Carapari and Ingahuasi
charged 10 per cent of the annual increment, they also took
one of each thirty rams and ewes. Bella Vista, San Andrés
and Nogalito charged an annual money head tax for all grown
animals in addition to the diezmo.

LABOR OBLIGATIONS

The labor obligations of arrenderos varied a great deal
from hacienda to hacienda. When queried about the
differences in obligations between neighboring haciendas,
informants always asserted that they were never exactly
alike in any two cases. But they claimed that arrenderos
dared not to try to leave their hacienda for another with

fewer obligations because their old patrón might do them
bodily harm.

Most haciendas required their arrenderos to do field
labor on the hacienda lands. The only exceptions in Table
5 are San Julián and La Ciénaga near Padilla. In neither of
those cases did the owner work a part of the hacienda; except
for some pasture land held by the patrón and in common use,
these haciendas were divided up entirely into arriendos containing both pasture and cultivated land. Since labor demands
were small here, the owners, as we have seen, took 20 per
cent of the arrenderos' crops at San Julián and 50 per cent
at La Ciénaga.

On some haciendas the arrenderos were expected to
work two weeks or fifteen days per month, often called the
quincena (Chuquichuqui, Media Luna, El Chaco, Cororo,
estancias around Camargo, Ingahuasi, Bella Vista and San
Andrés). In such cases the arrenderos were usually divided
into two groups which worked alternate quincenas. At Vila
Vila only one week per month was required. In some cases
three days out of each week were for the hacienda (La Brisa,
Huerta Cucho and around Azurduy). At such places the
arrendero was expected to work the entire week for the
hacienda during planting and harvesting. This schedule
most closely approximates the English manorial system.

At some haciendas there was a designated number of
days per year which each arrendero had to work: 150 at
Tejahuasi, 90 at Nazaret and Carapari, and 30 at Patanca,
Nogalito (on the road from Tarija to Bermejo) and around
Entre Ríos. Other haciendas employed the system of
yanapacu, by which each arrendero was given a certain
quantity of seed to plant. The area necessary to plant this
seed was then tended and harvested by him. The amount of
time required for yanapacu service was consistently
estimated at between 80 and 85 days nearly everywhere it
had been employed. This system was used at La Florida,
Cabeza Baja, Ñucchu, Cororo and Molleni.

At many places arrenderos also had to serve periodically as servants to take care of the hacienda house and
grounds. This service was usually performed for a week
at a time and in rotation. It was called semanería or

pongueaje. During service at pongueaje an arrendero might
be given duties as a messenger (to buy things in town or
carry letters). This duty was known as runacacha. Pongueaje
was practiced at Chuquichuqui, Media Luna, El Chaco,
Tejahuasi, La Florida, La Brisa, Cabeza Baja, Ñucchu,
Cororo, and Molleni. In the vicinity of Camargo free
service was given the hacienda by peones efectivos on Sundays,
a slightly different system, but a form of pongueaje nonetheless.

When the arrendero's wife or grown daughters were
required to work as servants in the hacienda house, the
service was known as mitanaje. This work consisted mainly
of preparing meals for the peons, cleaning the house, and
feeding chickens. Like pongueaje it was done in rotation
for a week at a time but seldom affected the same household
more than twice a year. It was practiced at Ñucchu,
Cororo, Vila Vila, Bella Vista and San Andrés.

Caring for livestock of the patrón was an obligatory work
service apart from field labor or pongueaje at only a few
places: Chuquichuqui, La Florida, La Brisa, Cabeza Baja,
and Molleni. Again it was done on a rotation basis and
usually by women or children. From each family it required
the work of one person for two to four weeks a year. At San
Blas and Molleni it was also obligatory for each arrendero
to raise and fatten one pig a year for the patrón. If the
animal died, the arrendero had to replace it.

Cacha was a very common service obligation and was
usually additional to the other services. It was included in
the general labor obligation only at Huerta Cucho, Carapari,
Ingahuasi and Nogalito. Cacha consisted of the obligation
to transport the patrón's agricultural products to a market
or road, almost always on burros and mules of the arrenderos.
If there were not enough of these animals, the arrenderos
had to rent them or exchange labor for them. An average
of about five or six days a year was devoted to cacha by
each arrendero.

Another very common service obligation, again additional in most cases to other requirements was to provide
the hacienda with firewood. The arrenderos had to look for
this wood, cut it, load it on their own burros, and transport
it to the hacienda, a procedure which took anywhere from

one to twenty days but averaged (for twenty haciendas) six days. It was included as part of the general work services at La Florida, Vila Vila, Carapari, Ingahuasi, and San Andrés.

Work services often required in addition to the others (but in a few places included in the general labor obligation) were: (1) to provide a certain quantity of construction materials each year for the hacienda including posts, roof beams and adobes; (2) muqueo, the obligation to make chicha from a certain quantity of maize given each family by the patrón (usually the work of women); (3) spinning and weaving a certain quantity of wool each year (also work of women); and (4) pisquero or pajarero, frightening birds away from the ripening hacienda crops, usually fruit trees. This task was often assigned to the children of the arrenderos.

Table 4 shows the total number of work days per year provided by the average arrendero family at each of the haciendas listed (but only for the tasks listed). These totals are computed from estimates given by discussion groups of informants in about half the cases. Information was obtained from only one informant in the cases of Nazaret, Cocha Loma, and Patanca. About two thirds of the totals (for men) fall between 100 and 200 days per year and about half of them at over 150 days. The highest figure, 350, was for obligatory wage labor. These figures seem consistent with very rough estimates made by the writer in 1953 for a few haciendas in Peru and Ecuador, and also seem consistent with estimates of the number of days per annum which the feudal villein was obligated to devote to work services for his lord. There seems to be an upper limit of tolerance to the amount of free labor which farm families will trade for perquisite subsistence plots under a loose feudal-type system. Only with greater centralization of power can the number of agricultural work days per family per year be increased to as much as 500 (as in the Russian kolkhoz) or 700 (estimated for the Chinese commune). The probable Israeli kibbutz average of 500-600 is the product of an entirely different kind of social phenomenon--a nativistic religious movement.

CONTROLS

The result of these inquiries about pre-reform labor
conditions in various parts of Chuquisaca and Tarija supports
the often-heard contention that those conditions became less
feudal toward the southern and eastern portions of this
region, where land was more plentiful and labor in greater
demand. The obligations were obviously lighter in Tomina
around Padilla and became negligible in the vicinity of
Monteagudo. In Nor Cinti around Camargo the peones
efectivos worked a full year, but they were wage laborers
(as their name implies) with a perquisite plot thrown in.
The Cinti canyon has always had a labor shortage, and
peons who knew the more specialized agricultural tasks of
the vineyard, such as proper pruning techniques, were in
demand. Even at Ingahuasi in the highlands of Sud Cinti,
the arrenderos were paid when they worked for the
hacienda. In the department of Tarija where the farm
population around the city of Tarija was most dense, work
obligations intensified again though they were much weaker
to the east, south and west.

The distribution of physical punishment and the taking
of prendas is also of interest. Prendas were objects of
value which the mayordomo took from the house of an
arrendero if he did not comply with labor or payment obligations. Mentioned most often as prendas were blankets,
cattle,and pigs. If the obligations were not fulfilled, the
prenda was sold. This custom was prevalent in northwestern
Chuquisaca, among arrenderos of estancias in Cinti and in
large haciendas around the city of Tarija; but its existence
was denied by ex-arrenderos around Padilla, Monteagudo,
the Cinti canyon (peones efectivos), and western and
southern Tarija. The distribution of this method of control
conforms to the area of the most severe obligations. The
distribution of corporal punishment is practically identical
to that for taking prendas. Apparently the worst offenses
of this nature were perpetrated at Molleni, the hacienda
which has come to epitomize the evils of the "feudal" era in
Chuquisaca. At Molleni the campesinos told of incredibly
brutal treatment at the hands of the hacendado, who not
only whipped them in anger but sometimes even cut them
with a knife. One elderly campesino woman cried as she
showed me her scars and told how don Crisólogo Reyes had

cut her with his knife. Ex-hacendados usually defend each
other but none deny the stories about Reyes. He was a self-
made man who had acquired several haciendas and lost them
all in the reform. But he was considered to belong to the
lower-middle class, and in the view of hacendados of "good
family" he was a "sick man," or a "sadist." It would not be
fair to regard the extreme situation at Molleni as in any
sense typical of pre-reform conditions in this region.

In most of Chuquisaca and Tarija there was on each
hacienda a large and imposing adobe dwelling where the
owner lived. Very few owners resided continuously on their
haciendas, for nearly all had town houses where they spent
some of their time. They were most likely to be on hand
at the hacienda during planting and harvest. Most haciendas
had mayordomos, work foremen, or both. A mayordomo
was an administrator who looked after the hacienda and saw
that all the arrenderos performed their work obligations when
the patrón was not present. When the patrón was present he
acted as a work foreman relaying orders and supervising the
work. Very often the mayordomo was an arrendero in whom
the patrón had confidence and to whom he made special
concessions such as providing him with a large and choice
arriendo. The mayordomo was spared most of the payments
and common work obligations, but it was up to him to perform
the odious police duties of the hacienda, such as taking
prendas.

On very large haciendas the mayordomo needed
assistants to direct the various work parties that might be
deployed in several places on the same day. At some
places, such as Nazaret for example, such a subsidiary
work foreman was called a capataz. These men were
selected by the mayordomo himself and were given special
favors such as higher wages and more land. Neither
mayordomos nor their foremen were ever chosen by the
arrenderos themselves.

At Ingahuasi, a huge hacienda of some 15,000
irrigated hectares on a plain in highland Sud Cinti was
divided for administrative purposes into seven sectors
(sectores). Each sector was under the administration of a
caporal and his assistant, work foremen who were picked
by the manager (gerente). These caporales were

arrenderos also, but they were excused from the quincena
and given larger parcelas. The caporales took prendas from
their neighbors when the manager ordered them punished but
it was said that their fellow campesinos did not hold such
acts against them, for a caporal had to obey the manager.

Local government was definitely on the side of the
landowner in pre-reform days. According to the
ex-arrenderos of San Blas, some who tried to leave the
hacienda were captured by police from Sopachuy and kept
in jail there until they agreed to return. Without any doubt
the most significant result of the Bolivian land reform has
been the complete destruction of the power of the wealthy
landed classes. This change in the power structure is a
topic to which we will return in a later chapter.

CHAPTER **5** LAND TENURE
AND REFORM

— Charles J. Erasmus

In order to gain some idea of the size and distribution of land holdings in southern Bolivia, statistics were abstracted from 335 expedientes (dossiers of agrarian reform proceedings) for the department of Chuquisaca. All of these expedientes were on file in the Sucre and provincial offices. Many more are available in La Paz, but there was not sufficient time for documentary research in the capital. No one seems to know on just what basis some expedientes are kept in La Paz, some are returned to Sucre and others filed in the agrarian reform offices of the provincial capitals. It appears to be a matter of chance, and for that reason the information extracted from the 335 expedientes and presented in the following tables may be a representative sample. At any rate, until a more detailed study can be made in the archive in La Paz, the following statistics may be better than none at all. Unfortunately it proved impossible to obtain statistical information from the expedientes in Tarija. As explained previously, at the time of this study the Tarija office of the agrarian reform was closed as a result of the political maneuvering which had led to the firing of the department director.

An expediente is the series of documents resulting from the legal action by which a farm property is affected by the agrarian reform. These papers are bound together under a title sheet bearing the name and location of the property. *

---

*For details on the complex sequence of procedures involved in land claims cases, see Chapter 2.

SIZE OF LANDHOLDINGS

From the several documents in the expediente it is possible to obtain data on the size of the hacienda or farm, amounts of cultivable and non-arable (or pasture) land, number of arrenderos and the range in size of their holdings, who initiated the proceedings (peasants, owner or judge), length of time to complete the proceedings, and so forth. As indicated previously, the size of a farm is important in categorizing it as a latifundio or as a small or medium property according to the type of geographic zone in which it is located. For example, the maximum size of a mediana property is 350 hectares in "semi-desert" regions of the Altiplano zone, 40 hectares in valles cerrados (closed valleys), 200 hectares in cabeceras de valle (heads of valleys), and in open valleys (valles abiertos) 60 hectares of irrigated land, 150 hectares of dry farming land or 24 hectares of vineyard.

Table 6 shows the relative frequency of each zone designation in our sample of Chuquisaca properties. Here the designation "head of valley" predominates to the virtual exclusion of almost all others and reflects the very mountainous nature of the terrain. This also means that the zone categorization is not a very diagnostic criteria in differentiating between classes of properties in Chuquisaca since most fall within this one zone-type.

Table 6

FREQUENCY OF ZONE DESIGNATIONS OF HACIENDAS
IN CHUQUISACA

Province	Valle Abierto	Valle Cerrado	Cabecera de Valle	Semi-desértico	Puna
Oropeza	1	6	90		5
Yamparaez	0	0	34	3	25
Zudañez	0	4	45		2
Azurduy	0	0	45		2
Tomina	0	0	67		1
Nor Cinti	1	7	7		0
Totals	2	17	2 88	3	35
%	1	5	83	1	10

Table 7 gives averages of hacienda sizes for the department of Chuquisaca. It shows that the difference between pequeñas and medianas is much greater than that between the latter and latifundios. This reflects the fact that a property can be declared a latifundio if it has been abandoned (sometimes because the owner is afraid to return), or is declared feudal in its former employment of the labor force. Many farms which would belong in the mediana category on the basis of size, have been declared latifundios for the latter reason. In the early days of the reform the accusation of feudalistic labor exploitation of arrenderos was an easy tool for political reprisal against hacendados who were enemies of the governing political party.

Table 7

DIFFERENCES IN CHUQUISACA PROPERTY SIZES ACCORDING TO TYPE*

	Latifundios	Medianas	Pequeñas
Number of cases in sample	45	188	102
Average total area of hacienda	1356.26	950.02	100.23
Average uncultivated land of hacienda	202.30	112.30	7.22
Average uncultivated (pasture) land	1142.61	835.24	92.93
Percentage of cultivated land	15	12	7
Percentage of non-arable (pasture) land	85	88	93

*in hectares

A comparison of Tables 8-10 shows that the smallest latifundios in Chuquisaca provinces range from 5 to 120

Table 8

SIZES* OF CHUQUISACA LATIFUNDIOS

	Oropeza	Yampa-raez	Zudañez	Azur-duy	Tomina	Nor Cinti
Number of cases	12	11	3	12	12	3
Total area* of largest	8,693	3,500	6,647	5,815	2,919	7,615
Cultivated area* of largest	3,060	1,249	194	230	233	267
Pasture area* of largest	5,633	2,251	6,453	5,585	2,686	7,348
Total area* of smallest	438	79	82	120	305	116
Cultivated area* of smallest	120	19	5	10	97	11
Uncultivated area* of smallest	318	60	77	110	208	105
Average total area*	2,487	1,345	2,292	1,299	1,241	2,905
Average cultivated area*	703	324	106	38	148	103
Average pasture area*	1,777	1,020	2,186	1,261	1,093	2,802
Percentage of total latifundio area in cultivation	28	24	5	3	12	4
Percentage of total latifundio area in pasture	72	76	95	97	88	96

*in hectares

Table 9

SIZES* OF CHUQUISACA PROPIEDADES MEDIANAS

	Oropeza	Yampa-raez	Zudañez	Azur-duy	Tomina	Nor Cinti
Number of cases in sample	69	34	36	23	21	5
Total area* of largest	5,237	8,013	14,423	6,944	2,328	936
Cultivated area* of largest	170	400	1,958	95	63	31
Uncultivated area* of largest	5,067	7,613	12,465	6,848	2,265	905
Total area* of smallest	15	60	23	54	38	11
Cultivated area* of smallest	5	37	2	13	12	11
Uncultivated area of smallest*	10	23	21	41	26	0
Average total area* of sample	715	1,194	1,408	1,075	583	204
Average cultivated area* in sample	103	200	151	42	35	21
Average uncultivated area* in sample	613	994	1,257	1,033	548	182
Percentage of total mediana area in cultivation	3	17	11	4	6	10
Percentage of total mediana area in uncultivated land	97	83	89	96	94	90

*in hectares

Table 10

SIZES* OF CHUQUISACA PROPIEDADES PEQUEÑAS

	Oropeza	Yampa-raez	Zudañez	Azur-duy	Tomina	Nor Cinti
Number of cases in sample	15	15	11	12	42	7
Total area* of largest	331	403	230	345	801	9
Cultivated area* of largest	17	18	4	16	6	9
Uncultivated area* of largest	314	385	226	329	795	0
Total area* of smallest	. 5	3. 7	20	. 9	1. 8	. 5
Cultivated area* of smallest	. 5	2. 6	5	. 9	1. 8	. 5
Uncultivated area* of smallest	0	1. 1	15	0	0	0
Average total area* of sample	106	106	113	94	111	2. 8
Average cultivated area* in sample	11	13	5	8	5	2. 8
Average uncultivated area* in sample	95	92	108	86	106	0
Percentage of total pequeña area in cultivation	10	13	5	9	5	100
Percentage of total pequeña area in uncultivated land	90	87	95	91	95	0

*in hectares

hectares (counting only cultivated land) and the largest
medianas from 31 to 1,958 hectares. This is a very considerable overlap. At the other extreme, however, the
largest pequeñas range from 4 to 18 hectares and the smallest
medianas from 2 to 37 hectares, an even more surprising
overlap given the greater gap in the average size of farms in
the latter two categories: average farm size of pequeñas
ranges from 2.8 to 113 hectares, of medianas from 204 to
1,408 and of latifundios from 1,241 to 2,905 in the various
provinces.

LAND USE

A noteworthy product of the statistics in Tables 7-10 is
the relatively small proportion of cultivated land in relation
to pasture in all types of properties. It ranges only between
7 and 15 per cent (Table 7) with the latifundios having the
advantage of the highest percentage of cultivated land. This
does not mean that large properties exploited more of their
available territory; it means that they had relatively better
land of which a higher percentage was arable. The
"uncultivated" or "non-arable," or "pasture" land of
Chuquisaca farms is usually mountainous terrain (steep
canyon sides, etc.) which cannot be exploited for farming.
It is surprising how often slopes are cultivated even though
they seem much too steep. Why latifundios in the provinces
of Oropeza and Yamparaez have a much higher percentage of
cultivable land than those in other provinces is difficult to
explain, unless perhaps this difference is due to some
irregularity in the sample. Another possible explanation is
that the farms in these provinces lie closest to the department capital, Sucre, where individuals of the wealthy upper
class were concentrated. These individuals undoubtedly
endeavored to consolidate the best lands within their farm
holdings.

A problem related to the above is why a much higher
percentage of cultivated land was worked by owners of
latifundios than of mediana properties (see Table 11; the
statistics for latifundios in Table 11 are derived only from
these same provinces of Oropeza and Yamparaez). Proceedings against these haciendas, which were close to
Sucre--the seat of political action in this area--were

Table 11

DISTRIBUTION OF LANDS* WITHIN DIFFERENT CLASSES
OF CHUQUISACA PROPERTIES

	Latifundios	Medianas	Pequeñas
Number of cases	45	152	102
Percentage of total cultivated lands worked by owners	33**	20	70
Percentage of total cultivated lands worked by campesinos	67**	80	30
Average arable land per campesino	4.0	3.2	1.6
Average non-arable land* per campesino	21.8	20.6	14.0
Average arable land* per owner	161.2**	27.9	5.1
Average non-arable land* per owner	204.0**	366.3	76.7

*in hectares
**only Oropeza and Yamparaez (23 cases)

initiated early in the agrarian reform when the data on the
land use patterns existing within the properties before the
reform were known and clearly recorded in the expedientes.
As can be seen in Table 12, the expedientes from the
remaining provinces of Chuquisaca tend to give the post-
reform land distribution; in most of these cases the owners'
land had already been "abandoned" by them and put to use by
the campesinos at the time of surveying. In most cases the
land in these latifundios was no longer being used by the
former landowners. This lack of information is unfortunate
since it makes it difficult to be sure of the pre-reform

Table 12

DISTRIBUTION OF LANDS* WITHIN CHUQUISACA
LATIFUNDIOS

	Oropeza	Yampa- raez	Zudañez	Azur- duy	Tomina	Nor Cinti
Number of cases	12	11	3	12	4	3
Percentage of total cultivated land worked by owners	43	19	0	0	0	0
Percentage of total cultivated land worked by campesinos	57	81	100	100	100	100
Maximum size arriendo*	228	169.39	73.74	413.58	201.50	---
Minimum size arriendo*	.03	1.00	6.36	.58	2.00	---
Average maximum size arriendo*	119	62.08	40.72	135.54	99.90	---
Average minimum size arriendo	3.47	4.80	1.03	9.51	11.91	---
Average largest parcela*	15.10	12.53	11.40	6.35	15.80	8.89
Average minimum parcela*	1.32	1.41	.53	1.33	1.19	.14
Average arable land per campesino	4.00	5.10	4.73	2.27	7.15	3.67
Average non-arable land per campesino	24.91	23.23	155.48	74.88	52.65	100.08
Average arable land per owner	295.18	61.03	0	0	0	0
Average non-arable land per owner	253.11	155.03	0	0	0	0

*in hectares

percentage of cultivated land in large properties which was
contained in the perquisite plots of the arrenderos, and the
percentage directly administered by the hacendado. In the
mediana properties (Table 13) the percentage of cultivated
land administered by the owner varies from 17 to 22 per cent
and averages 20 per cent. Oropeza and Yamparaez in this
case average a little lower than the rest.

It is questionable whether the data for medianas on the
division of cultivated land between owners and campesinos
give an exact picture of pre-reform conditions. In many
cases, apparently, when mediana haciendas were being
mapped, the holdings of arrenderos were increased by the
surveyors at the hacendado's expense without this increase
being recorded in the legal records. Moreover, in many
cases part of the owners' lands were taken from them to
give to recién dotados, usually grown sons of arrenderos who
were without lands of their own with which to maintain their
families. Working carefully with the expedientes available
in La Paz, it might be possible to make more exact estimates,
based on those expedientes with the most complete records,
of the percentage of hacienda lands, cultivated and pasture,
used by owners and by arrenderos prior to the reform.

From the information contained here, it would appear
that the percentage of cultivated land which was directly
worked by the owner averaged between one fifth and one third
of the total in the larger properties, the rest being contained
in the parcelas or arriendas of the campesinos. Until more
complete information is obtained, the amount can be roughly
calculated as averaging about 25 per cent. In other words,
owners of medium to large properties worked one fourth of
the cultivable land and the arrenderos the other three fourths
in their perquisite plots.

In the pequeña or small properties the percentages tend
to reverse themselves for the simple reason that the
majority of small properties in the sample were family-
worked parcels without any arrenderos. In Oropeza and
Yamparaez the small properties nearly always have some
arrenderos, but the expedientes for Zudañez and Nor Cinti
showed none and those for Tomina and Azurduy, only a very
few cases. Since the average amount of cultivated land in
pequeñas (Table 10) is nearly twice as great in Oropeza

Table 13

DISTRIBUTION OF LANDS* WITHIN CHUQUISACA
PROPIEDADES MEDIANAS

	Oropeza	Yampa-raez	Zudañez	Azur-duy	Tomina	Nor Cinti
Number of cases	69	34	36	23	21	5
Percentage of total cultivated lands worked by owners	17	20	22	19	22	37
Percentage of total cultivated lands worked by campesinos	83	79	78	81	78	63
Maximum size arriendo*	587.02	233.71	281.71	647.78	406.46	---
Minimum size arriendo*	.06	.14	.06	.27	1.55	---
Average maximum size arriendo*	56.94	68.48	93.63	---	---	---
Average minimum size arriendo*	3.41	3.80	1.71	---	---	---
Average size arriendo*	21.63	21.82	---	---	---	---
Average largest parcela*	8.21	13.95	8.66	7.53	5.08	1.60
Average minimum parcela*	1.13	1.00	.85	1.09	.90	.37
Average arable land* per campesino	3.51	4.28	5.19	2.94	2.64	.72
Average non-arable land* per campesino	18.12	17.54	33.17	76.86	43.12	.66
Average arable land* per owner	17.51	42.27	32.96	7.79	7.87	13.30
Average non-arable land* per owner	207.77	91.04	569.28	118.26	143.61	181.42

*in hectares

and Zudañez as in the other provinces, the greater number of
arrenderos there is understandable. The complete lack of
arrenderos on pequeña properties in Nor Cinti, which average
only 2.8 hectares, is again what one might expect.

The figures in Table 11 show that the average amount of
cultivable land worked personally by hacendados was by no
means extraordinarily large. Latifundio owners in Oropeza
and Yamparaez averaged 161 hectares; medium-size property
owners average only 28 hectares--by no means a large farm.
Even allowing for a considerable loss on the part of the
medium properties as a result of the reform (giving some of
the hacienda land to beneficiaries of expropriation) the
average probably did not exceed 38 hectares in pre-reform
times. The cultivable land worked by owners of small
properties averages only one hectare more than that worked
by arrenderos on large holdings.

REFORM AND REALLOCATION

The average amounts of cultivable land held by
arrenderos was and is extremely small. It seems difficult
to believe that three or four hectares can maintain a family,
yet in many cases families apparently subsist on much less,
as we shall see. Tables 12-14 list the minimum and maximum
sizes of campesino holdings as well as the "average
maximum" and "average minimum." These latter terms
require some explanation. The technical documents in most
expedientes list all the arrenderos by name and the size of
their holdings. Minimum and maximum size campesino
holdings were recorded from all expedientes. The largest
and smallest on all the expedientes from a given province
are given in the tables as well as the average of all the
largest and smallest recorded campesino holdings for that
province. Thus we see that a very few arrenderos had
holdings (including both pasture and arable land) of as much
as 500 and 600 hectares. Yet at the other extreme many are
far under a tenth of an hectare (in such cases the parcel is
all arable land). It is noteworthy that in very few cases was
anything done in this area to equalize the disparity in size of
campesino holdings. Ex-arrenderos were almost always
given title to whatever land they already occupied before the
reform. Inequalities in land tenure among the campesinos

Table 14

DISTRIBUTION OF LANDS* WITHIN CHUQUISACA
PROPIEDADES PEQUEÑAS

	Oropeza	Yampa-raez	Zudañez	Azur-duy	Tomina	Nor Cinti
Number of cases	15	15	11	12	42	7
Percentage of total cultivated lands worked by owners	43	55	100	81	90	100
Percentage of total cultivated lands worked by campesinos	57	45	0	19	10	0
Maximum size arriendo*	35.38	81.10	---	--	---	---
Minimum size arriendo*	.34	2.40	---	--	---	---
Average maximum size arriendo*	15.70	47.02	---	--	---	---
Average minimum size arriendo*	6.25	17.30	---	--	---	---
Average size arriendo*	15.35	26.71	---	--	---	---
Average largest parcela*	1.96	4.17	---	--	---	---
Average minimum parcela*	.62	1.29	---	--	---	---
Average arable land* per campesino	1.30	2.84	---	1.04	1.08	0
Average non-arable land* per campesino	65.02	22.25	---	17.21	---	0
Average arable land* per owner	5.02	6.91	5.48	8.25	4.36	2.79
Average non-arable land* per owner	8.48	32.82	107.95	60.25	106.00	0

*in hectares

themselves has for the most part been perpetuated by the
reform, and the inequalities are obviously enormous. The
same tables also give the average maximum and minimum
sizes of arable plots held by the campesinos (ex-arrenderos),
which range from one third of an hectare to over fifteen
hectares.

The sizes of arriendos (campesino perquisite plots which
included both cultivable and pasture land) are not given for
Cinti latifundios, for medium-size holdings in Azurduy,
Tomina and Cinti, or for small properties in Zudañez,
Azurduy, Tomina and Cinti. In these instances the number
of arriendos was too few to warrant comparison. Either
there were very few campesinos, as in the case of the small
properties, or the campesinos did not have arriendos. For
example, over half the medium properties in Azurduy did not
have arriendos. Each ex-arrendero or ex-colono has
cultivable parcelas and the pasture or non-arable land is
held and used in common. The same is true of most medium
properties in Tomina. What is not clear is how many of
these cases of common pasture are pre-reform and how many
post-reform. In some cases the initial document in the
expediente enumerates arriendos but they are ignored in the
final judgment, as far as the non-arable land is concerned.
Yet in many of the expedientes the documentation indicates
that collective pastures were the custom prior to the reform.
Azurduy and Tomina are provinces where collective pastures
were a frequent alternative to the arriendo system among
medium properties and in Cinti among latifundios. This
alternative was well known to the agrarian judges in this
area, who have sentenced many properties which formerly
had arriendos to change to the collective pasture system.
What geographic or social conditions may account for the
original prevalence of this alternative in these two provinces
would require more comparative data to ascertain.

Table 15 lists the average number of campesinos on
properties of different size. The variations are commensur-
ate with the size of properties. Table 16 shows the disposition of the cultivated lands which were formerly worked by
the owners of properties declared latifundios. In most cases
a "collective" is formed in which formerly landless
campesinos (often grown sons of the ex-arrenderos or
arrenderos with small parcels) participate. Officially the

lands of these collectives are supposed to be worked as one
farm; they are not supposed to be subdivided into family
plots. As we shall see, the campesino beneficiaries
invariably subdivide them into individual parcels regardless
of official wishes. In a few cases the hacienda lands were
actually subdivided by official action and in another large
number of cases the campesinos (ex-arrenderos and their
children) squatted on the lands long before surveyors working
for the agrarian reform could map them. In the latter case,
the campesinos were simply left with the parcels of land on
which they had squatted.

Table 15

AVERAGE NUMBER OF CAMPESINOS ON CHUQUISACA
PROPERTIES

	Oropeza	Yampa-raez	Zudanez	Azur-duy	Tomina	Nor Cinti
Latifundios	98	52	21	17	21	28
Medianas	24	38	23	11	10	11
Pequeñas	5	2.1	0	1.5	0.32	0

Table 16

POST-REFORM DISPOSITION OF THE OWNERS'
CULTIVATED LANDS IN THE CASE OF CHUQUISACA
LATIFUNDIOS

Province	Formed into Collective	Divided among New Beneficiaries	Taken Over and Divided by Ex-arrenderos
Oropeza	9	1	0
Yamparaez	8	4	1
Zudañez	1	0	2
Azurduy	0	0	12
Tomina	1	1	2
Nor Cinti	1	0	2
Totals	20	6	19

The data in Table 17 show who initiated legal action to
affect a property under the laws of the agrarian reform. The
campesino syndicates have been overwhelmingly the most
important initiators of action in the case of larger properties
--latifundios and medianas. Agrarian judges and landowners
become increasingly important as the size of the property
diminishes. This fact is related to the motivations of those
initiating action. The larger the property the more hopeful
are the campesinos that they can bring about total expropriation or at least obtain title to their own arriendos or parcelas.
As the size of the hacienda diminishes the smaller becomes
the chance that the campesinos will get title and the greater
becomes the chance for the owner to do so.

Table 17

PERCENTAGES OF TYPES OF INITIATORS OF LEGAL
ACTION FOR AGRARIAN REFORM IN CHUQUISACA

	Local Sindicate Leader	Agrarian Judge	Land-owner	Totals
Latifundios	89	11	0	100
Medianas	80	13	7	100
Pequeñas	25	28	47	100

It is of interest that the expedientes for small properties
in our sample are in general more recent in their date of
initiation than those for latifundios. With the passage of
time, smaller landowners have tended to lose their
temerity concerning the reform and have begun to petition
for an agrarian title to their land. However, since many
have no arrenderos on their holdings and do not feel threatened,
they often have to be pushed by the agrarian judge, who may
actually initiate the proceedings for them. As the number of
large holdings which have not yet been affected becomes
fewer and fewer, the judges keep busy by pushing the smaller
owners to petition for inaffectability--having their holdings
categorized as pequeñas.

Although the owner of a pequeña property receives title
to his entire holding, if he has arrenderos he is in practice
often left in very much the same position as the owner of a
medium property. His arrenderos do not receive titles to
their arriendos or parcelas as they do in medium properties,
but they are given the right to retain their plots until other
lands are found for them elsewhere. Since "other lands" are
never found in most provinces of Chuquisaca, arrenderos are
just as permanently benefited on the pequeñas as are those
on medium properties and latifundios who are given title.

Only in Hernando Siles around Monteagudo were cases
encountered where campesinos on landholdings declared
pequeña were moved to land expropriated from larger holdings
elsewhere. But around Monteagudo there is no great land
pressure and even squatters have been moving here in recent
years without causing much turmoil.

In reviewing the results which the agrarian reform has
had on actual land tenure in the most limited sense of land
use, it would appear that in this area little change has taken
place. Most farm families have continued to work the same
land they were working before the reform. If we add together all the landowners and peasants in the sample we
obtain a total of approximately 7,000 families. All the
latifundio owners (45) lost their lands and we can roughly
estimate that half the owners of medianas (95) lost some of
theirs. The 140 families in the sample who lost land constitute only 2 per cent of the total. It would be interesting to
know how many campesinos were beneficiaries of the land
lost by this 2 per cent, but the expedientes do not always
designate the number of beneficiaries (recién dotados).

To figure the percentage of cultivated land in the sample
which was taken from its original owners and distributed to
others, we must first estimate the amount of land expropriated and to do this we must work with incomplete data.
Oropeza and Yamparaez must alone serve as a measure of
the amount of latifundio land cultivated by the owners (i.e.,
about one third). For the medium-size properties we can
very liberally estimate that landowners had lost a third of
their original holdings in cultivated land. These amounts
total to 5,155 hectares or 17 per cent of all cultivated land
in the sample (30,953). So, 17 per cent of the best cultivated

land has been taken from 2 per cent of the users for redistribution to the other 98 per cent. While significant, this is
not a very large change.

The important fact is that the land which the campesinos
had for their own use even before the reform cannot now be
alienated from them. There no longer is anyone to threaten
them with loss of their parcels if they fail to fulfill certain
work obligations. The elimination of all the obligations
discussed in the preceding section has been the most
significant result of the land reform. The following chapter
begins with a discussion of the nature of this change in the
power structure of the labor force.

CHAPTER

6

FARM LABOR AFTER
THE REFORM

—Charles J. Erasmus

LABOR AND POWER

Before arriving in Bolivia, and even in La Paz after my arrival, I heard stories that in remote areas in the southeastern part of the country there were still haciendas operating in the pre-reform feudal style, areas which the agrarian reform had not yet reached. One of my reasons for trying to study such a large part of the Chuquisaca-Tarija region in so short a time was to find out whether this rumor was true.

In one very limited sense these stories possessed a germ of truth. As Table 18 shows, the number of properties affected by the reform (demonstrated by the number of expedientes) has been heaviest in the provinces nearest Sucre and smaller in the outlying districts. This table is a copy of a chart prepared by the then-director of the agrarian reform in Chuquisaca. He said it was incomplete for the early years of the reform before he took office. Its purpose is to show the number of expedientes processed each year within the Chuquisaca district and the differences among provinces. Unfortunately the expedientes processed by the two "mobile" judges were not broken down by provinces, but most were apparently from Oropeza, Yamparaez and Zudañez. Azurduy, Boeto, Sud Cinti, eastern Nor Cinti, Hernando Siles and Luis Calvo are the areas of least legal activity.

Around Monteagudo, for example, properties were visited where the campesinos simply were not interested in gaining titles to their plots of land and frankly said so. They feared that once they obtained title they would have to pay

Table 18

NUMBER OF EXPEDIENTES SENT FROM SUCRE TO THE NATIONAL COUNCIL
OF AGRARIAN REFORM, 1955-62

Agrarian Reform Districts within Chuquisaca	1955	1956	1957	1958	1959	1960	1961	1962	Total
Oropeza district 1	10	2	26	12	14	22	34	61	179
Oropeza district 2	6	9	26	32	27	11	27	58	196
Mobile judge 1			3	12	18	53	61	22	169
Mobile judge 2				37	16	18	54	25	150
Yamparaez				35	14	11	11	14	85
Zudañez				9	19	10	44	43	125
Tomina & Boeto				23	10	13	32	64	142
Azurduy						12	22	11	45
Nor Cinti				21	8	44	45	43	161
Sud Cinti								8	8
Hernando Siles & Luis Calvo						1	2	3	6
Miscellaneous				3	2	3	4		12
No identification				2					2
Totals	16	11	55	188	128	197	333	353	1,280

heavy taxes. Furthermore, some feared restriction of movement. This is still a slash-and-burn, or swidden, farming
area, and some wanted to be able to move on and clear a
fresh tract when the land tires. The agrarian judge in
Monteagudo attempts to obviate this difficulty by persuading
the beneficiaries of expropriated lands during the audiencia
to request enough so they will have some continually at rest.
Since there is always more than enough land around Monteagudo,
awarding the additional amounts is no real problem there.

In the Chuquisaca provinces where there have been
fewest expedientes, and in the Tarija province of O'Connor,
one often hears the complaint that the surveyors never come
to these regions to make the necessary property maps which
form the basis for legal action. There are, however, two
good reasons why surveyors do not come to these areas.
First, they are remote and transportation to them is
expensive and time-consuming. Secondly, after the
surveyors arrive there is never enough work for them to do
to justify the inconvenience of the trip. Even though the
local agrarian judge may stir up interest among the
campesinos, when the time comes for all the ex-colonos in
an hacienda to pay their share of the mapping costs, they
cannot raise the money. Surveyors soon learn to avoid
regions where the campesinos are likely to default in payment
of surveying costs.

Despite this sense in which the agrarian reform may be
said to be lagging in the more remote districts of southeastern Bolivia, there is a more important sense in which
it has reached every nook and cranny. As we have already
seen, well under a fifth of the cultivated land has actually
changed hands here as a result of the reform, a relatively
small proportion. The important result of the land reform
was the abolition of the quasi-feudal labor obligations, and
this is the change which has affected the entire area. There
is no farm today in this region where the feudal work regimen
persists. Everywhere it has been superceded by wage
labor, a change resulting from the growth and power of the
peasant labor union movement. In this movement rests the
real strength of the agrarian reform in Bolivia, a fact which
is reflected in the deep hatred which most large landowners
have for the campesino syndicates. I was told repeatedly by
landowners and ex-landowners that the syndicates were

Communist organizations, for "Communism" and "Communists" have become labels used by the former privileged classes to denigrate everything which has upset the old status quo.

Wage labor has replaced the former quasi-feudal obligations, and even in areas where the campesinos have not initiated legal action to obtain agrarian reform titles to their subsistence plots they virtually own them anyway. Table 19 shows the wages earned by informants at various places in Chuquisaca and Tarija in 1963. Wages are usually more if the workers are not given food, but they can vary as much as 1,000 bolivianos a day among nearby haciendas. In Chuquisaca the daily wage is generally between 2,500 and 3,500 with food, and 4,000 to 5,000 without. Wages in Tarija (the last four entries on the table) are somewhat higher.

Although the work obligations are gone, the idea or function of perquisite plots still persists in some places, for most peasants want a piece of land on which they can cultivate subsistence crops. The Cambas (Guarani-speaking Indians) in Hernando Siles are the outstanding example. They refuse to organize in syndicates and do not want title to land, but they insist on having use of a parcel where they can plant maize and manioc. A Camba is paid 3,000 bolivianos a day, and he and his entire family are fed by the landowner. He often sells his crops prematurely, at a reduced price; what is lent to him may be sold even before harvest in order to buy chicha or cane alcohol. He seldom receives his wages in cash. The landowner invariably has a small store from which he provides the Cambas with the clothes and articles they need. Although the wage goes to pay off these debts, this is not debt slavery. Landowners compete to woo Cambas to their farms and seldom do the Cambas pay for all they buy on credit. When a Camba decides to leave, he is not restrained by force, and other landowners are always willing to pay his debt in order to obtain his services. Small farmers are at a strong disadvantage in this game, and several complained that they had lost Cambas to larger operators who were able to entice them away with the promise of more and better clothing and goods.

In the province of O'Connor in Tarija subsistence plots are lent to permanent farm laborers in addition to the wages they earn. But only landowners who already have agrarian

Table 19

FARM WAGES IN CHUQUISACA AND TARIJA, 1963

Place	Province	Daily Wage*	Plus Food	Plus Coca
Hacienda Tejahuasi	Oropeza	4,000		
Hacienda La Brisa	Oropeza	3,000		
Hacienda Cabeza Baja	Oropeza	5,000		
Vicinity of Ñucchu	Oropeza	4,000		
Hacienda Vila Vila	Yamparaez	3,000		
Vicinity of San Pedro	Azurduy	2,500	X	X
Vicinity of Azurduy	Azurduy	2,500	X	X
Vicinity of San Julián	Tomina	5,000		
Vicinity of La Ciénaga	Tomina	2,500	X	X
Hacienda Huaca Huasi	Tomina	3,500	X	X

Farms Vicinity Monteagudo

Place	Province	Daily Wage*	Plus Food	Plus Coca
1.	Hernando Siles	5,000		
2.	Hernando Siles	3-3,500	X	X
3.	Hernando Siles	3-3,500	X	X
Hacienda Porvenir	Nor Cinti	5,000		
Hacienda Companía	Nor Cinti	4,500		
Hacienda San Pedro	Nor Cinti	5,000		
Hacienda Papagayo	Nor Cinti	4,000		
Vicinity Ocurí	Nor Cinti	3,000	X	
"	"	5,000		
Vicinity Ingahuasi	Sud Cinti	2,500	X	
"	"	5,000		
Vicinity Bella Vista	Avilez	5,000	X	
Campo de Vacas	Arce	6,000	X	
Vicinity Bermejo	Arce	9,000		
Vicinity Entre Ríos	O'Connor	5,000	X	
"	"	8,000		

*Wages are in bolivianos; Bs. 12,000 equal $1.00

reform titles (as <u>medianas</u> or <u>pequeñas</u>) do this. They feel
secure with their <u>new titles</u>, have sufficient cultivable land,
and face such a strong labor shortage that they are willing
to take the risk. In Nor Cinti at the winegrowing hacienda
of San Pedro (near Camargo), on the other hand, there is
need for more permanent laborers than the hacienda is
willing to provide with subsistence parcels. Unwilling to
risk the possibility of further losses of land, this hacienda
has a policy of compensating permanent peons who have no
subsistence plots. In addition to the 5,000 bolivianos they
earn daily, they are paid an annual bonus of 400,000
bolivianos.

I encountered several cases in Chuquisaca in which the
owner of <u>mediana</u> property had an agrarian reform title and
had lent them subsistence plots in addition to a daily wage.
In none of these instances, however, was the wage paid these
peons less than the prevailing rate. The subsistence plot
was an added bonus.

The feudal-like work conditions that prevailed over much
of the area prior to 1952 have definitely vanished, and the
change has been primarily due to a change in the power
structure. As we saw previously, prior to the reform, the
ruling landed class so completely controlled the government
that hacendados were able to use municipal jails to lock up
<u>arrenderos</u> who tried to leave them. Today they are very
much afraid of the "communist" campesino syndicates, and
large landowners frequently complain that the syndicates are
now in control of the country.

Discontent was apparently in the air even before the
reform. In 1946, at Hacienda Las Canchas in Nor Cinti near
the Potosí border, the campesinos refused to work, gathered
outside the hacienda house, played musical instruments and
threw a few stones. Troops moved into the area and several
campesinos were killed.

In 1948, the <u>arrenderos</u> of Hacienda Carapari in Sud
Cinti murdered their <u>patrón</u>, a man who not only charged them
a certain number of <u>cargas</u> of maize per year for their
<u>arriendo</u>, plus 100 days of free labor per year, but also
insisted on taking 10 per cent of all their crops. When they
refused to pay the latter obligation, he threatened a gathering

of campesinos with a rifle. After disarming him by force,
they stoned him and dragged him behind a horse until dead.
The first man to hit him was later executed before a firing
squad.

In 1957, long after the reform, some hacendados at
Huacareta (south of Monteagudo) attempted a revolt, creating
an incident which illustrates how completely the situation had
reversed itself by that time. Some twenty landowners
ambushed and murdered five syndicate leaders visiting
Huacareta from Monteagudo. They were resentful of these
outsiders entering their domain in order to organize their
peons, and they apparently felt Huacareta was far enough
away from the center of political activity that they would get
away with murder. When news of the atrocity got out, 200
armed members of campesino syndicates from the region of
Padilla marched on Huacareta and sacked the properties of
the landowners involved, killing and barbecuing many of
their cattle, and took the landowners to La Paz where they
were kept in jail for a year or two and then released. It is
said they paid bribes to regain their freedom. The ring-
leader of the assassins is now the alcalde of Huacareta and
has joined the MNR. Other large landowners near Huacareta
who had nothing to do with the murders, have since joined
campesino syndicates themselves. Some landowners around
Monteagudo refer to these individuals as "the cowards."
Nowhere else did I hear of prominent landowners joining
campesino syndicates.

These three incidents well illustrate the reversal in the
power structure which took place with the reform. The
larger landowners bitterly resent their loss of power and the
growing strength of the syndicate leaders, but there is no
organized resistance within their ranks. The old aristocracy
is demoralized and in many cases quite impoverished. It
should not be concluded from these facts, however, that the
campesinos of Chuquisaca were leaders of the agrarian reform.
They have been followers. If the revolution had not begun
elsewhere, it might not have happened at all in this area; it
seems certain that the peasantry of Chuquisaca and Tarija
would never have taken the lead.

Since the arrenderos belonging to a given hacienda tended
to form a community and were accustomed to working together

in the past, they were logical units for the formation of the
smallest farm labor union unit--the syndicate. Usually
haciendas falling in the latifundio and larger mediana class
had enough arrenderos to form a syndicate, which according
to the Chuquisaca federation should preferably have at least
forty members. In the case of pequeña properties there are
often less than this number, in which case a syndicate is
formed by grouping together the ex-arrenderos of adjoining
haciendas.

Where haciendas become coterminous with syndicates,
the new organization to a certain extent tends to parallel and
preserve the old. The arrenderos are referred to as "ex-
arrenderos" of the hacienda, and the syndicate to which they
belong is referred to by the hacienda name. If the hacienda
is a mediana, the members of the syndicate (ex-arrenderos
of the hacienda) continue to work for their old patrón but now
on their own terms and according to their own free will and
inclination, much to the patrón's displeasure. Intermediate
between campesinos and patrón is the work inspector, whose
job is to see that both parties live up to their labor contract.
He epitomizes the reversal in the power structure.

Many haciendas still have their own chapels attached to
the hacienda house. There the patron saint of the hacienda
is kept, waiting for the day each year when the campesinos
hold a religious celebration in its honor. This custom
usually persists on such properties and continues to
strengthen the social unity of the syndicate. When the property
is mediana the patrón (or patróna) often continues to assist in
the care of the chapel and the expense or arrangements of
the fiesta for the patron saint. Usually the ex-colonos continue to address the ex-hacendado as "patrón" and to treat
him with respect and courtesy. One hears of many exceptions
to this pattern, but in my experience it was the most common
one.

In the case of some latifundios many of the attributes of
the patrón's role have been taken over by the secretary
general usually referred to in this area as "el sindicato."
At Hacienda Molleni in Azurduy province, for example, the
sindicato was an extremely aggressive young man who
thoroughly dominated the membership (the ex-arrenderos of
the hacienda.) He was always collecting money for some

purpose, such as his transportation to Sucre to talk to "the authorities," then failing to give a satisfactory account of his expenses. He also fined members who failed to attend meetings, making them work on his own farm plot in payment. He expropriated the parcela escolar, land designated for the use of the school, and divided it up among his relatives and friends. He even decided that one old woman living near him was a witch and tried to bake her alive in his adobe oven.

One of the most interesting aspects of the Molleni case is that this was the hacienda which had had the most abusive and totalitarian patrón in all of Chuquisaca prior to the reform. Campesinos who grow accustomed to dictatorial treatment seem to fall victim to it again the most easily, although the authority figure may take a slightly altered form. The director of the Chuquisaca office of the agrarian reform became aware of the Molleni situation while attending the ceremony to distribute land titles to the campesinos. He encouraged them to send a delegation to Sucre to protest and to ask for the removal of their sindicato from office. They finally sent such a delegation and the leaders of the Federation were deciding the outcome in Sucre when I left. The executive secretary of the federation was reluctant to dispose of this man because he was a good political boss and very effective in organizing the campesino voters at election time.

At Totocoa near Sucre there was a syndicate strong-man, Palaguerra, who died of tuberculosis in 1962. When the university in Sucre was opened to all classes of students, those of the upper class staged a mild protest demonstration. Immediately Palaguerra appeared on the scene with his armed campesinos from around Totocoa, and Sucre was soon peaceful once again. Several hacendados tell of being beaten by Palaguerra's men when they fell into their hands. Palaguerra was one of the very few caciques (petty local dictators) who appeared among Chuquisaca syndical leaders, and he was mild compared to his counterparts in Cochabamba. It is significant, perhaps, that he was not a Chuquisaqueño but a miner from Potosí.

The second outstanding cacique in the Chuquisaca farm labor movement was Chumacero, also a Potosí miner, who

formed the second Chuquisaca federation, which includes the
two Cinti provinces. Since he was not an ex-arrendero he
had no plot of land with which to maintain himself, and so
charged his members dues from which he paid himself a
generous salary. Rivalry between two communities within
Chumacero's jurisdiction resulted eventually in his death.

These two examples of rather powerful syndicate
leaders, one of whom at Molleni was apparently quite abusive
to his membership, do not seem to be typical of this area.
Everywhere I went I tried to obtain information on authoritar-
ian leadership in the syndicates. Landowners or ex-
landowners often spoke of the abuses of syndicates in
charging quotas and fining members by making them work
on their own plots. These stories were always very much
alike, and formed a kind of oral tradition among hacendados.
Campesinos usually laughed and denied them, calling such
tales the propaganda of the rosca (former dominant class).
In some places campesinos admitted that when the reform
began, the first syndicate leaders tried to overcharge on
dues and assessments or fined members to get them to work
on their own lands. But the campesinos claimed they had
grown wiser over the years and no longer paid or allowed
syndicate leaders to take advantage of them. Around Entre
Ríos the situation has so reversed itself that syndicate
leaders were paying the expenses of their office out of their
own pockets because the campesinos refused to pay their
dues any longer.

Nowhere in the area was a case encountered where a
secretary general had been chosen for the office because of
his participation in the religious fiesta system. Sponsoring
fiestas does not lead to office-holding in the campesino
syndicates. In fact in most of the cases where they were
asked, syndicate leaders had never sponsored religious
fiestas or were opposed to sponsoring them. Everywhere
campesinos claimed that individuals picked for leadership
of the syndicate were chosen because of intelligence,
integrity, and ability to represent the membership effectively
with persons from outside the community, including the
ability to speak Spanish.

At most places visited, the campesinos said that there
had been no local school prior to the reform, but that since

the reform the syndicate through cooperative work parties
had constructed a school building. While true in part, the
role of the local rural school district directors (Directores
de Núcleos Escolares Campesinos) is not given sufficient
importance in these accounts. In practice these directors
have largely pushed the syndical leaders into getting their
fellow members to construct these buildings. A major part
of the impetus for school construction has come from this
quarter.

On expropriated latifundios which have irrigation canals
or reparos (walls to protect against the eroding action of
rivers), the secretary general organizes the work parties
which maintain these constructions. In a few places the
syndicates have even built community chapels where none
existed before.

In the second Chuquisaca campesino federation in Nor
and Sud Cinti there are no subcentrals, only centrals and
individual syndicates, which do not here regularly conform
to hacienda boundaries. Ingahuasi, for example, formerly
a very large hacienda, is an entire central. The previous
subdivisions of the hacienda called "sectors," which were
composed of work groups under the command of caporales,
are now the syndicates. Since the death of Chumacero there
has been a great deal of decentralization of authority in this
federation. One central wants to set itself up as a separate
federation, and the officers of some centrals complain that
their syndicate leaders pay them no heed, acting very
independently.

Subcentrals in Tarija often combine several cantones,
and all the haciendas in one canton make up one syndicate.
Very frequently, however, a large hacienda constitutes an
entire canton in the provinces of Avilez, Cercado, and
O'Connor. Around Bermejo on the Argentine border where
government lands are currently being settled by colonists
from farther north, the syndicate leaders do not get along
well with the agrarian judges; this is the only place where I
found such dislike to exist. Here the syndicates are all
relatively new, and the new leaders, anxious to strengthen
their power and to get money from the colonists, represent
themselves as authorities having the right to grant lands.
They actually attempt to dissuade settlers from going to

the agrarian judges. The latter feel that syndicates are
completely unnecessary in this area where there had never
been any feudal conditions previously and they consider the
syndicate leaders a nuisance.

The head of the main Chuquisaca federation, which has
its headquarters in Sucre, is Manuel Nava, a former
arrendero on hacienda La Florida bordering on the city of
Sucre. Not only is he head of the Chuquisaca federation, he
is also one of the congressmen from his department. Nava
is a self-educated man who did not even know how to read
and write before the reform. As a young man, just prior
to the reform, he was greatly influenced by the movie Viva
Zapata! starring Marlon Brando. Pictures taken of Nava
during the early part of the reform show him wearing a
large Mexican-style sombrero and a bandelier of cartridges
over each shoulder. He still likes to dress in this fashion
for parades. Extremely shy by nature, he warms up when
in his cups and may even begin to discuss international
monetary problems using the vocabulary he has learned as
a Bolivian congressman. He still speaks with a Quechua
accent.

Despite his emulation of Zapata and Pancho Villa, Nava
is not a cacique or strong-man. The day I left Sucre, for
example, the President's candidate for the vice-presidency,
a military officer,* was scheduled to visit Sucre. To show
their opposition to this further gesture of Victor Paz
Estenssoro's alleged growing favoritism toward the armed
forces, Nava was going to block the road from the airport
with armed campesinos. Instead, he finally asked to ride
with me to La Paz so he would not have to be present to
welcome the new candidate for vice president. This fits the
customary pattern of Chuquisaca campesino behavior, which
is to avoid a show of force which might lead to violence. In
the long run Nava has undoubtedly been a better influence for

---

*/ Editor's note: This was Air Force General Rene
Barrientos Ortuño, who was subsequently elected with Paz.
In November, 1964, however, Barrientos assumed the
Presidency of the military junta which succeeded Paz in a
"Revolution of Restoration," and was subsequently elected
constitutionally to the Presidency. -- DBH/

Chuquisaca than if he had been more like his heroes, Pancho
Villa and Zapata.

The recent growing importance of the military has been
a source of concern to some in the federation. Most
campesinos asked said that they would probably fight if anyone tried to take their lands away from them now, but they
seemed indifferent to any threat from the army. Nava is of
the opinion that the Bolivian campesinos are well enough
armed that they could oppose even the army if necessary,
but not all syndicate leaders are so optimistic. Some told
me that the Bolivian army is now equipped with new weapons
imported from the United States, which require different
ammunition from the older models in possession of the
campesinos. This change was deliberate, they feel, in order
to make the campesinos' weapons obsolete.

Although the board of directors of every syndicate
includes a secretary of "milicias armadas," few syndicates
actually have a large armed militia. At thirteen syndicates
in Chuquisaca and Tarija where inquiries were made, eight
claimed to have arms and five said they had none at all.
Of the eight with militia, only one was completely armed;
this was the San Andrés syndicate in Tarija which was also
known as a "regimiento campesino." (Any syndicate whose
members are all armed and who train regularly under the
secretary of militias constitutes a campesino regiment.) Of
the other seven, none had more than eleven armed campesinos
and five had only five or less. Although Manuel Nava has a
machine gun in his living room and feels optimistic about the
campesinos' chances of resisting a new military coup, the
apathy of the campesinos in this region and their relative
scarcity of arms does not make Chuquisaca look like an
area which would put up much of a defense. *

In many parts of Chuquisaca and Tarija the campesinos
still find it hard to believe their good fortune brought by
the land reform. Although many stated that if a new government gained power and tried to give their plots back to the

---

*/Editor's note: There was no active opposition by
 campesinos in this area during the military coup of 1964,
 and the military regime had little impact subsequently.
 --DBH/

hacendados they would fight to keep them, there seems a
widespread uneasiness that just such a reversal might occur.
Several syndicate leaders were of the opinion that the
campesinos' fear of losing their lands was abating with time.
At twelve different haciendas campesinos admitted that they
hadn't really believed they would be given their arriendos by
the reform even after it began. Then they were afraid the
government might change and they would lose the land again.
But after ten years many were beginning to feel sure that
the parcels were permanently theirs. However, at Nucchu,
Monteagudo, La Ciénaga, Bella Vista, and Entre Ríos
campesinos were still of the opinion that with a change of
government their plots would be taken from them. *

At several places campesinos stated that they would
prefer to have their land deeds signed by the former owner
rather than by the President, who signs them all. They feel
the transfer of ownership would be more legal and binding
if "our patrón's" signature were on the deed. One hacendado
said that a group of his ex-arrenderos came to him with
their hats and their new deeds in their hands to ask if he
wouldn't please sign underneath the president's signature.

The attitude of landowners toward the reform is almost
universally negative. The most common accusation is that
the entire reform program was simply a political device to
gain the support of the campesino masses and was put into
action without any technical planning or foresight. Moreover,
the Indians (propietarios and ex-propietarios still use the
word "indio") are not capable of managing their own affairs
and do not know how to make use of the land given them.
They simply loaf more now and drink more chica, and farm
production has consequently suffered drastically. "You
have to understand the Indian mentality," the upper class
landowner explains. "I have worked with them all my life
and I know they cannot be changed." The "blue-blood"
Chuquisaca landowner talks about Indians much as a conservative U.S. southerner talks about Negroes. Some explain
that their peons were "como niños de la casa" (like children

---

*/Editor's note: This dreaded alienation of land did not
come with the subsequent change in government. --DBH7

of the house). They were treated paternally by the patrón
and taken care of when they needed help. Almost every
landowner I talked to told how he kept medical supplies to
treat his peons and how his wife served as nurse and mid-
wife.

On one occasion an ex-hacendado who was my guest for
dinner at my hotel in Sucre spent most of the mealtime
relating how good he had been to his peons. A few minutes
later he was violently berating the waiter for what he considered to be slow and faulty service.

A very common complaint among landowners was that
the reform had created a new "lucha de clases" (class
struggle). Before the reform, as one hacendado's wife
explained it, the peon had "cariño al trabajo y al patrón"
(love for work and patrón). Now everything is different.
"Under the old paternal system we could all sleep peacefully.
Now the laborers sabotage their work for us, and there is
not the same fondness between peon and patrón."

This frequent assertion by the former aristocracy that
there was no class antagonism prior to the reform is
extremely interesting. There were, of course, social
classes, and they were apparently more rigidly defined then
than now. What this statement means is that the lowest
class, the peasantry, did not previously question its
inferior position but accepted its lot without complaint. The
"lucha de clases" really refers to the lower class's increasing
self-consciousness of its inferior position and the awakening
of new aspirations on its part. Thus, the growing "class
struggle" is actually the beginning of the dissolution of a
very rigid class system which preserved the status quo and
the favored position of the aristocracy.

The hatred of the landowners for the campesino
syndicate has already been mentioned. It is generally believed by the landowning class in Sucre that there is a
deliberate plot on the part of the campesino federation of
Chuquisaca to drive all the old property owners from their
lands. It is said to be Manuel Nava's policy to encourage
all campesinos in private conversation (though never in
public) to avoid working for their former patrón. Or better,
they may work for him to get a crop started and then fail to

appear when the land has to be cultivated or weeded or
harvested. If the landowner loses money on his crop so much
the better. Everything should be done to discourage him so
he will give up in disgust and abandon his farm. Then it can
be declared latifundio and expropriated in its entirety.

The directors of the federation laugh at these accusations.
Everyone admits that when the reform began, things were
carried to extremes and that at that time campesinos were
exhorted not to work for the patrón any more. But since then
they have been asked to cooperate with the former patróns
(of mediana properties) so that those lands can produce for
national markets and for the greater prosperity of Bolivia.
According to the federation authorities there is nothing
deliberate about what appears to be sabotage on the part of
the campesinos. In pre-reform days, say these men, the
campesino had to work on the patrón's lands when the time
was right for plowing, planting, etc. Only after the work
was done on the patrón's lands could the arrendero turn his
attention to his own plot, and by then very often it was too
late to get the best results. Consequently the crops of the
campesinos were the most likely to suffer from tardy
planting and cultivating. Now the situation is reversed, and
the former patrón does not like it. The campesinos work
their own lands first and then work for him. They are not
deliberately sabotaging him; they are simply looking after
their own interests.

Such are the arguments of both sides, and both are
probably partly true. Much of the so-called sabotage is not
deliberate. On the other hand, the directors of the federation are not at all concerned about the well-being of the
landowners. They hate them as much as they are hated.

Economically, many members of the old aristocracy who
lost their lands as latifundios are in desperate circumstances.
Families that once had hundreds of hectares, cars, tractors
and beautiful homes, now do not have enough to eat. Their
plight is all the more pitiful because they are used to a high
standard of living. They were accustomed to travel in
Europe and to send their children abroad for education. The
last thing they sacrifice, no matter how desperate their
situation, is the education of their children. Hacendado
families with scarcely enough to eat somehow manage to

send their sons to Brazil, Argentina, Chile, or the United
States to finish their education. Many have sold their household furnishings and even their homes to provide this one
last "necessity." An impoverished former ha cendado whose
sons have been educated and have found employment in
Venezuela or Brazil, proudly announces that they are earning
far more than they could in Bolivia. "They will never come
back to this country," he declares defiantly. "No one who
is well-educated and can earn a good salary elsewhere stays
here. I used to love my country, but I have lost all my
patriotism. If I had had the money, I would have left long
ago. "

     Two attempts were made to find a rapid means of
getting information on what had happened to upper- and middle-
class farming families of Chuquisaca since the reform. On
the first attempt a list of one hundred upper-class families
was obtained from the Sucre telephone directory. This
proved to be a biased sample since farmers are less likely
to have telephones than merchants and professionals. Nevertheless the results are interesting in giving some idea of the
diversity of employment among Sucre's "good families"
today. Of the 100 families, 20 per cent were professionals
(doctors, engineers, lawyers, etc.), 17 per cent lived from
investments (rented houses, stocks, etc.--and these
families were in the worst economic conditions), 16 per cent
were farmers still working mediana properties, 16 per cent
were employees (banks, government, etc., other than
college professors), 16 per cent were college professors
(Sucre is a university town), 10 per cent were merchants
(store owners, wholesalers, etc.), 3 per cent were manufacturers (alcohol, lumber, soda-pop), and 2 per cent were
in the transportation industry (truckers).

     In the second attempt, information was obtained on 176
members (half) of the Sociedad Rural de Chuquisaca, a
farmers' association. The membership list was from the
pre-reform period. Of the eighteen families in the sample
which were members of the first class and previous owners
of latifundios, 33 per cent had left Bolivia, 22 per cent were
professionals working in Sucre (doctors or lawyers, etc.),
33 per cent were unemployed (and in desperate economic
circumstances), and the rest were now employees or
merchants. Of the twenty middle-class families who lost

their lands as latifundios, 25 per cent had left Bolivia, 35 per
cent were unemployed (and being helped by relatives--usually
grown sons), 30 per cent were employees, and the rest owned
their own businesses (flour mill, distillery, etc.).

In the sample, 102 members had properties declared
medianas, and of these 50 were first class and 52 middle
class. Of the first-class medianas, 6 per cent had abandoned
their haciendas, 46 per cent were working their farms
personally and 48 per cent had placed their lands in hands of
sharecroppers, renters, or administrators. The latter were
professionals, university professors and merchants. Of the
middle-class owners of medianas, 77 per cent were working
their land personally, none were sharecropping or renting
and only 23 per cent had put their land in the hands of administrators. These data show that members of the first
class are still much less likely than members of the middle
class to engage in actual farm labor and administration.
The rest of the sample had properties declared pequeñas,
and of these 90 per cent were being worked by their owners
and only 10 per cent were in the hands of administrators.

Although Bolivians often mention the fact that many of
their countrymen have left Bolivia since the agrarian
reform, I was surprised to find that such a high percentage
of this sample had in fact done so. This statistic confirms
the often-expressed attitude of educated people who remain,
that they would abandon the country if they had the money to
do so.

Many people in the upper class feel that during the
early days of the agrarian reform properties were declared
latifundios and taken from their owners for purely political
and social reasons, and that many of such properties should
rightfully have been declared medianas. One man in particular is singled out as having been the spearhead of this
vindictiveness toward members of the upper class in
Chuquisaca; he was the man in charge of the agrarian reform
office prior to the present director. This man, an important
and powerful figure in Chuquisaca politics, is the
illegitimate son of a servant woman and a male of the upper
class. His father saw that he received an education (he is
a lawyer), but he grew up as a marginal man with the education and aspirations of a member of the upper class but

without full acceptance by that class because of his illegitimate birth and the low-class status of his mother. At the time of this study, he was a highly motivated, ambitious, extremely intelligent man with deep feelings of uncertainty that had made him a heavy drinker. That he employed the agrarian reform as an instrument for personal revenge against the social class he hated is an accusation which many members of the Sucre upper class make against him.

The present director of the agrarian reform, Enrique Arrancibia, is well liked and respected by all social classes. Some ex-hacendados and members of the upper class expressed regret that he was not director during the early days of the reform. "There would have been more justice."

There has been some dishonesty and graft in the execution of the agrarian reform in Chuquisaca and Tarija, but in an area where the poverty is so great there is little opportunity for large-scale dishonesty. What has occurred has been of a very petty and limited scope.

The surveyors for the reform got a considerable amount of petty graft during the early days. Since they were paid for the number and size of plots measured, they often measured off new arriendo plots in the hacendado's pasture simply to collect surveying charges which were paid by arrenderos. Other surveyors exaggerated measurements to earn more, and some were paid by landowners to reduce measurements so the property would not appear to be as large as it actually was. Other surveyors made measurements, collected fees from the peasants and then never turned over the plans. In some of these cases they were probably not real surveyors, but in other cases it is believed that they were paid by the landowners to disappear and destroy the plans.

Some petty graft-taking has also been engaged in by the agrarian judges. The Bolivian government is well aware of this and in the decennial report of CNRA, mention is made of the fact that campesinos were being illegally charged for their land titles by dishonest functionaries (Bolivia 1963:27). The campesinos are generally afraid to accuse these authorities in writing, which makes it difficult to bring charges against them. Despite the government's best

intentions, charging for titles still goes on even in Chuquisaca.
One judge who is a political appointee without legal training
charges peasants 17,000 bolivianos each for their titles, an
extra fee which he pockets. This is certainly graft on a very
minor scale, and the salaries of agrarian judges are so low
that it is surprising there is not more. The judges in
Chuquisaca who have law degrees earn the equivalent of only
fifty dollars a month! Although Arrancibia, the director, is
aware that his subordinate is illegally charging for titles, he
dares not bring action against the man because of his political
connections.

In a previous case Arrancibia was able to fire an
agrarian judge who was charging campesinos for his
sentences. At the hacienda Molleni in Azurduy this judge
promised the campesinos he would declare the hacienda a
latifundio if they paid him 3 million bolivianos. When they
raised 1 1/2 million, he told them that amount was only
worth a sentence of mediana. At Entre Ríos in Tarija the
agrarian judge claimed that previously many expedientes had
been conveniently lost as a result of bribes by landowners to
agrarian reform personnel. Most of the agrarian judges in
Chuquisaca are also of the opinion that considerable bribery
takes place in the Ministry of Rural Affairs where some of
their sentences have been reversed. Latifundios are sometimes reclassified as medianas for the proper price to the
proper individual, and for failure to make the appropriate
gestures some medianas have been reclassified as
latifundios.

In general this observer was favorably impressed with
the agrarian reform personnel he met in Chuquisaca and
Tarija. There does not seem to be a great deal of graft at
present, and the personnel are courteous and equalitarian--
without appearing patronizing--in their interactions with the
campesinos.   For the most part they seem to be young
energetic people with a sense of mission who believe in the
goals of the reform.

PRODUCTION

One of the biggest puzzles of the agrarian experiment
in Bolivia has been its effect on production. It is said by

many that after the reform agricultural production in Bolivia
went into a slump from which it has never recovered. A few
believe it has increased, and frequently one hears the opinion
that there was a decline during the early years of the reform
followed by a return to pre-reform production levels during
the mid-1960's.

These opinions are based on little more than speculation,
a condition which this report can do very little to improve
upon since production figures are hard to obtain either for
pre-reform times or for the present. All expedientes include
production figures; but since even the agrarian reform
personnel consider these data very inaccurate, one would not
be justified in constructing production levels from this
source.

As a social phenomenon in Bolivia, attitudes and opinions
on production are interesting and important. When I first
arrived in La Paz I made it a point to ask everyone I met
about the agrarian reform--taxi drivers, hotel clerks,
elevator operators, government personnel, and shopkeepers.
I found that city people in general considered the reform a
failure. People of the middle-or white-collar class seem to
look down on the peasant, whom they often refer to as
"Indian." As they view it, the Indians are only interested in
growing food for home consumption and sponsoring fiestas
and when there was no longer anyone to make them produce
for market there was a drop in the supply of foodstuffs for
the cities causing inflation and a more restricted diet for
city dwellers.

The above attitude, common among white-collar workers
in the city, is even stronger and more universal among the
ex-hacendados and landowners affected by the reform.
Members of the campesino federation consider these widespread opinions the result of destructive propaganda
deliberately aimed against the reform by the old aristocracy.
In Sucre I found the upper-class hacendados and former
hacendados very anxious to convince me that agricultural
production was much lower since the reform. To one such
ex-hacendado with whom I became well acquainted I proposed
that we go to the Sucre market and interview women who had
worked there selling foodstuffs for over fifteen years. We
would ask them whether in their opinion production was

greater before 1950 than now. He agreed to this proposal and
we went to the market. To his surprise and annoyance the
market women, interviewed separately, all gave the same
reply: agriculture production was much greater now than
they had ever seen it. These women claimed that before 1950
the campesinos cultivated their arriendos for family subsistence and it was the hacendados who supplied the market.
Today the campesinos bring in most of the market produce--
in small quantities to be sure, but so many of them come to
market that the supply is greater than ever. Moreover, the
campesinos do not hold their crops off the market until
prices go up as the hacendados used to do, which in the old
days caused periodic shortages and considerable price fluctuation. Now there is always food n season and the prices
fluctuate less.

My hacendado friend was not discouraged. These market
women simply did not know.what they were talking about. He
knew a Yugoslav merchant who had been a grain dealer in
Sucre for over twenty years. This man would know the true
story on production and set me straight. But the grain dealer
simply confirmed the opinion of the market women. There
was absolutely no doubt, he said, that agricultural production
has increased since the reform. My ex-hacendado friend
never mentioned production to me again.

Of course the above are only opinions, but they are
well-informed opinions, and I am inclined to believe that for
the Chuquisaca area at least they are probably correct.
Another indirect way in which we can calculate the extent to
which production may have been affected is to use data on
land tenure abstracted from the expedientes, plus field
observations and the results of interviews with owners of
mediana properties.

On latifundios visited in this study the land formerly
cultivated by the hacendado was under intensive cultivation
by the campesinos. In a few cases there was a period of
confusion immediately after the reform when the owners'
fields were not cultivated, but usually it did not take the
campesinos long to divide up the hacendado's lands and put
them under cultivation for their personal use.

What were the consequences of this change in land tenure?

Did it lower production per hectare? When lands were not
cultivated for a year or two, production per hectare was
lowered, but such cases were so rare that they could not
have amounted to more than 1 per cent of all the cultivated
land. Some argue that even where the peasants appropriated
and cultivated the hacendado's lands they did not have the
capital and means of exploiting it to its full potential; they
used inferior seeds, less fertilizer, and so forth. However,
hacendados did not as a rule invest large sums of money in
agricultural production and the ordinary Bolivian campesino
is a conscientious farmer who knows the value of fertilizer
and uses it whenever possible. A liberal allowance for the
possibility that the campesinos' lack of capital lowered production would be to estimate a drop of 33 per cent in production. Since the cultivated lands farmed by latifundio hacendados was less than 14 per cent of the total cultivated land in
our sample, the drop in total production as a result of this
change in land tenure could not have been greater than 5 per
cent.

The question as to whether this change in land tenure
decreased production for market is very difficult to answer.
Did the land formerly cultivated by the hacendados and subsequently divided among the campesinos change from market
production to subsistence production? At the haciendas
visited, the new lands were being cultivated by ex-arrenderos
and their sons who may have increased their food consumption.
If they did, and if the hacendados had been producing much of
the market crops on these lands prior to the reform, the
percentage of reduction in produce for market might have
gone as high as 50 per cent.

At the other extreme are the pequeña properties. Total
percentage of cultivated land in these properties is low and
no change in land tenure of importance took place in them.
Owners have continued to crop their parcels of land as before.

Many owners of mediana properties, which make up the
greatest part of the cultivated land, complain that they now
have great difficulty getting labor. Their ex-arrenderos no
longer want to work for them unless they receive a higher
wage than the owner feels he can afford to pay. However, as
we have noted before, the bulk of the cultivated land even on
mediana properties was contained in the arriendos, and since

the reform the campesinos have been able to give more attention to their own plots than they did before. When the time is
right for plowing, cultivating, and so forth, their own property
comes first and the hacendado's fields must wait. Since approximately the same amount of labor is going into agricultural
production the difference here is in whose lands that labor is
now being invested with the greatest intensity. The effect on
overall productivity per hectare may be in the direction of an
increase since the campesino can now intensify his efforts on
land that belongs to him and in which he has the greatest
personal interest.

To help gain some idea of the effect of the reform on the
production of the medianas, interviews were held with forty-
four owners of medianas living in Sucre. The farms of these
landowners, however, are not restricted to Oropeza (40 per
cent of the sample) but are located also in Zudañez, Yamparaez,
Tomina, Azurduy, and the department of Potosí. Owners
were asked how much land they had before the reform, how
much they have now, how much of their farm land is now under
cultivation, where they obtained their credit, whether they
sharecrop or pay wages, and what difficulties they have getting
labor.

The most surprising result of these interviews was the
difference in the amount of land held by owners of medianas
before and after the reform. Owners of such properties
supposedly are allowed to keep their own fields intact, but
according to this sample, two thirds of the owners' land was
given to campesinos. The expedientes show no such enormous
transfer of land ownership among medianas. The hacendados
explain that very often pressures were brought on them to
divide up lands among the campesinos without this allocation
ever being recorded in the expedientes. If this is true and
our sample represents a general occurrence among medianas,
two thirds of the medianas owners' lands have been expropriated from them and given to the campesinos. This two
thirds would represent 7 per cent of all the cultivated land in
our Chuquisaca sample. If we liberally estimate production
on this land to have dropped one third for lack of working
capital, and if we add this loss to the previous estimate for
the latifundios, the estimated possible production drop for
all cultivated lands would still total under 8 per cent.

Although 82 per cent of the mediana owners in the sample claimed they had great difficulty getting adequate labor, only 22 per cent of the cultivated land now in their possession was not being farmed, whether for lack of laborers or capital. If we assume that this 22 per cent would have been cultivated under the old system, its loss would lower total production another 1 per cent at most and only increase the estimated possible production loss for Chuquisaca to a maximum of 9 per cent.

The evidence at our disposal suggests that there has been little if any drop in production per hectare, and that it may even have increased. But if we take even the most pessimistic view and allow for the maximum loss of production wherever possible, total production could not have dropped more than 10 per cent. In this area agricultural production varies by as much as 30 per cent depending on weather conditions. Compared with annual variations in production caused by climatic conditions then, the maximum amount of production loss possible as a result of the reform is negligible. The fact that throughout the area of study, crops in the agricultural year 1962-63 were too abundant to market and were spoiling in considerable quantities makes the estimated possible loss even less significant.

Production for market is another story. It is virtually impossible now to estimate how much it dropped after the reform began, but at the present time there seems to be a greater abundance than ever. Production for market probably dropped considerably immediately after the reform, but has steadily improved to the point where it equals or surpasses that of pre-reform times.

Type of production has changed on many properties affected by the reform. For example, three latifundios along the Río Chico produced tomatoes in great quantities before the reform mainly for the Sucre and Cochabamba markets. Some tomatoes are still grown, but now under campesino cultivation, the cropping is more diversified with many varieties of vegetables being produced. On the other properties in the same valley the principal crop grown by the owners was sugar cane to be used to manufacture alcohol. Now these lands are truck-gardens supplying vegetables for Sucre. Where such changes have occurred, the trend has been toward crops requiring less investment or involving less risk.

The principal crops of the area and their distribution have been listed earlier.   Table 20 shows the planting and harvesting seasons for these various crops according to informants in different parts of the region.   Table 21 shows the ratio of harvest to seed informants claimed to have received and Table 22 their estimates of production per hectare.

The months of greatest activity in the farming cycle are the planting months of October, November and December and the harvest months of April and May.   The rains begin in September, becoming heavy by November, and last almost until harvest time.   Crops grown without irrigation are seldom planted before November.   The food staple most often irrigated is the potato, although as Table 21 indicates, the return on the seed is generally low.   Informants were much better at estimating harvest/seed ratios than production per hectare. Most of the places listed in Tables 21 and 22 are in the Spanish-speaking zones.   Quechua informants are generally poor at all production estimates.

High harvest/seed ratios are not necessarily indicative of high production per hectare.   Monteagudo has one of the highest such ratios for maize but is below Huaca Huasi in production per hectare.   The agronomist who owned the hacienda of Huaca Huasi claimed to get only 90 arrobas of maize for every arroba (25 pounds) planted in his irrigated fields, whereas numerous farmers around Monteagudo claimed a return of between 150 and 200 for one.   But the agronomist-proprietor at Huaca Huasi harvested 360 arrobas (about 9000 pounds) per hectare whereas the Monteagudo farmers were getting at most only 200 arrobas (about 5000 pounds) per hectare.

Estimates of the number of man-days of labor necessary to produce an hectare of maize for all stages from burning or plowing to shucking and shelling showed that production per man-day of labor was significantly higher in the tropical lowlands than in the highlands.   At La Ciénaga, Huaca Huasi and Ingahuasi the return per man-day of labor was between 1. 5 and 2. 2 arrobas and at Monteagudo and Bermejo between 3. 3 and 4. 0 arrobas.   While all these estimates are only

Table 20

CROPPING SEASONS IN SOUTHERN BOLIVIA*

Crop	Place	Jan.	Feb.	Mar.	Apr.	May	Jun.	Jul.	Aug.	Sep	Oct.	Nov.	Dec.
Maize	Medina Luna		H							P			
	Nucchu			H	H							P	P
	Nucchu I							P				H	H
	Cororo					H			P				
	Vila Vila			H	H					P	P		
	San Julián					H						P	
	La Cienaga		H									P	
	Huaca Huasi					H						P	
	Huaca Huasi I					H							
	Monteagudo			H	H							P	P
	Camargo I	H						P					P
	Ingahuasi I			H	H					P	P		
	Santa Ana				H	H	H						P
	Campo de Vacas			H	H							P	
	Entre Ríos				H	H					P	P	
Potatoes	Media Luna I							P				H	
	Nucchu		H										P
	Nucchu I							P				H	
	Cororo			H	H						P		
	San Julián		H									P	
	La Ciénaga		H								P	P	
	Huaca Huasi	H	H										
	Huaca Huasi I							P					H
	Camargo I							P					H
	Ingahuasi I			H					P				
	Campo de Vacas						P		H	H			
	Entre Ríos I							P					H
Wheat or Barley	Nucchu	P				H	H						P
	Cororo						H	H			P	P	
	La Ciénaga	H										P	
	Ingahuasi			H	H						P	P	P
	Santa Ana	P				H							
Peanuts	San Julián					H						P	
	La Ciénaga						H					P	
	Huaca Huasi					H					P		
	Huaca Huasi I					H	H		P				
	Santa Ana							H				P	
	Entre Ríos	H	H								P	P	
Chili Peppers	Huaca Huasi				H	H						P	
	Huaca Huasi I				H								P

H = harvest, P = planting.

146

Table 21

HARVEST/SEED PRODUCTION RATIOS IN SOUTHERN
BOLIVIA

Crop	Place	Ratio	Irrigation
	Cabeza Baja	20/1	
	Vila Vila	20/1	
	La Ciénaga	40/1	
	Huaca Huasi	60/1	
	Huaca Huasi	90/1	X
	Monteaguado	150/1 & 200/1	
Maize	Camargo	25/1	X
	Ingahuasi	20/1	X
	Santa Ana	30/1	
	Campo de Vacas	1 60/1	
	Bermejo	2 00/1	
	Entre Ríos	2 00/1	
	Cabeza Baja	5/1	X
	La Ciénaga	10/1	X
	Huaca Huasi	5/1	X
Potatoes	Camargo	8/1	X
	Ingahuasi	5/1	X
	Campo de Vacas	6/1	
	Cabeza Baja	5/1	
	La Ciénaga	8/1	
Wheat	Ingahuasi	5/1	X
	Santa Ana	5/1	
	La Ciénaga	20/1	
	Huaca Huasi	50/1	
Peanuts	Huaca Huasi	80/1	X
	Santa Ana	10/1	

Table 22

ESTIMATES OF AGRICULTURAL PRODUCTION PER
HECTARE IN SOUTHERN BOLIVIA

Crop	Place	Production* per Hectare	Irrigation
Maize	La Ciénaga	60 arrobas	
	Huaca Huasi	240 arrobas	
	Huaca Huasi	360 arrobas	X
	Monteagudo	150-200 arrobas	
	Ingahuasi	80 arrobas	X
	Entre Ríos	200 arrobas	
Potatoes	La Ciénaga	30 cargas	
	Huaca Huasi	80 cargas	
	Huaca Huasi	120 cargas	X
	Ingahuasi	40 cargas	X
Wheat	La Ciénaga	25 arrobas	
	Ingahuasi	15 cargas	X
Peanuts	La Ciénaga	100 arrobas	
	Huaca Huasi	250 arrobas	
	Huaca Huasi	400 arrobas	X

* arroba = 25 pounds; carga = 165 pounds.

crude approximations, they are accurate enough to add
further substantiation that tropical slash-and-burn farming
can give a higher return on seed and man-days of labor than
intensive highland agriculture even with its plows, fertilizer
and irrigation. Production per hectare, however, depends
on many factors, for a carefully cultivated highland hectare
with irrigation and fertilizer will readily outproduce a lowland hectare cultivated by slash-and-burn techniques. Nevertheless, if one chooses production per man-day of labor as a
measure of efficiency rather than production per unit of land
area, tropical slash-and-burn agriculture may be considered
a very efficient method of farming.

Slash-and-burn agriculture requires more land per farm
family not only because it involves less intensive farming
techniques but because after two to eight years of use, fields
must be left to recuperate four to ten years. This kind of
farming does not foster the same degree of attachment to a
particular piece of ground as highland farming, where fields

are left in fallow for no more than one growing season at
most. At places in the highlands where the land hunger is
greatest, fields are never allowed to rest although animal
manures are usually used to fertilize them. All over the
highlands, however, crops are rotated. The rotation cycle
usually begins with potatoes, which are fertilized, followed
by maize, then wheat, barley, or peanuts before returning
to potatoes again. Ideally land rests fallow one season before
being planted to potatoes, which means one fourth of a high-
lander's cultivated land is resting at any one time if he has
enough to permit it. But in most of the highlands of southeastern Bolivia, campesinos claimed they did not have
sufficient land to follow this preferred procedure.

If production per man-day of labor is greater in the
tropical lowlands and there is no shortage of land there, one
immediately wonders why more highlanders do not move east.
There are many reasons. First, profits are not any greater,
because the lowlands are far from markets, and transportation costs are high. For example, a man might produce
nearly twice as much maize per man-day of labor near
Monteagudo as near Sucre, but half the market price of his
maize delivered in Sucre would go to pay the truck freight.

When I was at Monteagudo farmers were feeding their
maize to hogs in order to get some return on it. A hog ready
for fattening could be purchased for about 100,000 bolivianos;
after fattening it on 40 arrobas of corn, it would be worth
Bs. 150,000 to 250,000 in Sucre, depending on the market
price at the time. After deducting the expenses of truck
freight and market taxes (a minimum of Bs. 40,000) the
return on the maize used to fatten the hog would vary between
Bs. 10,000 and 110,000 ($1.00 to $9.50). Figuring an
average profit of Bs. 60,000, the return on the maize would
be about Bs. 1,500 per arroba, a little under what they get
for it when they sell it in Monteagudo. Moreover, selling
maize "on the hoof" involves an added investment of the
farmer's time in raising the animals and the added risk that
some will die before reaching market. Obviously this is not
a profitable enterprise unless the price of hogs is very high
or the price of maize extremely low. Usually the second
factor is the deciding one, for the farmer with enough hogs
of his own that he does not have to buy them for fattening and
with maize that he cannot market is in no position to do

anything but sell the maize "on the hoof." This example
illustrates the gravest problems facing agricultural development in Bolivia: markets which quickly saturate, transportation difficulties, and risk-taking motivated by the incentive
to minimize losses rather than expand profits. It is because
of these circumstances that so much of Bolivian farming is
subsistence-oriented. And if one is farming mainly for subsistence wherever he is, why move east?

Throughout the highlands of this area of Bolivia, many
young men migrate periodically to northern Argentina to work
at harvesting sugar cane. Wages are much higher in Argentina and these migratory laborers are able to return with
money and such goods as radios and bicycles. In very recent
times some have begun migrating to Santa Cruz to work in
the cane harvest there. When it becomes clearly more profitable to live and work in the lowlands, the highlanders will
learn of it through the migratory workers, many of whom will
stay in the lowlands or encourage others to return there with
them.

As long as economic opportunities are not sufficient to
be an incentive to migrate permanently, those who move into
newly opened lowland areas will be predominantly families
from regions very close by. Interviews with twenty colonists
near Bermejo on the Argentine border revealed that almost
one half came from the same province and at least 90 per cent
from the same department--Tarija. At Monteagudo one fourth
(of 22 farmers interviewed) were from the same province, one
half were from adjoining provinces and the rest from the same
department, Chuquisaca.

A second major reason why more people do not move
into the lowlands is fear of sickness and dislike of the hot
climate. Campesino families in the highlands around Sucre
had heard that people who move into the lowlands often became
ill and that the heat and insects were unbearable there. A
few had relatives who had gone to the lowlands to work and
had either taken sick or returned with too little to show for
their work. However, several young informants in the Río
Chico area, a subtropical valley near Sucre, said they had
worked recently near Santa Cruz and that the rumors about
the heat and insects were exaggerated; conditions at Santa
Cruz were not much different from the Río Chico. Most said

they would move permanently to Santa Cruz if the government
would transport their families and give them a piece of land,
for none of these young men had sufficient lands of their own
in the Río Chico valley to support their families without
working part of the year as day-laborers.

Recent economic developments in the Santa Cruz area
have created relatively greater prosperity there and it is
beginning to look attractive to people in the highland zones.
As one might expect, those already living at lower altitudes
are likely to be attracted first. Many young families with
insufficient lands will undoubtedly make the move as the
economic situation in the lowlands becomes increasingly
inviting. Most older people, however, will not be tempted
to move; all men of middle age or older whom I queried on
the subject were not interested in leaving their land to investigate new areas. It was up to the young people, they
said, to go where land was more abundant.

It seems almost unbelievable how little land is necessary
to maintain a family in the highlands. Twenty families at
Huaca Huasi which claimed they lived almost entirely from
their parcels and very seldom hired out as day-laborers
averaged 4.2 members per household. According to the
expediente of this hacienda, which listed the size of each
family's holdings, they averaged 4.5 hectares per household
or about 2.5 acres per person. These family holdings were
not equal but ranged in size from 1.5 to 7.5 hectares. At
Chuquichuqui seven households averaging three persons per
household were living from only one half to three quarters of
an acre per family. The Chuquichuqui land is in an irrigated
subtropical valley growing vegetables and fruit for the Sucre
market whereas Huaca Huasi is a potato-, maize-, and wheat-
growing area. In the first case, plots frequently yield three
crops of vegetables per year.

Reliable production estimates for vegetable gardens in
the valley were difficult to obtain, but those for the area
around Huaca Huasi and nearby La Ciénaga indicated that
four hectares of land produced somewhat more than the amount
of potatoes, maize, and wheat consumed by a family of four
adults on the outskirts of Sucre during a year. The Sucre
farm family had income most of the year from jobs in town
and probably consumed more food per person than most

Chuquisaca families. Moreover, the production estimates
for the area around Huaca Huasi and La Ciénaga are probably
minimal. Although these production and consumption estimates
are only very approximate, they suggest that three to four
hectares of highland land will support a small family at close
to subsistence level. According to the estimate of several informants four hectares of highland farmland was about as
much land as one man could cultivate by himself.

Four-and-a-half hectares per family, however, was an
average and only for a very small sample. As Tables 11-14
show, the average amount of arable land per campesino
family varied between 1.5 and 4.0 hectares for different kinds
of properties. Families with less than four hectares often
sharecrop parcels of land belonging to families with larger
holdings.

Sharecropping is called by a variety of names depending
on the region: aparcería, a la partida, a medias, al partir,
a porcentaje, and compañia. Everywhere it occurs today it
seems to involve an equal division of the harvest between the
landowner and the sharecropper. Where the owner of the
land is a former patrón--a relatively large landholder--he
usually provides the seed, draft animals, fertilizer, and
tools. In some cases he even pays the sharecropper half the
normal wage for his labor, but always the division of the
harvest is in equal shares. Among the campesinos themselves sharecropping arrangements are a little more favorable for the landowner. The sharecropper may contribute
the seed; or if the landowner provides the seed, the cost is
deducted from the harvest before the profits are split. At
the indigenous community of Ocurí, the sharecropper provides the seed but the landowner contributes half the work
Undoubtedly some of the inequalities in landholdings are
compensated for through aparcería.

But as Tables 11-14 also show, campesino families
average between 14 and 22 hectares of pasture land each, and
the few head of livestock they normally keep are an important
asset. Cattle, sheep, goats, hogs, and chickens are like a
form of savings; when a family has bad luck and needs food
or medicine the sale of an animal or two can provide a ready
source of cash.

Although crude, these quantitative data are accurate enough to show why farming tends to be subsistence-oriented in this region. Not only are the market incentives for cash-cropping weak, but land is also in short supply.

There are various other indications of the subsistence orientation of the economy here. For one thing the tradition-al units of measure vary greatly even within an area as small as Chuquisaca, although fortunately the arroba and quintal are standard measures into which the others may be converted. (An arroba is 25 pounds and a quintal is 4 arrobas or 100 pounds.) Wheat is usually sold by the fanega, which is 185 pounds in Azurduy, or 160 pounds in Sucre. Potatoes are sold by the carga, which is 130 pounds near Sucre, and 165 pounds near Ingahuasi. However, the carga has different values for corn. At Ingahuasi a carga of maize is only 140 pounds, and at Padilla 110 pounds. The tercio, which is used only for maize, is 125 pounds around Yotala and Sucre, and 150 pounds near Padilla.

Other symptoms of the subsistence orientation of the economy are the very widespread use of reciprocal farm labor and the very limited supply of credit. The two forms of reciprocal farm labor which so commonly occur together among primitive farmers throughout the world are both found here. The festive form in which the host is less obligated to return the work of his guests but in which he treats his workers to a banquet, drinking, and sometimes dancing at the end of the day is called mingca in the Quechua regions and faena in the southerly Spanish-speaking part of the area. The con-tractual form in which there are no festivities and the "owner of the work" is obligated to repay his guests with an equal amount of labor on request is known as ayñi in the Quechua regions and torna vuelta in the Spanish-speaking parts. These are both means by which a campesino can obtain help during periods of peak labor load when the members of his immedi-ate family are insufficient to perform some urgent task such as weeding, land clearing, or harvesting. Often farmers claim more is accomplished on these occasions simply because of the competitive nature of the work when it is done in a group.

In most of Latin America there has been a tendency for the festive form of reciprocal labor to disappear over the

past thirty to forty years as agriculture has increasingly
commercialized. It persists in most places visited in
Chuquisaca and Tarija although some campesinos who were
more market-oriented than the majority criticized it as an
expensive and inefficient means of obtaining labor. Criticism
was greatest in the faster developing lowland areas around
Monteagudo and Bermejo. In these areas farmers are more
commercially oriented or are not so well known to one another
as in more stable highland communities. The more con-
tractual or exchange form is characteristic of all farming
areas where campesinos have little cash. It is common even
around Monteagudo and Bermejo, especially for landclearing.

Credit for farming is almost nonexistent in Chuquisaca.
In the entire department the Banco Agrícola makes loans
totaling only 300 million bolivianos (about $25,000) a year to
about 100 farmers. Over half of the money goes to the newly
developing lowland areas in the provinces of Hernando Siles
and Luis Calvo, where machinery is so important. The rest
is spread out over all of Chuquisaca. So few and far between
are the recipients of this supervised credit that I met only
one in my travels in the department; he was at Monteagudo in
Hernando Siles.

Occasionally campesinos lend money to friends or
neighbors at 5-10 per cent interest per month, but the
practice is extremely rare since few have funds. Around
Azurduy cases of selling crops in advance were encountered.
Called sacar reparto, this practice involves selling a crop
or a part of one to a storekeeper long before harvest in order
to buy food or clothing. The storekeeper usually pays about
half the market value of the crop. Repartos are not as common
in this area, however, as they are in parts of Mexico and
Venezuela.

Sometimes peasants in Chuquisaca lend seed to one
another at planting time. As is customary in most of Latin
America where this practice occurs, the creditor at harvest
time gets back double the amount of the loan--about 100 per
cent interest for half a year.

Before turning to the next topic, something should be
said about production cooperatives. According to article 82
of the Bolivian agrarian reform law, on all expropriated

latifundios an area equal to 10 per cent of the total lands
awarded individually should be cultivated in "collective form"
by the hacienda community. In other words, if on most
latifundios prior to the reform two thirds of the land was in
arriendos and a third cultivated for the hacendado (see Table
11), after the reform, approximately two thirds of the
hacendados' third would be divided into individual plots and
distributed to landless families and the remaining third
would become a collective worked by all of the beneficiaries
together. In practice these collectives or cooperatives have
had little success in southeastern Bolivia.

There is only one employee in the Regional Office of
Cooperatives in Sucre--the director. This young man is provided with a pick-up truck but since he never receives funds
for gasoline he seldom has an opportunity to visit any of the
six officially recognized cooperatives in the department of
Chuquisaca. The four on his list which I had visited were not
operating as production cooperatives, and the two I did not
visit were service cooperatives of small private farmers which
in his opinion were not successful. Without transportation to
visit these organizations regularly, it was impossible for
him to give them technical or even moral support. He had
on occasion visited latifundios listed by the campesino
federation as having cooperatives, but found that in no case
was this claim true. In this point my observations confirmed
his opinion. In every case of an expropriated latifundio I
visited, the so-called collective lands had been divided by
the campesinos into individual parcels. Nowhere did they
wish to work land in cooperation with others and divide the
profit; this attitude prevailed both among campesinos who
had participated in collectives and among those who knew of
them only by hearsay.

CONSUMPTION

Traveling about southeastern Bolivia, one is at first
impressed by the great hacienda buildings, many of them two
storeys high with tile roofs, huge verandas, and extensive
adobe walls. But on closer examination one finds roofs
sagging, walls eroding, paint worn away, windows broken,
and a general appearance of decay and neglect. Since these
buildings are the most imposing structures in the countryside,

the effect is to give the entire region a decadent look. The
visitor cannot but wonder if all agrarian reforms are so
economically destructive. Even these former oases in what
seems a desert of poverty are now in ruin.

But slowly, as the visitor investigates the situation further
the picture changes. First he learns that these structures
were built and formerly maintained by obligatory, unrenumer-
ated labor from serfs who had to supply even the building
materials. Second, he finds out that they are no longer in
good repair because the owners cannot afford such sumptuous
living quarters now that they have to pay a fair wage for the
labor necessary to maintain them. Third, on visiting the
humble dwellings of the ex-arrenderos, he discovers other
kinds of changes that have resulted from the land reform.
Although not so obvious and impressive on casual observation
as those on the hacienda buildings, they are very significant.
Some of the campesinos' shacks now have tile roofs instead of
the customary thatch; a few have windows, and some owners
proudly call attention to their new concrete floors. Labor and
materials that once went into the hacienda buildings are now
going into the houses of the ex-arrenderos. Before the reform,
the campesinos explain, they were never sure of staying on
the hacienda; the patrón could send them away. It would have
been foolish to fix up a house they might have to leave, but
now the land and the improvements they make on it belong to
them.

As the pieces of the total picture fit together, the decaying
hacienda buildings take on a new significance for the visitor.
He no longer sees them as evidence of decadence, neglect and
economic ruin but rather as the very opposite--the beginning
of hope of prosperity and a new way of life replacing one of
the most pernicious, decadent feudal systems to survive into
the twentieth century.

But realizing that profound changes have taken place
leads to a new question. Have living conditions for the rural
masses improved enough to make the campesinos really
better off than they were before? It soon becomes evident to
the investigator that agrarian reform is an operation which
involves two great steps, of which Bolivia has taken only one.
Land redistribution is the first step; it is a political reform
which opens the door to further progress. The second step

is economic, for redistributing wealth around a mean does not
by itself raise the mean.

Throughout southeastern Bolivia, campesinos are unanimously of the opinion that they are better off than before
the reform; now they are free from obligations to a patrón and
can work for themselves, and they do not have to work so hard.
But opinion varies greatly as to whether their material living
standards have improved. Some believe they eat better now
and can buy more clothes, but most feel their economic situation has remained relatively unchanged.

At Cabeza Baja, Ñucchu, Cororo, Molleni, Azurduy, San
Julián, Companía and Bella Vista, campesino families were
asked to estimate the frequency with which they replaced
blankets and each of their articles of clothing and the cost to
them of purchasing these various items or the raw materials.
All the estimates were so close that the calculated annual re-
placement costs for all such items (bedding and all articles of
dress including hats and sandals) for a man and his wife
ranged between Bs. 750,000 and 950,000 and for a child
Bs. 250,000 to 350,000 at these eight places. Half of these
same families were also asked to estimate the life span and
cost of their various tools and household utensils and the
annual consumption of various foods and household supplies
not produced on their own land (refined sugar, coffee, lard,
kerosine, rice, meat, spaghetti, etc.). Annual costs of these
two categories of goods for a family of four totaled about
Bs. 500,000 and 800,000 respectively.

These estimates are very crude and based upon informants' memories rather than detailed records. They probably come closer to representing what the family feels it
needs rather than what it actually consumes. For example,
men dressed in incredibly patched and tattered shirts would
claim they used up six shirts a year. Taking, then, the
minimal estimates, we may calculate that the basic cash
needs of a family of four during one year are approximately
Bs. 2 1/2 million (about $200). This may seem a high figure
for such impoverished people, but it must be remembered
that all of these estimates are from highland areas where the
climate is very chilly and sweaters, coats, and blankets are
needed for any degree of comfort. It also represents a
perceived minimal need rather than an actuality.

Table 23 shows how much land a peasant would have to devote to a cash crop to earn the necessary $200. The figures in this table are based on estimates of both high and low production of four prominent highland crops, and the extreme highs and lows in their price fluctuations. To obtain the figures in the left-hand column of the table, the lowest production estimates were multiplied by the lowest prices; and to get those in the right-hand column, the highest production estimates were multiplied by the highest prices. Maize is not very rewarding in the highlands, usually being a subsistence crop, while the price of wheat has suffered recently due to competition with the United States wheat surpluses flooding the limited local market. Potatoes and peanuts are obviously the most rewarding and reliable crops, but peanuts do not do well in all soils and potatoes require fertilization and irrigation.

Table 23

NUMBER OF HECTARES NEEDED TO EARN A GROSS
PROFIT OF $200, CALCULATED FOR
DIFFERENT CROPS

Crop	Number of Hectares	
	Poor Conditions	Excellent Conditions
Maize	20	5
Wheat	15	1 1/4
Potatoes	1 1/2	2/3
Peanuts	2	1/2

If an average family of four needs from three to four hectares to produce the food it consumes (including livestock) and its cultivated holdings are close to this amount, the family's cash purchases are obviously highly dependent on fluctuations in yields and prices. While our production and consumption figures are too gross to show exactly how the average campesino family manages to make its purchases in spite of everything, they are sufficiently accurate to substantiate the extremely low standard of rural consumption which is so visibly striking in the field.

Despite the very low standard of living of most Bolivian campesinos and their pessimism regarding improvements, there are some minor indications of consumption increases even in Chuquisaca. We have already noted that some are investing labor and money in housing improvements. Strangely, these consumption changes seem to vary with communities. In the Río Chico Valley, for example, half of the 43 families in Tejahuasi have constructed new houses with tile roofs since the reform, whereas very few families have done so in the surrounding communities. At Ingahuasi, located on a very large plateau with a scattered residence pattern, bicycles have become something of a consumption fad. One or two radios are encountered in most communities but they are never found in great quantities. Sewing machines are surprisingly prevalent in some places, as at Ñucchu where 60 per cent of the families have them, yet many other communities have none at all.

Close to Sucre some campesinos have bicycles to get into town where they work at least part of the year. Urban dwellers and those living closer to towns where they can secure occasional employment are more likely than most campesinos to have radios, bicycles, and metal beds; the same is true of those who have worked in Argentina. But the number and proportion of such families is low. In any case, whatever slight trend toward increasing affluence may be encountered from time to time does not seem to have resulted directly from the land redistribution program.

In conclusion, I shall present some observations on a form of consumption which is prominent among the peasantry and very typical of a primitive or household economy, which is primarily subsistence oriented and largely self-sufficient. The form of consumption I refer to may be called "ceremonial," "distributive" or "social" and is characteristic of peoples who do not consume a great quantity of manufactured goods. In this form of consumption, money and produce or both are expended to support public ceremonial activities which bring some measure of social recognition to the sponsors.

Table 24 lists the locations where data were collected on ceremonial consumption in southeastern Bolivia. In all cases fiestas are held for patron saints once a year, and the economic burden of the fiesta falls upon a sponsor usually called alferez but often alférez and sometimes el obligado or el nuevo. The fiesta is usually held at the hacienda and in many cases the hacienda has a chapel where the patron saint is kept during the year. In other cases the saint is "owned" by an individual or kept in the church of a nearby town.

Table 24

FIESTA FOR PATRON SAINTS:
COSTS AND SPONSORSHIP

Place	Total Cost in Thousands of Bolivianos	Cost Equivalent in Jornales	Cost Equivalent in Dollars	Selection of Sponsor					Respect for Sponsor
				wealth	turns	authority	picks	promise	
Chuquichuqui	3,000	750	250	X					--
Tejahuasi	2,985	746	248	X					--
Cabeza Baja	723	145	60		X				--
Nucchu	1,905	476	159	X	X				X
Cororo	3,253	813	270		X				X
Vila Vila	1,914	479	159	X	X				X
San Blas	766	191	64				X		X
Molleni	1,516	379	126				X		X
Azurduy	2,580	645	215			X	X		--
San Julián	934	187	77						X
La Ciénaga						X			--
Huaca Huasi						X			--
Monteagudo	1,000	250	83						
Ocurí	2,065	688	172						X
Compañía	100	20	8				X		--
Porvenir	310	62	26						X
Nazaret	2,115	529	176	X					X
Ingahuasi	2,000	40	166	X					X

The expenses incurred by the sponsor are various and
include food, drink, entertainment, and the priest's fee for
mass.   For expensive fiestas, cows may be butchered and
for less expensive ones sheep or goats.   In addition potatoes,
wheat, and maize are consumed and great quantities of chicha
fermented.   Sometimes cane alcohol is purchased and usually
there are sky rockets.   In many communities local musicians
play for the evening dancing, but sometimes the sponsor must
hire these as well.

At most of the places listed in Table 24 fiesta expenses
were itemized by informants who had served recently as
sponsors.   Only at Chuquichuqui, Monteagudo, Compañía,
Ingahuasi, and Patancá, were the total costs estimated by
informants without itemization.   While the cost of these
fiestas does not seem high in dollars, they are a considerable
burden to the peasants of this area as the local cost equivalents
in jornales (wage-rate for one day of work) shows.   Obviously
these people cannot afford to save their total earnings for two
and three years to pay the cost of a fiesta.   Much of the
expenditure comes from goods they have on hand or borrow
from friends and relatives.   The most costly ingredients of
the fiesta--the meat and the corn for chicha--are usually
products which the sponsor already has.   To buy those items
he cannot produce or manufacture himself, he may sell livestock.   One informant had sold his plow oxen to meet his
expenses as a fiesta sponsor.   Many persons, however, go
into debt at this time and it may take several years to make
repayment.

Although sometimes persons are encouraged to become
fiesta sponsors because they are "more wealthy" (usually
meaning they have more livestock which they can dispose of
to meet the expenses), fiestas are often given by very poor
families.   Some of the most expensive itemized fiestas in
Table 24 occurred in very retarded areas, as, for example,
Cororo.   Where "wealthy" individuals tend to be persuaded
to support fiestas, there may well be a "distributive, "
"leveling" quality to the activity.   That is, the community
may bring pressures on its more affluent members to force
them to share their greater wealth through ceremonial consumption at the same time making their economic situation
more like that of everyone else in the group.   In some cases
the sponsors are selected by the patron or the local priest.

In other communities the obligation is said to go by turns to
everyone regardless of wealth or lack of it, although in
practice there are some who never accept it. At several
communities, sponsorships were said to be undertaken to
fulfill a vow made during an illness. More intensive investigation in the area would probably reveal that most of these
reasons for serving as sponsor can co-occur in the same
community and that they are not incompatible with one another.

The column "Respect for Sponsors" in Table 24 concerns
the community's feeling toward persons who have ably
sponsored many fiestas. A minus indicates that informants
did not feel that fiesta sponsorship merited any special
respect. At Media Luna and El Chaco in the Río Chico Valley,
fiestas were no longer being given as often as they had been
ten years ago according to informants, and no one attained
prestige by giving a fiesta, even at Tejahuasi and Chuquichuqui
where fiesta expenses are high. Near Sucre (in Río Chico
and at Cabeza Baja) and at Azurduy, La Ciénaga, and Huaca
Huasi the greatest antagonism to fiestas was encountered. At
the last three places people used to be obligated by the priest
to serve as alferez but now at La Ciénaga and Huaca Huasi the
syndicate leader does not permit his members to sponsor
church fiestas. He has apparently been quite successful in
influencing local attitudes. Through most of the area there
is a belief in a supernatural sanction, a divine punishment
for people who refuse to sponsor fiestas. But at La Ciénaga
the syndicate leader laughed scornfully when I mentioned it.
"Hemos hecho la prueba ya y no cayó nada" ("We have tested
/the belief/ and nothing /bad/ happened"). I found no other
cases of syndicate leaders who had undertaken to oppose the
age-old fiesta system. Perhaps the fact that La Ciénaga was
formerly a church-owned hacienda has something to do with
this syndicate's unusual attitude.

At most of the more inaccessible haciendas informants
claimed that those men who had made the sacrifice to serve
as alferez were respected for this contribution to the community. There were various ways of indicating this. Ñucchu
informants said that in arguments among men of the community those who had given the most fiestas were paid the
most attention. Others were often quieted with the admoni-
tion that they should give fiestas before they contradicted
those who had. At Ingahuasi, men who fail to sponsor

fiestas are disparagingly referred to as evangelistas
(evangelists, or Protestants) and at Nazaret, as men who no
longer believe in the saints. Some say that an alferez is
respected because in order to serve he had to be a man of
good character, maturity, and one capable not only of
supporting his family but of serving his community as well.

Near the city of Tarija at Bella Vista, San Andrés, and
Santa Ana at the town of Entre Ríos, fiestas for the patron
saint are now supported by the community. At Santa Ana,
San Andrés, and Entre Ríos the alferez is simply a director
of the fiesta appointed by a committee of community members,
and the whole community contributes to the costs of the
fiesta. There are still small privately sponsored fiestas for
saints given by individuals at their homes at all three places.
At Bella Vista a committee in charge of the patron saint
levies a fee on each family in the community and no director
is appointed. Some individuals have begun to make a
business out of the fiesta for the Virgin of the Immaculate
Conception by paying for mass and then inviting everyone to
their house where they sell chicha. At Campo de Vacas near
the border of Argentina, families of landclearing colonists
had begun their own community fiesta two years before. All
families make an equal contribution to pay for the fireworks
and aguardiente.

Although the data on fiesta consumption are sketchy and
were hastily gathered, they do indicate several general
tendencies worth further investigation. First, the traditional
consumption goals of the campesinos are still strong here.
They are not buying bicycles and radios and other durable
goods in great quantity but they are capable of spending large
sums on their fiestas; the fiesta for the patron saint may be
only one of several, although usually the most important.
Every chapel and church contains many saints' images which
have their annual fiestas and sponsors and expenses. And in
addition to these, wakes, memorial ceremonies, and weddings
are common. The first two usually cost between 100,000 and
300,000 bolivianos and the last from 500,000 to 1 million.

Secondly, all of these festive consumption patterns tend
to be most persistent in the Quechua-speaking zones, particularly in areas farthest from major population centers. In
Spanish-speaking Tarija they have modified toward smaller

household fiestas and the community functions are tending to become commercialized. The fiestas there are losing whatever distributive quality they may have had.

Third, even in the Quechua-speaking regions there are some individuals in nearly every community who are not only uninterested in sponsoring fiestas but are antagonistic toward them. Thus, even at a place as much off the beaten track as Ingahuasi we find that "evangelist" and "Protestant" have become words of opprobrium directed at those who do not sponsor fiestas. Similarly at Nazaret some families who have never given fiestas and refuse to do so are no longer invited to social affairs. Nearly everywhere there are people who complain about the expense of fiestas and refuse to sponsor them when asked to serve as alferez, although most feel it is best to accept once and then refuse subsequent requests. Consequently the respect accorded the sponsor at a fiesta is no longer a subject of agreement. The variability of attitudes collected on this subject may have been as much a product of my small sample of informants as of any regional differences. But not everyone today looks up to the man who has given many fiestas. Status-seeking through fiesta sponsorship is still strong but by no means universal.

The hacienda buildings and the fiesta patterns of southeastern Bolivia very well exemplify the important changes and problems of the area. Both phenomena are major characteristics of the feudal-like kinds of societies which have prevailed in many of the underdeveloped countries where a very small controlling elite is superimposed upon lower-class masses with little between them. The hacendados were not modern capitalists in the sense that they sought to expand their operations by reinvesting in the tools of production. Any farmer willing to assign three fourths of his cultivable land to his work force in exchange for their labor is a conspicuous consumer of labor rather than an efficient producer or a conspicuous consumer of goods. Without markets for more than a small fraction of his farm produce and with only the poorest transportation facilities to get it to market, he traded his land for free services which he consumed as conspicuously as he could through his large retinue of household servants and his imposing living quarters. The decaying mansions represent the dissolution of this parasitic class and a great step forward.

But the rural masses in this kind of feudal society are the dispensers of the services. They make possible the peculiar consumption patterns of the elite and in so doing assign themselves to a subsistence-level existence. In a social order where status depends upon the consumption of labor they have none to consume; they are the producers of labor consumed in a situation where labor virtually becomes a good, in the economic sense. Among themselves the campesinos follow the only route to status-seeking left open to them--ceremonial consumption, which could just as easily be called "ceremonial production." As subsistence farmers they own and procure relatively few goods. Labor is the only good of which they have some surplus; it is what they supply the elite for its consumption and it is what they give to their own class through the community service of fiesta sponsorship in hope of some comradely appreciation. Labor devoted to augmenting subsistence crops or a family's small numbers of cattle, sheep, or goats can be converted into the requisites of a fiesta. While the cracks in this half of the feudal consumption pattern have begun to show, they have not yet seriously disrupted the ceremonial tradition. All such factors as population pressure on the land, poor transportation facilities, and lack of markets keep the campesino a subsistence farmer and a conspicuous producer of ceremonial services.

The decaying hacienda structures epitomize the political success of Bolivia's agrarian reform in its destruction of a parasitic elite conspicuously consuming labor. The persisting fiesta system epitomizes the economic failures of that same reform. But the growing dissatisfaction expressed toward ceremonial consumption or production suggests that the peasantry is now ripe for an economic revolution too.

PART **III**

LAND REFORM AND SOCIAL REVOLUTION

IN THE NORTHERN ALTIPLANO AND YUNGAS OF

BOLIVIA

7

—Hans C. Buechler

INTRODUCTION

The factors leading to agrarian reform were accentuated in this area because the northern altiplano, or high plateau, and the adjacent semi-tropical valleys constitute the most densely populated region in Bolivia. The peasant population there consists almost entirely of Aymara-speaking Indians (or campesinos). Of the estimated 868,147 Aymaras in Bolivia in 1962, nearly 90 per cent lived in the Department of La Paz (Comas, 1962:14).

Campesinos traditionally lived in three types of communities: comunidades, haciendas, and mixed Mestizo and Indian towns or villages. The members of a comunidad, or free community, enjoy direct control over all the produce they raise on family plots and they rarely work for anyone else. Most of the comunidades are the remnants of pre-conquest communities, and a few are the result of the Spanish system of grouping Indian families who had dispersed to avoid Spanish exploitation. According to Carter (1963), only 3,783 comunidades were left in the entire country in 1952. They are much more common in the altiplano than in the valleys or in other parts of Bolivia. The main integrative factors in the comunidad are the predominance of endogamous marriages, and the political hierarchy, linked with a complex system of fiesta sponsorship in which all landholding members of the community participate. Although title to land is held by the community as a whole, all agricultural land and most pasture land is exploited on a family basis. In effect, this is not a communal organization; on the contrary, the family is the most important economic unit.

169

The hacienda, as it existed before the agrarian reform, was constituted by a group of families who worked for a land-owner, or patrón, in return for subsistence plots. Many haciendas originated from comunidades, some as recently as the first part of this century, and therefore comunidades and haciendas resemble each other in many organizational details. But in the hacienda, the peasant, called a colono, was incor-porated into a complex organization headed by the patrón. He worked for him for a few days every week, and was obliged to render numerous services, some of which lasted as long as a year at a time. Usually a colono was not paid, and even when he was, wages were low.

Finally, some Indians live in or around villages with a considerable Mestizo population. In many of these villages, Indians have their own lands and have no obligation to work for landowning Mestizos, but hire themselves out for low daily wages or work the Mestizos' land on a sharecropping basis.

The first type of community has been the object of an intensive study by Carter (1963). Haciendas have never been studied intensively in Bolivia, although an extensive survey was undertaken by Carter in one altiplano province (1965). Regional variation in the Aymara area is so great, however, that an extensive study of its major subregions was impera-tive. For instance, land tenure systems in the subtropical yungas or valleys are as distinct from those of the altiplano as they are from those of the Oriente. In turn, differences between zones within the yungas themselves may, in certain aspects of organization, be at least as great as those between parts of the yungas and the altiplano.

The main areas of the Aymara habitat will, therefore, be treated separately in most of the chapters dealing with aspects of land tenure and related domains of culture; we shall also describe under different headings the situation before the agrarian reform and the transformations that took place after it.

The agrarian reform has effected a change paralleled in Bolivia's history only by the Spanish conquest. This does not mean that no important changes took place between the latter part of the sixteenth century and the twentieth

century but that change had never been so abrupt. It is therefore legitimate to take the date that the agrarian reform was
issued (August, 1953) as a kind of watershed and inquire what
the situation was before and what it later became. In this
section, the hacienda before the reform will be compared to
subsequent developments. It is often virtually impossible to
get detailed information on the patterns before the reform
even from older informants, for in a sense the old hacienda
system is already enveloped in a mist of unreality, having
attained an almost mythical character. I interviewed not
only campesinos, but also former and present proprietors of
the haciendas, who often appear to remember the pre-reform
situation better than do the campesinos. Within the latter
group, my principal informants were leaders of the local
campesino syndicates. The role of the secretary general is
so important that any outsider who did not initially establish
contact with him would be regarded with suspicion. Furthermore, these men were generally available for extended interviews, in part because it is one of their obligations to be at
the disposal of visitors, and also because many of them
proudly relish recounting the emergence of the independent
peasantry. In addition to work with informants, two weeks
were spent in the archives of the National Council for
Agrarian Reform (CNRA) abstracting data and copying maps
from the dossiers of haciendas.

Sixty-nine haciendas were chosen for study. They were
scattered through ten provinces of the Department of La Paz
as follows: Murillo, 17; Nor Yungas, 13; Los Andes, 12;
Sud Yungas, 9; Larecaja, 5; Inquisivi, 5; Manko Kapac, 4;
Omasuyos, 2; Ingavi, 1; Aroma, 1. (See Map 4). They
represent the main ecological variations in the region
studied.

ECOLOGICAL ZONES

The department of La Paz is probably the most ecologically diversified political division of Bolivia. All variations
in habitation zones are present, from the cold heights of the
Andes to the heat of the tropics; and all degrees of population density occur also, from the densely settled shores of
Lake Titicaca to the barren southern altiplano and the
virtually empty Alto Beni.

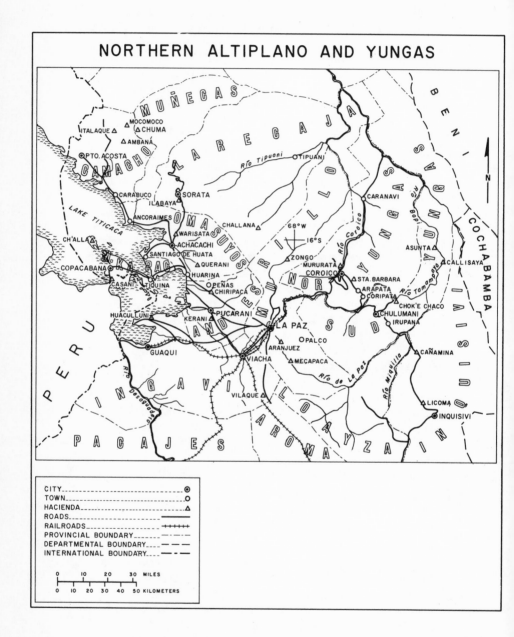

NORTHERN ALTIPLANO AND YUNGAS

CITY..⊚
TOWN...o
HACIENDA.......................................△
ROADS..
RAILROADS......................................+++++
PROVINCIAL BOUNDARY.........................−·−·−
DEPARTMENTAL BOUNDARY.......................− − −
INTERNATIONAL BOUNDARY......................−·· −·· −

0   10   20   30   MILES
0   10   20   30   40   50 KILOMETERS

One way of classifying haciendas is by the ecological zone which they occupy. Such a classification is valuable for the area studied because of the manifold correlations that can be made between the various ecological zones and land tenure, organization of work, and other domains of culture. It is, for instance, not unusual that two haciendas lying only a few miles apart but in different zones, differ much more from each other in these respects than do two haciendas lying in distant but similar valleys or even on sections of the plateau.

We shall distinguish two main ecological zones: the altiplano in the broad sense, encompassing arable land between the altitudes of 11,500 and 16,000 feet, with a generally cold, dry climate; and the yungas, rugged subtropical valleys in the eastern Andes, from about 2,000 to 8,000 feet. Time did not permit a detailed study of the intermediate temperate valleys between 8,000 and 11,500 feet.

The Altiplano

The altiplano can be further subdivided on the basis of suitability for agriculture. The highest reaches of human habitation are on the foothills of the Andean peaks, to about 16,000 feet, a zone often called the puna. Only bitter potatoes, fodder barley and a little quinoa will grow here; at about 15,000 feet agriculture ceases to be profitable. The upper limits of the punas are used for grazing llamas, alpacas, and a few sheep, horses, and cattle. The high plateau, or alti-plano which lies between the two ranges of the Andes, has an altitude of between 12,000 and 13,500 feet. Within it, two main subzones can be distinguished (following the classification made in the agrarian reform law): the area influenced by Lake Titicaca, and that outside its influence. This division has no clear-cut boundaries. The area around Lake Titicaca is relatively fertile, and barley, quinsa, and all the highland root crops will grow there, although the lower parts of it are often inundated during the rainy season and are therefore of little use for agriculture. A coarse and hardy grass (pasto bravo) provides abundant natural pasturages between the many stream beds most of which at least partially dry out during the dry season. About thirty miles south of La Paz, the pasto bravo abruptly gives way to low shrub vegetation, which in turn thins out toward the desert-like southern plains. On the altiplano south of Lake

Poopo, agriculture is virtually restricted to the hillsides,
the parts of the plateau sheltered by them, and the lower
reaches of the puna.

The Yungas

The term "yungas" has a triple meaning. In the most
restricted sense it denotes two provinces of the department
of La Paz, Nor and Sud Yungas. Among the people of the
altiplano, it is used to refer to the rugged subtropical Andean
valleys between 2,000 and 8,000 feet. Finally, the people of
Cochabamba call the flat Chapare region the "yungas of
Cochabamba." We shall here follow the altiplano usage,
which is similar to that in English.

Some yungas are continuations of higher more temperate
valleys, while others descend abruptly from the cordillera
with little transitional vegetation. The main access to the
yungas from the altiplano is a dizzying 6,000 foot descent by
car from the punas. Here the haciendas are situated on
extremely steep slopes. Toward the east, at lower altitudes
the valleys gradually widen toward the colonization zone of
the Alto Beni.

Access to city markets is perhaps a better criterion for
subdividing the yungas than is ecology, since cash crops
predominate in this relatively uniform area. The area that
has probably been colonized for the longest period is the
southwestern part of the provinces of Nor and Sud Yungas,
around the towns of Coroico, Coripata and Chulumani. The
population is densest in this region, where haciendas most
closely resemble the landholdings on the altiplano. This
region, close to the markets of La Paz, has long had great
importance for coca production, and, to a lesser degree, for
coffee and citrus fruits. In the southern yungas, located
almost entirely in the province of Inquisivi, the market is
primarily Oruro. Communication with the altiplano is less
easy here, and attracting people to work as colonos was
harder, not only because of its inaccessibility, but also
because much of this area was infested with malaria and
yellow fever. The area around Irupana, midway between
Chulumani and the province of Inquisivi, is intermediary
between these two types.

The lower Tamampaya Valley and the Bopi Valley form a third region. It was colonized early in this century by Indians who went to collect cinchona bark, and only later did it become a coffee-growing area.

8

—Hans C. Buechler

BEFORE THE REFORM

With a few exceptions, the basic pattern of land tenure of haciendas in the whole area studied revolved around a triple distinction between lands used for the direct benefit of the patrón, lands used by the colonos for their direct benefit, and land open both to colonos and the patrón. Land under cultivation invariably belonged to the first and second categories in haciendas. Pasture land could belong to any of the three categories, and normally included all three, while jungle, puna, etc., usually belonged to the third category.

The Altiplano

Most land on the northern altiplano is used practically all the time, wherever possible. Many haciendas before the reform resembled the free communities on which they were ultimately based, especially regarding many aspects of land tenure. This resemblance was reinforced by two factors. Many free communities had lost their status and had become haciendas quite recently, some even during this century. Moreover, entire comunidades, or parts of them were often incorporated into existing haciendas using the labor force, but leaving their land intact. The land tenure patterns on haciendas appear then as simple parcels of land cultivated for the benefit of the patrón; in terms of land use, they merely duplicate the holdings of the colonos, with some alterations dictated by the larger size of the land parcels. Land tenure patterns in the hacienda are therefore best described by taking the campesinos' plots as a starting point.

Lands to which a campesino had access fall into at least three categories in almost all altiplano haciendas: the

176

houseplot or sayaña, scattered plots called aynokas which
follow a common rotational pattern, and wastelands usually
used for sheepraising.

The Sayaña

In almost all haciendas, each peon had a plot of land
around his house, ranging in size from a few hundred square
·meters to a few dozen hectares, to which he and his family
had exclusive access at all times and where he could plant
whatever he pleased and pasture his livestock. This was
usually inherited from his father, and not even the patrón
dared challenge his right to it except in grave cases of mis-
conduct, such as consistent refusal to work for the patrón,
theft, or murder. Since the patrón was virtually omnipotent,
there were occasional exceptions to this rule. For instance,
on one small island visited, the patrón had felt that he had
too many colonos and forced some of them to leave, giving
them only food to eat on their way. Usually, colonos could
be moved to other plots only if they had just recently settled
on the hacienda or if they did not have the status of the full
colono. In one case, however, new owners (foreigners with
little knowledge of the habits of the colonos) had changed all
campesino plots to another site.

The sayaña may consist of a single plot, but it is often
fragmented because of inheritance patterns, additional land
given to the colonos by their patrón, and so forth. Sayañas
are absent in some puna haciendas where houses and llama
corrals are surrounded by common pastures.

Aynokas

Another basic type of campesino holding is the aynokas,
sections of land on which a rotational pattern of crop cultivation prevails. Each campesino, like the landlord, had one or
more plots (kallpas) in as many sections of land as the succession of different crops and the fallowing period demanded--
as many as nine, depending on the quality and amount of land
the hacienda possessed. In contrast to the sayaña where
pasture rights are private, aynokas are usually used as
common pasture when lying fallow. This pattern differs from
that of some comunidades where the aynoka is divided into
individual parcels of pasture land when lying fallow. Such

parcels usually are prolongations of the sayañas into adjacent aynokas and do not coincide with the division of the aynokas while they are under cultivation. Aynokas are absent in only a few haciendas near La Paz; in other regions they frequently account for all the arable land.

Wastelands

Uncultivated hillsides or other wastelands were used as common pasture land both by the campesinos and by the patrón.

Holdings of the landlords were often classified in much the same way as those of the campesinos. The hacienda usually had lands similar to the sayañas, often near the hacienda buildings. These lands, called jachojja, were usually the best on the hacienda and were cultivated continuously, with manure as fertilizer. The hacienda also had its own aynoka parcels, cultivated in the local rotational pattern.

Throughout the plateau, and on many lakeshore haciendas, grazing lands were extensive. These lands, the ahijaderos, differed from common wastelands in that they were of superior quality and could just as well have served for cultivation. They were used exclusively for animals belonging to the patrón and his shepherd. Where stockbreeding was important, the ahijadero was sometimes divided into various sectors, each with its enclosures where sheep of similar age were kept. In spite of frequent fines, the campesinos often did use the ahijadero clandestinely, unless it was encircled by an adobe wall.

Access to Land by Colonos

In most haciendas on the altiplano, colonos did not all have the same status. Usually there were at least two different categories of peons, and sometimes as many as four. In general, the amount of obligation to the patrón was in proportion to the amount of land held: personas mayores, or full colonos had the largest parcels of land and also the most obligations toward the patrón. The personas segundas (also called medias personas, or sullka personas) had access to aynoka plots about half the size of those of the personas mayores; however, their sayañas were often of the same size.

In at least one hacienda there was a category of terceras
personas, whose obligations were the same as those of
personas segundas but who could be moved to another site if
the patrón wished. In one lakeshore hacienda there was
another category of persons, called konuris, with aynoka
parcels but no sayañas. Widows with no means of fulfilling
the entire hacienda obligations were changed to the status of
medias personas on the Sun Island; half of their sayaña passed
to the hacienda, and for the other half, the widow had to do
only half as much hacienda work as a male head of household.
Unmarried women with children in this hacienda also received
land and became medias personas.

The sayaña could be inherited by all the male offspring of
a colono or by the youngest or the oldest son alone. In the
first pattern, which was most frequent, the house standing on
the sayaña was eventually passed on to the youngest son after
the older sons had built their own houses when they married.
Women seldom inherited land in haciendas on the altiplano,
although they occasionally did in some free communities.
Land was often worked jointly by all a man's heirs and divided
only after some time, as for instance, after his widow's death.
Where only one son inherited the sayaña, the hacienda often
gave land to the other sons if it was available. This could be
reserve land, sayañas for which there had been no direct
heirs. Colonos were usually given land at the time of marriage.
In at least one case the young peon first became a tercera
persona, then a media persona, and eventually advanced to
become persona mayor.

Usually a colono inherited aynoka parcels with the
sayaña and retained them throughout his lifetime. In a few
rare instances, however, there was some redistribution, the
plots being equalized every time a new aynoka section was
cultivated by the hacienda officials, so that land could
actually pass from a less numerous household to a more
numerous one; for instance, in Chálla each colono would
stand in his aynoka plot every time a new aynoka section was
opened for cultivation, and the hacienda officials would
measure every plot and equalize their size. I know of a few
cases where land in aynokas was newly distributed for each
rotational period, a custom still practiced in at least one
hacienda. The variety of patterns of redistribution should
dispel the widely held belief that annual reallocation of all

land was the general pattern, a belief that resulted from the
myth that Aymara land tenure was communal in nature. As
Carter (1965) has pointed out, this is as untrue in the free
communities as it is in haciendas.

In probably every hacienda and comunidad there are also
persons who have no land; these are the utawawas (literally:
"children belonging to the house"). The term can have either
of two meanings: it can denote all the younger males in a
family who are of age but who have not yet received land
because their father survives or because they are not married,
or it can denote orphans or other persons who have been
adopted into a family. The adopted persons had almost no
rights before the reform; they did the heaviest work and
received board and lodging as their only remuneration. At
least, they could get some produce for themselves through
share cropping with landed persons. Utawawas rarely
inherited land if there were no direct offspring in the adoptive
family, but more often the children of their adoptive parents
eventually forced them to leave.

Some haciendas comprised a single integrated community
with no subdivisions; however, many of the larger ones were
subdivided into smaller territorial and organizational units
called estancias. Estancias had varying degrees of independence in some domains of the hacienda organization. Sometimes access to pasture land was restricted to residents
within the estancia; quite often each estancia furnished an
equal number of officers for hacienda duties, or took them up
by turns. Individuals from the different estancias could
alternately sponsor fiestas. In haciendas where estancias
lay in different ecological zones there were even differences
in obligations toward the hacienda.

The origin of the estancias is obscure. A similar division in free communities has been attributed to the fact that
groups from different localities were thrown together through
forced settlement in the Spanish reducciones. The estancias
in some haciendas may be vestiges of the Inca division of
communities into an "upper" and "lower" moiety, the social
significance of which is not yet clear. This could be the case
for instance in Wacullani where certain ritual elements (e.g.,
dancing in different parts of the plaza during fiestas), are
attached to the two estancias. Some estancias probably

resulted from the purchase of land at different periods: thus
at least two haciendas visited consisted of one estancia where
the patrón had all his cultivable lands and pastures, and
another which seems to have been added later, from which he
drew only labor.

Patterns of Land Use

Communities on the altiplano generally belong to the dispersed settlement type. Houses lie spaced at a distance of
fifty to a few hundred meters and form small groups separated
by aynokas, wastelands, or hacienda lands. Less common are
nucleated settlements with a chapel in the center and houses
grouped closely around it. Some campesinos, of course, live
in predominantly Mestizo towns and walk to their fields every
morning.

Although a few land tenure patterns are shared by all
haciendas, there are also considerable variations. The most
important factor making for variation is the ecology of
haciendas. Haciendas on the shore of Lake Titicaca usually
form a special category of land. Every colono had a plot on
the border of the lake called the milli, and the hacienda had
similar lands. The millis were similar to the sayañas in
that anybody could plant what he pleased there. They are
usually cultivated continuously, with manure and reeds as
fertilizer; since the land is always slightly moist it produces
good crops. Millis, however, have one disadvantage; they
are periodically submerged because of the fluctuating level
of the lake. At present, the situation is particularly adverse;
the lake has steadily been rising since about 1946 and is
higher than at any other time since its level was first measured
about sixty years ago. The only thing which can be done where
a plot is inundated is to plant totora which is valuable as
fodder for cattle and can be used for making reed boats and
for thatching roofs. Totora is important enough to have
received special attention in formulating land tenure patterns.
The patrón usually had a large plot of it, and colonos either
had equal strips a few yards wide, or strips varying in size
according to the number of cattle the colono owned. In one
case, the campesinos held a totora patch in common and had
planted on their own initiative and in their spare time. Strips
of totora are distinguishable either by the different height the
totora has attained (because all colonos do not cut the reed

at the same time) or by trenches too deep for totora to grow.
The owner can also indicate these boundaries by tying a few
reeds into a knot.

The valleys at 11,500 to 12,500 feet elevation around La
Paz are especially valuable because they are sheltered from
the winds and frost of the open altiplano. Furthermore, they
usually have some means of irrigation and are situated near
the important city market. The basic pattern here was to
have the sayañas in the best lands, sometimes in the form of
scattered plots, and to put the aynokas farther up on the valley
slopes where land is less fertile and not irrigable. Many
haciendas in this subregion have considerable stands of
eucalyptus trees, invariably belonging to the patrón. Where
the river beds are broad, peas may be planted there during
the dry season. The river bed either formed part of the
sayaña or constituted a distinct category of land; in the latter
case, every colono and the hacienda had a tumuyu, or parcel
of land in the river. The pastures of the colonos were limited
to those aynokas that were lying fallow, and to the upper
barren reaches of the hacienda, while the patrón often had
grass and alfalfa fields for his cattle.

Rules concerning access to pastures differed according
to zone. In the puna, sometimes the boundaries for grazing
were those of the estancias, and colonos could put their
animals anywhere within their estancia. This was often the
case when an hacienda's puna lands were grouped together to
form one estancia, separating the colonos on the plateau from
those in the puna, or when the puna lands themselves were
subdivided into a number of estancias. In other instances,
colonos kept their animals in a more or less well-defined
area around the house.

Haciendas whose lands were limited to the high puna are
rare. They usually belonged to mining companies, since
their value would be small if these were no subsidiary
activities. Although there were usually a few Indians who
lived exclusively by herding in such haciendas, most colonos,
at least in the punas near La Paz, also worked in mines,
gypsum factories, peat bogs, or other enterprises. Even
those who were primarily miners and factory workers, kept
llamas or alpacas, which were herded by members of the
household as an additional source of income. Other high

puna haciendas incorporated at least some agricultural land
in the lower puna or higher altiplano. Great importance was
attached to these lower plots, for a shepherd always seeks to
supplement stockbreeding with some other activity, even if
he has unlimited access to pasture. Regardless of estancia
boundaries, colonos usually had plots in every aynoka so
that each colono might have access to arable land. In one
hacienda, for instance, most of the aynoka land lay within
only two of the fourteen estancias.

In haciendas on the plateau, with predominant sheep and
cattleraising, a different situation prevailed. In the province of Los Andes, the hacienda owners used much of their
best lands, often irrigable, for pasturage (ahijadero). The
campesinos, in contrast to their neighbors in the puna, had
their pasture land in form of sayañas. Both the hacienda
and the colonos held most of their arable land in the form
of aynoka plots, usually not on the plains but at the foot of
hills, where they shared the aynokas with puna dwellers.

In the northern part of the provinces of Aroma, Manko
Kapac, and parts of Omasuyos, sayañas were small and used
mainly for agriculture. The colonos pastured their few
animals on fallow aynokas and on the unproductive hills, while
the patrón usually had at least one ahijadero in the flat
country.

In the province of Aroma people designate a special
category of pasture land, the loma uyu (literally: "a place
on the hillside"). Each peon, like the patrón, had small
parcels of land on the hillsides. Each plot is encircled by
stone walls, giving the hillsides a honeycombed appearance.
These plots are used for grazing sheep and cattle or for
growing barley for fodder. Apart from the loma uyu, each
campesino had a series of enclosed plots which were part of
his sayaña, and which he alternately used for cultivation and
for grazing his cattle.

The main crops on the altiplano have long been potatoes,
barley, ocas, broad beans, and quinoa. Apart from these,
a host of other tubers and a few other seed crops are grown
in small quantities. Agricultural land use patterns in this
area appear to have continued, with little change since before
agrarian reform.

Potatoes are the most important crop almost everywhere on the altiplano. The bitter variety can grow up to altitudes of 16,000 feet but, in general, agriculture is not profitable above 14,000 feet. The best land is often assigned to potatoes, alternating with fallow periods. Barley grows anywhere, even at higher elevations than potatoes, but it is usually grown for fodder rather than food.

Ocas and habas (broad beans) are somewhat less hardy than potatoes, and are not grown on the open altiplano. Quinoa is also hardy, but in the last two decades it has inexplicably declined in importance as a food. Quinoa and ocas are often raised together in the same fields.

On the shores of Lake Titicaca, in very sheltered places, even maize will grow. Onions are frequently planted near the lakeshore, while other vegetables are rare and are grown only by a few hacienda owners and Mestizos for sale in the villages and towns. Eucalyptus trees, which furnish the only construction wood available on the altiplano, are fairly common in the sheltered valleys and around Lake Titicaca.

Crop rotation is practised and differs somewhat from zone to zone, and according to the size and population of an hacienda. When there is not enough land, and where land is good, the rotation period is shorter. Where land is plentiful or of poor quality, fallowing periods are lengthened and the years of successive cultivation decreased. An hacienda may also have more than one rotational pattern, depending on the altitude at which the rotated parcels, or aynokas, are located.

On lands immediately bordering the lake, one can plant continually, sometimes harvesting twice a year. For instance, one might alternate potatoes and ocas, or potatoes and barley. Fertilizer, often in the form of dung mixed with totora, is used. In his own sayaña, a campesino will plant what is most necessary or what he thinks is best suited to the land. If he has manure he will use it there. Normally, he will leave a part of his sayaña fallow and use it for sheep. The rotation of a sayaña is similar to aynoka crop rotation, but with less fallowing.

The cultivation of the basic altiplano crops has already

been described by a number of authors, but the growing of
totora, or lake reed, as a cultivated plant has often been
overlooked. Totora grows wild in many parts of the lake,
but since the level of the lake rises and falls, the strips of
totora growing along the lakeshore are often submerged or
left on dry land. Therefore, in order to have a constant
supply of totora for livestock, for thatching roofs, and for
building small boats, or balsas, it has to be planted. Totora
roots may be obtained by digging them from places where the
reed grows wild, or by thinning out previously planted totora.

Usually, the roots are cut into pieces about four inches
long and planted under shallow water by pushing them down
into the mud, one step apart, where the roots soon grow
into a dense network. More rarely totora seed is broadcast
on the lakeshore in August. During the rainy season a few
months later, the lake rises and the reed soon grows even
more densely than when transplanted. Totora can be
harvested at any time and is generally cut at about four-month
intervals, except when it is to be used for house-thatching
or boat-building; then it is cut only after going to seed.

On the altiplano north of La Paz, many haciendas have
some irrigation. Irrigation covers only a small part of the
haciendas, however, and before the reform was often used
by the hacienda owners, especially for pastures.

The Yungas

While the northern altiplano is characterized by a
chronic shortage of productive land and by overpopulation,
most of the yungas, by contrast, have an abundance of land
and a shortage of labor. Even where there are many
colonos, occasional outside labor is frequently required--
by hacienda owners and colonos alike. This pattern of
chronic labor shortage is reflected in pre-reform as well
as contemporary tenure patterns. Although most of the land
in the yungas was held in the form of haciendas before the
reform, only a tiny percentage of it was actually cultivated
in most areas. The most important problem with such an
abundance of land was to attract people to settle on the
haciendas. Therefore, to attract new settlers, the hacendado
gave every new colono a house, a small coca field taken from
the hacienda's older stands, some young fruit trees or some

coffee plants (usually already bearing) as well as a cleared
plot on which he could cultivate yuca and other tropical root
crops. The colono's obligation to the hacienda started only
after he had become well established and had made his first
harvest. In addition to the cultivated lands which he
received at the start, he could usually cultivate as much
other land as he wanted. If he left, he could sometimes even
sell to the hacienda the improvements on the land which he
had cleared. In some cases, with the hacendado's consent,
he could even sell to other individuals. In one instance,
peons who had in this manner freed themselves from the
hacienda obligations bought land in nearby communities and
settled there.

Sometimes different categories of persons were distinguished. For instance, the yanaperos were a category of
colonos who cultivated less land for themselves, and who
had fewer obligations to the patrón. As on the altiplano,
there were also landless utawawas who worked for their
"foster-parents." Because both colonos and patrón could
clear land almost anywhere within the boundaries of the
hacienda and because the steep terrain made for ecological
variation at different elevations, holdings were in the form
of scattered plots sometimes at considerable distances from
each other. One farmer near Irupana, for instance, had his
coca plantings, orange groves, and stands of banana trees
in ten fragments. In another hacienda near Coroico, a
campesino's lands were distributed in the following manner:
Bananas, 0.17 hectares; coca, 0.22; bananas and coffee,
1.12; coca and bananas, 0.32; citrus grove with coffee and
coca, 1.78; and coffee alone, 0.29; totaling only 3.9
hectares. In the same hacienda the patrón had the following
plots: 3 stands of coca, of 0.33, 4.35, and 8.18 hectares;
citrus, 4.33; coffee in several plots: of 21.40, 1.41, 1.02,
1.60, 0.15, and 0.8 hectares; totaling 43.57 hectares.

Usually the hacienda had some pasture for mules; by
and large, cattle and other livestock have never been
important in the yungas. In some inaccessible parts of
large landholdings which the owners rarely or never visited
land was even held by squatters.

Land was usually given by the hacendado to sons of
colonos when they married. The plots which a colono had

worked (including both the plots he had received in production from the hacienda and those he had cleared himself) were inherited by all of his children; contrary to the practice on the altiplano, women inherited land as well as men.

The yungas valleys were settled primarily for the cultivation of coca. The leaves of this plant, from which cocaine is derived, are dried and chewed, often with lime to heighten the effects, by Indians of the highlands. The use of coca to keep Indians contented on altiplano haciendas and in mines was so well established that before agrarian reform, the hacienda owners in the yungas were authorized to send two cestos (32 pounds) of coca, tax free, for their colonos in their altiplano haciendas. Coca could also be exported to neighboring countries. It has been and still is, in many regions, the ideal cash crop. Light in weight and not apt to spoil easily once they are dry, coca leaves provided a good return, even when they had to be transported by mule to the altiplano.

Today coca is still the dominant crop in most of the older inhabited regions of the yungas. It is still grown almost exclusively in the Arapata-Coripata region.* Coffee is next in importance. It has gained great popularity in all the newer colonization zones which lie at appropriate altitudes. Like coca, coffee is profitable in spite of high transportation costs. Citrus fruit and bananas are grown everywhere in the yungas. Their success depends largely upon transportation facilities, so that in regions far from roads, surplus citrus fruit regularly rots.

Coca is grown in a distinctive fashion by which the steep yungas slopes are turned into an advantage. The coca shrub is planted on a series of terraces, like steep steps less than a foot wide. These are made in the following manner: after the brush is cleared, trunks burned, and stumps uprooted during the dry months, the earth is dug to a depth of eighty centimeters just as the rainy season begins. Then the stones are picked out and piled in rows, to be covered with earth to make steps--some forty centimeters

_____

*/Editor's note: This is the region that was subsequently studied by Léons (1966). --DBH/

high and thirty centimeters wide. Behind each step a ditch
is dug which is later used for planting the coca. The steps
are usually shaped with a distinctive local style of pick-
mattock and are hardened by beating with a wooden paddle.
Only in the flat terrain around Callisaya and Asunta in the
Bopi Valley, is coca planted in normal furrows. Coca
seedlings are set out when they are one year old. The young
plants are protected against the sun with banana or other
leaves, a crude shade-frame being raised as the plant grows.
The first harvest may be made after six or seven months.
The cocal, or coca plantation, reaches normal production at
the outset of the third year. The leaves may be picked three
or four times a year, in January, March, June and July, and
sometimes late during the dry season. This task is done
mainly by women, while the men do the weeding immediately
after each harvest. Harvesting and weeding are easy in the
step-like cocal. Every four or five years, or when the
plants are weakened by blight or drought, they are pruned
to about ten centimeters. A well-cared-for cocal may last
for as long as forty years, after which the land is frequently
planted with coffee or citrus.

The harvested coca leaves are winnowed of twigs, and
spread out on an open platform made of slate, the kachi, to
dry in the sun. If not dried with care, the leaves turn
black and are worthless. They are later pressed into
bundles, wrapped in banana fronds, and transported to the
altiplano.

AFTER THE REFORM

The effects of the agrarian reform on land tenure may
be classified into three different categories: 1) the effect
on the conditions of access to land; 2) the effect on land
tenure categories; and 3) the effect on the distribution of
land.

Of all the changes which took place after the reform,
those concerning the conditions of access to land were the
greatest. After the reform, no tribute labor of any sort
could be demanded from the former colonos in return for
the land they occupied. They were transformed from serfs
into landowners who may work the land and pass it on to

their heirs with no obligations to any other person.

The effect on land categories was not as great. Where haciendas were entirely expropriated, such categories as the ahijadero were sometimes abolished completely, but otherwise, everything usually remained the same as before.

The agrarian reform had a double aim with respect to the distribution of land. First it was intended to give every person, completely and almost unconditionally, ownership of that land which he had previously worked for his own benefit. Furthermore, it held that each former colono should also get a part of the land which he had worked for his patrón. The first of these two goals presented the least problem, since access rights to individual parcels were fairly well established. However, controversies were not entirely absent. These controversies arose mainly because the status of the colonos' holdings is not quite the same as that of the free peasants' holdings, nor is it identical to the general European conception of ownership. First, the inheritance patterns are often different, and many of the members of a family were often forced to leave the hacienda to seek land or employment elsewhere, since a fairly common pattern was for only one son to inherit the land his father had cultivated. The rights of persons who had left the community were not the same as those who had remained. The hacienda had the right to redistribute the land of colonos who had left their holdings. Thus, from the standpoint of the hacienda pattern, the persons who had left the hacienda before the reform, whether because they were excluded from inheritance or for some other reason, no longer had claim to land in the hacienda of their origin. However, from the viewpoint of the free community, the colonos who had left the haciendas had been wrongly dispossessed and had a right to reclaim their plots. Since these parcels had in most cases been given to other colonos, in accordance with the hacienda's policy of giving land to the young peasants who had come of age, and since especially in the altiplano there was rarely any surplus land to be distributed, the claims of the "dispossessed colonos" encountered strong opposition, both from the hacienda owners and from the established campesinos. In general the outsiders were defeated, but not before having put up a strong fight.

The case of an hacienda on the southern shores of Lake
Titicaca serves as an illustrative example. At the time
when expropriation proceedings were initiated, twenty
hectares were described as having been reclaimed by
campesinos who had previously been dispossessed. The
dossier reveals that, some time after the original map was
made, the secretary general of the local campesino syndicate
expressed resentment against these newcomers, who,
according to him, had abandoned their land before the reform
and had no right to come back. Later he stated that these
newcomers had formed a syndicate in La Paz where many of
them lived, and tricked the colonos of the hacienda to join.
They had then persuaded the colonos to take a number of
persons from other places into the hacienda. These outsiders arrived with flags to mark off plots which they claimed
had belonged to their grandparents and, in so doing, they
dispossessed the established campesinos from part of their
pasture land. The dossier continues with the reply of the
ex-comunarios, as the newcomers called themselves, that
they had been violently driven from the hacienda by the
patrón and had a right to come back. Some months later the
secretary general called for action on the part of the authorities. In a letter written in broken Spanish, he described
how the ex-comunarios had arrived with the agrarian judge,
taking possession of land (including land that had been set
aside for the school), respecting not even the plots of the
colonos. At that time, the property had already been declared latifundio, to be expropriated in its entirety. Nothing
more on the subject appears in the dossier until in 1958,
almost two years later, when it is recorded that the property
had been sold to the ex-colonos for 7 million bolivianos
(about $585), and the machinery and other facilities for 13
million, both sums paid in cash. The protest from the
ex-comunarios came eight months later. Their secretary
general stated that--in spite of the fact that the hacienda had
been declared latifundio, so that the former landlord no
longer rightfully owned it--he had agreed to sell it to the
colonos. He claims that then the colonos not only got
possession from the authorities and proceeded to divide the
hacienda among themselves, but also destroyed the houses
and plantings of the ex-comunarios, and drove them out,
killing one old ex-comunario in the process. The ex-colonos
immediately replied insisting on their right to buy the
hacienda, and stating that this seemed the best way to rid

themselves of any debt they might have to the patrón for the
land. In the end, only one of the ex-comunarios eventually
received land.

Although the struggle with former colonos over land is
not always as dramatic as in this case, the sequence of
claims and counterclaims is fairly typical. In a few cases,
the persons who had left the hacienda before the reform did
succeed in returning in considerable numbers. On one
island in Lake Titicaca, for instance, where a few colonos
had been forced by the patrón to leave the hacienda before
the reform, they and their sons have recently been able to
come back. This does not mean, however, that those among
them who had entered other professions have reverted to
farming again; they have built houses on the island but their
land is cultivated on a share-cropping basis by relatives.
They come to the island only for fiestas, and occasionally at
harvest time. In one hacienda in the Valley of Río Abajo,
quite a number have returned, taking the patrón's land by
force. Only rarely, however, were more than one or two
persons able to re-establish themselves on an hacienda.

The second goal of the reform, the reduction of the
patróns' lands to a fixed limit and the total expropriation of
the latifundio, has caused more difficulties than the handing
over to the peasant of the land which he had occupied before.
Whereas the parcels cultivated by the campesinos for their
own benefit were (at least in theory) immediately handed
over to them in August, 1953, all questions over what should
be done with the rest of the land were settled through an
elaborate process of affectation, as described in Chapter 2.

The Altiplano

Theoretically there were two major possibilities for the
redistribution of land that had belonged to the patrón. Either
there could be a complete reorganization of lands resulting
in the equalization of individual parcels of land, with each
campesino receiving a consolidated allotment, or the
pre-existing land allocation could be taken as a basis for the
final distribution, with hacienda land simply being divided
up to provide supplementary plots for all campesinos, or for
those with too little land.

The first approach has rarely been followed. However, it does seem to have been done sometimes with respect to the aynoka lands. In such instances, land has usually been redistributed in a manner similar to the pre-reform pattern of some haciendas. Thus, the quantity of land a campesino had in the aynokas depended on his place in the classification of colonos, so that a persona mayor got most, a media persona less, a konuri still less, and so forth. For instance, in Ch'alla there are now four categories of persons with respect to access to land. Two of these categories existed prior to the reform; two are new and include persons who did not have any land before. In every aynoka each of these has the following amount of land: primera persona, 2,000 square meters; segunda persona, 1,500; tercera persona, 1,000; and cuarta persona, 500. This type of distribution is quite frequent and is often made by the campesinos themselves in aynokas which have been declared "common lands" by the CNRA. In some rare cases, campesinos have gone so far as to reallot aynoka plots annually to compensate for population increases.

The second type of distribution, a simple addition of hacienda lands to existing sayañas and liguas, is much more frequent. A minimum may be set, and all campesinos who have less then receive a compensating amount of land. Even landless utawawas have sometimes received land in such situations. In one hacienda, small plots were given to them from the lands near the hacienda buildings, but they did not have access to the ahijadero which had been divided among the full colonos. Thus, redistribution has often accentuated differences among campesinos rather than equalizing their landholdings.

Land tenure categories, as such, were affected very little. However, in a few haciendas, some change did occur. In two of the haciendas studied, aynokas were abolished and transformed into sayañas. In one of these haciendas, the aynokas on the hillsides were merely divided in such a way that each campesino now has his aynoka lands in one large parcel, instead of having parcels in every aynoka as was the case before. Crop rotation thus becomes an individual rather than a collective concern. In the other case, the aynokas on the hill were transformed into sayañas, so that some persons now have land only in the flat part of

the hacienda while others have lands only on the hillside.
This proved to be unsatisfactory, because the level part of
the hacienda is often inundated during the rainy season and
some of the campesinos who used to enjoy the security of
the produce from their aynoka plots on the hills, now lose
their whole crop during rainy years. A similar situation was
recorded by Carter (1963:174) in an hacienda where the
aynokas were simply considered collective lands by the topographer, and were in part divided into new sayañas, and in
part consolidated in favor of the hacienda, which now has
access to more land than it did before the reform.

The Aymara ideal of having land in different ecological
zones is realistic, based on the observation that when crops
fail in one zone they often do well in another. Those who
oppose land fragmentation on logical grounds alone seem
sometimes not to be aware of such considerations. An
interesting situation was encountered in a puna hacienda
where each campesino had been given all his land in a single
parcel without consideration of the aynoka, which in this
hacienda accounts for all of the cultivable land. Now each
man holds legal title over a section of aynoka land which
previously consisted of a great number of kallpas, or aynoka
plots, of different owners. The campesinos have avoided
confusion by simply continuing the old aynoka system, dis-
regarding legal titles. A person's kallpas may now lie in
lands that legally belong to other persons, while in his own
land there are aynoka plots of many other persons. Thus,
titular ownership and customary access are completely
divorced and form two incongruent systems.

The ahijadero has been divided among the campesinos
in different ways. In some instances it is used in common;
in other cases it is divided into small individual pastures.
Sometimes both systems are continued so that during the
rainy season the ahijadero might be divided into small
parcels while during the dry season campesinos may pasture
their sheep anywhere. The ahijadero may also constitute
part of the sayañas after redistribution. In some haciendas,
for instance, the ahijadero was divided into very long strips
containing different qualities of land and was added to the
sayañas which had been used as pasture before the reform.
In one hacienda the new sayañas are about one kilometer in
length and only one tenth as wide. Especially in the province

of Los Andes, the ahijadero is now being used primarily for cultivation, while only parts of it are retained for pasture.

Sometimes land has been handed over to the campesinos to be cultivated cooperatively, with the idea that its revenue either be divided among the campesinos or be used for community improvements, such as schools. In general, this has not been very successful, although there are a few haciendas where the system of school lands seems to work fairly well. Usually, however, cooperative lands are viewed as a temporary solution for exploiting hacienda lands which have not yet been expropriated, or as a means of keeping a reserve of lands to be distributed later.

Some campesinos even buy land from the former patrón. The owners of most haciendas have been eager to sell land to whoever would buy it: sometimes piecemeal to former colonos individually, or in bulk to the ex-colonos as a group, with each paying the same amount and receiving an equal share of land. This applies not only to land which may be expropriated; sometimes land that has already been consolidated in favor of the hacendado is also sold in this manner. Campesinos can sometimes get money by selling oxen; on the altiplano, a campesino invests money in cattle during good times and sells them when he has to sponsor a feast, cover the costs of holding a political office in his community, or when he has some other major expense. Another method of financing the purchase of hacienda lands is to give all the produce from the hacienda lands to the landowner for several years, foregoing one's share in a sharecropping arrangement.

A peculiar case is constituted by the haciendas on the periphery of the city of La Paz. These have been, in part, parcelled as building lots, and the campesinos on the unaffected part live in the midst of factory workers, artisans, and so forth. Some people in these sections own a few cows without having land; fodder is bought from the altiplano and is supplemented with malt residues from breweries. Six to eight cows is about the maximum number of animals owned, and women sell the milk directly to the customers.

The Yungas

The reform has produced quite different results on
haciendas in the yungas. Although land quality, the slope of
land, and other factors are important, improvements on the
land are of even greater importance in determining its value.
Coca plantations and fruit groves of the landowner are
coveted by the campesinos and therefore the hacendado has
difficulty retaining his cultivated parcels even if he had been
granted them by CNRA. Where the ex-patrón's cultivated
areas were given to the campesinos, they have usually been
divided among families. Sometimes they were given to the
campesinos to be worked cooperatively; but here, as elsewhere, cooperatives have been at best only a temporary solution. Cultivated areas are exploited in this manner only
when there is no immediate possibility of dividing them, and
the cooperative arrangement does not often function satisfac-
torily. In some haciendas, particularly around Coripata,
there is little uncultivated land, and campesinos have merely
received their former plots. However, in some cases,
peasants whose parcels totaled less than a set minimum
received compensating amounts of land. Where land was
plentiful, all ex-colonos were given five to ten hectares,
depending on the region, while all the rest of the land reverted
to the state to be distributed to future colonists. This situation is unusual in that access to land by campesinos was
actually restricted by the agrarian reform rather than
expanded, since they could previously use as much land as
they could cultivate. Land cannot be cultivated continuously
for very long periods of time in this region, since the soil
becomes exhausted and should be left fallow. Terraced coca
plantations may last as long as forty years, but most other
crops produce well for only a few years. It is quite likely
that exhaustion of land will soon become a widespread major
problem, as it already has in some areas. Therefore, much
more attention should be given to soil conservation. Only in
rare instances are provisions for conservation adequate and
even these result more from chance than from planning. For
instance, in Callisaya in the Bopi Valley, every campesino
has received ten hectares of land. Most of them have only
about three hectares under cultivation at one time; this con-
serves the soil since it allows for adequate periods of
fallowing. In some haciendas land has been set aside for the
future formation of cooperatives. It is doubtful whether such

land will ever be used for the intended purpose, but this
could be regarded as another reserve to be tapped. The need
here is less for the settlement of new colonists than for future
expansion by established families with too little land.

Some haciendas, particularly in the province of Inquisivi
and in the Tamampaya and Bopi Valleys, have recently become
major areas of colonization. Miners who have been discharged
from nearby mines are often settled in the province of
Inquisivi. Campesinos from Turco and other communities
which lie in particularly arid regions near the Chilean border,
came to Inquisivi as wage laborers and received land which
they cultivate during part of the year, living on the altiplano
during the other part. One family is usually left to watch
over the crops (mainly maize) while the others are away. In
Cañamina, for instance, five hectares have been given to
each new settler. They work for the established campesinos
during the first years until they have enough production to
become independent. In Callisaya the new colonists get land
from the syndicate leader.

In most areas, no effort whatsoever has been made to
regroup the scattered holdings of the former colonos. In
contrast, some of the hacendados have consolidated their
holdings into single parcels. Even if they still own various
plots of land, they usually concentrate their planted areas,
often in anticipation of eventual affectation. For instance,
coca terraces may be rented to the syndicates or sold to
them gradually, with the idea of keeping only the lands
around the hacienda buildings. Sales of land among campesinos are relatively frequent in the yungas. An interesting
case occurred near Coripata where some of those who had
left the hacienda had sold their land outright but others sold
only the right to the plantings they had made. In the latter
case, the "buyer" is not allowed to make new plantings when
these are exhausted. The "buyers" in some cases have
renewed plantings anyway, paying the syndicate some Bs.
100,000 for permission to do so. However, the former owners
sometimes return and reclaim their land, basing their claims
on the widespread belief that land awarded under the agrarian
reform cannot be sold, so that such sales are, in effect,
leases. Land is often sold when a campesino moves to one
of the new colonization areas; and in at least two instances,
powerful syndicate leaders forced campesinos to sell their
lands to the syndicate and to leave.

The frequent transactions of land are understandable in
the light of ancient patterns. We have mentioned that the
campesinos, if they wished to leave, were often allowed to
sell their improvements on land to the patrón or sometimes
even to other campesinos. If, for some reason, this was
impossible, they might still leave the hacienda. There has
always been greater geographical mobility in the yungas than
on the altiplano or in the valleys, and the small holding probably never attained the same stability in these areas. An
important aspect of land tenure after the reform is the
psychological impact on campesinos of gaining legal title to
their land. It is a widespread phenomenon that, as soon as
former colonos get definite titles, they stop working for their
former patróns, or must be coaxed to do so.

In recent years, even where coca is still the prime crop,
some farmers are beginning to diversify and not to renew
coca plantings. This is more true of the large landowners
than of the campesinos, who openly ignore the recent law
prohibiting the setting-out of new coca plants. Cocaine
production and smuggling have caused some international
incidents in recent years, so the government sought to curtail
production. Of course, another reason why the landowners
are gradually shifting to citrus and coffee is clearly the high
cost and the difficulty of getting laborers for the exacting
preparation and care of coca. In spite of the official ban,
however, it is not rare to see new coca terraces being added
by campesinos around Coripata and Arapata.

Some campesinos in the yungas have abandoned other
crops, however. Bananas and tropical root crops can be
bought more cheaply, even after being trucked half a day,
from Caranavi.

Rice grows below 1,500 feet elevation. In Asunta, rice
is grown in the lowest part of the community. The forest is
cleared and after the vegetation has dried for about a month
it is burned. Rice is sown in October and can be harvested
in March. It is still hulled by hand just before buyers are
expected, since rice can be stored longer in the hull. Rice
is sold both to Chok'e Chaca where the mule path meets the
road, and in neighboring Callisaya which lies slightly higher
than Asunta and where rice, therefore, does not grow.

Alcohol production is also profitable, and sugar cane is planted on hot lowland haciendas, as in the Miguilla Valley. Cinchona bark is a wild jungle product which brings a high price periodically, as the source of quinine. Campesinos in the region collected the bark and sold it in a brief but spectacular boom during World War II and again in the mid-1960's. One of the areas originally colonized by cinchona collectors, the Bopi Valley, has also become a good source of coffee during past decades. Some of the older areas of settlement have been converted from coca to coffee production during this same period.

Pineapples are grown in quantity in a few areas; they are planted in furrows running down the hills. Production starts in two years, after which pineapples can be harvested continually, during the rainy season.

The cherimoya is a wild tree which produces a highly perishable fruit that brings a high price in the cities. The forest around such a tree is cleared and the tree is cared for in situ.

It has become fashionable for richer campesinos to own houses in the villages. People buy building-lots from the alcaldía, or town council, for as much as Bs. 100,000 per square meter. New houses line entire streets in towns such as Coripata and Arapata in the province of Nor Yungas, and the Mestizos who previously formed the great majority of the population of these towns are complaining that most of the town dwellers now are campesinos. Generally these new houses are not inhabited during the week, however, because campesinos continue to live on the ex-haciendas in dispersed houses, and come to town only during weekends and fiestas. In some places a group of new houses has been constructed to form a whole village where none existed before the reform.

Such houses are usually two-storey buildings of adobe, with corrugated metal roofs. Only down in the Bopi Valley and Alto Beni does one still find houses of the tropical forest type with palm leaf roofs and bamboo or wattle-and daub walls.

The landowners, especially around Coroico, have had to
leave their hacienda houses because of unrest among their
former colonos. Even those who still work their lands often
have had to move to their houses in the town. Many hacienda
houses, once magnificent villas, are falling to pieces. Some
are used as school buildings and as assembly rooms for the
syndicate, but these too are neglected and are little more
than ruins. Around Coripata, by contrast, a few patróns
still live in their elaborate hacienda houses.

CHAPTER **9** PATTERNS
OF
WORK

— Hans C. Buechler

BEFORE THE REFORM

As has been pointed out earlier, a system of forced labor
was the general pattern throughout the altiplano and the yungas.
A fixed number of days had to be devoted to working in the
fields of the patrón in return for a subsistence plot. Whereas
unpaid labor by resident peons was the rule on the altiplano,
in parts of the yungas the colonos were paid small wages, and
occasional labor from the outside was employed for harvests.

The Altiplano

In all the haciendas on the altiplano, colonos worked a
fixed number of days per week for the hacienda and had the
remaining days to work on their own plots. Reliable figures
on exactly how much work had to be done for the hacienda
are difficult to obtain, but three or four days with two persons
from each family working seems to have been the average
amount of labor demanded by the hacienda on the altiplano.

In some instances, the only compensation given by the
hacienda was a ration of coca, and sometimes not even this.
In at least one instance, however, food was given during the
major tasks, such as sowing and harvesting. During fiestas
the patrón might also hand out coca and alcohol. Furthermore,
the patrón would usually help his colonos when they got into
trouble with the law.

Sometimes a colono was obliged to work for his patrón
in another of his haciendas. In at least one instance, the
colonos were sent to work in the patrón's yungas hacienda

for a few weeks each year. In another, colonos sometimes
had to go to work in the patron's valley hacienda.

In addition, colonos had to perform certain services by
turns. These services, which lasted for periods varying
from one week to one or more years, had the character of
tributary assignments. During his lifetime, a colono fulfilled them according to a more or less fixed order, starting
with those which demanded least responsibility. The posts
were thus ordered hierarchically, coordinate with a parallel
hierarchy of prestige. In this respect, they resembled the
social organization in the free community (cf. Carter, 1965),
and were probably an adaptation of the ancient Aymara socio-
political order to the demands of the hacienda. Above this
hierarchy were the patrón and some permanent salaried
employees.

The hacienda was administered directly by the patrón, by
a permanent administrator, or by both. As absentee
landownership was frequent, there was usually an administrator, at least in the large haciendas. A mayordomo, or
foreman, was present in most haciendas. In most instances,
he came from a Mestizo town and was a permanent salaried
employee, while in others, his position was the top rung in
the hierarchy of colono offices. In either case, however, he
was named by the administrator or the patrón, and if he was
a colono, he was generally one who had served in most of the
lower offices, and so earned prestige and authority. The
mayordomo took orders from the administrator, and closely
supervised the colonos at work in the fields.

If the mayordomo was a Mestizo, the jilakata was
principal among the Indian offices. All haciendas, with very
few exceptions, had a jilakata, who had the same functions
as the mayordomo, but on a lower level. He frequently also
served as the hacienda's judge in minor cases, the major
ones being heard by the administrator; outside authorities
rarely intervened. The jilakata was always named by the
administrator, the patrón, and the mayordomo. The ideal
pattern was to change jilakatas every year, as in the free
community, but in practice, if he did his job well, one
could stay in office as long as ten years. Although the patrón
and the administrator usually chose him among the older and
more respected people who had already occupied many of

the other offices, they could choose anybody they felt was
qualified. The relationship of the jilakata to the other
campesinos caused ambivalence. On one hand he was
respected as their judge, and as the top figure in their social
organization. On the other hand, they often felt that he was
taking sides with the patrón and using his power to his own
advantage, especially if he stayed in office for many years.
He was, in fact, often less a leader of his people than an
instrument of the patrón to make them work. His insignia
were a staff symbolizing authority and justice, and a silver-
handled whip, which he did not hesitate to use on his people.
The prerogatives of a jilakata were few but valuable. He did
not have to do any other work for the hacienda during his
tenure. He sometimes received food during work days,
especially during the harvest period. In one hacienda, he
and other higher officials had the right to keep sheep in the
ahijadero. In another, he was in the position to secure more
land for his relatives by giving them preference in allotting
sayañas left by owners without heirs, etc.. In some smaller
haciendas where there was no mayordomo, the jilakata took
over his functions.

The next lower rung in the hierarchy was that of alcaldes.
They helped the jilakata, called people every work day,
supervised work, etc.. They were also appointed by the
administrator. In a few cases, this was the top post the
segundas personas could hold. There was usually one
alcalde for each estancia, or section of the hacienda.

The campos, or camanas, were in a sense the messengers
of the jilakata. They helped him readjust the boundaries of
the aynoka plots each year in the haciendas where this was
the practice; they called together the colonos, etc. Some
specific functions of the campos were to make fires on the
hilltops to drive away hail, and to pray that hail and frost
would spare the fields. The campos were usually appointed
by the jilakata and the alcaldes. Sometimes there was a
campo for every hacienda field, or for each aynoka.

The awatiris, or shepherds, had about the same prestige
as the campos. Like them, they were usually married
persons. They lived in huts on the ahijadero with parts of
their family, while the others took care of the crops at
home. The awatiri did not have to tend the flock personally

all the time; he could send his wife or his children to keep
watch. Usually the awatiris had no other simultaneous
hacienda obligations, and were allowed to keep their sheep
in the ahijadero during their year of service.

The chuño camana and the tunta camana either made or
supervised the making of chuño and tunta, different kinds of
frozen and dried potatoes. For every three measures of
potatoes they received, they had to return one measure of
the dried product. In smaller haciendas, one person could
do both jobs, while in larger ones there could be one or two
in each office.

These are the most frequent annual offices although there
are a number of less general ones. The aljiri, for instance,
was a person who had to spend six months or a year in La
Paz where he sold the hacienda's produce in the hacienda
store. In at least one case, he also directed the pongos, or
servants, who were of inferior rank. As remuneration he
received food and lodging. On one hacienda, there was a
person who had to water the young eucalyptus trees every
Sunday. Other cargos found in some haciendas included the
ch'awa jake, who milked the cows and the sheep, and the
alcalde de agua, who regulated the distribution of irrigation
water.

Apart from the yearly offices, there were a series of
obligations of one week's duration. The mulero, or vaquero,
took care of the mules, cows, and horses of the hacienda,
and sometimes also was charged with feeding the pigs and
chickens. During his week in office, he lived in the hacienda
buildings. The pongo had to work as a servant in La Paz, or
wherever the owner lived, for one week. Sometimes there
were one or two pongos who went to La Paz, and another one,
often called mit'ani or islero, who cooked for the administrator in the hacienda, and was in charge of goods in storage
there.

Case Studies

In order better to illustrate patterns of work and social
organization, let us consider in some detail two specific
cases. Kerani is an hacienda near Peñas in the province of
Los Andes. Its main revenue came from sheepraising for

which extensive areas both of lands of the colonos and of the
hacienda were reserved. According to the person who owned
the hacienda between 1939 and 1946, it had a population of
over 300 families and at that time was considered one of the
most prosperous haciendas of the region, in terms of both
the income it brought to the owner, and the standard of living
of the colonos. The patrón owned more than 4,000 sheep
which were kept in an extensive irrigable ahijadero. Neither
the patrón nor the colonos owned any alpacas or llamas. The
main crops were potatoes, barley, and quinoa.

Labor obligations for full colonos consisted of three days
of work each week, from Monday to Wednesday, during which
the family of each full colono had to provide three persons.
This arrangement had remained unaltered for generations.
Personas menores, who had less land than personas mayores,
also worked three days per week but furnished only two
persons. Terceras personas, who could be moved when the
patrón wished, had the same obligations as personas menores.
A clause in the written labor agreement stated that for
secondary tasks (specified as winnowing quinoa, repairing
walls and other constructions, planting trees, etc.) only two
persons per family had to work. These tasks were done on
Monday. If a person had to be absent for one reason or
another, he made arrangements with another to replace him.

At 8 A.M., the alcalde de campo, and sometimes some
of the other officers called from the hilltops, naming the
work to be done that day so that the colonos would bring
appropriate tools. Work began at nine when the peons
arrived in the field, hurried along by the jilakata and his
helpers, who brandished their silver-handled whips. Coca
was handed out to all the workers around mid-morning, and
again at noon when an hour's break was called. Then, too,
campesinos usually ate food they had brought from home,
except during sowing and harvesting time, when they received
a meal consisting of chuño, cooked potatoes, tunta, and meat,
in addition to coca. Harvest was a gay affair when the men
arrived to work playing flutes, and the girls, following an
ancient custom, were towed across the fields which were to
be reaped.

Any campesinos could also be told to carry produce with
their animals to La Paz, or to get firewood, in addition to

their three days'obligated labor. About twenty to thirty
Indians would make the trip to La Paz once a year. In the
city their animals were taken care of and they slept in
special quarters in the patrón's house. This service was
called the cumunta. In the same way, any person could be
asked to be a propio, that is, he could be ordered to carry a
message to the priest or to the village, or to carry something
or run an errand for the administrator or the patrón. All
other obligations formed a hierarchy of offices through most
of which a colono passed during his lifetime. A young colono
would start out as a pongo and serve the patrón in La Paz
for one week. One served as housekeeper; another worked
in the kitchen and was expected to bring forty or fifty eggs
and six or seven bags of llama dung for fuel. The two
pongos worked under the direction of the aljiri, who stayed
in La Paz for six months to sell the hacienda produce. Even
an illiterate campesino could keep accounts using the quipu,
a mnemonic device of knotted strings, to register his sales.
After his term as pongo, a man might become one of the ten
hacienda shepherds. After serving as a camana de campo,
making fires as defense against hail, keeping sheep out of
cultivated fields, etc., he would be eligible for one of the
alcalde positions: alcalde de agua, in charge of irrigating
hacienda lands; alcalde de quezo, in charge of cheese-making;
alcalde de isla, comptroller of the herds of sheep; or alcalde
de campo, helper of the jilakata. The alcaldes or the
jilakata were named by the administrator or by the patrón,
as were many of the other offices. At Kerani, the mayordomo
was a local campesino. Usually the mayordomo was changed
regularly but the patrón had taken a liking to one who had
stayed for ten years. The other campesinos resented this
because it meant that the hierarchy of offices stopped at the
post of jilakata, with no possibility of further advancement.
Above the mayordomo, there was the administrator who
acted as a judge in minor disputes, as well as administering
hacienda affairs.

     As much a part of the social system as the various
obligations were the frequent fiestas, which were sponsored
and organized by individuals. In contrast with the free communities, fiesta sponsorship on haciendas was not part of
the hierarchy of offices. Generally, the campesinos decided
who should become preste, sponsor of a fiesta. The preste
had to provide alcohol and food for the fiesta, so he had to

have some surplus wealth, although he did not bear the total
cost of the fiesta, but was helped by the jilakata and the
patrón. The administrator always sent invitations to the
heads of the neighboring free communities to attend the
fiesta; good relations with the comunidados were important,
since the water used for irrigation of the hacienda flowed
through them. Relations with neighboring haciendas tended
to be more strained because of disputes over water rights.

The island hacienda Ch'alla had a slightly different
socio-political hierarchy. The posts at Ch'alla were
associated more with agriculture than with stockbreeding,
reflecting an overall difference in emphasis from Kerani.
Thus, instead of one set of posts connected with watching the
fields during the growing season there were two: a set of
campos and a set of uñjiris.

The four campos formed a hierarchy of responsibility
and prestige: the campo mayor was in charge of the potato
aynoka; he also acted as judge. The second campo was in
charge of the aynoka planted in oca; the third in charge of
the aynoka planted in broad beans; and the fourth, of the
barley aynoka. The first three had to be married, and their
activities in crop rituals required the cooperation of a woman.
All built huts on their aynokas and watched over the aynoka
parcels, especially those of the hacienda. If somebody
allowed his animals to stray into the cultivated fields of the
hacienda, the campo brought them to the hacienda building
where their owner would have to pay a fine consisting of
firewood, as well as paying damages. The campo also acted
as messengers of the jilakata, measured the aynoka parcels
every year, and strove to keep away hail by means of fires,
dynamite, and prayers. A fifth campo, who stood outside
the hierarchy, was responsible for guarding the boundary
with another hacienda. This was necessary because there
was always considerable tension between the two haciendas,
and the danger of trespass was always present.

The uñjiris had responsibilities similar to those of the
campos. They were, in a sense, their helpers, and, like
them, built huts in the aynokas. They did not have to run
errands for the jilakata, and they did not form any hierarchy
among themselves.

A person could start his political career by becoming
either an uñjiri or a campo. After having filled these posts
two or three times and after having been awatiri a couple of
times, and perhaps captain of the hacienda boats, a colono
was eligible to become alcalde or jilakata. It was usual even
for a retired jilakata to take up other posts because, as in
the free communities, the more posts he had filled, the
greater was a man's prestige.

The Yungas

There have always been at least two systems of work in
most haciendas in the yungas: permanent obligated labor in
return for land, with or without wages; and seasonal paid
labor from within or from without the hacienda. The systems
varied in different subareas. In many haciendas there were
only peasants who worked for land. In others, there was a
category of renters who could pay their rent in money. In
practice, however, all paid rent at least partly by labor.
One case of expropriation listed four different classes of
workers on one hacienda: colonos who worked for the patrón
in return for the usufruct of land; yanaperos, who worked
fewer days for the patrón and had smaller plots; arrenderos,
who paid in kind, according to the quantity of land they
occupied; and habilitados, who worked for daily wages.
Landless utawawas, who worked for the colonos who had
adopted them, also existed in the yungas.

The area where yungas haciendas most closely resemble
those of the altiplano lies between the three towns of Coroico,
Coripata and Chulumani. Before agrarian reform, these
haciendas demanded two or three days of unpaid labor per
week. In Nor Yungas, five out of eight haciendas visited
had two days' obligation, and the other three had three days.
According to some informants, including a landowner, the
obligation had been four days until about 1940. These
haciendas also employed varying amounts of labor from the
altiplano during certain months. Many of the colonos had
originally come as temporary laborers from the altiplano.

Other obligations were somewhat fewer than on the
altiplano and usually lasted for shorter periods. Obligations
of a year's duration included the jilakata, or sutta (as he was
sometimes called in the yungas). Like his altiplano

counterpart, he could stay in office for more than one year if he pleased the patrón. In some haciendas there was one sutta who supervised men's work and another who supervised women's work, such as harvesting coca leaves. On one hacienda in Sud Yungas, he stayed at the hacienda house and had little time for work in his own fields. But if his fields suffered, the hacienda helped him to catch up. Suttas were appointed by the owner of the hacienda or by the administrator.

Another important office was that of camani, who received the coca as it was brought from the fields. He dried the leaves in the sun, and stored them. On one hacienda, he was helped by two or three persons if the harvest was big. In the same place, he had two weeks' vacation after the harvest. On some haciendas he also packed the coca leaves. If the leaves spoiled because of careless drying techniques, he sometimes had to pay for the damage. The camani was in office for one or two months, until all the coca of one harvest was dry.

Weekly offices included the pongos, or semaneros, who acted as house-servants, like their altiplano counterparts. Their wives lived with them in the hacienda house during their week's service, and did the cooking. The mulero took care of mules; in haciendas with cattle, these were taken care of by a vaquero. Minor obligations could include going to the village to get the mail, and running other errands.

In the province of Inquisivi, all work for the hacienda was paid, although wages were very low. In general, the campesinos worked for ten to fifteen successive days each month. Usually work beyond this was paid immediately or discounted from the next month's obligations. Food and clothing were sold in the hacienda store, where the colono could purchase goods against his allowance. Adjustments were sometimes made every two or three months, sometimes only once a year. Payment seems to have depended on the kind of work done; for example less was paid for weeding than for clearing the jungle. Work could also be paid by the cato, or quarter-hectare, of land cleared or weeded. According to one informant, payments were made directly with goods: for seven days the colono would get one pound of rice or noodles, one pound of sugar and one pound of jerked meat daily; and for the next week he would work for clothing. To what extent the colonos were indebted to the

landlords could not be ascertained exactly, but both colonos
and hacienda owners agree that when a peon wanted to leave
he usually left by night, selling his harvest before he departed.
Even such a peon could probably settle on another hacienda
easily since landlords strove to attract new colonos in that
area of labor shortage.

The faena, which consisted of work such as pathmaking
which benefited both the hacendado and the colonos, was done
on Sundays and not remunerated. In the Inquisivi area,
cargos, or tribute posts, either did not exist or people from
the hacienda itself were permanently employed to do the
work. Where coca was grown, a kachiri (as the camani there
was called), was usually recruited among the older men, for
coca drying is one of the lighter agricultural tasks. He would
usually remain in office until his death. In one hacienda in
the adjacent Irupana zone, this office was even so coveted
that it became hereditary. Cattleherders were permanent
employees in the haciendas visited. A special category of
colonos, the arrieros, acted as muledrivers in exchange for
land. In a zone between the two areas described patterns
were variable, sometimes resembling those of the first area
and sometimes of the second. One hacienda, for instance,
had changed from unremunerated labor to paid labor less
than thirty years ago. Others belonged essentially to the
Inquisivi type; still others remained more feudal in nature
until the reform. In the smaller ones the conditions were
usually better than in the larger ones, in that all labor
beyond two days was paid.

Colonos in Callisaya, in the Bopi Valley, were settlers,
slowly paying for the land and help they had initially received
from the patrón in order to become established. They could
work on the hacienda for wages, but were under no obligation
to do so. The owner of Callisaya nevertheless could dictate
a plan for the development of each settler's land, and so he
had the guarantee that the land would be amortized. The
neighboring haciendas had the same system, but the
hacienda owner had no cultivated land there. This system
had been introduced at the time when cinchona bark became
important in this region in the late-1930's.

In a few regions of the yungas, especially around Coroico
and Irupana, Negro slaves had been imported at various

times from Brazil and Peru. The government of General
Sucre declared in 1826 that slaves, although they had been
freed by article 11 of the Constitution, were to remain in the
service of their patrones as debtors until they had paid for
their value. In 1827, it was added that freed slaves who had
abandoned haciendas without the consent of their patrones
would be considered vagrants and could be captured by the
police and put to work on public works. In 1830, former
slaves could no longer buy their freedom. After this, General
Andrés Santa Cruz imported some eighty Negro families from
the Peruvian coast and put them to work in his hacienda in
yungas. Finally in 1851, Negroes were again allowed to buy
their freedom, but few did so, and they remained as colonos.
On the few haciendas where Negroes lived, there were rarely
any Aymara colonos; stereotypes and reciprocal prejudice
persisted between these two groups whose status as peons
was similar.

AFTER THE REFORM

The agrarian reform laws did not provide clear-cut means
by which an hacendado could continue utilizing the land which
remained under his control. Wages were fixed by the
Ministry of Rural Affairs, and it was clear that all labor had
to be paid. But the questions of who would be working the
hacienda lands, and who would be directing this work, have
occupied both the former landowners and the campesinos for
the past ten years. Some suggested that the ex-colonos had
the obligation to go on working for the former patrón, if some
minimum wage were paid. It was not altogether clear whether
other forms of compensation for labor, such as sharecropping,
could be substituted for cash. Such questions were of great
importance, and had to be given at least temporary answers.
In order to continue working, owners of haciendas have
chosen among the following solutions.

First, they could mechanize their farms. This has only
rarely been done, however. One reason is lack of capital;
another, no less important, is the lack of guarantees that
their ownership would be respected. Moreover, many
haciendas, especially in the yungas, do not lend themselves
to mechanization because of their rugged terrain.

A second possible solution would be to make individual working contracts with campesinos, or a collective one with a syndicate. Both forms of contract, often in combination, have been adopted. Collective contracts have the disadvantage that the landowner is then dependent upon the good will of the syndicate, but they have the advantage of having all the campesinos as a labor supply, and not having to expect reprisals as are frequently made against campesinos who contract individually.

Individual contracts, however, have the advantage that the patrón can choose a capable person whose interests coincide with his own and who will be interested in using the land as intensively as possible. This latter method also **seems** a better solution to another grave problem: that of directing work. Although there is no law prohibiting administrators from staying on hacienda, they have generally left, together with the mayordomos. Where administrators remain, the campesinos often try every means to get rid of them. The landowners themselves can now, in most cases, visit their haciendas again; but, especially during the first years, it was dangerous for them to do so. Moreover, a great number of landowners did not live on their haciendas before and had no intention of living there after the reform. Thus, the task of supervising work had to be entrusted in most cases to the syndicate leaders.

A third possible solution would be to try to find an external source of labor; this was rarely possible on the altiplano, although in the yungas, it predominated.

Especially during the first years, considerable resistance was met for any type of working arrangements and in many regions this continues to be the major problem for hacienda owners. Nevertheless, some regional patterns can be distinguished, as follows.

The Altiplano

For various reasons, wage labor has proved unsatisfactory on the altiplano. Most haciendas soon reverted to sharecropping arrangements. Sharecropping has generally proven the most satisfactory arrangement, especially for the landowners, and has therefore persisted—even in times

when, as now, it was illegal. Sharecropping is more satisfactory than wage labor because it requires less direct control on the part of the owner of the land. Also, sharecropping
has always been a familiar pattern on the altiplano and in the
valleys, and has been practiced in a number of variations.
Not only do the campesinos work on a sharecropping basis
among themselves, but also, on occasion, small-scale
Mestizo landowners in the villages will adopt this system.
Many sharecropping arrangements are practiced between
landowners and their former colonos. The most common
system is an adaptation of the old hacienda pattern of work.
The syndicate leader directs work on the hacienda lands,
much as the jilakata had before the reform, with the exception
that instead of all the produce going to the patrón, 50 to 70
per cent is divided among the campesinos. In this type of
arrangement, all work is done jointly, and the produce is
then divided. In a somewhat different system, the hacienda
land is divided into a great number of small plots, and each
campesino has the obligation to work one or two of these
plots. In Ch'alla on Sun Island where this system is employed,
one of the hacienda's aynoka parcels is divided into three
sections, in each of which the colono has to work a plot of
land. Persons who own less land than a full colono only
have a plot in one section. The parcels are separated by
narrow strips of grass. Every campesino works these plots
on the same day; as in pre-reform times, they are called
together in the morning for work and go home when work on
their plots is terminated. Instead of working a few days
each week, the campesinos are called together only when the
weather seems appropriate for a particular phase of cultivation, and they have much less land to work for the landowner
than before. The produce is pooled, as in the system of
common labor, with two thirds of the harvest being divided
among the campesinos. The same method was encountered
in two other haciendas. On one of them, the system of small
plots had existed before the reform. This system has an
obvious advantage in that individual effort is recompensed
proportionately, and therefore work tends to progress more
rapidly. Another method of sharecropping corresponds
closely to the Aymara arrangement known as waki. The
land is parceled out to individuals who sharecrop independently, each according to his own time schedule. At harvest time
the land is divided into halves, the produce of one half going
to the landowner, and the rest to the sharecropper. In all

of these arrangements, the landowner usually provides the first year's seed from his reserve, with the seed separated out before dividing the produce between sharecropper and the landowner in subsequent years.

A kind of sharing arrangement is also practiced with sheep. The sheep are entrusted to the care of one or more campesinos who receive half of the lambs born in that year. The shepherds may either be the same for many years, or they may change every year, as before the reform. I have never seen this arrangement practiced when the hacienda still had a substantial number of animals, in which case the shepherds are always paid in cash.

A peculiar case of sharecropping is encountered in Chirapaca, which had been declared an agricultural enterprise due to large investments in machinery and pedigreed sheep and cattle. The owner handed the hacienda and machinery over to the army, which works it with soldiers and pays for fuel and fertilizers. The produce is then divided equally between the army and the owner.

Salaried labor is advantageous only when the landowner or a permanent administrator can be present to supervise agricultural work, or when large herds of animals must be cared for. Salaried labor for farming was encountered in only four haciendas on the altiplano. In one hacienda, Bs. 2,400 ($.20) is the daily wage for men, women, or children. In another, a proposal for Bs. 3,000 per day for men, 2,000 for women, and 5,000 for an ox team was made to the landowner as an alternative to sharecropping. Salaried labor is more frequent in stockbreeding. Wages paid to shepherds amount to Bs. 60,000 per month on two haciendas.

Almost all hacienda offices were either abolished completely or replaced by offices in the campesino syndicate. A frequent exception to this was the campo, who remained, principally because he was indispensable to the campesinos themselves.

Among the Campesinos

The foregoing discussion has dealt with working arrangements between landowners and campesinos after agrarian

reform.   Another important complex of patterns of work
obtains among the campesinos themselves.

One of the most common working arrangements on the
altiplano is aini, or reciprocal labor. This occurs most
frequently within the framework of the extended family, but
on occasion help from outside the family may be enlisted,
although outside labor is more commonly paid with produce
or money. Paid labor, or minga, can also be arranged among
members of the extended family. If persons from outside the
hacienda are employed they are usually personal acquaintances.
For example, in Vilaque persons from neighboring free communities are employed both for agricultural labor and for
herding sheep. Laborers are always paid with produce, the
rate being about half a sack of potatoes or other product for
each five to six hour day.

On Sun Island, only the aini and the minga are practiced.
Minga payment may be delayed until harvest, reminiscent of
sharecropping. The amount is the same, regardless of sex
of the worker or time of payment. As in Vilaque, money is
not used; the type of product to be paid is determined by the
employer.

When a campesino does not have enough land, or does
not have a team of oxen, he may enter into a sharecropping
arrangement with another person. One such is the sathakha,
which is an agreement between a person in need of help and
a person in need of land. In the variant encountered in
Vilaque, a person helps in the sowing of potatoes, bringing
with him some seed potatoes which he may sow in one or two
rows on the side of the field, the yield from these rows
being his at harvest time. The sathakha is practiced only
with potatoes, and was unknown in other haciendas where
inquiries were made.

Throughout the altiplano, an arrangement called waki is
often practiced between a person who does not have enough
seed and a person who has a surplus of seed but not enough
land. In Vilaque, one person provides the seed and helps
only with the sowing, while the other provides the land,
prepares the soil, and tends the field until harvest. At
harvest one person first harvests alternate furrows, and
then the other harvests the rest. At Vilaque, this is done

only with potatoes, although it is commonly done elsewhere
with barley as well. Another system, called kañuñjasiña in
Vilaque, is practiced between a man who has land but does
not have a team of oxen and one who has oxen but not enough
land. The seed is provided in equal quantities by both
parties, while the manure is provided by the man who owns
the land. The man with the oxen prepares the soil and helps
with the sowing. In this case, the land is divided into halves
and each party harvests his part.

Arrangements involving the sharing of animals are also
made. In Vilaque, the person who takes care of another
person's cow will get the first calf, while the second will go
to the owner. Piglets born under a similar arrangement are
equally divided between the two parties, as are lambs born
during the year of contract. The above is a means for the
poorer peasant to enlarge his flock, by a sort of "adoption."

Land is rarely rented on the altiplano; I encountered it
only in one hacienda and one comunidad on the shore of Lake
Titicaca, both of which were overpopulated. In these communities, a few small plots were rented, cash in advance,
for a full three-year rotational cycle.

The Yungas

In the yungas, unlike the altiplano, migrant wage
laborers are indispensable. This pattern was and still is
characteristic not only of the patróns, but also, to a lesser
degree, of the colonos themselves.

On the Haciendas

Some wage laborers came from neighboring villages in
the yungas. These are employed almost exclusively for
specific tasks that require skills distinctive of the area.
More younger men generally work in the yungas during the
dry season and sometimes also for a few weeks or months
during the rest of the year. The laborers generally come
only from the free communities, since the haciendas have
enough land so that people need no subsidiary activities.
This does not seem to be the case in the Sorata Valley;
many persons, even from haciendas there, work in the gold
fields of Tipuani, or in the yungas.

Two types of arrangements with wage laborers prevail, contrato or jornal. A person working by contrato agrees to do a certain job, such as weeding which is paid according to the size of the area weeded. The rate per unit of area varies according to region and type of labor. The other system of payment, jornal, is a daily wage. The rates paid by the patrones to their colonos today are usually lower than what they pay to outsiders. They range from Bs. 3,000 to 4,000 ($.25-35) without food or lodging, for colonos who work for their patrón, to Bs. 5,000 with food and lodging, for people coming from outside. Colonos pay similar rates when they occasionally hire part-time laborers.

Very often contratos and jornales are combined. One task may be done by contrato for a few days, followed by another task done by jornals, or a wage laborer may arrange with a campesino to work by jornal during the week and to work by contrato on Sundays.

Wage laborers generally go to the yungas to look for work; previously, landowners used to send contractors to the altiplano, who would contract for labor in the presence of the town authorities, paying advances to the laborers. The town authorities, who were paid by the contractors, were then responsible for seeing that the laborers complied with the agreement. This method was more expensive than hiring laborers who came down to the yungas independently, but it brought the security of an adequate labor supply.

On medium-size properties, which were not subject to expropriation as were latifundios, landowners were also affected by the agrarian reform inasmuch as ex-colonos often refused to work for their former patrones. The difficult labor situation probably stems largely from vengeful pressure by syndicate leaders, but there are also other causes. The campesinos themselves have to use labor from the altiplano, and see no advantage in working for a landowner for wages lower than what they themselves pay migrant workers. Contracts between a syndicate and a landowner specifying a certain number of working days per week from each campesino, therefore, are generally unsatisfactory even where they can be negotiated. Campesinos usually honor them only casually, especially during the last few years.

An alternative to wage labor as a means for landowners
to derive a revenue from their land, is renting cultivated
land. Land is leased annually to individuals or syndicates
for a fixed amount, paid either at the beginning or the end
of the year. Renters usually run into the same problems as
the landowners; they, too, have to get their labor from outside the hacienda. In one hacienda, the secretary general
finally agreed not to interfere, since the renter was not
cultivating much more land than the campesinos themselves.
On no medium property which I have seen in Nor or Sud
Yungas was the land under as intense cultivation as before
the reform.

In some cases, the former patrones are concentrating
their cultivated areas, slowly making themselves independent
of their former colonos, to whom they are selling the rest of
their coca plantations. Where they still live on the hacienda,
they may hire one or two permanent employees, apart from
occasional laborers.

The normal work day lasts only six hours. Many
patrones complain that laborers, especially hacienda residents, work even less than that. The laborers, one hacienda
owner said, prefer to start late and work during most of the
day, rather than to start early and have part of the afternoon
to themselves. With the opening of the new colonies in the
Alto Beni, wage labor has become even more important than
before the reform, since the colonists themselves employ
much occasional labor.

Among the Campesinos

Most of the labor of a campesino in the yungas is paid.
Labor is hired from the altiplano, as described above; and
minga laborers, groups of persons from the hacienda or from
nearby, are hired for the harvest. Persons who have little
land, as the utawawas, hire themselves out as mingas. Contrary to their situation before the reform, utawawas are now
usually paid, even by the family who adopts them. In some
instances, especially in the province of Inquisivi, payment
may be made in the form of fruit or other produce, but
payment in cash is more usual.

Reciprocal labor, or aini, is also frequent here.
Sharecropping, however, is rare in the yungas for various
reasons. Since land is plentiful, sharecropping is unnecessary
on virgin land. Also, returns from plantings are high, making
sharecropping less profitable to their owners than hiring wage
labor. Thus sharecropping occurs only in rare cases, for
instance, when labor is extremely scarce. For the same
reason, land rental is rare. In one hacienda, people rented
virgin land for temporary cultivation of waluza (a tropical
root crop), yuca, maize, and squash, but never for permanent
plantings. A cato of land was rented for some three days of
labor per year. Land was also occasionally rented in
Callisaya.

Around Licoma new settlers make arrangements with
established campesinos reminiscent of the patrón-peon
relationship; the new settler is given land in return for labor,
and the relationship ends when the newcomer's own fields
start to produce.

There is no doubt that many Negroes have freed themselves from hacienda bondage since emancipation. A considerable number lived in the villages. The village of
Chicaloma near Irupana, and Chijchipa and Mururata near
Coroico, for instance, are populated almost entirely by
Negroes and mulattoes; and elsewhere Indians and Negroes
live side by side. The Negro in the yungas has not presented
any particular racial problem. Marriage between Indians
and Negroes is not as rare as stereotyped views of both
groups insist it is, and Negroes have no difficulty in getting
high political positions in the campesino syndicates. Mestizos
discriminate against them as much as they do against the
Aymaras, although the stereotype they have of "the industrious Negro" is more charitable than that of the Indians.

It was difficult to gether even a little data on what
happened to the utawawas, or adopted children. They now
generally receive wages and, in some instances, they have
even received a little land. Although their status has
improved, it still remains lower than that of the full
ex-colonos. One informant told me that on his hacienda the
guardians of utawawas had asked for land for their adopted
children, but that that land was then used for the benefit of the
foster-parents.

CHAPTER **10** HERDING
AND
MARKETING

—Hans C. Buechler

HERDING

The raising of cattle and sheep has been and continues to be a major activity in most highland haciendas. Campesinos who live only by stockraising have always been rare in the area studied, but there are a few in the punas toward the Chilean border. In the punas on the northern altiplano, pastoralists almost always have plots, however small, in the form of aynoka parcels on the lower part of the hacienda. Thus, there never was a dichotomy between pastoralists and farmers as there is, for instance, in the Near East. A shepherd who can get a plot of land--even if it is far away-- will not hesitate to do so. One informant even mentioned shepherds who supplied farmers in another hacienda with llama dung in return for the usufruct of a small plot.

Before the Reform

In pre-reform days, there were neither landlords nor campesinos who specialized entirely in animals. Specialization in llamas was found among some campesinos, but haciendas generally had more sheep.

The number of animals a family owned has always varied according to region and hacienda. Variation is vividly illustrated in the holdings at the time of expropriation of Tocopa, a lakeshore hacienda: 69 colonos owned 508 sheep, 84 cattle, 91 swine, 145 burros, and 1 mule (averaging 7.4, 1.2, 1.3, 2.1, and 0 respectively), whereas the patrón owned 1,000 sheep, but only 2 cattle, 1 mule, and no swine or burros. In most haciendas, sheep, pigs and burros were

kept in mud or stone corrals adjacent to the houses of the
colonos while cattle were tied to stakes nearby. Llamas were
kept in large circular corrals or in harvested fields encircled
by stone walls. In some haciendas and free communities
southwest of La Paz, many of the members used to build
small huts in their aynoka parcels from which they would herd
their sheep while the aynoka was lying fallow.

The division of the patrón's sheep into flocks was made
on the basis of sex and age of the sheep. Also, the purebred
sheep (usually merino or corriedale) were separated from
the indigenous sheep (raza criolla). In Comanche, for
example, the 2,810 sheep were cared for by thirteen
shepherds; there also was one shepherd for the alpacas and
goats; another for cattle and horses, and seven for the
burros.

In Kerani there were ten shepherd huts, each of which
was used for only one of the following categories of sheep:
lecheras, mothers separated from their young and used as
milk sheep; pichoras, older ewes destined to be butchered;
genitores, rams; puitos hembras, female lambs after separation from their mothers; pata orko, castrated males; and
mothers not yet separated from their young.

The cattle and burros were divided among the huts
except for the milk cows, which were tended by the mulero
and kept near the hacienda house.

The shepherd or awatiri cared for the sheep of the
patrón, which were divided among the ahijaderos and kept
in corrals. He would stay in a nearby hut. He had the
right to put his own sheep into the ahijadero, a privilege
which on one hacienda was also conceded to the mayordomo,
the jilakata and other high officials. The awatiri went to
live in a special hut with part of his family during the year
of duty, but he did not have to tend the flocks personally all
the time.

Other assignments connected with sheepraising include
the following. The alcalde de isla, who controlled the herds
and brought lambs which had died to the hacienda, to be
counted by the islero. The islero lived in the hacienda
buildings and had the keys to the storage chambers; he made

jerked meat (charqui), cooked for the administrator and
kept all the hides of the sheep which had been butchered and
sent to La Paz, and of the lambs that had died. The alcalde
de quezo was in charge of cheese-making and directed the
milkers and the awatiris who helped in the milking. He made
cheese molds out of grass, prepared the curd from lamb
intestines, and, together with the milkers, made the cheese.

Each month the old ewes were butchered after the women
had sheared their fleece. Every year, around mid-November,
all animals were counted and reclassified. This task was a
joint undertaking of all higher officers, and took about two
weeks to complete, with counting sometimes still done by
illiterate campesinos with the aid of heaps of stones of
various sizes and with quipus (strings with knots in them),
as in pre-Columbian times.

There was some seasonal variation in pasturing sheep.
During the rainy season, the flat parts of the hacienda might
be inundated, while the hillsides would be green and could
be used for pasture. In the dry season, sheep were brought
from the barren hills to the flat lands. In one hacienda,
part of the family moved to huts at a higher altitude during
the rainy season. In the punas, llama and alpaca herds were
sometimes forced to move from the higher to the lower puna
when snow fell. Women would sometimes search for fodder
for the cattle when it was scarce. On lakeshore haciendas
cattle could always feed on totora.

A number of Indians and Mestizos raised cows on the
outskirts of La Paz, and sold the milk from house to house;
usually they did not own any land, but bought straw from the
altiplano and malt residues from breweries to feed their
cows. They rarely would have more than eight cows, and
usually fewer.

In the yungas, stockbreeding was relatively unimportant,
and differed from that on the altiplano. The colonos had few
or no cattle; they rarely kept more than a few sheep around
the house and a few mules in the upper reaches of the
hacienda. The patrones usually had mules for transport, and
a few cows for their own needs, but rarely more than that.
Three haciendas were observed which had between 50 and
150 cattle; they were left to run wild in stretches of land

which was cleared jungle, covered with grass and brush, and were rounded up once or twice a week to be counted and treated for vampire bat bites and other ailments. All work associated with cattle was done by the patrón personally or by a permanent employee. Cattle were raised mostly for meat; only in one hacienda was milk regularly sold to a nearby village.

After the Reform

In no other agricultural activity did the reform have a greater effect than in livestockraising. In all regions studied, sheep and cattle belonging to the former patróns disappeared or were greatly reduced in number.

This was true not only in properties which have been declared latifundia but also on medium properties and in agricultural enterprises. In most haciendas, the patrón's pasture lands were reduced, since only purebred sheep were taken into account when land was distributed on a per capita basis according to the reform laws, and no hacienda had a large proportion of purebred sheep. Another reason for the disappearance of livestock was that the campesinos often hoped, by reducing the herds of the patrón, that they could more easily force him to give up the hacienda. Often animals were mistreated, for instance, by taking them out to the pasture late during the day and bringing them in early; in some cases, they were beaten or even fed barbed wire mixed with the fodder. Stealing was also quite frequent, on the part of both colonos and administrators, who sometimes took advantage of the period of anarchy in the early 1950's to sell animals for their own profit. However arbitrary the reduction of herds might seem, there is certainly a long-range advantage in this. Land can sustain many more people if it is put to cultivation, an observation which has been made almost everywhere agrarian reforms were introduced.

MARKETING

Before the Reform

One way of marketing produce from haciendas was to sell it in hacienda stores which were frequently run by a

colono, who would stay in La Paz for six months or a year.
Some of the produce was also sold in nearby villages.   For
example, Ch'alla hacienda on Sun Island provided the nearby
pilgrimage center of Copacabana with meat and cheese,
especially during major pilgrimages.   The campesinos sold
their produce either directly in local markets or to middlemen, usually Mestizos, who bought as large quantities as
they could, for sale in the capital city.   The patrones also
frequently sold to middlemen.

Marketing posed a major problem in the yungas because
of inadequate transportation facilities.   Transportation of
yungas produce, consisting primarily of coca, was all done
by mule until 1924 when a railway reached the entrance of
the yungas valleys, and not until 1928 was a truck road started
in the area.   The difficulties of transportation can easily be
appreciated by considering the many important areas which
even today can be reached only by mule.   For instance, the
coffeegrowers on the Bopi Valley still have to take out all
coffee by mule.   In this valley, the people of Asunta have to
pay 30,000 bolivianos ($2.50) per quintal (46 kilograms) of
produce to mule drivers who, once a week during harvest
time, make the three-day trip to the nearest road.   During
the rainy season, transportation is even more expensive
because landslides make paths and roads dangerous and
difficult; tariffs reach as much as Bs. 15,000 per quintal per
day's journey.   Only coffee, coca, and rice can repay such
high transportation costs.

Produce was brought to the road and sold there during
large Saturday markets, when people from all over the altiplano arrived to sell and exchange their produce.   Many of
the traders in these markets were semiprofessional middlemen, who sometimes also bought produce in situ.

Coca was often packed and distributed by the hacienda
itself which frequently also bought coca from its colonos.
There were also various firms with coca-packing presses in
the villages, and they also acted as middlemen.

After the Reform

Since the reform, traffic between the yungas and the
altiplano has increased.   People from the altiplano go down

to yungas and sell dried or fresh fish and meat, eggs, chuño, and other altiplano produce, and come back with fruit, rice, and other lowland products. Such trips were not infrequent before the reform, but have been greatly stimulated by the improvement and extension of roads, the extension of credit to truck owners, and other factors. Campesinos, especially from poor comunidades, make such trips to complement subsistence farming. They frequently buy up produce in their own and neighboring communities and sell it in yungas areas. These middlemen sometimes excel in very complicated business transactions. One man in Río Abajo, for instance, regularly buys twenty to thirty mules, which he exchanges for cattle, which he then drives to La Paz and sells to the slaughterhouse.

Also, more and more peasants from all three zones have started to bring their produce to the cities personally. In La Paz, there are a few streets where Indians may sell their produce on Saturdays and Sundays without paying a fee. It is probable that the fact that Indians are selling their produce themselves has hurt the professional market women in La Paz, who formerly had little competition.

CHAPTER **11** INDUSTRIAL AND
LABOR ORGANIZATION
ACTIVITIES

— Hans C. Buechler

NON-AGRICULTURAL HACIENDA ACTIVITIES

Not all haciendas devoted their entire efforts to agriculture and livestock raising. One important subsidiary
activity was mining. It is even probable that some haciendas,
especially in the punas near La Paz, were originally bought
as part of mining concessions. Although there are many
miners who had neither animals nor cultivated land, a considerable number of campesinos also worked part-time in
the mines. In one of the puna haciendas, there are still a
gypsum factory, various small mines, and a peat bog. The
gypsum factory used mainly full-time workers before the
reform, while the small tin mines and the peat bog employed
colonos whose principal activity was herding llamas. In
another hacienda at an altitude about 15,000 feet most workers
in a gypsum factory have llamas which are cared for by part
of the family. In a chalk factory belonging to an electric
power company, a few permanent employees own sheep which
they pasture in the lands around the factory; although the land
belonged to another hacienda, they simply paid a small
annual fee for each animal to the patrón of the hacienda. Now
they pay a similar fee to the syndicate which has taken control
of the hacienda.

On one hacienda, the mines and the land belonged to
different patrones. The shepherds all had a site along the
gold-bearing river, paying their rent in gold. Almost all of
these persons had a parcel in aynoka farther downstream,
and some worked in La Paz or served as musicians in fiestas
during the dry season when gold is hard to pan. A few
haciendas were combined with factories of soft drinks,

furniture, etc.   In the yungas, some haciendas are also
lumbering enterprises.

The reform had various effects on these haciendas.   In
one mining hacienda, the syndicate of the gypsum factory not
only demanded rights to keep animals on the hacienda, but
also demanded arable land.   Although the campesino syndicate
opposed this, their request was accepted by the government.
In view of the frequency of multiple occupations in these
haciendas, this is not surprising.

Sawmills in the yungas have proven to be advantageous
after the reform, since not much labor is involved and they
do not often involve quarrels with syndicates over land.

Craft specialization frequently brings subsidiary revenue
to peasant communities on the altiplano.   Surprisingly, it is
as frequent in haciendas as it is in free communities, in spite
of the former labor obligations to the hacienda.   In some
haciendas, pottery is made by the campesinos during their
free time and sold at markets far and wide.   In one group of
three haciendas, all belonging to the same patrón, every
family makes musical instruments.   The material, a type of
bamboo, is collected once or twice a year in the tropics, and
the finished flutes and panpipes of various sizes are sold
throughout a wide area, including the altiplano, yungas, and
valleys.   The patrón respected this trade, which had probably been practiced in these communities for centuries before
they became haciendas.   Baskets made in the valleys are sold
in major cities throughout the country.   Some haciendas on
islands in the southern part of Lake Titicaca complement
farming on their too-small plots by building totora rafts or
small boats during the dry season, and selling them in
various shore communities.

Fishing is an important subsidiary activity in many lakeshore haciendas.   In the early 1950's, net fishing was com-
plemented by trolling with spinners when lake trout were
introduced into Lake Titicaca.   On Sun Island, for instance,
some informants calculated that trout fishing accounts for
about fifty per cent of their income.   Fish are sold in the
nearest village, where they are bought by middlemen and
taken to La Paz.

THE CAMPESINO SYNDICATES

As part of the program for agrarian reform, the Bolivian government felt it necessary to create a new and different type of social organization which would at the same time be an instrument for the realization of the reform and for local government. This new organization, called the sindicato, or syndicate, was not based on any structure which had previously existed in either haciendas or free communities. Rather, it was modeled on industrial labor unions, modified only slightly to fit an agrarian context. The syndicates were supposed to be uniform throughout the country, regardless of population and size of an hacienda, with thirteen officers, each with definite responsibilities.

The secretary general (secretario general) is the head of the syndicate. He is responsible for initiating and furthering affectation of the hacienda. He directs the meetings of the syndicate. The secretary of relations (secretario de relaciones) replaces the secretary general when the latter is absent. The recording secretary (secretario de actas) keeps the minutes of the meetings. The secretary of justice (secretario de justicia) acts as judge in minor internal disputes. He is frequently quite active. More difficult cases are turned over to the secretary general or settled in a meeting of all secretaries. The secretary of roads (secretario de vialidad) is in charge of roads and the construction of football fields. He is not always active. In one case he had the role of the former jilacata and distributed aynoka parcels every year. The secretary of sports (secretario de deportes) organizes a soccer club, stages matches with neighboring hacienda and comunidades, is in charge of equipment, etc.. This is probably the best-defined post. The secretary of education (secretario de educación) controls school attendance and admonishes parents to send their children to school. In one hacienda, he sells produce from school lands to buy school supplies. The commander of the militia (jefe de comando) is in charge of the militia and enforces orders from government agents. The secretary of agriculture (secretario de agricultura) is supposed to procure insecticides, see that people are using their land efficiently, etc.. This post and the secretary of livestock tend to duplicate the functions of pre-reform offices. Their attributes seem poorly understood by the campesinos. The secretary of livestock

(secretario de ganadería) is supposed to buy medicine for
animals with dues collected from each member of the
syndicate. The secretary of the treasury (secretario de
hacienda) is responsible for the treasury; he collects the dues
of the members, pays expenses of the secretary general when
he has to travel to the capital, keeps the funds which derive
from cooperative lands, etc.. The secretary of hygiene
(secretario de hygiene) should visit members who are sick,
bring them to a doctor, and collect dues for buying medicine
for poor members in need of medical assistance. The
secretary of press and propaganda (secretario de prensa y
propaganda) should inform the members of current events.
The secretary of welfare (secretario de beneficiencia) should
collect dues for persons in need of financial aid; this office
was rarely encountered.

Apart from the secretaries, there are subsidiary posts
such as the alcalde escolar --a post which had been created
previous to the reform--who helps the schoolteacher keep
order, and who acts as an intermediary between the teacher
and the parents. There are also vocales, who replace the
secretaries when any of these is absent, and who call the
members together for assemblies.

Although this list includes thirteen secretaries as well
as a few other functionaries, they were never all encountered
in any hacienda. The ideal functions listed are based on what
the campesinos understood from government agents who
explained the functions of each secretary, and the secretaries
do not even always know what they are theoretically expected
to do. The system of thirteen secretaries was probably meant
to supplement any existing organizational patterns, although
it is doubtful whether those who formulated it had any clear
idea about previous patterns. In effect, much was done on
the part of the government agents to destroy former patterns,
since they seem to have felt that everything of the pre-reform
period should be done away with as outdated relics of
feudalism.

To be certain, many aspects of the social organization
in haciendas had to be changed when the haciendas were
divided among campesinos. For instance, self-government
with direct connections with the national political system
soon supplemented the old system that had been directed by

the patrón for his own ends. The change also had to include
formation of an organization which would hold together a
number of small independent landowners. To do this, the
character of the campesino leader had to be changed. Before
the reform, the jilakata represented the interests of the
patrón. After the reform, the secretary general, who took
his place as head of the community, and also the other
secretaries were to be elected by the campesinos, and were
to represent them more directly. This meant, then, that a
break with the past was necessary in certain domains. However, it should not be overlooked that the former hacienda
organization was more than just a means of exploiting
campesinos. It also included mechanisms for ordering
relations between men and between men and land which were
vital to both the patrón and the peons. For instance, as we
have seen in our analysis of land tenure, the patrón had
access to the same categories of land as did his colonos.
Like the campesinos, he had only limited lands where he
could plant what he wanted, and on others he was required
to follow a rotational pattern; even his grazing lands were
treated in a manner similar to the private grazing lands
which a colono had in his sayaña.

In a very real sense, the organization required by the
tenure patterns of hacienda lands was often only an enlarge-
ment of that demanded by the people's land categories.
Similarly, the cleaning of irrigation ditches and the building
of dams and other public works were of interest to both
landowner and colono. Thus, many activities directly related to access and the conservation of natural resources,
were common to both hacendado and campesinos. There
was no reason for changing the old system in this respect.
But here the radical attitude of the reformers led to confusion rather than betterment because they hesitated to permit
the continuation of any former office.

In other domains, the changes that had to be made were
even more complex, for example, in the maintenance of law
and order. Before the reform, the administrator usually
had most to say in this area, although the jilakata also sometimes acted as a judge. In some areas, the problem has not
yet been resolved whether justice should be meted out by the
syndicate leaders or should be transferred to nearby government authorities outside the hacienda.

The influence of the patrón did not, of course, cease to
exist from one day to the next, even with the reform. In
many haciendas, things continued much as before during the
first few years, except that wages were paid or a system of
sharecropping was introduced. However, the syndicates
sought--sometimes violently, sometimes slowly and peace-
fully--to have more influence in determining not only affairs
related to the campesinos and their newly won land, but also
those related to the administration of the former patrón's
land. Mayordomos and even administrators were generally
forced to leave, so that the landowner was obliged to arrange
activities directly with the syndicate leaders, on whose good
will he became increasingly dependent. The ambiguous
situation to which this led is well illustrated by the attitude
of one of the first secretaries general of Ch'alla. Immediately upon leaving the patrón's house in La Paz, where they had
discussed work on the hacienda, he would loudly proclaim
that he would do just the contrary of what they had agreed
upon. Despite this symbolic defiance, however, he would
always fulfill his commitment precisely.

Resistance to the patron was promoted both by agents of
the Ministry of Rural Affairs and by regional syndicate
leaders. During meetings, the campesinos were told in what
ways they could still collaborate with the landlords and in
what ways they should not. Also, there were pressures on
the more moderate haciendas from those of neighboring
haciendas who had chosen a more radical path. The patrón
lost his role as judge and advisor of his people after the
reform. Some of the patrones feel that the persons who
carried out the reform should have discussed with them
problems such as quarrels over ownership of certain sayañas,
and claims of persons who had left the hacienda before the
reform, since they or their administrators usually knew much
about each individual colono. It is hardly surprising, however,
that this has rarely been done.

The settlement of quarrels among campesinos, in which
the administrators previously played a decisive role, are
now often arbitrated by the syndicate, although the more
difficult cases are sometimes brought before the village
judges.

An important change in leadership was the transformation from a system of appointment by the patrón to election by the campesinos themselves. The change was not as radical as might appear; even before the reform, the jilakata was often nominated by the older men so the appointment of the jilakata was by no means always an arbitrary decision of the patrón or administrator.

It is difficult to generalize about the degree to which the election of the syndicate leader actually follows highly touted democratic principles. However, a few principles of recruitment are apparent. Usually the secretaries are married men who own land, with the exception of the secretary of sports who is usually a young man interested in sports. Utawawas rarely seem to become members of the board, and when they do, they never get to be secretary general. If the hacienda is divided into different estancias, care is taken that each estancia is represented in the directorate. Some haciendas have split into two or more syndicates. The reason usually given for this is that the size of the hacienda or its topographical characteristics rendered the hacienda unwieldy for a single syndicate to control. Sometimes such sections had been semi-independent before the reform. In Huanca Pampa, each estancia had had a separate jilakata and other officials; all they had in common were the aynokas and the work for the patrón. Another unusual reason for division is the formation of different interest groups. In one hacienda, three men formed a syndicate of campesinos-without-land, for the sole purpose of strengthening their claim for land. In still another hacienda, a group of persons whose fathers had once owned land, formed a syndicate led by the militia chief of a neighboring hacienda.

In contrast to the offices before the reform, there is no hierarchy among the secretariat. It is not necessary for a secretary to have passed a lower office before becoming eligible for a higher one. Even the secretary general need not necessarily have been a member of the board before. Usually, however, a secretary general is supposed to be a "person of responsibility," which means that he should not be very young, that he should have been a jilakata before the reform, or have shown in some other way that he is a mature man.

The ability to speak Spanish has probably helped some campesinos to gain positions of responsibility, but this is by no means a prerequisite. Of the secretaries general from the altiplano and the valleys whom I have met, seven did not speak Spanish at all, and only seven were more or less fluent. This is not surprising, however, for few persons over 25 years of age have a good knowledge of Spanish. Moreover, when a secretary general goes to La Paz, he will usually find people who speak Aymara in the offices he is interested in. If, on the other hand, he has to deal with topographers or officials from La Paz who come to visit, he will always be able to find an interpreter among the younger people.

A secretary's term in office varies considerably from hacienda to hacienda. The usual practice is yearly election, after which a delegate from the government should be called to install the secretaries in office. Re-election of the same secretaries is frequent, however, so a secretary may stay in office for three years or more. In other instances, however, elections take place less regularly. In some haciendas only those secretaries are replaced who do not do their jobs well, or who have died. In some cases, a secretary has stayed in office since the reform; sometimes only the secretary general has remained the same, and the others have changed more frequently, whereas in other instances all change at the same time, even if the change takes place only after several years. Of those haciendas of the altiplano and valleys where data were collected on this subject, eight changed their secretary general every year with few re-elections; in five cases, he stayed in office for two or three years (in two of these, the secretary general was changed regularly every year during the first few years after the reform, and only recently has he been allowed to stay for longer periods). On one hacienda, the same person had been in office for five years; on another, for seven, and on one, for nine years; on three others he had not changed since the reform. One of those who has stayed since the reform is an energetic, middle-aged person who has recently been elected provincial syndicate leader, another is an old man who probably proved to be a good counterpart to a particularly difficult patrón, and the third once led an open revolt against the patrón, wounding him and distributing his lands among the campesinos. A special case was encountered in an hacienda bordering the city of La Paz. There, the secretary general, who had been in office for nine years, was at the same time president of

the junta de vecinos (neighborhood council) which organizes
the inhabitants of the recently urbanized sector of the
hacienda.

Probably the major confusion with regard to the new
campesino organization was--and still is--the delimitation of
the functions of each of the secretaries. In most haciendas,
many secretaries still do not have any specific assignment
apart from attending syndicate meetings. Very frequently,
the secretary general completely overshadows all the rest
and is for all practical purposes the only person who counts.
Only a few functions are beginning to crystallize into widespread patterns, but most are local adaptations.

The primary function of the secretary general is to
initiate the petition for affectation of land, and to keep the
process of affectation going until the titles are ready. For
this purpose, the secretary general and the recording secretary, frequently have to travel to La Paz to lobby for expedi-
tion of the process of affectation, to fight against outsiders
who want land in the hacienda, and so forth. The secretary
general incurs considerable expenses, both for transportation
and for stays in the capital, where his trips from office to
office often take many days, and where he may have to spend
money on bribes to assure that officials will help him. Some
secretaries pay such expenses themselves; more often, however, per diem comes from dues. A few secretaries doubtless take advantage of this system, but ex-landlords probably overstate the case when they call this a common abuse
of the rank and file by their officers.

The secretary general also has to entertain visiting
officials, and to attend meetings of the regional syndicate
organization, sometimes weekly.

On those haciendas where the hacendado is still in
residence, the secretary general usually serves as mayordomo. He oversees the cultivation of the lands which still
belong to the hacendado, divides produce in sharecropping
arrangements, etc.. He also organizes communal work such
as the cultivation of school lands, clearing of irrigation
ditches, and, in valley-bottom haciendas, the construction
and repair of dikes. For this purpose, he keeps track of the
persons who have fulfilled their obligations. Finally,

together with the secretary of justice, and often with the whole syndicate, he may also act as judge.

The secretary general's power enters many domains, but is by no means unlimited. Major decisions generally require the support of the members. It is, for instance, often possible for individuals to avoid collective tasks. The power to punish is limited, and the rise of almighty caciques, or despotic autocrats, among the secretaries general is rare on the altiplano, contrary to popular opinion. Caciquismo, when it appears, is usually on a level higher than the local syndicate. The secretary general's power of decision is restricted not only from below, but also from above. Town mayors and higher level syndicate leaders can have a great deal of influence. Often decisions concerning affection of a hacienda, labor relations with the former patrón, purchase of land from the hacendado, and so forth, are regulated from this higher level, and, in some instances, higher level officials even influence the election of secretaries general.

As we have mentioned, some of the other secretaries have functions which are quite similar from hacienda to hacienda. These were functions which were understood by campesinos, and which did not duplicate those which they believed should be attributes of the highest official. With a few exceptions, then, their actual jobs are very much like those prescribed for their statuses. For example, the secretary of relations does generally serve as assistant to the secretary general; the recording secretary usually does keep minutes of meetings   (and so is the only one who should certainly know how to read and write).

The functions of other secretaries have already been out-lined in general terms, although they show much greater variation, either because they were not well understood, because they duplicated pre-reform offices which still per-sist, or for some other reason. For example, the jobs of the secretaries of agriculture and livestock tend to duplicate the functions of pre-reform offices, such as the campos or campanas, who were in charge of keeping animals out of cultivated lands. Their official functions can only rarely be performed: the curing of animals, for lack of medicines, and seeing that the campesinos are cultivating their fields, which no longer has meaning for the campesino. Therefore,

in practice, they have the choice of doing nothing at all, or of
fulfilling some of the functions of pre-reform offices. In
order to determine what the campesinos would do with such
ambiguous statuses, I tried to find out their specific jobs on
most haciendas I visited. On five of the twelve haciendas on
which data were gathered, the secretary of agriculture has
no job whatsoever. In one hacienda, he buys vaccines for
animals. In four he acts as campo; in two of these four cases
he is even identified with this pre-reform office; in the other
two, the campo continues to exist as assistant to the secretary
of agriculture. All impose fines on persons whose animals
have strayed into fields, and the fines are then used to pay
for the titles of land of the poorer members of the syndicate.
In one hacienda, the agricultural secretary directs work on
cooperative land, and in two other haciendas he has replaced
the jilakata, directs work on hacienda lands, and is even
known by that title. The secretary of livestock has no job in
four of the cases studied. In two instances he acts as campo;
in four he occasionally purchases vaccine with dues paid by
the campesinos.

The secretary of finance collects dues in three of the
haciendas where his activities were checked, while in one he
directs hacienda work together with the secretary of agriculture. The real functions of the secretary of welfare are even
more obscure. Usually the title exists, devoid of any function.
On many haciendas in the yungas and in the valleys near
Sorata, there is a secretary of propaganda, who does little
more than call people to meetings. Aside from the several
secretaries, in some haciendas there is also an encargado
who represents the interests of the hacendado. His job
resembles that of the jilakata of hacienda times but has, of
course, much less power. On one hacienda, the encargado
distributes seed to be sown on hacienda lands, directs work,
as well as giving offerings to Mother Earth and conducting
the annual sacrifice of a llama before the potato planting.
The encargado was originally installed after the crops failed
in the year that all the functions of the jilakata had been
abolished by the secretary general; the crop failure had been
interpreted as the response of the Earth for not having received the customary offerings.

In certain parts of the yungas, the change after the
agrarian reform was much more violent than on the altiplano

and in the valleys. The change from the patrón-oriented
system often meant the adoption of a system where neither
the patrón nor his interests had any place whatsoever.
Hacendados were often chased away; their plantations and
houses were neglected, or even destroyed. Those who did
remain or who could come back later usually had little to do
with the syndicate, and where contacts did exist, they have
tended to diminish with time as the hacendados try to become
as independent as possible of their former colonos. Where
the landowners have transmitted their land to renters, there
is often considerable resistance toward them on the part of
the syndicate.

It is on the level of the province that some syndical
leaders have become omnipotent caciques and directed the
syndicate members to resist the hacendados. During the
1960's such abuses lessened, and they were virtually ended
by the downfall of the MNR late in 1964.

In many ways the secretary general in the yungas resembles his counterpart in the valleys and on the altiplano,
although he sometimes has more power. In two out of seven
cases, the secretary general changed every year; he stayed
for two or three years in three cases; and nine and ten years
in two cases. One of these last cases is remarkable in that
an hacendado from one hacienda became secretary general of
three neighboring haciendas, while in his own hacienda another
was syndicate leader. Hacendados sometimes feel that
secretaries general acted harshly toward their own people.
In two instances, the secretary general supposedly told
people to move off their land because they were not wanted
there, promising them that the syndicate would pay for the
land. The secretary general also sometimes made allotments
of land without permission from any authorities above him.

In the few instances where data were obtained, the
secretaries of relations, of justice, and of sports had functions similar to those on the altiplano. The secretary of
press and propaganda has various functions from hacienda to
hacienda. In Callisaya, which can be reached only by a two
days' mule trip, he brings newspapers from outside and, in
general, is charged with finding out what is going on in the
world. On another hacienda, he simply does whatever the
secretary general orders him to do, while on a third hacienda,

he only calls people together for assemblies. The secretary
of welfare collects dues for medicine in one hacienda, has no
functions in another one, and had died but not been replaced in
a third one. The secretary of roads is important in Callisaya,
where he is in charge of keeping the mule trail open.

The secretaries general are responsible to leaders on the
level of the provinces, or on the level of sections, some of
the larger provinces being divided into two secciones. It is
unfortunate that no one has investigated in detail the roles of
these leaders, recruited sometimes among the syndicate
leaders of the haciendas, and sometimes among the town
Mestizos. Obviously, they press for affectation of haciendas,
tell campesinos when to collaborate with the hacendado, and
when not to, and act as judges in quarrels between ex-
haciendas such as boundary problems, but extensive study at
the local level disallowed intensive study at the provincial
level.

Some provincial leaders whom I did meet were energetic
men and commanded general respect. One, recently elected
in the province of Murillo told me he would soon be touring
the haciendas together with inspectors from MAC to see if
there were still haciendas which retained old customs.
Another in Sud Yungas succeeded a leader who had terrorized
the province by instigating strikes, demanding money from
the campesinos, and antagonizing hacendados and campesinos
alike. The new leader, a Negro who had been leader of one
section of the province for two years before and is also
secretary general in his home hacienda, told me he would
have to "mend the broken plates" of his predecessor. He is
paid by the government and, unlike his predecessor, will
not depend on exacting tribute from the campesinos. On the
altiplano, a third "natural" leader has a job in MAC and at
the same time is slowly gaining control by undercutting the
authority of the incumbent provincial leader in a power struggle
that involves a curious combination of agricultural moderniza-
tion, smuggling for profit, land-grabs, championing of individual campesinos, and other maneuvers, alternately beneficent
and selfish. The fact that such men get virtually no direction
from the government offers an interesting study in the dynamics
of leadership, but it also allows manifold abuses in the
countryside.

IMPLICATIONS FOR ACTION

It would be pretentious to suggest detailed methods for solving rural problems on the basis of so short a study. Nevertheless, judging from the present research and from past experience on the altiplano, a number of observations appear to have direct bearing on policy.

Throughout this study we have emphasized organizational aspects of the hacienda before and after the reform, i.e., we have stressed qualitative rather than quantitative aspects. This was done in the conviction that the general way in which people in a given society go about solving their problems should be the guideline when introducing change, rather than imposing a closed, or ideal, system without reference to the particular socio-cultural situation. If this criterion is accepted, the study of Aymara society and of the society of the landowners offers some interesting considerations.

It has frequently been repeated that the Aymara and Quechua free communities are strongly integrated entities, whose members act as a unit in many aspects of life, including the exploitation of land. Recent studies seriously challenge this view, especially the work by Carter (1963, 1965) on the northern altiplano. Contrary to popular opinion, there appears to be little general cooperation in Aymara communities, beyond the extended family. The myth of working cooperatively is most firmly entrenched in reference to the exploitation of land. As we have mentioned, the aynokas or rotational lands are exploited individually; the only common organizational pattern involved is the sequence of planting crops and then leaving land fallow, which is a common right, is general only in ha-ciendas; in at least some free communities even this is indivi-dualized. Therefore, the aynoka cannot be taken as exempli-fying cooperativism in any meaningful sense. And yet the question remains whether cooperatives of some sort might be advantageous for altiplano haciendas and comunidades.

One syndicate leader wants to try a cooperative system for growing garden vegetables. Not only would this assist crop diversification, but the vegetables might find an easier market if grown in quantities. To be sure, this would demand very little cooperative effort and would take into account existing patterns of social organization. Marketing would probably not pose any major problems, for the attention of middlemen from La Paz would be attracted to the local weekly markets as soon as vegetables became available in large quantities. As an alternative solution, agreements similar to those we have described for valley-bottom haciendas could be made with a market vendor in La Paz who could regularly come to buy produce from the campesinos.

Another problem appears in this connection with the question of how far the influence of higher campesino leaders should be used for the undertaking of rural development projects. Many of these leaders tend to be preoccupied with personal political aspirations, and so practical problems are often neglected. With adequate direction, however, they could presumably become a valuable asset to rural development, especially if their power were harnessed for other than purely political purposes.* The people on the altiplano today are in search of direction; the proliferation of syndicate meetings on all levels is one manifestation of this. If the campesinos have adequate leadership coming from their own ranks, positive results could be expected.

On the level of the hacienda organization, more efforts should be directed toward the education of persons eligible for secretarial posts. Courses should be taught by persons who are well acquainted with the specific problems of their area. To make this possible, the area of responsibility of each teacher or group of teachers should not be too large.

It has repeatedly been pointed out, in this book and elsewhere, that there should be more guarantees for the owners of medium-size properties (propiedades medianas) in order to foster investment in modern agricultural methods. We feel obliged to repeat and underscore this necessity here. The absence of guarantees has led to the neglect of land by many landowners, ranging from a reluctance to invest in machinery to the abandonment of entire haciendas because of threats on the part of campesino leaders, as in yungas. These guarantees should not require the campesinos to work for

─────────

*/Editor's note: The degree to which some syndicate leaders in the yungas realize their power, and effectively use it for the common good, is illustrated in Heath, 1966 -- DBH/

their former patrones, but rather should guarantee that no
sabotage be tolerated against whatever contracts have been
made with campesinos, whether they be from within or without the hacienda.

Land fragmentation is a major problem, and will become
increasingly serious if mechanization is introduced. On the
altiplano, fragmentation has its justification in that the
rotational pattern of the aynokas presupposes it. In this
case, other methods for better exploitation of land resources
could probably be devised, such as mechanized farming of
aynokas with adequate marking of the plots. However, in
many haciendas the sayañas are also fragmented and the
reform has usually not helped the situation, since fragments
of land were added to the sayañas in many cases; regrouping
seems to have been achieved in only a few instances. Considering the benefits of land consolidation, as practiced in
Switzerland, more attention should be given to the problem.

Soil conservation is another crucial problem, especially
in the yungas. Prohibiting campesinos in the yungas from
planting just anywhere, as they could have done before, will
force them to use land more intensively. However, they are
still ill-prepared to make more intensive and efficient use
of land. Soil conservation is also crucial on the altiplano
where, because of population growth, the fallowing periods
have been drastically reduced which, in turn, is diminishing
yields.

PART **IV**

LAND REFORM AND SOCIAL REVOLUTION

IN

THE BOLIVIAN ORIENTE

12

INTRODUCTION
TO THE REGION

— Dwight B. Heath

In eastern Bolivia, most people derive their livelihood more or less directly from the land. A different means of subsistence predominates in each of the three regions studied within the Oriente, and yet each involves a fairly immediate relationship between the people and the land: agriculture in Santa Cruz, herding in Mojos, and the collection of forest products in the Northeast. Ecological and demographic similarities and differences allow a degree of controlled comparison within this area. Even more striking are comparisons with the highland regions described by my colleagues.

The Oriente is of special importance for a number of reasons. It compels our attention in terms of sheer area, comprising almost two thirds of the nation. In ecological terms, its hot, wet, tropical climate offers a striking contrast with the cold dry altiplano or the temperate valley zones to the west. Historically and culturally, it has been distinctive since pre-Columbian times. But most people phrase the importance of the Oriente in demographic terms: it is a sparsely populated frontier in a nation where old population pressure is fast being aggravated elsewhere.

Little social science research has been done in the tropical and subtropical plains of eastern Bolivia, and the bulk of it has dealt with the northern Santa Cruz area, the center of the greatest population within the Oriente, and the zone with most intensive and extensive agriculture, immigration, and incipient industrialization. As such, it is focal but by no means typical. For this reason, I felt it important to work not only around Santa Cruz, but also in other regions of the Oriente which are different in many significant respects.

Brief visits provided some familiarity with the Mojos region in the state of Beni. This open grassland is more tropical, even more sparsely populated, and subject to seasonal flooding. Investigation around Trinidad and Santa Ana de Yacuma yielded valuable information of patterns of land tenure and use in a prairie region where cattleherding is the predominant economic activity. The northeastern area, including Pando and northern Beni, comprises still another ecological zone: tropical, even more sparsely settled than Mojos, a dense jungle area where the collecting of forest products is virtually the only occupation. I worked briefly in Riberalta and vicinity, and found striking contrasts with all of the other regions. In each of the following topical discussions, a final section is devoted to Mojos and the Northeast, in order to indicate briefly how they differ from the Santa Cruz area.

METHODS

Fortunately, some of my previous research was of immediate relevance: I had already gained an intimate familiarity with the Santa Cruz area in 1956-57, and subsequent study in 1962 and 1963 provided insight into recent changes, as well as greater historical perspective.* An excellent study by Crossley (1961) summarizes much of the work published to that time, including statistical data which I shall not repeat here. Although my previous experience was helpful in one of the areas studied, the factor that contributed most to my accomplishing so much was the generous and ample cooperation of virtually everyone with whom I had any dealings. In such research, it is just as important to deal with a "representative sample" in the lay use of the term, as it is impossible to seek a "random sample" in the strict sense.

---

*Field research sponsored by the Henry L. and Grace Doherty Charitable Foundation, Social Science Research Council, Brown University, and Land Tenure Center has yielded a variety of data and conclusions on life in the Santa Cruz area: general (Heath, 1959d), historical (1961b, 1964a, 1965a, 1966b, c), emphasizing agrarian reform (1959a, b, c, 1960a, b, 1963, 1964b), and cultural change (1965b).

As explained in the introduction to this book, courtesy
visits to Bolivian officials at all levels yielded discussion
that was unexpectedly full, frank, and fruitful. Employees
and advisors in national and international agencies generally
were helpful within the realms of their competence; the same
held true at the local level, even in isolated communities
where the subject matter of research was more acutely sensitive. Land tenure is a concern to large-scale commercial
farmers who control thousands of acres and also to peasants
cultivating small subsistence plots; cattle ranchers and
rubber collectors derive their living from the land; merchants,
labor leaders, truckers, lawyers, landlords, lumberers,
and a host of others are intimately affected by patterns of
land tenure, and the social revolution of the past decade has
certainly touched every Bolivian in some way. It is a tribute to the Bolivian people that no one declined to discuss
the subjects, although, to be sure, they were not always
careful to distinguish between fact and opinion, both of which
were relevant to the investigation.

A variety of field methods were used, among which the
predominant technique was informal interviewing. While
attempting to get information on similar subjects from a
variety of respondents, it was most useful to take cues from
the informants themselves and to pursue their concerns
rather than restricting myself to a predetermined set of
categories. On no occasion did I have to use an interpreter,
nor did I pay informants, except by sharing cigarettes, beer,
meals, and so forth. During most interviews, I took abundant handwritten and shorthand notes without asking permission. These included verbatim quotations as well as
summary paraphrases, sketches, maps, and so forth. Maps
and portions of legal dossiers were copied, with permission,
and are similarly cited. Photographs provide an important
supplementary form of documentation for the subject of land
tenure and use; I took photographs openly, without asking
permission. A special phase of the project was documentary
filming by Fritz Albert, a skilled and sensitive photographer
of the University of Wisconsin's Department of Agricultural
Journalism. Footage shot in the northern Santa Cruz zone
provides effective documentation which will presumably be
of special value as a training tool, and in communicating
some of my findings to a broader audience than will read

this book. *

One of the advantages of previous warm acquaintance in the area was my being welcome at a variety of hearings where controversies over land tenure were aired, and differences sometimes settled. Such sessions were especially fruitful because values and attitudes were thrown into sharp relief, and litigants mustered tradition, law, and their beliefs about law (which were often far divergent from juridical reality). The bulk of research in documentary sources such as published books and journals, administrative archives, and so forth, had already been done on previous visits. An appreciable amount of the descriptive data on society and culture had also been collected earlier, using traditional ethnographic techniques.

In reporting my findings, the primary aim is to present a succinct description of land tenure and use, in socio-cultural context. It seems pointless here to wrestle at length with the old question of what is meant by the broad term "land tenure"; the anthropological perspective stresses the view that aspects of culture are interrelated, and I conceive of "land tenure" as involving economic, political, evaluative, and other social aspects as well as the juridical. In the simplest terms, I view patterns of land tenure as patterns of social relations inasmuch as they define man's relation to man in the use of land and of goods derived from it (cf. Hallowell, 1943; Heath, 1960a). For this reason, I feel that discussions of rules, laws, traditions, or other pronouncements concerning claims to land are pointless without an understanding of the uses and meanings of land itself. The scope and implications of my conception of land tenure should emerge from the report that follows.

---

*Three 16mm color films, each about thirty minutes with narration, have been produced and are available through University of Wisconsin. They constitute a series on "The Santa Cruz area of eastern Bolivia, August 1963," and are entitled: "Changes in agriculture, population, and utilization of resources," "Immigration of Japanese from overseas, ⎾and⏌ highland Indians," and "Changing land tenure in the rural area around Montero."

Pseudonyms are used for individuals throughout this study, because of the confidential nature and political sensitivity of many of the attitudes expressed. Political units and geographic features are correctly named, and archaic names which have historical relevance are noted. Fincas, however, are distinguished by pseudonyms in order to respect the trust of residents who are identified with particular landholdings. In many instances, relevant statements by individual informants are much more revealing of the full significance of cultural elements than could be any analytic summary by the investigator. For that reason, I include colloquial translations from my field notes; translations from materials published in other languages are also mine. For the convenience of the reader, my spelling of Indian tribal names follow Métraux (1942; 1948). In many instances, his orthography does not accord with local pronunciation; in such cases, local variants are noted at the first occurrence of the name.

CHAPTER **13** THE ENVIRONMENTAL,
HISTORICAL, AND
SOCIAL SETTINGS

—Dwight B. Heath

The vast but little-known tropical eastern lowland area of
Bolivia is distinguished from the populous mountainous western
part of the country, by the term "Oriente," and comprises all
of Beni and Pando departments, most of Santa Cruz, and small
portions of Chuquisaca and Tarija.

THE ENVIRONMENTAL SETTING

For our purposes, the Oriente must be subdivided into
regions where different types of land use predominate. Three
of these which I visited in the course of the research are:
northern Santa Cruz area, Mojos, and the northeast. In this,
as in subsequent sections, detailed description of the northern
Santa Cruz area constitutes the major portion, and a final
section is devoted to pointing out the distinctive features of
Mojos and the Northeast.

Physical Factors

Most of my research was conducted in the sixty-mile square
which is the only zone of relatively intensive agriculture in the
Oriente, and that which contains the bulk of the population. This
region has long been called "the northern Santa Cruz area"
(Leonard, 1948; Bolivia, 1954). It lies near the geographic
center of the continent, but natural barriers have combined with
sheer distance to isolate it from outside influences until the past
decade. The city of Santa Cruz is the point of articulation between
this area and the rest of the world; settlement extends about
sixty miles north, and is largely bounded by the Yapacaní and Grande
(formerly Guapay) Rivers, an area about the size of Delaware. The
whole of this zone lies between lats. $17^{0}10'$ and $17^{0}50'$S, and longs.
$62^{0}55'$ and $63^{0}50'$W (See Map 5).

The northern Santa Cruz area can be characterized as sub-tropical; seasons are marked more by differences in rainfall than in temperature. Bright sunny days predominate from February to October, and virtually all of the year's 60 to 100 inches of rain normally falls between November and January when cold winds come from the south. Heat, humidity, and precipitation all increase toward the north.

Two very different types of ecology dominate in the Oriente, that of the pampa and that of the rain forest. The former predominates in Mojos, and the latter in the Northeast, whereas the northern Santa Cruz area is intermediate, with pampa in the south and jungle in the north. The pampa is sandy, with little cover other than stiff grass, broken by patches of cactus or thorny bushes. In nearby but contrasting tropical forest, moist black soil supports luxuriant growth including an immense variety of hardwood and palm trees, balsa, and a profusion of undergrowth such as orchids, vanilla, and lianas. Birds are everywhere; rivers abound with fish; animals and insects are so profuse as to defy cataloguing.

The Oriente is an alluvial plain, with the rugged escarpment of the Eastern Cordillera of the Andes rising abruptly to almost 10,000 feet to mark its western limit. That portion studied contains some of the headwaters of the Amazon: rivers run northward from an altitude of about 1,430 feet at Santa Cruz to about 560 feet at Riberalta. Transportation--or lack of it--has played an important role in the history of this area. In the south, rivers which become broad raging torrents in the rainy season are little more than streams lined with quicksand during most of the year. There is virtually no transportation on the waterways south of Puerto Grether on the Ichilo River, and motor launches come upstream only as far as Cuatro Ojos on the Piray, both of which are north of the present area of settlement.

The northern Santa Cruz area had no rail connections until 1955 when a line was opened connecting the city of Santa Cruz with Corumbá, just across the Brazilian border. Until early 1964, wood-burning locomotives made weekly trips along the 422-mile track which was constructed with Brazilian capital under a treaty providing for repayment in petroleum products. This railroad was the avenue of introduction of cheap manufactured goods which had not previously been available in the area. Since Bolivia declined to assume responsibility for maintaining the line in 1964, service has been halted, and the roadbed and rolling stock are said to be fast deteriorating. Another railroad, connecting Santa Cruz with Yacuiba, Argentina, has recently been opened, although many

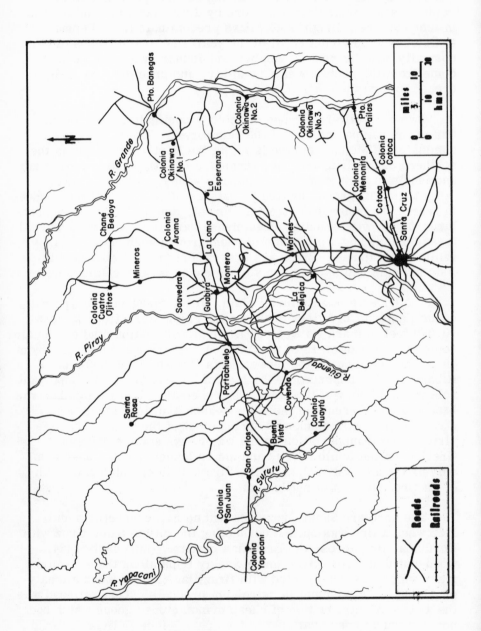

NORTHERN SANTA CRUZ AREA

Pto. Banegas
R. Grande
Colonia Okinawa No.2
Colonia Okinawa No.3
Pto. Pailas
Colonia Cotoca
Colonia Okinawa No.1
La Esperanza
Colonia Menonita
Chané Bedoya
Colonia Aroma
La Loma
Mineros
Montero
Warnes
Cotoca
Santa Cruz
Colonia Cuatro Ojitos
Saavedra
Guabirá
La Belgica
R. Piray
Portachuelo
R. Güendá
Santa Rosa
Covendo
Colonia Huaytú
Buena Vista
San Carlos
R. Surutu
Colonia San Juan
Colonia Yapacaní
R. Yapacaní

miles
5 10
0 10 20
kms

Roads
Railroads

bridges remain to be built, also with foreign capital which is
to be repaid in oil.

Connections with the western portion of Bolivia have
only recently been opened. Markers left by three successive
surveys are the only indications that a railroad between Santa
Cruz and Cochabamba is "under construction" as it has been
characterized since 1900. Although this line would be the
last link in a valuable transcontinental railway system, it is
doubtful that it will be completed; the project would be
enormously expensive and difficult because most of the route
is through rugged mountains which are still uninhabited and
even in large part unexplored.

Although the technical, economic, and administrative
difficulties involved were almost as great, Bolivia's only
paved highway was opened early in 1955 (see Bergmann, 1966).
Constructed with Point Four funds, this road was planned to
serve as an outlet for the produce of the Oriente as much as
a link with the rest of the nation. Unfortunately, the highway
has not been adequately maintained, so that erosion, landslides, and heavy freight are taking their toll.

Air service for freight and passengers is expensive but
fairly regular (except in the rainy season), even in several
remote towns which have no other means of transportation or
communication. The national airline and the Army dominate
this field.

The Environment of Mojos and the Northeast

The flood plain of Mojos (or Moxos) sprawls over the
central portion of Beni department, between lats. 13° and
16OS, and longs. 64° and 67^OW. The population is extremely
sparse, scattered in a dozen small towns and in far-flung
ranches on bits of land that rise slightly above their surround-
ings. For purposes of this researc h, brief studies were made
in the vicinity of Trinidad, capital city of the immense department, and Santa Ana de Yacuma, a smaller town which also
has desultory river traffic on the Río Yacuma. The land is
almost entirely used for grazing; cattleherding is the only

industry. A little slash-and-burn agriculture, for subsistence,
is practiced in the narrow well-watered strips along the
river banks, and some cocoa is collected, but agriculture and
collecting are of minor importance in relation to herding.

The climate is tropical, hot throughout the year, with
heavy rains from November through April and drought during
the other six months. The land is low and flat; sluggish
rivers flood the country-side and change their courses annually, leaving swamps and ephemeral lakes erratically scattered
across the plain. The flora is xerophytic, mostly grass with
occasionally thorny shrubs and palm trees. The fauna consists of little more than rodents, snakes, crocodiles, and a
dazzling array of waterbirds.

Distances are enormous, and the people sense themselves
isolated in a wasteland where roads are nonexistent. Horse
or saddle-ox are the means of overland transportation; canoes
and launches ply the major rivers, as far south as Puerto
Villarroel. Since the 1920's, weekly service by the national
airlines has carried passengers and freight; a few slaughterhouses now fly beef and hides to La Paz in their own B-17's.
Neither telephone nor telegraph service is available, and
there is a sort of chauvinistic exultation in the region's isolation from "political intrigue" and "the hurried life" which are
thought to typify more settled areas.

North of Mojos, the jungle closes in again, and dense
forest covers Pando and that portion of Beni which together
constitute the northeastern portion of the nation. Here,
again, difficulties of transportation are such that immense
areas remain unmapped even today; for purposes of our
research, it seemed feasible to work out from the administrative center of Riberalta, visiting nearby portions of both
departments by foot and canoe. In this area, still another
kind of land use predominates; the economy is based on
gathering of forest products, especially rubber and brazil
nuts.

Both heat and precipitation increase toward the north,
and the Northeast is a typical Amazonian tropical forest in
flora and fauna as well as in climate. The population is
extremely sparse, with few settlements of more than thirty
persons. Rivers have generally cut somewhat deeper channels,

so that flooding is not an annual problem as it is in Mojos.
Launches and canoes serve for local traffic, and will presumably become more important when the road from La Paz
through the Alto Beni colonization zone to the Río Beni is
made passable throughout the year. In the meantime, air is
the only means of communication with most of the nation. The
Madeira-Mamoré Railway was planned during the rubber boom
in the late nineteenth century in order to bypass the series of
rapids just below Riberalta and connect that rubber center
with ships which could come up the Amazon to Puerto Velho,
Brazil. But construction was halted at the Brazilian border
when the price of rubber fell, and only since 1965 has there
been any serious hope that a road to Guayaramerín might at
least provide one route for overland contact with the rest of
the world.

THE HISTORICAL SETTING

The Bolivian Oriente is one of the few frontier regions
remaining in the world. Much of the Northeast is still unexplored; there are tribal Indians in the Mojos region whose
indigenous cultures have been little affected by contact with
Europeans since the expulsion of the Jesuits, and the northern
Santa Cruz area is gradually expanding northward into
territory unsettled except for Indians. Even the few enclaves
of self-styled "White" population scattered throughout the
Oriente represent an emergent Mestizo tradition; descended
from Spanish colonists and members of indigenous tribes,
their culture and physical type reflect both sides of their
ancestry. A brief discussion of historical perspectives is
indispensable to an understanding of the emergence of these
peoples and their multiple heritage.

Prehistory

The prehistory of the vast tropical plain which sprawls
across the center of the South American continent is still
virtually unknown. Little archeological research has been
undertaken there, and the few sites which have been located
have yielded little material from which to reconstruct the way
of life of pre-Columbian inhabitants. The northern Santa Cruz
area appears to have been occupied by the Arawakan-speaking
Chané (Sanabria, 1949), until conquered by the Guaraní who

came from the southeast to raid the nearby Inca, perhaps as
early as 1490 (Means, 1917). The problem of ethnohistorical
reconstruction in the area has been succinctly stated by
Métraux: "The numerous Indian tribes mentioned by the con-
quistadores seem to disappear suddenly and we do not know
whether they were exterminated or whether they continued to
live under other names" (1942:123). There are few ethnographic data on any of these groups during the period of early
Indian-White contact. They can probably all be broadly
characterized, however, as semi-nomadic groups with
cultures corresponding approximately to the generic "Amazon"
or "Tropical Forest" culture types, with some influence from
the Andes. Slash-and-burn agriculture was widely practiced;
yuca and maize were staples, while beans, camote, peanuts,
pumpkin, and squash were also common. There were no
domesticated animals, and such desultory farming was precarious, so that hunting and gathering were important supplementary economic activities. Most of the natives lived in
small villages and had no political federation.

The Colonial Period

Colonization progressed slowly throughout the Bolivian
Oriente and even today remains incomplete. Before the first
White settlements were established there, a series of explora-
tory expeditions penetrated the area, both from Paraguay and
from Peru, in quest of the legendary El Dorado. The city of
Santa Cruz de la Sierra was established in 1559 as an outpost
midway between Asunción and the supposed riches of "El
Gran Paitití," or "the Great Tiger Lord."

The problem of administration was far more complex in
this region than in the more densely populated area of Latin
America, such as Peru and Mexico. There was no pre-
existing complex bureaucratic structure in which the Spaniards
could simply usurp the dominant positions of native leaders;
on the contrary, control had to be local and personal. The
encomienda system which worked efficiently throughout most
of hispanic America was ill-suited to the peculiar conditions
which settlers encountered in lowland South America.

Encomenderos were required to remain in the area, and
many of them took native women as wives and concubines.
Acculturation took place rapidly under such conditions. The

sons and daughters of the original conquistadors were already Mestizos and were reared in modified Spanish culture. Native laborers, servants, and wives retained some native ways in agriculture, food preparation, and so forth, so that Spanish culture began to undergo change during the earliest years of colonization in the Oriente. As mestization increased, the number of encomienda Indians decreased and control became more direct and personal, resulting in accelerated reciprocal acculturation.

Isolated from the governmental centers by distance, natural barriers, and by Indian tribes who were often hostile, the inland regions of South America generally remained poor and undeveloped. The northern Santa Cruz area continued to be a neglected frontier which contributed little to the crown and received less in return. Because of its size, the Bolivian Oriente was granted a degree of autonomy in civil and religious administration, with the city of Santa Cruz as the effective center of control, although the region was officially under the successive jurisdictions of the Audiencia of Charcas within the Viceroyalty of Lima, the archbishopric of La Plata, and the Audiencia of Buenos Aires within the Viceroyalty of Río de la Plata. As an intendancy, Santa Cruz was among the first to secede from Upper Peru in 1810, and was the largest of the "six little republics" from which guerrillas harassed royalist troops throughout the fifteen-year War of Independence. It was important as a place of refuge and as a source of supplies even though its location was not strategically significant. The history of this period has been summarized by Gandía (1935) and Sanabria (1958).

When the liberation of Peru from Spanish dominion was secured in 1825, a general assembly was called in order to determine the future political status of Upper Peru. The representative from Santa Cruz had been in Buenos Aires for several years awaiting convocation of the Assembly of the United Provinces of Río de la Plata, from which there finally emerged the Republics of Paraguay and Argentina. Santa Cruz was not fully represented, however, at the Assembly of Provinces of Upper Peru which met in Chuquisaca and resulted in the formation of the Republic of Bolivia.

The Republic to 1952

The fact that the people of Santa Cruz were not even consulted about the crucial question of national affiliation presaged
the neglect of the area which was to continue under the republic
much as it had under the crown. For fifty years, a dreary
succession of weak presidents and short-lived military despots
passed through Sucre, capital of the young nation. These
"revolutions" were only small political or military coups
which comprised little more than changing the palace guards
and the cabinet; they had no popular support and little impact
on the local citizenry.

The northern Santa Cruz area continued to be an outpost
of administration and Western culture, while most of the
Oriente remained even more distant and isolated. Agriculture predominated, and the semi-feudal haciendas produced
little commercial surplus. Apart from subsistence crops,
little was grown other than sugar cane, which was rendered
into alcohol for sale in the highlands. Provincialism
characterized the isolated Oriente, and although this meant
complacent indifference among the great majority of people
there, it found occasional expression in vehemently chauvinistic revolutionary moments among a few political actionists.
Short-lived secessionist uprisings occurred in rapid succession, protesting the domination of the region from the highlands. When the national capital was removed to La Paz at
the end of the last century, federalists undertook to break
down the traditional isolation of the Oriente. A tortuous but
heavily traveled road was built to connect Santa Cruz with
Cochabamba at about the same time that erratic air service
was established between the two cities. However, the out-
break of the Chaco War disrupted any plans there may have
been for integrating the Oriente with the rest of the nation.
Ever since the Standard Oil Company bought concessions for
exploitation of the southern portion of the Department of
Santa Cruz in the early 1920's, rival claims of Paraguay and
Bolivia over the undemarcated boundary through the Chaco
area increased in both frequency and vehemence. When a
national oil company was formed and some of Standard's concessions were revoked, it became clear that the Bolivians
intended to hold and exploit the region. Minor border
skirmishes flared into open warfare in 1931, and there began
a tedious struggle in which thirst and disease took as high a
toll as modern firearms.

Bolivians speak of the Chaco War as a turning point in modern history, in part because it gave the Indians a sense of participation in the nation, and in part because it demonstrated the weakness of the old social order. Near Asuncion, Paraguay, a group of prisoners of war founded the Republic of Santa Cruz de la Sierra in 1935, but the leaders of the movement never dared return to Bolivia even after a treaty favorable to Paraguay was finally negotiated in 1938. The experience of the war served to discredit the political and military leaders and a struggle for power ensued. Among those who held office briefly was a young army officer, German Busch, whose progressive social legislation made him the intellectual godfather of the MNR, a coalition party which was violently ousted in 1946, but whose successful nationalistic revolution has transformed Bolivia during recent years.

The Recent Revolutions

Bolivia has experienced dozens of "revolutions" in her short history, but most of them have been anything but revolutionary in their effect. The revolution of the MNR, on the contrary, resulted in a large-scale overhaul of the national social system, with drastic effects in political, economic, and other terms. Although the impact has been negligible in some parts of the Oriente, it has been enormous in others. A brief characterization of the principal currents of change will set the stage for an understanding of our subsequent analysis of the impact of agrarian reform.

In August, 1949, control of Santa Cruz was quickly won by revolutionary forces and it became the seat of a major popular revolt for reinstallation of the exiled MNR. True civil war spread throughout the country, with outbreaks in the capital of each department, but fighting petered out in a couple of weeks. Rebels in Santa Cruz were the last to capitulate, and the leaders again fled to Argentina.

When the MNR regained power through an armed revolution in La Paz, April 9-12, 1952, it became clear that the people of Santa Cruz had been fighting against the former government for their own reasons and not in support of the newly incumbent party. Local uprisings continued with some

frequency, until one insurrection in 1959 was ruthlessly suppressed by a horde of "kolla " campesinos (Quechua Indians)
brought from Ucureña, near Cochabamba. Murders and
atrocities committed by the kollas , who stayed several
months as an occupying force, served both to break the back
of active resistance and to confirm the hatred of easterners
for highlanders.

Governmental neglect of the Oriente can no longer be cited
as justification for secessionist movements, however. The
MNR attempted to overcome the traditional isolation of the
region and to integrate it with the rest of the nation. Almost
immediately upon coming to power, President Victor Paz
Estenssoro asked for economic as well as technical aid from
the United States. A "crash program" suddenly made Bolivia
the recipient of the largest per capita Point Four aid program
in the world, and North American officials were induced to
try to make the northern Santa Cruz area a showplace because
of its reputation as a land of enormous agricultural potential.
Millions of dollars have been poured into a variety of projects
including the improved Cochabamba-Santa Cruz highway,
large-scale landclearing, immigrant colonization programs,
establishment of a large government sugar refinery, and
others.

By the time the 1964 elections came around, many
Bolivians were restive about Paz's having assumed a paternalistic role as the personification of the revolution. Dis-
gusted by his having railroaded through Congress a constitutional amendment allowing him to succeed himself, all
parties except the MNR boycotted the elections. Having
broken with even veteran MNR leaders like Juan Lechín and
Hernán Siles, Paz did accede to the insistence of the party
congress that he accept Air Force General René Barrientos
as running-mate. Presumably this was intended to serve as
a demonstration that the armed forces were strongly on the
side of the MNR and thereby discourage militant uprisings
among the opposition. Some strong campesino leaders had
used the militia arms and organization to set themselves up
as virtual warlords, and the miners were a powerful bloc
more devoted to Lechín than to the party. The military was
strengthened in order to keep Paz in power, but, ironically,
it was the military that unseated him a few months later.

There was active guerrilla fighting in the eastern Oriente
in mid-1964, apparently directed by the Falangists, the principal rightist opposition. It was hit-and-run harassment, not
aimed at any confrontation with government troops but a constant annoyance to them and a rallying point for the opposition.

   Meanwhile, Genl. Barrientos knew that he had not been
Paz's choice and avoided close or sustained contact with him.
In fact, he spent most of his time in his native Cochabamba,
where he enjoyed strong local support. Stringent censorship
imposed by Paz after the supposed discovery of an anti-
government coup led to noisy opposition by miners and
students alike. Barrientos spoke out against such strict
measures, and at the end of October, in three days of confused skirmishing, it became clear that the armed forces
were not disposed to defend the president. Paz finally left
the country on November 4, 1964, and Barrientos was named
head of the junta that came to power. * Their so-called
"Revolution of Restoration" was proclaimed as an attempt
to restore the principles of the revolution of 1952, that had
been corrupted through abuses of the MNR regime. It did
not, as some had feared and others had hoped, presage a
return to "the military boot," oppressive domination of the
campesinos by the army as guardian of the feudal oligarchy.
Neither did it fulfill the early hopes of the bourgeoisie for a
long-awaited "return to order," with the junta remaining
apolitical and fostering a new climate of "work, discipline,
and honesty," while laying the groundwork for truly democratic elections. Brief but violent civil wars flared in which
labor fared badly, and the junta adopted some of the suppres-
sive tactics of their discredited predecessors. Army General Alfredo Ovando Candia was named co-president, and
then succeeded to the top position in the junta when Barrientos
resigned in January, 1966, in order to run successfully for
the presidency on a partisan ticket. Despite widespread
premonitions, Ovando stepped down to make way for Barrientos, whose tenure has seen local outbreaks in the mining
area and guerrilla activity just south of Santa Cruz, neither
of which constituted a significant danger for the incumbent
regime.

_____

*The rapid decline and fall of Paz is discussed in more
  detail in Heath, 1965c.

The self-styled "National Army of Liberation" made news
out of all proportion to its numbers or activities in the Oriente
throughout 1967.   They were clearly Castroite guerrillas, able
to elicit little local support in an area where the basic social
revolution had already occurred years before it did in Cuba.
They never posed a real threat to the national government nor
even committed significant acts of sabotage, and certainly did
not provide a rallying point for any movement among native
Bolivians.   They did not even follow the simple precepts of
guerrilla warfare formulated by "Che" Guevara (1961), who
is said to have been their leader.   Whatever their purpose,
they succeeded only briefly in providing what their companion
Régis Debray (1967) called an "insurrectional focus," demon-
strating that a guerrilla band could survive in an outlying area
where the government had only tenuous control, and that armed
action was a viable alternative in response to dissatisfaction
with an incumbent regime.   Although they did not threaten the
economic and political stability of the country, their mere
presence had symbolic value for potential guerrillas else-
where--probably greater symbolic value throughout the rest
of the hemisphere than among Bolivian campesinos a few
miles away.   Since 1967, the guerrillas appear to have been
dispersed; Debray is no longer a cause celebre*, and it is
still unclear whether Guevara was, in fact, at the head of the
guerrillas. **

---

*For a discussion of "the Debray affair," in which a strong
   personality and a confusing context combined to lend apparent
   historic weight to an intrinsically trivial event, see Heath,
   1967.

**Evidence for "Che's" death in Bolivia will probably remain
   confused and confusing because, for different reasons, it
   is advantageous to Castro, CIA, the Bolivian government,
   and USA at the same time.   In a very real sense, however,
   it doesn't matter whether this is "really true," since "Che"
   as a mythical figure had already displaced the historical
   figure of Ernesto Guevara, as evidenced in his supposedly
   having been seen in various trouble spots throughout the
   world--often simultaneously--and his even having been
   reported killed in Cuba in 1965, in the Dominican Republic

Opposition parties continue to be vocal but generally ineffectual. The MNR is still the favorite party among the majority of campesinos (except in the Oriente, where Falangist sentiment remains dominant). A large number of other parties, representing a wide spectrum of political sentiment, comprise a splintered opposition that could never realistically hope to unseat the incumbents or either of the major parties.

It is clear by now that the "Revolution of Restoration" is neither revolutionary nor restorative. Their experience is significant, however, in suggesting that the social changes of the MNR's thoroughgoing revolution of 1952 are irreversible, and that this is a rare instance in Latin America where a military coup could not impose a rightist dictatorship. At the same time, the junta and Barrientos's administration have tended progressively to drift away from their early liberal stance, and the key question seems to be whether they can succeed in their effort to sustain economic growth at the high rate which has finally been achieved, and to establish political stability on a firmer basis than sheer military force.

The History of Mojos and the Northeast

The prehistory of the northern Oriente is little better known than that of the Santa Cruz area. A few urn burials were excavated in Mojos by Nordenskiöld, and impressive earthworks there (Denevan, 1966), suggest that a much denser population than today's may have been supported by large-scale intensive agriculture before the arrival of the Spaniards. Speculation about the scale and complexity of pre-Columbian civilizations in the area will undoubtedly continue until at least some systematic archeological exca-

-----

later that year, and in Bolivia in 1967. It is ironic that he has become so important a concrete symbol of revolutionary potential when he himself stressed the supra-individual "inevitability" of revolution in situations of social exploitation. It matters little when--or even whether--"Che" may have died; what matters more is how the myth of "Che" may survive.

vation is undertaken. Virtually no meaningful pre-historic finds have been made in the Northeast.

After a series of fruitless and often tragic forays north-ward during the first decade of conquest, Spanish soldiers were disillusioned about El Dorado and left Mojos and the Northeast to the missionaries. The latter area remained virtually unchanged until late in the last century; but in Mojos, several missions were bound into a prosperous theocracy under the Jesuits (see Burges, 1781; Tormo, 1966). Trinidad was founded in 1687 as a mission for Indians of several of the Arawakan-speaking tribes that came to be called collectively "Mojos"; Santa Ana de Yacuma was one of several other missions founded for Indians of other unrelated languages (in this instance, Móvima). After the Jesuits were expelled from the entire New World in 1767, their Franciscan succes-sors never quite regained control (Cardús, 1886), and many of the Indian groups returned to earlier levels of culture and commerce.

The livestock abandoned by the Jesuits apparently went wild and multiplied profusely in Mojos, so that cattle became a ready source of food for the few rugged Mestizos who moved in, men who fit the adopted term "los frontırsmen," and became the ranchers of today.

Not until the rubber boom began in the 1880's was there any great interest in Bolivia's Northeast. In this region, everything is on a grand scale; immigration, wealth, and abuse of native laborers seem to have been no exception during the three decades when the immense world demand stirred this remote and, at that time, sole source of supply. When rubber became available more cheaply from plantations in southeastern Asia around 1910, the boom ended as abruptly as it had begun.

The Suárez brothers from Santa Cruz seem to have dominated the economic and political scence throughout Mojos and the Northeast around the turn of the century. Some critics claim that don Nícolas ruled the entire depart-ments of Beni and Pando as if they were his private fief. Whatever truth there may be to such charges cannot be judged until systematic historical investigation is under-taken, but there remains today no vestige except a few rusting launches, abandoned warehouses, docks scattered along riverbanks, and a village at Cachuela Esperanza, which used to be headquarters of the so-called "Suárez Empire." Inhabitants of each community visited took special delight in pointing out that the firm of Suárez Brothers was defunct-- "not a hectare of land, not a head of stock, and not even an agent remains." The company's economic and political dominance had apparently been gradually diminishing for decades when the MNR came to power, and the threat of nationalization and persecution seems to have led them to abandon the enterprise.

The nature of the population and the economy in both of these regions is such that land reform has had a far less dramatic impact than in other parts of the country. Nevertheless, there have been some noticeable changes during the past decade which will be discussed below. Although political control is exercised from La Paz, even the MNR did not succeed in bringing Mojos and the Northeast into close and sustained relations with the rest of the nation. The potential value of natural resources in these regions is recognized, but they appear to have minimal priority in terms of both economic development and political organization. Difficulties in transportation and communication undoubtedly combined with sparcity of population in determining the MNR's continuation of earlier policies of neglect.

During the 1960's, a new political force appeared in the Northeast. Cobija and Riberalta are among the few centers of real Communist activity remaining in Bolivia, but small-scale agitation there seems to be primarily the work of a few Castroites who infiltrated from Peru and enjoyed very little success. The junta seemed for a while to be creating problems for itself by sending leftist dissidents to "internal exile" in the isolated Northeast, but they soon realized that although this provided some immediate relief to pressures in the factories and the mines, it could eventually result in new problems with the emergence of guerrillas in precisely those areas that are most difficult to control.

THE SOCIAL SETTING

Throughout the Oriente, life has remained essentially primitive in large areas, and even the scattered towns of Europeans or Mestizos have been basically colonial until recent years.

Internal Social Organization

The Spaniards came as conquerors to occupy the land of the native Indians, but the caste line broke down readily and the lack of Spanish women during the early years of settlement led to rapid and progressive mestization. The Spanish conquistadors took native wives and concubines and often recognized the children as their own. On the basis of comparative data from other areas, it is doubtful that Indian men were allowed to marry Mestizo women, but specific data are not available on this point.

Social Classes

Despite the universality of miscegenation in the early years of colonization, many of the Spanish-speaking residents of the region even today assert that "There are still a few of us who have pure White blood. We are of pure Andalusian stock, those of us who are direct lineal descendents of the original colonists. You can tell clearly from the delicate features, white skin, gallant manners — in sum, we carry the entire aspect of a finer race." Such people call themselves "Whites" (los blancos), in contrast with campesinos, the lower class-acknowledged Mestizos who compromise the overwhelming majority of the population. Essentially the same duality in social status is described by the campesinos, although with different connotations. To be a campesino does not have racial implications because, as one informant perceptively observed, "With respect to race, everybody is all mixed up-- Guarayú, Chiriguano, Chiquitano, Spaniard, gringo, and all the rest. There's no pure race since the Garden of Eden." From the point of view of the campesino his label suggests his poverty in relation to "the rich ones"(los ricos), which is his term for those who call themselves "Whites." Because extensive questioning revealed virtually universal

agreement on the subgroup membership of any individual, I
have chosen to call these subgroups "social classes,"
following Goldschmidt's comprehensive definition as "...
segments of the community, the members of which show a
common social position in a hierarchical ranking" (1950:491).
For the sake of convenience, I shall hereafter refer to the
self-styled "Whites," who are also called "the rich ones," as
"the upper class," while the majority of the population, be
they tenants, day-laborers, squatters, small farmers who
work their own plots, or market vendors, will be called "the
lower class," or, interchangeably, "campesinos."

The distinguishing characteristics of members of the
upper class were not difficult to determine, despite some
apparent inconsistencies in the reports of the people themselves. The criterion of wealth used by members of the
lower class is vague and relative; that of racial purity used
by the upper-class people is not subject to objective verifica-
tion. The crucial factors are an inseparable combination of
wealth, and source of wealth. People whose wealth allows
them to live in a leisurely manner, without attending to work
except the administration of their own property, constitute
the upper class in the local society. Urban residence is not
a factor of any importance in determining class membership:
all finqueros belong to this group, as do those towndwellers
who live on rents or who have their lands cultivated by hired
hands. They are, in effect, the gentry whose wealth,
derived from the land, is a major factor in determining the
lines of social interaction and provides the basis for a few
manifest differences in way of life.

The development of commerce has opened new
opportunities for enterprising men who would formerly have
remained campesinos, but who now constitute an incipient
middle class. One indication of a growing awareness of a
new class is the fact that both upper-and lower-class
informants repeatedly declined to assign a large number of
people to either subgroup but instead consistently identified
their social status with their occupations. Among those
whom they consider neither "Whites," "rich ones," nor
"campesinos," and whom I call "the middle class" are
shopkeepers, truckers, politicians, and others whose income
derives from sources of wealth other than land and wage labor
which have only recently developed within the local culture.

The majority of the population are campesinos,* members
of the lower class, whose meager income is derived from
their own labor, either for wages in the employ of someone
else, or in cultivating or selling the produce of their own land.

Kinsmen and Compadres

Each person enters an important subsystem at birth,
that of kinsmen. Throughout childhood, family relationships
usually continue to be of cardinal significance and in many
societies the main lines of communication and interaction are
those of kinship. In the northern Santa Cruz area, however,
frequent isolation of individual households (which usually
comprise only the nuclear family), and a high degree of
geographical mobility tend not to favor the elaborately
patterned extension of reciprocal role relationships between
kinsmen which so often characterizes rural societies.
Nevertheless, patterns of relationship which are meaningful
to the local people do occur among household and family,
other kinsmen, and compadres, sometimes called "ritual
kinsmen" or "pseudo-kinsmen."

Relationship is traced horizontally as much as vertically;
the emphasis is more on social than genetic affiliation.
Among campesinos, descent is seldom traced more than two
generations in either direction, that is, grandparents and
grandchildren, are often unknown to an individual. Inheritance is by primogeniture, patrilineal in theory but bilateral
in practice; that is to say, it may cross the sex lines at one
or more points if, as is sometimes the case, a family
fortune should pass to a daughter in the absence of a son. In
such instances, the relatives from whom wealth derives gain
importance in the family history. Among the upper class
there is more concern over ancestry than among the rest of
the people, and most finqueros can trace their descent from
the original founder of their finca, although relatives not in
the direct line of inheritance are seldom known. The
differential emphasis on lineal relationship in different social

---

*The most common synonym of "campesino" is "peasant."
For a searching critique of the burgeoning literature by
anthropologists on peasantry as a social type, see Wolf,
1966.

classes is related not only to the justification of inherited wealth and pride is supposed racial superiority of the "old families" but to different patterns of marriage as well.

Nominally Roman Catholic, these people are monogamous. The mode of marriage of campesinos, however, can more accurately be characterized as "serial monogamy." Common-law marriage is the norm, and such consensual unions are extremely brittle. Adolescents of both sexes are allowed considerable freedom in sexual activity as long as they are discreet in their liaisons. Celibacy is abnormal, and "a young man may marry as soon as he starts to earn regularly, while a young girl ought to marry a short time after she begins to bleed," according to most informants. When a couple do choose to marry, they usually simply start living together. A campesino will rarely solemnize his union, "... because it costs too much. There's not only the rite-- you have to pay the Civil Registrar at least, and the priest too if you marry in church--but you also have to give a fiesta for all your friends. That is an obligation which could not be ignored, so most of us don't get married. It's all right; a few words don't count for anything." Even mission- ary priests show no prejudice against common-law mates or   their children, nor does any public stigma attach to them. Just as there is no disgrace associated with a common-law union, the few couples whose relationships have been legalized or sanctified derive no special prestige from that fact.

Adultery is rare and despised, but nevertheless, common-law marriages among campesinos are often short- lived. Separation is unceremonious and easily secured. A man simply fails to come home one day and goes to another finca or town where he is likely, before long, to take another common-law wife. Most members of the middle and upper classes, by contrast, do have their marriages formalized and their unions are more stable. They also evince con- siderable concern over genealogy and trace contemporary relationships widely in recognizing a broad extended family.

Members of the upper class, unlike campesinos, usually pay considerable attention to relatives in all consanguineal and affinal categories, and any social functions take on the aspect of a family reunion.

As among many Latin peoples, another kind of relationship is important, that of compadrazgo, often called "pseudo-
kinship," "ritual kinship," or godparenthood. This involves
the extrafamilial extension of certain reciprocal rights and
obligations on a level of intimacy similar to those which
obtain among close relatives. Such an extension of relationship is usually dramatized through a ritual observance; each
infant boy is "sponsored" at baptism by a godfather (padrino),
and each infant girl by a godmother (madrina). The immediate responsibility of the godparent on this occasion is to pay
for the rite of baptism and to contribute alcohol for a party
which follows. His long-term responsibility is greater,
however, inasmuch as he is expected to stand in loco parentis
to his godchild (ahijado,-a), offering counsel and aid whenever asked. The bonds between the child's own parents and
his godparents, who call each other "coparents" (compadre,
comadre), are even more close. Warm friendship is the
rule and each is expected to help the other in time of need.
In many Latin American societies, the institution of
coparenthood is exploited by poor people who invite wealthy
individuals to enter such a relationship with them. To
decline such an invitation would be a grave insult; to accept
it may be to assume unwanted obligations. The people of
Santa Cruz also occasionally employ this stratagem. Another
pattern is to ask a respected friend or relative so that
godparenthood often serves to reinforce pre-existing bonds
among kinsmen as well as to extend them to other persons
not already related by descent or marriage.

Individuals also recognize social groupings beyond those
of class and kinship which function as primary reference
groups in various contexts. Among the units which may
sometimes be meaningful in this social universe are locality
groups and sodalities.

Locality Groups

It has already been noted that campesinos are very
mobile within the limits of the northern Santa Cruz region.
A significant proportion of them were, until recently, tenants
who lived on fincas which are remote from the few villages
where administrative and commercial activities are concentrated. These fincas were, in effect, hamlets clustered
around "the big house" of the finquero, often several hours'

walk from the nearest village.   The population of these communities ranged from 20 to almost 200; and they are almost
self-sufficient, producing most of what was locally consumed.
Each finca is named and, although they are not political units,
campesinos would sometimes say "I'm from Monterico," or
"I'm a Guapureño," identifying themselves with the finca
rather than with the nearest municipality or with the province.
Despite the fact that means of transportation have improved
markedly during recent years, some of the more remote
fincas are still literally inaccessible during the rainy season,
and campesinos venture out from the more isolated ones only
to spend the major national or religious holidays in town.
Membership in locality groups is fluid, however, because
campesinos frequently moved.

Relations among tenants who were also neighbors were
cordial but rarely warm.   Interaction among members of such
locality groups was often limited to their working together
for a common employer; the individual household was and
is the functional economic unit and the only social grouping
in which daily communication is the rule.   Fiestas are
usually attended by most neighbors, but friends and passers-
by from elsewhere are also welcome, although there is no
pressure for all neighbors to take part.   In brief, the
locality group is recognized by the campesino, and he may
sometimes relate people to each other in such terms, but it
is not an important social unit in terms of function, manifest
or latent, from the point of view of the individual or the
group.

Sodalities

These campesinos are little given to group activity, and
the virtual absence of voluntary associations among them
provides a concrete demonstration of this fact.   One exception is a sodality which cuts across all class lines: Veterans
of the Chaco War meet each year to march and reminisce
about their experiences as comrades-in-arms.

An innovation of the MNR is the sindicato, a group of
campesinos ostensibly working for their common good.
Although the syndicate sindicato is nominally a local
campesinos' union, it was also a means of securing partisan
allegiance through patronage.   Membership is free, and

carried with it several perquisites, so that many joined who
had no interest in the potential force of collective activity in
labor-management relations. The benefits of membership
have been discussed in Chapter 11, including discounts on
foodstuffs, weapons, and even land. Although campesinos in
the Oriente were never as ruthlessly eager to invert the old
social order as were those in the highlands, they were
actively wooed by MNR and the syndicates gained considerable
importance. In some areas they have even taken on the
aspect of primary reference groups, with members calling
each other "compañero" ("comrade"), and sharing a sense of
community that was rare among tenants before the reform.

This discussion of the major axes of social relationship
illustrates the diffuse nature of the Camba social system.
Social classes are recognized, with subcultural differences
between them. The isolated household, usually comprising
only a nuclear family, is the basic unit in social and economic
activities, and yet common-law marriage is so unstable that
even this group may change frequently. Neither locality
groups nor voluntary associations appreciably fostered social
solidarity. I have elsewhere (Heath, 1958) suggested that for
most campesinos the most important reference groups were
the drinking groups who spend a day or two at a time in continuous drinking bouts with cane alcohol. In fact, in this
atomistic social system, alcohol served very real functions
of social integration, although the Camba are among the
heaviest drinkers on record for normal members of any
society. It appears that the campesino syndicate may be
providing an alternative in recent years, and drinking is
declining (Heath, 1965d).

Inter-Societal Relations

The integrative factors within this society are few and
tenuous. Inter-societal relationships which affect the Camba
may be characterized under four general rubrics which together comprehend the relevant out-groups in their social
universe: savages, kollas, the government, and gringos.

Savages

It has already been noted that most of the local campesinos
have at least partially Indian ancestry, and that members of

nearby indigenous tribes are even today "becoming" Cambas on the frontier. The attitude of the Camba toward the surrounding peoples is not so warm as one might expect on the basis of such relationships. The indigenes are invariably called "savages" (salvajes) or "barbarians" (bárbaros), in a deprecatory tone of voice, even by people whose own parents did not speak Spanish. Only rarely are distinctions made among the different tribes.

The present-day distribution of indigenous peoples which surround the region is similar to that described early in this century by Burela (1912), although the Camba frontier is slowly advancing northward. To the east, across the Río Grande, are the hostile Tapieté (locally called "Yanaygua"); to the south, scattered remnants of the Chané and Chiriguano groups. Along the cordillera which forms most of the western boundary of the Camba region live Quechuas (kollas), but in the lowlands to the northwest are the Yuracare (locally called "Yuracaré," or "Yura"), and directly to the north, the Siriono (locally called "Sirionó"). The culture and societies of these groups are apparently little changed from the descriptions in Steward (1946. 1948).

By and large, savages live beyond the frontiers of Camba settlement and try to avoid contact with them. Because most of the tribal peoples are seminomadic and travel in small bands, it is not difficult for them to remain isolated and unacculturated. Sporadic attacks by savages in quest of food, livestock, tools, and guns still present a threat along the north and east of the Camba region, especially in times of drought. Not all contact with savages are so unpleasant, however. During the 1950's, finqueros sometimes hired small groups of savages to work in the fields at harvest time and paid them in metal tools, gunpowder, and shot. To them, the savage was a cheap part-time laborer. Guarayú Indians from the old Jesuit reducciones to the northeast were especially popular because they often had learned Spanish from Franciscan missionaries, were reputed to be unusually intelligent and obedient, and ate little. One cane-planter put it this way: "They are the best workers I've ever had. They work hard all day; they are quick to learn, and even though they are very short, they are nevertheless very strong-- immensely strong. . ... All they need is their little cup of alcohol, like diesel fuel in a bulldozer." A few labor

contractors made regular annual recruiting trips to the
Guarayú, despite the dangers of having to cross Tapieté
territory and the illegality of their trade on the tribal reserva-
tion. The Guarayú who come to work for Camba finqueros
were frequently cheated and abused, so that they usually
returned to their homes within a year, leaving little impression on Camba culture and changing their own ways of life
only briefly. During the 1960's, kollas have displaced
savages as season laborers, as described below.

Kollas

    In Camba usage, the term kolla refers to any person from
"the interior," the highlands which comprise the western
one third of Bolivia. This derogatory label, which is applied
indiscriminantly to Quechuas, Aymaras (locally called
"Aymará"), and Mestizos alike, presumably derives from
Collasuyu, the name of the southernmost quarter of the Inca
Empire, which once included this area. The Camba pride
themselves on their sophistication and worldliness, in contrast to the stereotyped "dirty, lazy, ignorant kollas," who
"live like animals" and "don't even know how to speak
Spanish."

    Few local campesinos had any immediate contact with
kollas until the mid-1950's. With the opening of the Cochabamba-
Santa Cruz highway, a large influx of kollas began and has increased. Quechuas from around Cochabamba came to work in
the government sugar mill and on road-construction crews,
and to serve in the Colonial Division of the Army, while
Quechuas from Sucre, Potosí, and other highland departments
came to take part briefly in resettlement projects sponsored
by CBF, or by the United Nations. By the mid-1960's, kolla
"colonization" had extended the frontier of agricultural settlement almost to Puerto Grether, some 100 miles northwest of
Santa Cruz. This "colonization" is an outgrowth of the earlier
programs of resettlement, but contrasts in being "spontaneous" rather than "planned," i.e., unsponsored rather than
underwritten. Highlanders who came on their own have been
given plots of 20 to 50 hectares in previously unsettled areas,
and have homesteaded without any credit, tools, or other
organizational assistance. It is perhaps ironic that kollas
who came under such circumstances have tended to stay in
considerably greater proportion than those who came aided

by a national or international program. One of the crucial
factors is undoubtedly self-selection. Those who came
"spontaneously" obviously intend to stay; often they have nowhere else to go, whereas those who came in planned colonies
often return to their highland homes after satisfying their
curiosity about the lowlands, at no expense to themselves.*

   Another kind of contact with kollas also developed since
my original study in the mid-1950's. Increasing numbers of
Camba campesinos took advantage of the land reform allotments and deserted fincas where they had been tenants, in
order to establish their own small farms. Finqueros, having
lost resident laborers at the same time that they were expanding
commercial production (of sugar cane and rice) sought new
workers and found them in the southwestern part of the country.
Kolla campesinos there used to work in the cane harvests in
Argentina, until restrictions were imposed by the Argentines
in the mid-1960's, and they were a ready pool of efficient
seasonal workers. Hired in teams, through labor contractors,
they spend about half of the year working on fincas near Santa
Cruz, and return to the highlands for the rest of the year.
Paid by the ton, they work about twice as fast as Camba
tenants used to, and earn about twice as much.

   These kollas are distinctive from the Camba in many
obvious even if insignificant respects. Physically, they are
stocky and robust with sound teeth, both of which contrast
markedly with the Camba. Their colorful woolen dress sets
them apart also, as does their speech--both Quechua, which

_____

*An amazingly large body of myth still exists concerning
  Andean Indians. Buechler and I have above questioned the
  widespread presumption of a communal orientation among
  them, that is basic to many aid projects. Another remarkably persistent myth is that of the geographically isolated
  and immobile Indian. The idea that the Quechua and Aymara
  have horizons that rarely extend beyond the valley in which
  they are born is a romantic vestige of a reality that probably was never very widespread in fact. There is ample
  historical and archeological evidence that they have long
  participated in far-flung markets, traveled appreciable
  distances for seasonal wage-work, undertaken religious
  pilgrimages, or just struck out for considerable periods of
  time (see Heath, 1966a).

they use among themselves, and the sibilant accent of those who do speak Spanish.

There are a number of sources of conflict in relations between these groups. It is by no means an irrelevant historical fact that the forces sent into Santa Cruz to quell successive attempts at revolution or   secession have been kollas , and that the Camba have each time resented them as a foreign army of invasion and occupation.   There are still slogans painted on walls in the city of Santa Cruz condemning the militiamen who ruthlessly suppressed demonstrations there in 1959: "Be patriotic, kill a kolla;" "Death to the kollas , sons of bitches;" etc.   For the lower class, another source of conflict is the realization that some kollas have far more money to spend because their earnings are higher in more specialized and technical occupations. In Cotoca, violent resentment has grown from the fact that a large number of native people were dispossessed and their lands taken over by the U. N. to be used as a resettlement project for Quechua colonists.

The growing middle-class merchants scorn the supposed racial inferiority and "rude customs" of the kollas , but are grateful for the increased amount of business which they bring to any village near where they work. Resentment against kollas in general, rather than against just those who had come into the region, is especially strong among the local upper class. They are most acutely aware of the fact that the western portion of the country has, throughout history, enjoyed the benefit of whatever public works projects were undertaken, while the Oriente has been utterly neglected. This discrepancy is attributed, with some reason, to the fact that the majority of politicians in La Paz or Sucre have been kollas. The secessionist movement in Santa Cruz has enjoyed a long history as outlined above, and was increasing in popularity as the profits from oilfields in the Chaco began to contribute substantially to the national economy while the mines in the altiplano diminished in economic importance. It has never regained momentum since campesino militiamen from Ucureña crushed a large civil disturbance and occupied the region for several weeks in 1959.

The Government

The predominant attitude toward politics is well expressed in a popular riddle: "What's the difference between politics and water? The dirtiest water can still clean, but the cleanest politics can only dirty one." The long-enduring vitality of the movement for independence is ample demonstration that regional patriotism far outweighs national allegiance in this area. "The government" is spoken of as a powerful and avaricious entity by people of all social classes, and each group has its own reasons for resenting the national adminis- tration. Bolivia is constituted a republic with a democratically elected bicameral congress and president. In practice, how- ever, the government has usually been an oligarchy of the incumbent party. Although informants were universally reticent until I had won their absolute confidence, people of every social status spoke with intensity about politics, and referred to the subject often when there was no chance of their being overheard.

According to the upper classes, "The government is worth nothing--worse yet, it's a plague. It's an abuse. We pay taxes like everybody else, and there is nothing to show for it. Whatever doesn't go directly into the pocket of some politician is used to better the commerce of the kollas. The Oriente has always been ignored by the government--they only want the riches that they can take out, but never are willing to invest anything to develop or improve the situation here." The informant who said that is a finquero who had been favored by the MNR with special dispensation to keep land in excess of the maximum allowable under the agrarian reform; other advantages accrued to some finqueros who were outwardly sympathetic to the MNR, of which the most noteworthy during the mid-1950's was the privilege of buying imported food-stuffs and machinery at the artificially low official rate of monetary exchange. Informants who did not receive such patronage were even more outspoken in the criticism which they leveled against "the party," "MNR," or "the government," terms which they used interchangeably. A complaint often voiced was:

Bolivia is a rotten country! She could be rich with such natural resources, but never will be. Mismanagement in politics is the cardinal fault.

All politicians are thieves, rascals. They have
no honor, no shame. They always use high-sounding
words, but their actions are not just. ...liars,
murderers, thieves--all politicians are rats. No
wonder Bolivia is a poor antiquated country of poor
people with no hope for anything. And the MNR is
the worst ever, because it impedes any individual
who may have some interest in working for
progress...

Members of the emergent middle class were almost as
vehement in their condemnation of "the party" and "the
government," which were virtually indistinguishable terms
to them as well. The conviction that all public officials are
interested only in personal gain and that the consequent
"...poor administration is at the root of the utterly lamentable
present condition of the country" was widespread, even among
those who have themselves profited from political patronage.
Those merchants who were able to buy import licenses made
enormous profits from buying goods at the official exchange
rate of Bs. 190 per dollar, and selling at the black market
rate which ranged to 16,000:1. Nevertheless, they were
among the most vociferous in asserting that "Without a
doubt, Bolivia is the only country in the entire world where
things always are getting worse. ... There's no business,
no commerce, no money. It's all because no one has faith
in the government. And why should they? The politicians
care for nothing but filling their own pockets..."

Often, in fact, members of the MNR who held appointive
positions and mouthed party slogans in public confided in
private that:

The people don't trust the government. They
have learned through the years that it doesn't
pay. The party is secure only as long as the
miners are faithful. One must buy votes, even
if one cannot buy friends. Here in the Oriente
the party is weak, as all previous governments
have been. But the syndicates of miners and
kolla campesinos in the interior will defend the
government because they know no better.

Minor officials, including mayors, judges, and others, are
not elected but receive appointments from the departmental
or national capital, and so are under no pressure to please
their local constituents.   The irregular quality of perform-
ance reflects the varied qualifications of people holding
administrative posts.   Grossly inadequate salaries offer
some justification for a variety of abuses, including large-
scale extortion and misappropriation of public funds.   One
subprefect admitted that:

> Salaries don't suffice at any level of government.
> It is necessary that one earn a little extra however
> he can. All right, so everyone calls it stealing.
> But one must eat. Sometimes we put a special tax
> on butchering. Or we make trucks pay so much in
> order to pass through the town. What we gain that
> way is for our own use. It is true, what everybody
> says about how politicians take graft, but it's a
> necessary supplement--we don't get rich on it.

Few campesinos evince any interest in political activity,
although they were willing to vote for the MNR when party
agents provided transportation by truck to polling places in
the market towns.   Even members of syndicates who have
profited from party patronage are not always enthusiastic
supporters of the government; their interest is usually
limited to the question of what benefits they are to enjoy.
"The government" is, in fact, a remote and nebulous entity
from the point of view of the individual campesino.

The people of Santa Cruz are generally outspokenly
opposed to Communism, even in conversations among themselves, but hold that, "It can't happen here in the Oriente
because there's so much money, good working conditions,
high salaries and so forth."

Although I have not had the opportunity to return to the
Oriente since the "Revolution of Restoration" in November,
1964, there are ample indications that local attitudes toward
the government have changed little, if at all.   Abusive MNR
politicians have been unseated, but there seems to be no
significant support or opposition to the junta and its elected
successors.

Gringos

"Gringo" is not a derogatory term in local usage; it only refers to someone born outside Bolivia who remains distinguishable in his social relations and other behavior. Despite the fact that this region has never been in the mainstream of population movements, there have probably always been a few gringos living there. They do not constitute a unitary social group except from the point of view of the Camba. That gringos come from many nations and are diverse in race, language, and culture is irrelevant to a campesino although some finqueros perceive the patterns which typify the local adjustment of members of each ethnic group.

Few Spaniards ever came to the region after the first century of occupation. The early settlers were usually soldiers or public administrators who married local women and set the pattern of mestization which laid the basis for the emergence of the Camba as a new society. Other Europeans who came later generally tended to remain aloof and to retain as much as they could of their heritage. A number of Germans and Austrians came to serve as administrators and accountants for the immense private enterprises which were widespread throughout the northern Oriente during the rubber boom late in the last century, and retired to Santa Cruz after the market dropped and trade came to an end. Other central Europeans came to Bolivia again in the 1930's as refugees, and the outspoken anti-Semitism of the MNR is explained by party spokesmen as "... a recent and very just reaction against abuses by the Jews who were admitted to the country on the condition that they become agricultural colonists in the Oriente, but almost all of whom stayed in the cities and started shops, hotels, or restaurants in competition with Bolivian nationals." Another wave of European immigrants, including several Nazis who chose this refuge in the 1940's, follow this pattern of middle-class mercantilism and service industries in Santa Cruz just as in the rest of the nation. One notable exception is an enclave of thirty-eight families of German Mennonites who came from Paraguay in the early 1950's to farm a small isolated area northeast of the city. A small group of fifteen young Italian men were given land near Montero in 1954, and their agricultural cooperative has prospered, on the basis of their own hard work as well as technical and economic aid from CBF. A

few European missionaries have had little impact on the local
people over the years. In sum, gringos of European extraction have specialized occupations and take no part in the daily
life of most of the Camba, so that it is easy for them to cling
to their own cultures.

Gringos of Asiatic derivation appear more likely to assimi-
late to the local society. For half a century, Syrians and
Lebanese have been shopkeepers in the provincial capitals
as well as in the city of Santa Cruz, and many have become
respected "pillars of the community." About 250 families
of Okinawans have been brought to the region as agricultural
colonists since 1954. After a series of calamities, they have
been settled in three colonies along the western shore of the
Río Grande, and have achieved unusually good agricultural
yields. A group of Japanese immigrants from the main
islands have had more success with less outside aid--their
agricultural cooperative flourished and their colony (San Juan
Yapacaní) is a virtually self-sufficient community. Their
location in the northwestern corner of the area was a frontier
until kollas began settling along a road from Río Yapacaní to
Puerto Grether, in 1963.*

There are even gringos from South America in the Camba
region. Of the Argentine cowboys who trade mules for cattle
in Beni, a few have settled around Santa Cruz as ranch hands
or tenant farmers, and some of them have "become" Camba
by abandoning their foreign customs and entering the Camba
social system through marriage and/or coparenthood. An
even smaller number of shopkeepers originally came from
Chile or Argentina as fugitives from justice or political
pressure, and most of them remain gringos, not participating
in the local social order.

North American gringos have lived in this area only since
the 1950's, but they had an impact out of all proportion to their
numbers. Protestant evangelists enjoy little success, but
Catholic missionaries from the United States have taken control

---

*A detailed study of the Japanese colony was undertaken by
  Thompson (1968); and a film made during my 1963 field
  work compares the Japanese colony and the nearby area
  of kolla "spontaneous" migration (Land Tenure Center, 1964).

of many parishes, and the appointment in 1957 of a Maryknoll priest as Auxiliary Bishop of Santa Cruz is said to have been the first such investiture in Latin America.

An unusual group of gringos who have had some effect on the way of life there did so without having more than a minimum of personal contact with the people--they were Point Four employees who administered the extravagant program of technical and financial aid aimed at developing the proverbial agricultural potential of the Bolivian Oriente, with road and highway construction, supervised credit, machinery rental, experimental stations, extension agents, a "model finca," and so forth.

From 1957 to 1960 a different kind of gringo from North America appeared. Geologists prospecting for oil, and, later, oil-well "hands" were like Point Four administrators in that they remained aloof from the local people and were resented as boorish, but they were also viewed as harbingers of the long awaited economic development of the Santa Cruz area. Petroleum was not found in the quantities expected, and only one U. S. company continues to operate there.

A small contingent of young Peace Corps volunteers scattered throughout the area since 1962 have made modest efforts, especially in agricultural extension and public health. Their warm friendliness is reciprocated. In brief, people from North America, the gringos who have been among the Camba for the shortest time, are, paradoxically, the gringos whose impact on the culture and society may be the greatest. The products of United States technology are universally held in awe; the contribution of United States economic aid to the national budget is appreciated and the United States is admired as a sort of idyllic never-never land.

The Social Setting of Mojos and the Northeast

Few Spanish settlers came to the northern Oriente in colonial times, and fewer stayed. The Jesuit and Franciscan missionary-administrators were officially celibate, so that miscegenation began relatively late and on a small scale. Even today, most inhabitants of the area are tribal Indians except in the ten or twelve towns where Mestizos predominate. Our scanty knowledge of these peoples, based primarily on

d'Orbigny (1835-47), was well summarized by Métraux (1942);
members of the Summer Institute of Linguistics are studying
several groups that were unknown even then. This remains
one of the few areas in the world where there is still terra
incognita in ethnographic terms.

Even Indians in villages which were missions throughout
the seventeenth and eighteenth centuries (e. g. , San Ignacio
de Moxos, Beni) retain their language, dances, folklore, and
many other aspects of indigenous culture. The same is true
of Móvima Indians who live on cattle ranches scattered around
Santa Ana de Yacuma. Local Mestizos tend to take a
patronizing attitude toward such people, and sometimes pride
themselves that "ours is a pure White town; the Indians know
their place and come in only for annual fiestas. "

Among Mestizos, there are class differences based on
wealth and "name"; it is possible that these differences are
growing rather than diminishing in Mojos as stockmen progressively move into town, leaving their ranches in the care
of mayordomos. Wealth is reflected in the quality of dress
and housing as well as in leisure.

Foreigners include a few so-called Turcos or Arabes,
Syrian and Lebanese peddlers and shopkeepers who came in
the 1920's and seem at best to be grudgingly admired for
their acumen and success. "Japoneses" are actually those
100-some Ryukyuans who were brought as laborers during
the rubber boom, but stayed on to manage cafes, pool-halls,
and other small-scale service industries (Tigner, 1963). A
few central Europeans who came as administrators during
the rubber boom continue to dominate shipping and the
wholesale rubber and brazil nut industries in the Northeast.
Only the Europeans have tended to remain aloof.

Maryknoll Catholics and various Protestant missionaries
were virtually the only North Americans in the region until
Peace Corps volunteers began to serve in major towns in
the 1960's. They are generally liked if not admired.
Recently, Cuban and Peruvian Castroites have had little
success with an active program for political agitation in the
Northeast.

CHAPTER **14** ECONOMIC ACTIVITIES
IN THE ORIENTE

—Dwight B. Heath

Bolivia is generally considered an underdeveloped country, and the Oriente has less economic activity and diversification than most of the rest of the nation. The predominant occupations have persisted for centuries: agriculture in the northern Santa Cruz area, herding in Mojos, and collecting in the Northeast; other industries have languished. Bolivians savor the irony of a local joke: "The Oriente is the land of the future--as it was four centuries ago!" Crossley (1961) is more optimistic in the light of recent developments, and cites encouraging statistics.

AGRICULTURAL ACTIVITIES

By far the most important economic activity of the northern Santa Cruz area is farming. There has been little change in agricultural techniques or crops since the Spaniards first settled in the area. The region lies on the southern fringe of the tropical heartland of South America which is so lush that it was once hailed as the site of the original Garden of Eden (Léon, /1650/). This particular area has long been viewed as a potentially rich source of foodstuffs, and agricultural development is advocated by many as a means of helping Bolivia attain economic self-sufficiency. The recent concentration of effort and funds on the part of various national and international organizations to stimulate agricultural development in the area stems from enthusiastic reports on the part of supposedly critical investigators. A report by the Bolivian government asserted that "The development of the northern area of Santa Cruz is the best way to increase, within a short time, production of these /food/ articles now being imported" (Bolivia, 1954:57). The U.S. Point Four mission held that, "The Santa Cruz area of Bolivia contains

282

presently uncultivated land of sufficient size and acceptable
climate and soil condition to produce, in a short period of time,
practically all foods for which the country is now spending
sorely needed foreign exchange" (Foreign Operations Administration, 1954).   Even the United Nations lamented that
"Relatively little has so far been done to develop the agriculture in Bolivia. . . .   The Santa Cruz area, by reason of its
favorable situation as regards future communication and
labor supply, deserves first consideration' (U. N. Technical
Assistance Administration, 1951:51).

Although there have been some significant accomplishments in agricultural production, they have by no means fulfilled these extravagant expectations.   A more intensive and
temperate evaluation of the agricultural potential indicates
shortcomings in soil and climate which limit the variety of
crops which can suitably be grown there (Misión Británica,
1962).

For a discussion of agricultural activities, it is important to distinguish between finqueros and campesinos.
Finqueros are those who own large farms (usually with more
than 20 hectares under cultivation) and who hire wage laborers
for at least half a year.   Campesinos rarely have as many as
10 hectares under cultivation, and rarely hire wage laborers
for more than a few weeks.   Only a few campesinos are able
to do farming on a commercial scale, theirs is primarily
subsistence farming, producing little surplus beyond the needs
of their families, and selling only small quantities of produce
in local markets.   Fincas also have subsistence plots, but
since the mid-1950's have progressively emphasized crops
for sale.   Commercial farming and subsistence farming are
treated separately here, primarily because different crops
are emphasized; techniques for raising particular crops
differ only in a few respects between the two classes of
agricultural production.

Subsistence Farming

Despite enormous investments and elaborate programs
for stimulating the expansion of commercial agriculture
during recent years, small-scale subsistence farming is
still the predominant economic activity in Santa Cruz.
Campesinos work small plots with primitive techniques, and
their resources in capital and labor are limited.

Most subsistence farming is done in deep moist soils,
rich in organic matter and covered with huge trees and dense
undergrowth. Preparing land is, therefore, a major undertaking even before planting is possible. The usual method of
clearing a plot is that of slash-and-burn, or swidden
(locally called chanqueando)--cutting down trees, vines, and
brush, and leaving them where they fall. Whatever has dried
sufficiently after a few weeks is burned in situ. This kind of
landclearing is heavy work, and a steady industrious worker
can, in four to five weeks, hack out of the virgin jungle only
a hectare of land suitable for cultivation with his primitive
tools and methods. Even then, charred tree trunks sprawl
in all directions, and enormous stumps remain untouched.
The litter does not impede planting or harvesting because
neither machinery nor draft animals are used. In fact, this
method of landclearing has particular advantage beyond
economy--the ash from burnt brush provides a mineral
supplement to the undisturbed top soil, and the fallen trees
prevent wind erosion. This procedure is so time-consuming,
however, that one man can clear and cultivate no more than
two hectares in a year.

Planting is begun as soon as the land is cleared and
burnt. Men do the bulk of the work, although women may
help. The farmer's equipment is simple. After a field has
been cleared and planted, it may be weeded once or twice
within the first two months, by men swinging the pala (a
long-handled shovel with cutting edge along the straight side
of a flat D-shaped blade), in a low cutting motion. The plow
is unknown and the axe, machete, and pointed stock are
virtually the only other tools used in farming.

Seeds are selected in an impressionistic manner.
Campesinos say that "It is best to save seed from one harvest
for the next planting, because then you know what you have to
work with. Those plants with the best yield--usually they're
the largest, but not always--you should keep their seeds or
cuttings from them. When you buy seeds, you don't know what
to expect. It's an expensive way to gamble."

Crops are rotated periodically because people believe
that "the soil becomes tired, and serves for a single crop

only one or two years." Rotation is haphazard, however,
because there is no conception of restoring specific elements
previously extracted from the soil. No fertilizers or manures
are used, so that cultivation, combined with the leaching
action of heavy seasonal rains, presumably leaves the soil
in poor condition. Informants agree that "You can use land
three--maybe five--years, but no more. If you try to use it
more, it won't work. There is nothing to do but let it rest.
It makes itself good again in a few years, so that you can
clear it and use it again." Within six months of its abandonment a plot is overgrown with brush, and after lying fallow
for six to eight years, dense woods must again be cleared if
it is to be reused.

Watering, mulching, and fertilizing are all techniques
unfamiliar to the Camba. "To clear the land, to plant, and to
weed is work enough if the land is rich. If the land is not
rich, one can do nothing, so why try?" is their attitude.
Insecticides, introduced by Point Four, are little used because they are not only expensive but ineffective against the
farmer-ant which is the greatest pest in all seasons.

Important grain and vegetable crops are the following
(in alphabetical order): garlic, maize, onion, peanut, hot
pepper, plantain, rice, squash, sweet potato, and yuca.

Domesticated fruits also play a part in the diet. They
include: avocado, several varieties of banana, bitter orange,
cherimoya, guava, lemon, lime, mango, papaya, pineapple,
tangerine, and watermelon.

An approximate calendar of major activities in subsistence farming is as follows:

June: clear and burn new land--weed
                         maize - weed rice - seed yuca -
                         harvest citrus

July-August: clear and burn new land - seed yuca
                         - harvest citrus - harvest second
                         crop of maize and rice (if they have
                         survived dry season)

September-   seed yuca - seed rice - seed maize
   October:

November: weed yuca - weed rice - weed maize
                     - harvest mango

December: seed plantain - rainy season begins -

January-February: - rainy season; virtually no activity -

March: harvest maize - harvest rice

April-May: seed maize - seed rice

Yuca is a staple food in the Oriente--prepared in various
ways it is eaten with virtually every meal. Sometimes called
manioc, mandioca, or tapioca, this is the "sweet" variety,
unlike the "bitter" which requires elaborate processing to
render it non-toxic. "Yuca is the bread and meat of the poor,"
they say. Producing a tremendous yield with a minimum of
effort, it is the first crop most people plant.

Since tubers grow fast without becoming tough or woody,
some can be harvested after a few months and others can be
left for the entire two years of the plant's life, attaining a
diameter of up to seven inches and a length of up to forty.
Rodents and rot account for only minor losses. Because of
its long productive period, it is difficult to estimate the yield
of yuca, but it would appear that twenty-two tons per hectare
annually is not unusual.

Of almost equal importance and frequency is rice of the
"dry" or "upland" type. Although it is more delicate than
yuca and produces a lesser yield, it provides a source of
cash income for some families as well as their food.

Seed is a hardy local variety which bears heavily and has
large grains. Young seedlings are vulnerable to the climatic
extremes which characterize the area--they may be burnt in
a hot drought or washed out in torrential seasonal rains.
Those plants which survive are harvested in the fifth or sixth
month. After a good harvest, a few farmers gamble that a
second planting may survive the dry season; the small investment pays off handsomely in some years.

The rice harvest is one of the few occasions in which
people of the Oriente show any preoccupation with time as
well as sustained deliberation in their work.   There is a
peculiar urgency about the harvesting of rice because, "If
you don't harvest the rice immediately when it's ripe, the
grains fall.   Only a week, sometimes two, and there would
be no harvest.   You have to cut it spear by spear, carefully,
so the grains don't fall."   Timing is so critical in this phase
of the agricultural cycle that women even help in the fields,
although they rarely take part in other farming activities.   In
a good moist season, a hectare may yield as much as five
tons of grain.   Rice is spread on hides or twilled palm mats
to dry in the sun before being stored, still on the spear, in
palm baskets.

Plantain, like rice and yuca, is eaten in small quantities
with almost every meal.   Because the yield is high and care
slight, almost every family grows at least a few trees in
their yard.

By the sixth year a tree's yield has diminished so that it
can profitably be cut and as many as thirty shoots spring from
around the trunk.   During the first year when such shoots are
set out in a field, another crop such as yuca, maize, or rice
is often seeded between them.   After the trees have attained
their growth and begin to produce, they cast so much shade
that interplanting is not feasible, except with fruit trees or
coffee.

A plantain tree produces fruit at one year, and continuously thereafter.   The fruit becomes larger and more numerous
as the tree matures.   Plantain is a favorite crop among
campesinos; one man summarized its advantages as follows:
"You don't have to care for it every year with planting and
weeding.... You don't have to clear the land so much.   With
just one hectare you can have enough to eat, with two hectares
you could have enough to sell."   A tree produces a full stem
(of about 200 fruit) each five or six weeks.

Maize is almost as popular a crop as the three staples,
although it is rarely eaten as a grain.   Ground into flour,
however, it is frequently used in baking, and is the base of
a sweet unfermented chicha drunk as a refreshment.   A few
ears are usually roasted green as a special delicacy (choclo).

A nondescript local variety of maize predominates; it is white, soft-shelled, with large kernels irregularly spaced on small ears. In the early 1950's, agronomists of Point Four introduced "Cuban Yellow" that has almost twice the yield of the local maize. This new variety, however, is too hard to grind manually and so is used mostly to provide food for livestock. The failure of this program has been widely cited as an example of unexpected deleterious outcomes of a planned innovation. Certainly the new crop did not accomplish the intended purpose of improving the diet of the local people, but no evidence was found to support the allegation that it increased the supply of locally produced alcohol (Erasmus, 1961:23-24 and Foster, 1962:85; following Kelly, 1959:9-10).

Maize is seeded and cared for in the same manner as rice; in fact, almost half of the time they are interspersed in the same field. Maize has the same growing season as rice but need not be harvested so quickly. As with rice, some farmers occasionally gamble on a second maize harvest in a single year, and sporadic success is enough to perpetuate the pattern.

A campesino once observed that "There's just one difficulty with maize--it needs so much care. No, I don't mean in cultivation, but in guarding against pests. All the animals--monkeys are the worst--and birds, too, like it. A troop of monkeys or a flock of parrots can consume as much as one fourth of the crop. But you can't watch it all the time, so there's danger.... But what can you do? They are God's creatures too." Despite such ravages, a yield of five tons per hectare is not extraordinary for the local white variety of maize. Stalks are sometimes cut to serve as fodder for horses, although more often they are simply left standing.

Ears of maize, unshucked, may be piled like cordwood on low platforms, although they are more often hung on strands of liana out of reach of rodents and fowl. Storage is usually near the fire "because the smoke dries it faster and guards against insects."

A few fruit trees, such as orange, grapefruit, papaya, and others are seeded in the yard of almost every rural house. With virtually no care, they bear heavily, providing vitamins which significantly supplement the normal campesino diet.

No wine is made, and bitter-orange marmalade is the only way in which fruit is cooked.

Onion, garlic, peppers, squash, sweet potato, and peanuts are raised in insignificant quantities for domestic consumption.   They receive little care but usually produce a good yield.   Worms and rot occasionally damage all of these crops.

Commercial Farming

Farming can be done on a commercial basis in the Oriente only by finqueros who have large tracts of land and can regularly hire employees.   Even they have only in recent years begun to think of agriculture as a large-scale commercial enterprise in which the goal is progressive increase of efficiency and production in order to maximize profits. Finqueros used to farm only to feed themselves and their workers and to have a small surplus for sale or exchange in local markets.   Until the 1960's, the ease and few comforts the finqueros enjoyed were those of the semi-feudal landlord whose riches consist not in a large income but in an abundance of labor and the security of a moderate current income.

Extensive landholdings, therefore, long had value in terms of prestige which far outweighed their negotiable economic value.   Even in the largest fincas, agricultural techniques were traditionally primitive and investment of capital minimal.   Vast expanses of land were left uncultivated, and tenant farmers did virtually all work by hand.   By and large, the techniques of commercial farming were the same as those of subsistence farming, and it was the abundance of land, together with the concentration of manpower on a finca, which allowed production of sugar cane and coffee, the principal cash crops.

Landclearing by the slash-and-burn method was employed by the finqueros as well as by campesinos.   Crop rotation was equally haphazard, and betterment of the soil equally neglected. Planting and harvesting were likewise similar in both subsistence and commercial farming.

It was the enactment of the agrarian reform law in 1953 that precipitated a variety of changes in this pattern.   The threat of expropriation of "surplus" holdings shattered for many finqueros the feeling of security in land which they had enjoyed. The law provided for immediate total expropriation of all underdeveloped "latifundias," but with the explicit aim of increasing agricultural production, allowance was made for the retention of up to 2,000 hectares by a progressive "empresa agrícola."

In reaction to this threat many finqueros endeavored suddenly to make their latifundia eligible for the advantageous classification of "agricultural enterprises," and so defend their claim to large areas of land. At about the same time, Point Four's program of agricultural credit was started and finqueros were the only ones who could post land and future crops as collateral sufficient to get large loans. Many of them were glad to have funds for investment in the fincas, in order to retain the land on which their status as finqueros was based.

In 1954, an agricultural machinery pool was established at Santa Cruz, and finqueros with loans were able to rent a wide variety of mechanical aids at rates lower than actual operating costs. There was no specialized landclearing equipment in the pool, but large bulldozers were used for that purpose around Montero, Warnes, and Portachuelo. A bulldozer and operator, rented at Bs. 20,000 (about $2.00) per hour, could clear a hectare of high jungle in eight or nine hours, not only uprooting trees but pushing them aside to form long mounds on either side of a bare field. Clearly a finca where so much capital was invested and such large machines used should not be expropriated as a latifundium under the agrarian reform law. Furthermore, this major change in landclearing techniques meant not only a small saving on the initial costs of having land cleared, but the consequent huge saving in time allowed earlier planting and harvesting. Other savings were possible in that mechanized plows and seeders could be used in the uncluttered fields. Rental rates were so low that commercial farmers invariably realized profits from newly cleared land during the first year of use.

The market for agricultural produce in the northern Santa Cruz area had traditionally been limited. The population was sparse, and almost everyone raised crops which met a large portion of his own needs. Transportation to other outlets was too slow and costly to be feasible for foodstuffs. Large-scale commercial agriculture, in brief, required a change in facilities for distribution and consumption, and that change occurred in the late 1950's.

A huge modern sugar mill and alcohol distillery built at Guabirá by CBF stimulated finqueros to grow more cane, especially after a network of graded "feeder roads" was made by Point Four. By 1964, the area was already producing more sugar than was consumed in Bolivia. Unfortunately, production costs were such that it could be exported only at a loss. A new quota system imposed on producers has evoked considerable dissatisfaction, and the area is paradoxically suffering from "too much" success in the brief drive to increase sugar production.

The railway to Brazil and the highway to Cochabamba promised to serve as channels for the ready distribution of any surplus agricultural production. Thus, several finqueros who started commercial farming on only a small scale in order to protect their land from expropriation happened, by a peculiar accident of history, to be put in a position where they became wealthy in a single year, with a minimal investment both in capital and labor and with virtually no economic risk. Monetary inflation was such that invariably they were not only able to amortize the loan during the first year but also had a cash balance which far exceeded their usual income.

Describing the situation of 1957 required an extended discussion of reasons why finqueros had not then attempted to increase production or to look to an expanded market for greater profits (Heath, 1959b). In the course of subsequent work in the area, however, I have been struck by the extent to which commercialization of agriculture has progressed. An interpretive comparison of two such different periods would be especially fruitful.

One obstacle to earlier commercialization which still holds is the fact that the land reform law is not applied in a universalistic manner. In many instances, MNR sympathizers received preferential treatment, while opponents of the party suffered losses, even in violation of the law. This kind of illegal favoritism by differential application of sanctions is described and illustrated below; for the present discussion it should suffice to say that the threats implied in the agrarian reform law proved to be of no importance to many finqueros, while others ran the risk of losing their properties even if they complied with the specifications of the decree.   One major effect of this discrimination was a marked ambivalence toward expansion of commercial farming.   Those partisan finqueros who were assured of being able to keep their land no longer felt pressed to expand or intensify work on their latifundia, and other finqueros were for a time reluctant to invest in the development of properties which they might soon lose.   The attitude of this former group was well summarized by one man who in 1957 proudly welcomed me to his 1,200 hectare finca with this telling speech.

> Here you see a really primitive finca.   The tenants
> here work just as they did in colonial times.
> Nothing has changed; there's no progress; every-
> thing is as it always has been.   Does that seem
> strange?   I'm going to explain something to you.
> I'm a finquero--do you know what that means?
> It means that the land is my life, as it was my
> father's, and his father's, etc.. It's not that we
> are so rich--look--there are no luxury items, not
> even electricity.   But we have our land and our
> servants, and enough to live on.

He went on to explain:

> Sure, I took credit from Point Four.   I even had
> a few hectares cleared by bulldozer.   They even
> fixed the road out here--it used to be just mud.
> But that was some three or four years ago.   No
> more!   I know that the syndicates won't touch my
> land, so why cultivate it?   We have enough this
> way.   To expand the planting would need more
> tenants.   That means more work for me, too.
> No, thank you.   I have security; I have enough
> food and enough servants.   What more does a man
> need?   My finca remains backward--almost primi-
> tive--and why?   Because I prefer it, my friend.
> It's that simple.

His views were typical of the vast majority of finqueros.

It was just such complacent conservatism, however,

that another finquero decried as the greatest fault of his
neighbors. He himself had other reasons for not investing
heavily in the development of his property, although he was
enthusiastic about its commercial potential. His complaint
was that:

> The government opposes progress. Sure, they
> always say that they favor economic diversifica-
> tion, agricultural development, the progress of
> the country, etc.. But, to the party, those are
> just high-sounding words with no meaning. The
> MNR doesn't stimulate progress; it crushes it.
> This is especially a problem around here. The
> Camba are lazy, backward. They seem still to
> live in the sixteenth century. With the campesinos,
> you can't expect any better. They are ignorant--
> not stupid, mind you--they just don't know any-
> thing more than their own primitive way of life,
> and that probably hasn't changed much since they
> were savages. But the finqueros are worse. I'm
> a Camba, you should know; it is because I am a
> Camba that I know so well the fault of my kinsmen,
> my compadres, and friends. Finqueros don't know
> how to work. They have enormous landholdings
> and they do nothing but raise food for their families
> and those of their tenants.... Nobody earns much.
> They only cultivate a little, using archaic means.
> They don't know modern technology and worse, have
> no interest. Now I'm sure you must want to know
> how it is that I can say this when I myself have a
> finca very little developed. That is another story,
> very different, and a little sad. The sadness is
> not for me but for my country--she will suffer as
> well as I.

He continued sadly:

> Do you know why I, too, have a backward finca? It
> is not that I know nothing else--I have read much,
> and I have seen progress in Argentina. It is not
> that I am too poor to develop the land.... I know
> how to farm; I have plenty of good rich land; there
> is no lack of money; I am not lazy like most of the
> other Camba. I cannot progress because I don't

dare. That is difficult for you to understand, I'm
sure, so I'll explain. It's the party, the MNR. Do
you know that I'm called "an enemy of the party"?
It doesn't matter why. What is important is that,
as an enemy of the party, I have no rights whatsoever. Let's say I clear so many hectares; then I
plant cane. Then--poof--all of a sudden a new
campesino syndicate is formed and they steal my
land. They do it through the agrarian reform judge,
but I still call it stealing. According to the law, an
"agricultural enterprise" is exempt from expropriation up to 2,000 hectares. "The land belongs to
him who works it," they say. They also say, "We
must stimulate agricultural development, and for
this we will protect the landowner who augments
production." High-sounding words again, nothing
more. Do you know what happens to the finquero
who tries to develop his property, to augment pro-
duction--in short, to make progress? He loses
everything. There is such discrimination against
those of us who are not of the party that it is not
safe to show that you have anything. They are
thieves, that's all, but the party is the government;
law counts for nothing. We have only to work a
little harder than they, and, immediately, they take
what we have done. There is no recourse; they
have complete power. It has happened too often, to
me as well as to others. But no more. I can wait
and hope that someday the MNR will fall and it will
be safe for a man who wants to work for progress.

Although this man may sound paranoiac, his description
of the situation was accurate. His experience and that of
many others included illegal abuses and quasi-legal machinations that completely justify such bitterness. In such a
situation, commercial agriculture was understandably slow
to expand despite the efforts of national and international
organizations toward that end. But in 1963, such finqueros
had the feeling that they had already lost all the land they
were going to lose. Often, after partial expropriation, they
received titles confirming their inalienable ownership of the
remaining portion. However bitter may be their remembrances
of the early losses, they feel confident that they will suffer no
more such, and so do not hesitate to work it.

The partisan finqueros are also increasing their production for sale. Their eagerness to buy luxury goods (such as
radios, electric generators, and so forth) suggests new wants:
it may be that consumption patterns grew after others provided
an example, or it may simply be that their earlier denigration
was little more than a "sour grapes" reaction in an area when
such things were not available at any price.

Differential application of the agrarian reform law was
not the only factor that retarded the rate of expansion of
commercial farming in the area. The new technology of
mechanized agriculture had the unfortunate effect of speeding
up deterioration of the soil. After the loamy topsoil had been
scraped off by bulldozers, the sandy substrata were subject
to increased leaching by heavy seasonal rains, and erosion
became worse as winds blew unhindered down the long narrow
fields. One well-educated finquero who had observed agricultural methods in neighboring countries was well aware of
these shortcomings. As he phrased it, "Hand-clearing is
much better. But the problem is time. It takes so long with
just machete, brush-hook, and axe. But when you're
finished the land is still rich. Not like the bulldozers that
scrape off the best soil, some ten inches at least. . . . When
you clear by hand, the best soil is left on top, and the ashes
from the burned brush are good, too. So on land cleared by
machine you can only grow cane or rice, but on land cleared
by hand you can grow anything. " The disadvantages of
mechanized landclearing were not long a problem, because a
singular technological reversal took place late in 1956, when
many of the wealthy finqueros stopped using bulldozers and
reverted to the traditional method of slash-and-burn to clear
new fields for farming. A subsequent abrupt rise of 575 per
cent in the rental rates for machinery during January, 1957,
made the new technique more expensive than the old. By
October, 1958, only four of the original twenty bulldozers
remained in the area, and they were used almost exclusively
for roadbuilding and maintenance. In 1963 these were in the
hands of a commercial contractor who rented them at profitable rates to those who wanted land cleared for a variety of
purposes.

Crops raised on a commercial scale in the Camba region
now are the following: sugar cane, coffee, rice, and cotton.
The approximate schedule of activities connected with

commercial crops is as follows:

June:	clear and burn new land - harvest
June:	old sugar cane - seed new cane - weed rice - harvest cotton
July-August:	clear and burn new land - harvest cane - seed cane - weed new cane - harvest rice (if it survived dry season) - plow and harrow for cotton
September-October:	weed cane - seed rice - seed cotton - seed coffee
November:	weed rice - seed cotton - seed coffee
December:	weed and thin cotton - rainy season begins --
January-February:	-- rainy season; virtually no activity -
March:	harvest rice - weed cotton - weed coffee - seed rice - harvest cotton
April-May:	seed rice - harvest cotton

The most important commercial crop in this region is sugar cane from which are derived the two principal products of the area: sugar and alcohol. Since the cane is only a raw material which must be further processed, it is grown primarily by finqueros who have the equipment and manpower to deliver it in large quantities to mills. Until the late 1950's, crude sugar and molasses were produced by primitive labor-intensive methods on at least eighty fincas, and there were several small distilleries scattered through the area. Now, the production of both sugar and alcohol is concentrated in only four highly mechanized mills.

The economics of sugar cane cultivation is complex, involving not only large areas and considerable labor but also producing a long-term return. Cane sells for Bs. 100,000 per ton at the mill; in the Santa Cruz area, the annual yield is 60 to 120 tons per hectare, beginning nine months after planting and increasing until it reaches a plateau from the

second until the fifth year, after which it diminishes so
rapidly that most farmers abandon it and replant. The cost
of freight is so high that small plots are feasible only where
farmers can deliver by oxcart, and large-scale farmers
usually own trucks and/or tractors with 5-ton cane-carts.

Land is cleared in the same manner as for other crops,
and the primitive techniques of planting and weeding are the
same as used by subsistence farmers for other crops. The
first crop begins to ripen in about a year. Harvesting by
hand is a slow process. Each stalk is cut and trimmed
individually before being stacked. After the cane is hauled
away by truck or tractor-drawn wagon, the entire field is
burned over, in order to dispose of the leaves and waste
ends and "to lighten the soil." Subsequent crops mature in
about ten months. In the first year a stand of cane should
produce about seventy tons per hectare, and yields of almost
double that amount have been reported from older plantings.

Cane has always been a popular crop in this area, but
it was especially favored during the late 1950's because the
Bolivian government invested heavily in the sugar industry,
as described above, and almost the entire crop was sold to
a few large sugar mills. In the early 1960's, however,
production caught up with demand so that the boom in cane-
growing is over and farmers resent both government attempts
to limit their production and the fact that they already have
unsalable surpluses.

Most finqueros raise coffee for domestic use and for
sale. Coffee plants are a good long-term investment, but
have never been popular as a commercial crop in this area
because they require far more care than cane or rice and do
not give such immediate returns. The bushes do not bear
until the fourth year. Coffee, like rice, must be harvested
in a critical few weeks after ripening or the berries fall and
the crop is lost. After being hulled and sun dried, berries
are stored or sold, with roasting and grinding deferred until
just before use. A good yield for the first harvest is 1,000
pounds per hectare; plants bear for eight or ten years during
which time the maximum yield may reach almost 3,000
pounds per hectare.

A single finca has been recently devoted to the production

of cotton. The plant is a local perennial variety with short fibers, subject to several diseases and insect pests. The wealthy kolla owner who had been experimenting there for about a decade is vague about his success. His is one of the best-equipped and best-managed farms around Santa Cruz, and it is apparent that cotton is a commercially feasible crop, although detailed data on costs and yield are not available.

Rice is a staple food of the Oriente which has also become an important crop in commercial farming. Finqueros have always required large plantings of rice in order to feed their tenants, but there was seldom any appreciable surplus for sale. The method of landclearing, planting, cultivation, and harvesting by primitive manual techniques was the principal factor limiting production, even though finqueros hired the wives and children of tenants, as well as families of squatters and any other day-laborers they could find to help with the harvest.

A new kind of agriculture, very different from anything known in the region before, was developed with the introduction of mechanized agricultural implements in the pampa near Portachuelo. Fairly rich soil lies open and flat in this area, so that plows can be used to break the sod and seeding machines and harvesters can also be employed. With the introduction of mechanized agriculture it is now possible to produce a large harvest of dry rice with a minimum of manual labor in a year of good rains. Irrigation, fertilization, and crop-rotation are ignored by these finqueros as they are by others, so that the yield per hectare is about the same as by slash-and-burn techniques as used in jungle land--the greater efficiency of mechanized rice cultivation appears to have been offset by the relative poorness of the soil. New techniques do, however, allow the harvesting of much larger areas in the crucial brief period after ripening and before the grains fall, so that far greater quantities can be produced than are feasible where harvest is by hand. Furthermore, costs of production are far less, because of the immense savings on labor.

The 20-some finqueros who produce rice in this manner were well aware of their advantageous position with respect to the market, and resent the fact that the first Okinawan colony and the Japanese colony, using slash-and-burn techniques, produce more and better rice. By the early 1960's however, production already exceeded demand so that, as in the case of sugar cane, farmers have been disappointed by "too much" success in commercial agricultural production.

A few other crops are grown on a small scale for sale in the region. When finqueros have plantain, yuca, orange, grapefruit, banana, maize, or other crops, even after allowing for the needs of their family and their tenants, the surplus is sold in local markets. Such overproduction is not systematic, however, and methods are the same as those used by campesinos in cultivating their subsistence plots. Commercial farming, therefore, is largely restricted to the crops discussed individually above.

EXPLOITATIVE ACTIVITIES

Like most peoples, those of the northern Santa Cruz area derive some of their food and wealth from direct exploitation of the natural environment. Hunting, fishing, grazing, and collecting are activities which involve only minor human intervention in the production of economic goods from raw materials.

Hunting and Fishing

Unlike their forebears and the Indian tribes which surround them, the people of the northern Santa Cruz area get only an insignificant portion of their food from hunting. Although it is economically unimportant, men occasionally use slingshot or shotgun to hunt peccary, monkey, porcupine, or roe deer in the jungle. Tapir and capybara are especially prized, both for their size and for the quality of the meat; a few professionals hunt sloth, jaguar, and rhea for their valuable fur or feathers.

Casual fishing with dynamite has in recent years decimated the varied supply in the rivers around Santa Cruz. Commercial fishing, with nets and line, yields a small but regular supply for sale in the department capital. Fish do not figure significantly in the diet of the Spanish-speaking population of the Oriente, as they do for Indians.

Grazing

The Indian tribes from which the local people are descended had virtually no domesticated animals in pre-Columbian times. Stockraiding was introduced by the Spaniards and remains an important source of food, although subordinate to agriculture. Livestock are rarely fed, and generally get very little care of any kind.

There are almost no milch cows, and the scraggly creole stock are kept for beef only. A lack of selective breeding is just one aspect of an utter lack of interest. There are a few large herds which roam the open range between seasonal roundups for branding or selling. The majority, however, are owned, in twos or threes, by townspeople who simply let them forage where they can. It is because cattle without pasture present such a threat to crops and a nuisance around houses that barbed-wire fencing is so widely used despite the great expense involved. In strictly quantitative terms, beef would appear to play an unimportant role in the local diet; in the opinion of the people themselves, however, it is virtually indispensible.

Oxen are the only animals used for draft purposes. They are castrated young and yoked by the horns to a trained ox. A team remain tied together even when turned out to graze. The oxcart, a massive thing which can bear up to one and a half tons on its solid wooden wheels which are sometimes hewn from a single five-foot log of mahogany, was the standard means of transportation until displaced by trucks during the early 1960's.

Horses, like cattle, are of the small unimproved brown or brown-and-white creole type introduced by the Spaniards. Although they are widely used as saddle mounts, they generally receive no better care from their owners than do cattle.

A hardy long-legged breed of swine are raised in insignificant numbers for their fat. Most males are castrated and roam free to forage. They are staked and fed maize only for two days before being butchered. Lard, which is rendered from the fat, is the most important product. The skin, fried crisp, is a delicacy, and the meat is sold to a few people at a price one half higher than beef. Curing and sausage pro-

duction are unknown, although CBF plans a pig farm and
processing plant at Todos Santos near Guabirá. Sheep,
goats, and other small animals are not found in the area.

"Chickens are the poor man's livestock," according to
Camba campesinos, almost all of whom keep a few in order
to sell the eggs in town. Most are a hardy mixed breed which
thrive on the same minimal care afforded all other animals.
A few finqueros have begun, in recent years, to raise purebred chicks from Brazil with systematic feeding, immuni-
zation, and so forth.

Collecting

Collecting activities provide a minor supplement to the
predominantly agricultural economy, both for food and for
items of trade value. Wild fruit are numerous and plentiful;
diverse forest products have commercial value; and minerals
may come to play an important part in the development of the
area in the near future.

One of the few elements of the Indian heritage which persists even in the towns of the Oriente is a knowledge and use
of wild plants. In many cases, even the old names are still
used because the Spaniards were not familiar with the local
flora. Wild fruits which are collected by women and children
for family consumption have been mentioned; the nuts of
virtually every palm are collected and eaten also.

The jungle holds a wealth of other products which are
exploited on only a small scale. The costly slowness and
difficulty of transportation prevented any extensive development of the lumber industry until the late 1950's, but enormous
virgin stands of valuable timber are being fast exploited. Firewood is used not only for all cooking and baking, but even in
the four large sugar refineries. The collection of firewood
for sale to townspeople or to factories was an occasional
source of small cash income for lower-class men and women
until a few years ago, but landclearing has proceeded to the
point where firewood can now be cut feasibly only by those
who can truck it to market.

Balsa, cinammon, cinchona, kapok, and rubber trees
yield products which are occasionally valuable in international

commerce and could perhaps eventually lessen Bolivia's
dependence on a few mineral exports for foreign exchange.
At present, however, exploitation seems not to be economically feasible because of the shortage of labor and difficulty
of transportation in tropical areas where they abound.

The northern Santa Cruz area, as an alluvial plain,
provides few surface indications of mineral wealth. Small
deposits of gold to the north and east did not long sustain
commercial exploitation. The extraction of petroleum from
the Chaco to the south in the 1920's, first by Standard Oil
Company and later by the Bolivian national company (Aguila
Doble), is considered by some to have been the major issue
in the fateful Chaco War (see, e. g. , Marsh, 1928). The oil
fields remained in Bolivian hands after the war, but were
neglected until 1953, when the MNR took a gamble by investing
almost $2 million in modernizing and expanding operations of
the inefficient new state oil company (Yacimientos Petrolíferos
Fiscales Bolivianos, YPFB). More wells were dug and pipe-
lines constructed from the Camiri fields to modern refineries
at Cochabamba and Sucre, and the gamble paid off. Within a
year Bolivia became self-sufficient in the production of diesel
fuel, kerosene, and low octane gasoline, effecting an annual
saving of $8 million in foreign exchange. During the years
that followed, production increased so that YPFB was export-
ing light petroleum products to Brazil in partial payment for
construction of the Corumbá-Santa Cruz railroad, to Argentina
under an agreement providing for completion of the Yacuiba-
Santa Cruz railroad, and to Chile for cash. During the mid-
1960's, production has been falling off slightly, although
impressive new finds of oil and natural gas are reported.

In the late 1950's, the Bolivian government acted to
stimulate the exploration and exploitation of petroleum by
foreign companies. Gulf is the only survivor of about a
dozen North American companies which took advantage of
the liberalized tax and permission system to survey large
concessions throughout the Department of Santa Cruz.
Although most of the oil fields which are now producing
are located around Camiri, far south of the city of Santa
Cruz, a new area of exploitation is the midwestern portion
of the region studied, around Caranda. Furthermore, the
state-oil company is exploring the region just west of
Puerto Grether. The clearing of a road from Yapacaní

to Puerto Grether, and the construction of a provisional
bridge across the Yapacaní River in 1963, were undertaken
to facilitate movement of heavy machinery to the area but
also attracted kolla colonists who have already settled in
most of the plots staked out for them by CBF along the road.
In this way, the frontier of settlement has been expanded and
the economy has been stimulated.

Not only is petroleum benefiting the national economy but
it is especially beneficial to the Oriente. After a series of
bloody demonstrations against federal exploitation and neglect,
the central government acceded in 1958 to demands that 11 per
cent of petroleum profits revert to the Department of Santa
Cruz.

INDUSTRIAL ACTIVITIES

Industry has languished in the Oriente for a number of
reasons. The one most often cited by the local people themselves and by visitors to the area has long been the difficulty of transportation to distant market centers. Since the
late 1950's, however, transportation facilities have improved
and industry is fast gaining importance in the regional economy.

Alcohol and Sugar

The soil and climate of the northern Santa Cruz area are
well suited to the cultivation of sugar cane. However, neither
sugar nor molasses could have been sold for enough profit to
offset the cost of the two-month mule trek over the mountains
which until recently was the only route to the nearest market
city in the western portion of the country. But the margin of
profit from alcohol was sufficiently great to justify the expense
of transportation. Hence, nine distilleries were operating in
the area in 1956, ranging from a small homemade contraption
that produced about 200 liters a day during the four-month
season, to a huge mill with modern French machinery and a
daily capacity of 12,000 liters. The alcohol was shipped
throughout the country in 16-liter cans. Watered to 30 or
40 per cent, alcohol becomes aguardiente so often encountered
in the Andean region, but it is drunk undiluted by the local
people themselves and seems to be valuable in terms of social
relations (Heath, 1958).

Most finqueros had long made sugar cane their principal
cash crop, and sold to distilleries whatever they did not use
in the home production of molasses and crude sugar.   Every
finca of any size had primitive equipment for the rendering
of cane: a massive wooden rotary press powered by an ox on
a turnstile, and large conical clay pots for boiling the juice.
The average yield of sucrose was estimated at 10 per cent by
weight.

Since the early 1950's when regular truck traffic was
initiated to Cochabamba, production of granulated sugar
has become a major industrial activity in Santa Cruz.   The
production of two private mills (La Bélgica and Esperanza)
with annual capacities of approximately 4,500 tons and
500 tons respectively, was augmented in 1956 by the opening
of the CBF refinery (Guabirá), with an annual capacity of
about 20,000 tons.   None of the mills regularly operated at
capacity, because of inefficient workers, frequent mechanical
breakdowns, and periodic shortages of cane.   Each sugar mill
contracted early in the season for the cultivation of certain
areas of cane in order to have at least a portion of their
supply assured, but these areas rarely produced more than
10 per cent of their requirements so the rest had to be
bought from independent farmers who would erratically
bring loads by truck or oxcart from a radius of about
20 miles.   Obviously it was impossible to schedule milling
operations efficiently under such circumstances.   During
the early 1960's, the capacities of La Bélgica and Guabirá
were doubled, and another private mill (San Aurelio) was
established just south of the city of Santa Cruz.   The
Ministry of Economy developed an elaborate quota system
among cane-growers to assure a regular supply of cane at
the mills, until, during the 1963 milling-season, it became
apparent that existing facilities could not process any more
cane.   This appears to be a rare instance in which the nation
has reached a ceiling in one aspect of economic development.

The opening of the CBF refinery was part of a national
program of economic diversification.   It not only stimulated
agricultural development in the Santa Cruz region but also
helped to strengthen the economy of the nation by appreciably
increasing domestic production of sugar which had long been

a large item among costly imports. A number of changes have already come about locally because of the large mill. Contrary to expectations, it did not provide industrial jobs for the local people; nearly all of the workers are kollas who came from around Cochabamba only for the duration of the milling season. There is still widespread resentment of this fact as "a typical demonstration of the government's favoritism toward kollas in all things," although the large influx of workers brings money to the area, and the market in Montero thrives. A long-term benefit has been the construction and maintenance of a network of roads radiating from each of the mills to large cane-producing fincas. At each of the mills, alcohol is an economically important by-product, and this has forced all other distilleries out of the market. It is a bitter joke that during 1962 all the locally produced sugar was sent to Tarija from which it was smuggled to Argentina, while Bolivia imported sugar from Germany for consumption in Santa Cruz.

Other Industrial Activities

The Oriente produces virtually no other goods for export. Even manufactures for local consumption are few. Building materials such as adobe blocks and fired bricks and tiles are made by a few full-time specialists near each village, by a simple process requiring a small labor force and little equipment, on land owned in fee simple.

In Buenavista, a considerable portion of the income is still derived from the manufacture of fine "Panama hats." This local cottage industry, utilizing the dried leaf of the jipijapa palm (Carludovica palmata), dates from the eighteenth century when Jesuits founded a mission among the Churapa Indians there. Leaves are gathered in the jungle, and there is no conception of tenure of trees.

Each town has a few carpenters who make windows, shutters, doors, chairs, tables, beds, and wardrobes as well as caskets. With few tools and little skill they produce plain but serviceable goods from unseasoned mahogany at low rates.

COMMERCIAL ACTIVITIES

The limits of the internal market and of trade with
other areas impeded the growth of capitalism in the Oriente,
but commercial activities have become increasingly important in recent years.

Markets and Merchants

Until the early 1950's the village or hacienda community
was a self-contained economic unit. Each finca produced
most of the goods that were consumed there, and weekly
markets in each of the towns provided occasions for the
exchange of a small surplus of agricultural products for a
few imported necessities such as kerosene, clothing, barbed
wire, salt, and so forth. With the growth of towns and the
improvement of means of transportation, the northern Santa
Cruz area has become an integrated market system with
Santa Cruz and Montero as foci of daily commercial activity
and other villages retaining special market days.

Professional shopkeepers constitute a large portion of
the middle class, and the 1960's have seen a rapid shift from
tiny general stores to more specialized establishments in
each town. Shopkeepers keep friendship and business distinct, and no campesino is favored with special prices or is
extended credit; furthermore, prices are fixed and haggling
is in very poor taste.

Vendors often sell fresh fruits and vegetables in the
open-air public markets which are usually located near the
plaza of each town. These vendors are women of the lower
class who have much smaller and less varied stocks, mostly
produce from their husbands' fields. They seem to enjoy
being in the center of town and talking for hours on end, even
if many days yield no monetary profit. Like the shopkeepers,
they also charge standard prices for similar produce.

A few peddlers in the public markets handle manufactured
goods rather than fresh agricultural produce. These people
spread their wares on the sidewalk or on low tables during
the day, and collect and store them each night. Their stock
is diverse and comprises mostly cheap imports such as
cosmetics, plastics, costume jewelry, knives, mirrors,

ballpoint pens, pins, enamelled tableware, plus innumerable notions and sundries. These intrusive goods are welcome additions to the small inventory of local material culture but there appears to be no element of competition or ostentation in the acquisition of them.

A few butchers use their front rooms as shops for the occasional sale of fresh beef. These people are not fastidious buyers and the entire carcass yields only two distinguishable cuts: "meat" and "bone," apart from certain portions which are considered special delicacies.

Still another type of mercantile establishment exists on large isolated fincas where landlords provide commissaries for their employees--far less often now than a few years ago. Stocks are restricted to a few staples such as alcohol, kerosene, matches, salt, and sugar. Unlike the notorious North American company store of song and story, prices are normally lower than those of retail outlets in the towns, and short-term credit is available to campesino workers.

Money and Measures

The medium of exchange in most Camba commercial activities is Bolivian national currency. Barter persists only in rural areas where friends sometimes exchange goods in small amounts.

Chronic inflation has been an unpleasant reality in Bolivia during most of this century, as it has in most Latin American countries. Always a deficit nation because of a gross imbalance between the values of exports and imports, Bolivia has been especially vulnerable to fluctuations in the world market of minerals, her major product which alone accounted for more than 97 per cent of her foreign exchange income in 1953 (Bolivia, 1954:1). The discrepancy between production and consumption has been aggravated by chronic misdirection of public investment and poor administration. The government's maintenance of multiple artificial exchange rates killed many embryonic industries by making it possible to import goods less expensively than to produce them domestically.

Shortly after the MNR came to power in 1952,
"featherbedding" and gross incompetence in the newly
nationalized mining enterprises, together with a drastic cut
in the world price of tin, sharply decreased the nation's income. Several economic reforms aimed at curbing hyper-
inflation were passed in May 1953; nevertheless, the value
of the boliviano decreased from 60 per U. S. dollar at that time
to more than 16,000 per dollar. A further program of
elaborate reforms aimed at achieving economic stabilization
was instituted in December, 1956, and it achieved notable
success. After several months of widespread unrest, most
Bolivians came to accept the necessity of a wage freeze and
relatively free market. During the early 1960's, the
exchange rate varied little around an average of 12,000
per dollar; the new peso ($b) will replace bolivianos (Bs.) at
the rate of one per thousand. Foreign aid no longer contributes 30 per cent of the annual national budget; galloping
inflation has been halted, and there are some signs of vitality
in parts of the economy (see Zondag, 1966).

The development of private enterprise is difficult where
credit is available only at interest rates normally considered
usurous, as high as 50 per cent monthly. A program of
supervised credit for agricultural purposes was established
by the Interamerican Agricultural Service (Servicio Agrícola
Interamericano, SAI, a joint organ of U.S. Point Four and
Bolivia's Department of Agriculture), and only late in 1963
came under direct administration of the Banco Agrícola de
Bolivia. Based on a United States model, interest rates are
extremely low but qualifications for such credit are so
stringent that loans are only made to those who, in Bolivian
eyes, are wealthy already. In order to secure money at 10
per cent per year, it was necessary to post 100 per cent
collateral; this has recently been lowered to 50 per cent for
livestock; 60 per cent for mortgages; and 65 per cent for
agricultural production. In the Santa Cruz area, where the
smallest loan made was Bs. 5 million (over $400), the rate
of delinquency is slowly falling after having reached a peak
of 60 per cent. This situation has confirmed the conviction
of small-scale farmers that "it takes money to make money,"
and demonstrated in their eyes--justifiedly or not--that aid
from the United States is administered with the same class
favoritism that they had come to expect from their own
government.

A national law of many years' standing established the metric system of weights and measures as standard throughout the country.   The traditional isolation of the Oriente from commercial relations with other regions is demonstrated, however, in local retention of a number of archaic measures, many of which are no longer used elsewhere.   Among these units which persist are the following:

almud -- 1,000 square varas (of land); 32 pounds (of
            grain

arroba -- 25 pounds (of grain, coffee)

carga -- 200 pounds (of grain)

fanega -- 384 pounds (of grain)

libra -- 1 pound (of meat, vegetables, sugar, grain,
            coffee)

quintal -- 100 pounds (of grain, sugar)

rastrado -- 50 units (of palm leaves)

tarea -- 4 cubic varas (of firewood, sugar cane); 1,000
            square meters (of land)

vara -- 84 centimeters (of firewood); 85 cm. (of land);
            86 cm. (of cloth)

Now that transportation facilities have improved and the people of the Oriente are coming into closer and more frequent trade relations with kollas, these measures are gradually being displaced by metric units.   Weights are only approximate because each vendor or shopkeeper has her own assortment of stones and bits of scrap metal which, in various combinations, are supposed to give standard units of weight on homemade cross-beam scales.

OTHER ECONOMIC ACTIVITIES

Even a relatively homogeneous society such as that of the Oriente has an appreciable amount of occupational diversity.   Specialization is slight in rural areas, with the

great majority of the population engaged in agricultural
activities. Not all fincas even have foremen, and the typical
local finquero takes pride in overseeing much of the work
himself. Sometimes a tenant who has special skill will be
singled out on occasions to do carpentry or butchering, but
he is afforded no preferential treatment and works most of
the time with the other tenants.

Within villages, the number and variety of specialists is
in approximate proportion to the density of population. Be-
sides artisans and merchants, there are self-styled "nurses"
and "pharmacists" as well as a few lawyers and, recently,
even doctors. In most towns one can find some people who
work, at least part-time, as teachers, truckers, cooks,
maids, laundresses, blacksmiths, masons, butchers, bakers,
barbers, cobblers, or dressmakers.

ECONOMIC ACTIVITIES IN MOJOS AND NORTHEAST

Agriculture is far less important as an economic activity
in Mojos and the Northeast. Extensive flat-topped mounds
provided cultivable land above the floodplain in pre-Columbian
times, but these have been abandoned, and cultivation is now
limited to the narrow well-watered strips along riverbanks.
The vast savannah of Mojos serves only as natural pasture.
In the Northeast, indigenous peoples are primarily hunters,
and Spanish-speakers live by the commercial exploitation of
forest products. Only a few scattered campesinos practice
subsistence farming, using crops and techniques like those
described for Santa Cruz. Commercial farming is similarly
less important in both of these areas, being virtually limited
to the production of a small surplus of staples such as
plantain, yuca, maize, banana, and citrus fruits, by a few
farmers who sell in village markets.

Exploitative activities predominate in the economy of
the northern Oriente. Hunting and fishing are the principal
means of subsistence for tribal peoples, and a few professional hunters specialize in crocodile (caymán), jaguar, and
wildcat whose skins are valuable. But grazing supports most
of the Mestizos of Mojos and collecting supports those of the
Northeast.

Almost the only products of the vast grassland of Mojos

are beef and hides, and they are so valuable that they are
periodically flown to La Paz, since there is no other ready
means of transportation. Overland cattle-drives to Santa
Cruz or the Brazilian frontier are month-long ordeals,
gruelling for man and beast alike, so they are lessening as
"small-scale'stockmen (those with fewer than 150 adult head)
sell to local slaughterhouses which fly meat and hides in
their own B-17's. Some operate on such a scale that they
send two planeloads a week to La Paz.

The cattle are generally a lean and hardy creole variety
which are left to forage in open range. They are descendants
of stock introduced by the Jesuits, which roamed freely until
this century, when the enormous herds of virtually wild
cattle were decimated by indiscriminate slaughter; during
both World Wars, hunters took only their hides and left the
meat to rot. Even now, few ranchers keep accurate count of
their stock, which get no supplementary feeding and virtually
no care. Some stockmen estimate that only one calf in ten
survives the first year. There has been talk of introducing
selective breeding, but this rarely involves more action
than adding a zebu bull or two to a herd of a thousand or more.
In the same way, ranchers who speak in glittering generalities
about the potential value of "rational care," with immuniza-
tions, cultivated pasturage, fenced ranges for seasonal
rotation of grazing areas, and so forth, have generally made
no move in this direction, and are quick to point out that
credit is not available--which appears to be true. Around
Santa Ana de Yacuma, people say "we are crazy about livestock; it's in our blood," and some ranchers still count
their cattle in tens of thousands, although everyone laments
the decline in cattle population from "the old days, when even
the poorest campesino had 50 head."

Those that are butchered are usually the three-year-old
males, and females too old to reproduce. For example, one
rancher with about 400 head lets his lone cowboy kill one each
month for himself and his family, and sells about seventy-five
each May and December, when they bring about Bs. 3,000
per kilo of live weight at the slaughterhouse. Another rancher,
with a herd of about 15,000 can sell about forty each week.

In the Northeast, the predominant economic activity is
collecting, of rubber and brazil nuts. Although

plantation-grown rubber undercut the boom which this area
enjoyed at the turn of the century, and synthetics are used
increasingly, pure latex is still in demand for special uses,
so it commands a premium sufficient to cover the heavy costs
of transportation.   Labor-intensive methods remain unchanged,
with the collector (siringuero) living in an isolated hut along
the riverbank, from which he goes out daily to collect raw
latex from as many as 300 trees, which grow wild in the
jungle.   The sap trickles into a metal cup, from a deep gash
in the bark.   A good tree may yield nearly one eighth pint
daily; it is dripped to form a ball which is laboriously turned
over a smoky fire to yield a dry compact mass.   The
50-pound balls are exchanged with representatives of commercial houses, who make the rounds monthly in steam-power-
ed launches which are itinerant general stores.   Because
accounts are kept on the company's books, money is rarely
used and the exchanges look like barter, with machetes,
cloth, dried meat, gunpowder and shot, and other manufactured
goods being traded for rubber.

The brazil nut business is generally conducted in a very
similar manner, with scattered collectors working in assigned
areas where the trees grow wild, and exchanging their nuts
with the representative of a paternalistic wholesaler who
occasionally visits them by launch.   Shelling and selling are
done in Riberalta, where Europeans dominate the few commercial enterprises.   A striking innovation has occurred at
Blanca Flor, a few days upstream from Riberalta, where a
producing and marketing cooperative has been formed and is
thriving under the direction of Maryknoll missionaries.   After
a slow start, and continual reinvestment of capital rather
than payment of dividends, the co-op has repaid several large
loans from Point Four and now operates its own processing
plant with 190 employees working fourteen hours daily.
Nearly seven tons of nuts are flown out every other day, and
the people are turning now to housing, lumbering, and other
developmental projects in what is probably the nation's only
successful cooperativa integral (all-purpose cooperative).

There are few manufacturers in either Mojos or Northeast, and commerce is generally in the hands of a few
large-scale operators.   Two or three slaughterhouses
dominate the trade in beef and hides in Mojos; a half dozen
wholesalers handle most of the forest products of the

Northeast.   In the latter instance, Europeans who came during the rubber boom still predominate.   Costs of manufactured goods are high, because of dependence on air freight, and general stores predominate rather than weekly markets, in contrast with much of the rest of the country.

15

—Dwight B. Heath

The Bolivian Oriente is part of an enormous plain which stretches through the center of the entire South American continent. Soils are alluvial in origin, and of varying age. Large areas have been modified by the action of wind and water, and erosion is a continuing process. It is in this area that the prairie, or pampa, of the Gran Chaco merges with the jungle of the Amazon drainage, and these sharply contrasting ecological types both occur here.

Three main types of soil occur in the northern Santa Cruz area. These soil types have been roughly characterized as follows: predominantly deep, well-drained, medium-textured fertile soils; light-textured soils with a wide range of drainage conditions; and predominantly dry sandy soils (Foreign Operations Administration,1954:31). The deep rich soils occur predominantly along waterways and support the luxuriant growth of "high jungle." The second type of soil (locally called pampa negra or pampa isla), lies in broad stretches between waterways and is covered by a variety of vegetation, which appears to vary with the amount of moisture, from pampa grass to scattered brush and small trees sometimes called "low jungle." Dry sandy areas (locally referred to as pampa blanca), support little more than scattered clumps of coarse wiry grass; dust and sand storms are frequent discomforts in areas which lack adequate ground-cover. The people of Santa Cruz savor the irony of a local joke to the effect that one of the major aims of MNR can be so easily achieved in their zone. "Tierra propia para todos!" ("Private land for all!") is a catch-phrase which has brought the Quechuas of the altiplano and valleys rallying to support the MNR, but, according to the Camba, "Here we need only open our mouths to have tierra propia para todos!"

314

TYPES OF LAND USE

Areas of settlement are dispersed and account for only a tiny fraction of the land. There are seven towns in the Santa Cruz area which are bounded, in the classical colonial pattern, by a square which joins the points one kilometer in each cardinal direction from the center of the plaza. Only in the capital city, however, have streets been laid out within the entire urban radius, and only in a few other towns are houses regularly spaced more than one block deep on either side of the main street. The predominant hamlet and homestead patterns of settlement consume only small areas of land in total, and lands in public use include little more than the plaza of each municipality, the few roads, and small governmental holdings such as schools, cemeteries, town-halls, and police stations.

The few industries in the region also occupy little land area. Sugar mills and alcohol distilleries are not large establishments. Lands used for the cultivation of sugar cane are not considered industrial because cultivation is almost always done by people different from those who do the processing of the crop. A few tanneries occupy about a block each, and even the largest brick and tile factory has used less than six hectares in twenty years.

A North American rural sociologist who briefly visited the region quoted the estimate of a "long-term resident in the area, who has traveled extensively throughout the region" that "no more than 2.5 acres per thousand are in cultivation" (Leonard, 1948:26). This estimate was probably low at the time, and certainly now the ratio would be more than twice as large. Even so, farming areas are still scattered throughout expanses of jungle and pampa. The fact that new lands are continually being cleared for agricultural purposes does not mean that the total area of cultivated land is increasing at the same rate. Intensive farming, without fertilization or systematic crop rotation, and the leaching action of heavy seasonal rains are thought to leave farm plots exhausted in three or four years in this subtropical region, so that plots are abandoned and left fallow for as long as eight years before being cleared and used again.

No attempt has been made at irrigation which could
presumably open vast new areas for agriculture. The dry
sandy pampa supports no farming; it is essentially wasteland,
although it provides sparse pasturage for lean herds of
cattle and horses which belong to a few wealthy landowners.
Natural forest products are extracted from the jungle, including lumber and firewood which are consumed at progressive rates throughout the area. These activities are beginning
to leave a scar, although forest and wasteland still predominate in this region of rapidly developing agriculture.

     The broad generalizations which have been made about
land use in this area are more meaningful when related to
specific bodies of data. To this end, the ways in which a few
large and small landholdings are actually utilized by their
owners serve as illustrative examples.

     Monterico is a finca which comprises 2,250 hectares,
after expropriation and reallocation of 210 hectares to a
campesino syndicate. Until enactment of the agrarian reform
in 1953, it was virtually neglected and produced only a little
coffee; recently it has become one of the most progressive
commercial farms in the entire region. In July, 1963, there
were fifty-six hectares planted in sugar cane (including 8 of
two-year old, 18 of one-year old, and 30 newly planted). At
the same time, seven hectares were planted in rice and
fifteen in maize and rice interspersed. Three hectares were
devoted to plantain, and two to plaintain and yuca interspersed.
Houses of the owner and employees, together with outbuildings, surrounded a cleared plot of one hectare where a
few sheep and horses were grazed. Fourteen hectares of
high jungle were being cleared at the time, and twelve lay
fallow and served as pastureland for cattle. Coffee grew in
the shade on six hectares of jungle land which had been
cleared of undergrowth. The long winding road which led to
the settled area at the approximate center of the property
occupied no more than a few hectares, and the rest of the
land remained virgin jungle. During the subsequent twelve
months, the owner planned to clear six more hectares and to
have half planted in sugar cane and half in rice. He had some
doubt that he would be able to get enough manpower to allow
him to expand the area of cultivation. He had eighteen
regular employees at that time, and hired day-laborers
whenever he could.

A neighboring finca, Guapurú, had a resident labor force as large as that at Monterico but the owner had brought only a few of his 3,500 hectares under cultivation. Twenty-six were in sugar cane of various ages, two in citrus, four in plantain, four in yuca, three in maize, five in rice, seven in maize and rice interspersed, and six in shaded coffee. Three hectares were set aside for natural pasturage, and twelve lay fallow after having been farmed for varying lengths of time.

Among other fincas in the zone, the following examples illustrate the variation in land use at that time. One extreme is represented by a property of 2,500 hectares, with only nine in cultivation as follows: 2 1/2 in yuca, 1 1/2 in corn, 1 in plantain, and 5 in planted pasturage. The opposite extreme comprises 6,400 hectares, with 270 in rice, 50 in wheat (a recent experiment), 9 in sugar cane, and 3 in kenaf (another innovation), as well as portions for subsistence farming of yuca and plantain. A finca of 594 hectares had 54 in coffee, 25 in sugar cane, 12 in plantain, 6 in citrus, 5 in yuca, and 40 in fenced pasture, while 20 were being prepared for rice. Another property of 1,704 hectares was using only 30 in sugar cane, 4 in citrus, 4 in coffee, and 1 each in plantain and yuca.

Small plots which are cultivated on a subsistence basis by campesino families rarely are planted in anything but staples. One small farmer of my acquaintance had cleared 3 of his 14 hectares, and half of that was planted in maize interspersed with rice while the rest was in yuca. Another used one hectare for maize and rice, and half a hectare for yuca, while more than 12 hectares remained unclaimed from the jungle.

Few who have recently been granted 50-hectare plots make use of even 20 per cent of the area at any time. The following are typical patterns of use of such areas: three hectares in sugar cane and three in interspersed maize, rice, and plantain on one such holding; another had 2 1/2 hectares in sugar cane, 2 1/2 in plantain, and 1 in corn and yuca; a third devoted 1 1/2 hectares to sugar cane, 3 1/2 to rice, 3 1/2 to maize, and 1 to yuca; another had 3 hectares planted in rice, 1 in yuca, and 1 1/2 in mixed maize and plantain.

The striking difference between Mojos and the other areas of investigation is that as much as one fourth of the land is unusable for any purpose, in terms of the present technology. Even when rivers recede after four or five months of annual flooding, water remains in low spots creating lakes and islands which sometimes endure for years. Unlike Indians in the fifteenth century, contemporary inhabitants do nothing in the way of drainage, levees, and so forth. In some areas, colonies of ants have made the land useless--their nests of cement-like mud are three feet wide and five feet high, scattered at intervals of five or six feet across dozens of hectares, and cannot be broken with hand tools. Narrow strips along the riverbanks (not more than 500 feet wide) are the only areas where even desultory agriculture is practiced. There is abundant water, but no efforts have been made to develop irrigation systems.

Cattleherding is the principal occupation, and the sparse natural vegetation of open range is not supplemented with cultivated pasturage. In June and July cattlemen deliberately fire large areas in the belief that this will help next year's grasses; the land receives no other attention. Holdings are so enormous that the normal unit of measure in Mojos is not the hectare but the estancia (a 25-kilometer square).

In the Northeast, there is little concern for land at all, since collecting of uncultivated forest products is the principal industry. The striking difference in man-land relations is dramatically illustrated in the fact that one rarely refers to measures of area; the significant unit is the estrada, a group of 200 trees which may be concentrated on a few hectares or scattered over a hundred. There are, of course, small plots devoted to subsistence farming and to commercial production of small quantities of rice, plantain, and yuca to feed the few townspeople, but the bulk of the land is not "used" in the sense of serving as productive capital.

TRADITIONAL PATTERNS OF LAND TENURE

Among the few constants which have emerged from cross-cultural studies of economic systems is the fact that property is a social institution (Hallowell, 1943). The importance of land is certainly not intrinsic in the soil as such, nor even in its real or potential value as income-producing capital. Land is the focus of socio-cultural values which are often quite distinct from its economic value for production or consumption. Its fundamental importance, then, tends to be variously defined in different cultural contexts.

Whatever other values may be relevant in the study of land and society, those which refer specifically to tenure unquestionably carry the greatest affective charge throughout most of the world. "The institution of property in land is the focus of attention in land economics," according to a specialist in that field, "since it determines the major relations of man to the land..." (Renne, 1947:8). This way of looking at patterns of land tenure in economic terms is concerned with defining a formal relationship between an individual or corporate group and land as an entity in itself.

The legalistic view of property in land is somewhat broader. In discussing principles of land tenure among the Ashanti of West Africa, Rattray (1929:340) asserted that "...we should cease to regard land as a single immovable entity or possession; it is necessary to consider it as comprising three distinct attributes, or as having three distinct aspects: 1. The land itself, in its most literal sense.... 2. The usufruct, the use to which the soil may be put.... 3. The all-important fact that crops, trees, and even houses, were not regarded as 'part of the realty'."

Both the economic and legalistic views provide valuable ways of looking at patterns of land tenure and of comparing them cross-culturally. My own analysis of the functional interrelations of land and society suggests, however, that land tenure rights do not merely define the exclusive relationships of persons to land as a specific object of property, as the economist views it. Even the outlook of the anthropologically sophisticated legalist, who distinguishes between land, its use, and "improvements" on it, does not subsume many of the characteristics of land tenure relations which have been observed. The need for a somewhat broader concept of land tenure is evident.

The intricacy of covariance in patterns of land tenure and other aspects of social organization suggests that a

feasible approach is to consider land tenure as other kinds
of property ownership, as a relationship involving differential
rights and obligations of all members of a society rather than
as a relationship between one or a few individuals and land as
an enduring, non-human object (Heath, 1960a). Although the
conception of property as a social institution is not a new one,
it is apparent that this aspect of land tenure as a social
relational system has not always been clearly recognized.
Therefore, it is important to consider land tenure as a
category of behavior and values quite distinct from actual
uses to which land is put. The close interrelation of land
tenure with most economic activities in the area, the importance of land tenure in delineating social systems, the value
of land as a basis for political power, and other factors
presaged earlier are more fully explored in this chapter.

Aboriginal Land Tenure

The several Indian tribes who originally occupied the
northern Santa Cruz area have already been described as
typically "Tropical Forest" agriculturalists who lived in
small villages and often supplemented their desultory
farming by hunting and gathering. The only concrete refer-
ences to aboriginal patterns of land tenure are very recent
and refer specifically to the Chiriguano. In that group,
chiefs had eminent domain, although a plot of land that had
once been cultivated by a man belonged to him and his
descendents, according to Métraux (1930). Early conceptions of real property may possibly have been similar to
those of the present-day Siriono, among whom a garden plot
belongs to whoever cleared and planted it, while hunting
grounds, fishing sites, calabash trees, and stands of arrow
reeds are regarded as public property (Holmberg, 1950:21).

Colonial Land Tenure

Land was never scarce in the Oriente, and even today
this area lies on "the pioneer fringe" (Bowman, 1931). The
early Spanish explorers were bent on finding El Dorado and
had no designs on the unspectacular Indians whom they found
scattered across the pampa and through the jungle. When
White colonists began to settle permanently in the area in the
middle of the sixteenth century, however, they sought to

concentrate the native population in permanent settlements
(reducciones) in order to facilitate the imposition of political
and military control, and to create a sedentary labor force.
It was in these new settlements that mestization became widespread, reciprocal acculturation took place between Spaniards
and Indians, and the basis was laid for the emergence of a
Mestizo society and culture.

　　Several types of title to land have been recognized during
the different periods of Bolivian history. Under the Crown,
eminent domain remained predominant, and the allocations
with which victorious conquistadors were usually rewarded
carried no title. Unfortunately, during the early colonial
period the term repartimiento was applied in this region both
to outright grants of land, and to encomiendas. In Santa Cruz,
the latter meaning was plain and, in fact, the allotments were
specifically called "encomiendas" in the earliest letter of
authorization (Mujía, 1914:71). There are other bits of
evidence in this letter which suggest that the original grants
issued at the time of the founding of Santa Cruz were
encomiendas and not land-grants. For example, the author
cited the lack of metals, frequent drought, and the sparse
population as justification for asking that grants in this poor
area be for four or five generations rather than the customary
two. On the same grounds, he requested that colonists be
allowed to exact personal service from the Indians for a
period of twenty years, contrary to the general specifications
of the Law of the Indies (Mujía, 1914:72, 77). The original
list of encomiendas around Santa Cruz gives no indication of
the numbers of Indians involved, but rather lists only the
names of "chieftains" (prencipales) whose "peoples"
(pueblos) and "clans"(?) (ayllos) were put under the charge
of each of the seventy-nine named conquistadors. It was
clear that here, as elsewhere, such an allotment did not give
the encomendero any rights to the land itself, but the conquistadors generally had other ideas.

　　The Bolivian Oriente, like many isolated inland areas,
was characterized by a subsistence economy and produced no
exportable wealth. Because there were no mineral riches
and hardly any commerce, native labor was exploited in terms
of the local barter economy only, and Spaniards were in large
measure dependent upon Indians in order to derive a meager
existence from the land, and could not expect to gain great

wealth from them. The indigenes were considered slaves or serfs, but opportunities for escape were so great that colonists probably did not normally abuse them. In open defiance of Crown policy, there was little attempt in the interior lowlands to indoctrinate the Indians. Wages were rarely paid; and settlers usurped large blocks of land for their own unrestricted use. Soldiers who chose to settle in the area were presumably unchallenged in their authority, and doubtless many assumed the role of encomendero without being officially granted it by the distant administration.

Throughout the sixteenth and seventeenth centuries the predominant kinds of titles to land in this region were eminent domain of the Crown, and the traditional usufruct of indigenous tribes. Without official recognition, however, large tracts of land came under the control of encomenderos and their descendents, and a landed gentry emerged who were concerned with expanding as well as maintaining private estates which they held as if in fee simple, although technically only by sufferance. This conclusion is inferred from the frequent reiteration, in decrees and official letters, of the prohibition on such acquisitions and on the enslavement of the Indians.

The Crown was soon obliged, however, to adjust to the realities of the inland situation, which differed from that of the wealthy coastal and highland areas. Provision was made for legal acquisition of land, but still few in this region availed themselves of the opportunity. Even late in the eighteenth century, a royal inspector related that, "None of the residents have titles to the land which they till, not to the pastures for livestock, since none has had occasion to avail himself of the provisions of the law: they have only precarious claim to their holdings which lasts as long as they graze stock and cultivate fields, otherwise, the first person who comes along takes the opportunity to occupy the land" (Viedma /1787/:76-77). He considered this a fault and attributed to it the fact that "...the city of Santa Cruz, during almost three centuries since its foundation, has not prospered like the rest of Peru: because one cannot dispose of land either in life or in death, this causes people to care little about the betterment and cultivation of /the land/ and to be satisfied with doing only what is necessary from day to day."

In the Mojos region, the situation was strikingly different during the early colonial period. Occasional expeditions northward from Santa Cruz proved by the 1620's that the supposed riches of the area were fables. The first European settlers were Jesuits who began to establish missions half a century later. The introduction of livestock, new arts and crafts, and a benevolent theocracy transformed the Mojo, Baure, and related tribes around Trinidad and the Móvima around Santa Ana, but also laid them open to exploitation when the Jesuits were expelled in 1767 and the missions were taken over by Franciscan curates and civil administrators.

Of the Northeast, we know nothing before the nineteenth century. The Panoan-speaking Pakaguara occupied the area investigated, but the sparse ethnographic information available includes nothing on land tenure.

Modern Land Tenure to 1953

The constitution of the republic, established in 1825, was patterned after that of the United States and recognized several types of ownership, including fee simple, fee limited and leasehold, as well as eminent domain. This feature has been retained in the several revisions of the constitution which have accompanied the manifold revolutions in recent Bolivian history. Four types of land tenure are recognized in the Bolivian legal system: eminent domain, under which the state retains sovereign power over all property for the common good; fee simple, whereby property belongs to an individual without limitation as to heirs or restriction on alienation; leasehold, providing for temporary shift of use without shift of fee to a lessee; and sufferance, possession without leave of the owner. Prior to the agrarian reform nearly all of the land within the Oriente was "baldía," vacant and unclaimed property of the state. Free access to land was tantamount to ownership, and there was not sufficient pressure on the land to prompt people to concern themselves with legal title to holdings which remained uncontested. The few titles which are more than fifty years old are treated almost as relics.

We have already observed that the great majority of the people of northern Santa Cruz, of both the upper and lower classes, are agriculturalists who derive their income

immediately from the land. In such a situation, patterns of
land tenure and use play an important role in determining the
organization of social relationships and the integration of
other aspects of the culture. Before agrarian reform, five
types of farmers were distinguished on the basis of modes
of land tenure and use: finquero, tenant, small farmer,
squatter, and renter. The relationship of these types are
briefly discussed below. The many changes which have
occurred during the last decade will be treated separately.

Finqueros

A finquero was an upper-class agriculturalist who owned
a finca, in local usage, a farm where hired laborers other
than the family of the owner were resident throughout the
year. Probably the smallest such establishment comprised
twenty hectares; the largest, more than 50,000.

As described in Chapter 13, finqueros normally derived
not only an income from the land, but much of their prestige
as well. Absentee landlords were unknown, and the fortunes
of "an old family" and their land were inextricably identified
with each other. The traditional wealth of the local upper
class was singularly relative and restricted to the immediate
social context, and the situation was such that a very small
real income could provide a comfortable way of life for
finqueros whose wealth would count for little anywhere else.
The description of patterns of land use above illustrates the
fact that only a small portion of the total area of most fincas
was in cultivation, and large expanses remained undeveloped
jungle or pampa.

Land itself had almost no resale value in rural Santa
Cruz prior to the agrarian reform, and its non-negotiable
value derived from two major considerations. In the first
place, as long as a landlord had access to an adequate labor
force, control of land allowed production of most goods required to maintain the finca and the people on it, and a small
surplus could be exchanged in local markets for those few
goods which the finca did not produce. Furthermore, the
feeling of security derived from self-sufficiency prompted
many finqueros to spend almost all of their current income
to maintain their traditional way of life. Since the difference
between the local upper class and others in terms of material

property, diet, education, and other goods was more
quantitative than qualitative, leisure was the greatest luxury
of the upper class and a surfeit of labor was the major item
of conspicuous consumption. Most of the finqueros' employees
were tenants.

Tenants

In local usage, a tenant (jornalero) was a year-round
resident laborer on a finca. Wages and perquisites have
already been discussed. During the pre-reform period, most
tenants were also allowed to cultivate small plots of land for
their own use. Each tenant was offered as much jungle land
as he wanted to clear and cultivate during his free time--
rarely more than one hectare, and often nothing at all. Such
allotments carried usufruct privileges only; the tenant was
free to use the land as his own for a few years but had no
legal title or permanent rights to it. All preparing, seeding,
weeding, and harvesting of such plots was done by the tenant
and his family. Implements used usually belonged to the
finca, but the finquero had no claim to the produce unless he
had contributed the seed. Often, however, a tenant preferred
to forfeit 10 per cent of his harvest in repayment of seed
rather than to make the original cash investment at planting
time. Produce from such a garden usually served to feed a
tenant's family on Sundays and holidays when the finquero
did not provide food, and if a small surplus remained, it
could be sold or bartered. Such a liberal policy of tenancy
was feasible only because labor was more scarce than land
in this sparsely populated region. A Bolivian economist has
remarked that "Santa Cruz is one of the few places in the
world where the work of a farm laborer is much more
valuable--within a short time--than a hectare of land. The
shortage of labor and the abundance of land are such that
there is no one who would pay 10,000 Bolivian pesos for a
league of good fertile land situated on the outskirts of the
city, while, on the other hand, the same amount or more
which a tenant had contracted in debt would be paid in order
to have his labor" (Sanjines, 1943:393). Tenants made their
living by cultivating the finqueros' fields; farming for themselves was, at best, a spare-time supplement to their income. Most of the campesinos who make a living at farming
on their own behalf are called small farmers.

Small Farmers

Small farmers (pequeños proprietarios) are those Camba
who own homesteads (quintas) which are farmed by members
of the family, sometimes with occasional help from day-laborers. Such holdings are scattered throughout the countryside and, before agrarian reform, rarely exceeded twenty
hectares. Usually, in fact, their total area was more nearly
eight or ten hectares, less than half of which was under cultivation. The ideal of every small farmer is self-sufficiency,
but this is rarely realized and it is normal for them to take
occasional wage-work in order to earn cash. Staple foods
are their major crops and usually the only ones. Because
they cannot afford to store goods after harvest, it is the
small farmer who sell when prices are low and must often
buy back the same produce several months later at much
higher prices.

Nevertheless, to have control of even a small portion of
land is a source of prestige as well as satisfaction and can
lead to a degree of economic security. Most campesinos
agree that "the best is to have a little plot of your own and
have no boss /literally: patrón/. It's a good thing to work
your own land on your own account instead of always cultivating someone else's fields for theirs." Nevertheless,
despite the fact that a superabundance of land was easily
and inexpensively available, many men remained tenants on
fincas because "...there's also a danger of being fully independent. You spend everything to get tools and seed; you
spend many months clearing land, building a hut and a fence;
and then you still aren't sure of a good harvest. There are
droughts, pests, sickness--all these are enemies of the
lone campesino. If one could only have security as a small
farmer!" Although the actual income of a small farmer may
have been less and his labor expenditure and risks greater
than those of a tenant, his apparent independence was the
ideal of most Camba. Despite this fact, small farmers comprised only a small portion of the lower class until the early
1960's.

Renters

Although vast areas of land could still be had for the
taking on the fringes of the northern Santa Cruz area, a

number of campesinos rented small plots on a crop-sharing basis before the agrarian reform. A renter (inquilino) was usually a commuter farmer, living in a hut in or near a village. He would contract with a finquero to rent a plot of from one to three hectares, as near as possible to his home, and would walk as much as eight miles each way whenever he went to work his fields. In such a contract, the finquero supplied only the land; tools, seeds, and labor were all provided by the renter. Rental rates were liberal, in the view of the local people as well as in cross-cultural perspective: 10 per cent of the harvest went to the landowner and the rest belonged to the renter. A renter, like a tenant, enjoyed only the privilege of usufruct, and had no permanent rights to the land or to any improvements which he might make on it. One informant reflected nostalgically, "It was a good way to work. I could still live in town where my wife could sell dinners in the market to earn a little, and I worked as a day-laborer sometimes when we needed money for something. And renting let me be near enough the market to sell a part of the harvest. Sure, there's plenty of land way out in the jungle, but there's no way to carry things out. What good is a big harvest if you can't sell or trade a little?" Few tenants have the capital or the initiative to become renters, although they envied the relative freedom of the latter group. Finqueros were glad to have renters work their land because, however small their contribution, it was virtually something for nothing; the finquero invested neither capital nor labor for the tithe of the harvest which was his, but only provided land which would otherwise have lain idle. Renters themselves were mostly men who wanted greater independence than they could have had as tenants, who chose not to be small farmers, or who could not afford to start their own farms. Another group of campesinos who shared these characteristics but who were even more assertive in their independence were squatters.

Squatters

A small minority of the people in the Oriente have always been pioneers, men who are continually extending the frontiers of settlement. Most of these men were squatters (tolerados) who carved small homesteads out of the jungle on the unoccupied fringes of large fincas, and farmed them as their own until dispossessed. Remote from market towns, they

were usually almost self-sufficient. They used the same
method as did savages for getting goods which they needed but
could not themselves produce; that is, they hired themselves
out as day-laborers on fincas during critical periods in the
agricultural cycle. Finqueros were glad to have squatters on
their land who provided a source of labor and often made
some improvements, such as planting fruit trees, building
huts, and so forth, on the small plots of land which would
otherwise have lain idle. Two or three hectares are as
much as a squatter could cultivate in a year, and when the
soil was depleted he would usually move on to another site
rather than stay to clear other fields near the same place,
where the game had become chary of his hunting skill.

Interrelations of Land Tenure Patterns

It is important to note that the great majority of people
in the Oriente, including finqueros, were technically landless
until enactment of the agrarian reform, inasmuch as few held
legal titles to the areas which they used and claimed as their
own.

A demographic study noted that:

The abundance of land and the dearth of population
in the Department of Santa Cruz have not been con-
ducive to interest in and concern for land surveys,
sound property titles, and an accurate system for
determining exact and permanent property boundaries. As a result, much of the land in the
/northern Santa Cruz/ area is held through little
more legal authority than physical possession.
Little less than threat of actual dispossession
drives anyone to seek sound legal title and definite
boundaries for his property (Leonard, 1948:66).

Free access to land had been tantamount to ownership, and
the frontiers of the region had been expanded through simple
appropriation of land from savages, with no concern for the
acquisition of legal title.

Some people within the region, to be sure, had bought
their land or received it from the government. After each
of Bolivia's many international wars, areas of land were

ceded as compensation for military service, and "to those who want to work them." These grants, however, failed to accomplish the avowed purpose of stimulating settlement and agricultural development in the Oriente, and most of the land remained unproductive jungle or pampa, while small plots came under desultory cultivation by itinerant squatters. Late in the nineteenth century, public lands were sold cheaply at auction, but even so, few people came to the lowland plains from the densely populated highland areas of western Bolivia, and few of the local people themselves bothered to confirm the rights which they felt they had to land. During the first few decades of this century, the federal government even let down some of the restrictions on immigration in the hope that European colonists would stimulate development of the eastern lowlands. U. S. Senator "Alfalfa Bill" Murray's pioneer outpost in the Chaco is a well-known failure; Belgian and German experiments in colonization just east of the Camba region likewise ended in retreat to the cities (Torrico, 1956). The few individuals who did accept federal land grants or who bought land from the government were virtually the only ones who, in a technical legal sense, held land in fee simple. Most of the finqueros and small farmers who "owned" land, in actuality only held state land under sufferance even though they regarded it as though they had rights in fee simple and their claims were generally respected. Renters, of course, held small plots in leasehold only, as did tenants; squatters occupied land only on sufferance.

The isolation of the northern Santa Cruz area allowed survival there until this decade of many social and cultural patterns from colonial times. Many of these were intimately related to patterns of land tenure. By monopolizing land in proximity to market centers, finqueros were able to increase costs and risks for the individual who remained independent. Using the slash-and-burn technique of landclearing and associated primitive methods of cultivation, a small individual family would require, over a period of years, access to at least eight hectares. If a campesino could neither rent nor buy land nor claim squatters' rights, he was more likely to work for a finquero than if any of those other alternatives were open. Because they held effective control of bulk of production and distribution, finqueros were also able in large measure to regulate prices and to dominate the market. By investing even small amounts of capital in buildings, tools, fencing, and so forth, they were able to offer greater security to a tenant than he might have as a squatter or small farmer, assuming these capital outlays himself. Renting land became feasible as population increased, and small portions let in leasehold brought nominal income from towndwellers who would presumably not be available as tenants, nor competitive as small farmers or squatters. In these ways, finqueros and campesinos held complementary statuses on the basis of patterns of land tenure.

Elaborate patterns of social relationships also developed within the lower class on the basis of different patterns of relationship to land. The tenant, numerically predominant, remained a free agent unless bound by debt. But he rarely attained the courage or the capital to change his status. To become a squatter required capital (for tools, landclearing seed, and so forth), as well as courage to assume the risks which are the price of independence; to become a renter required at least as much capital and some courage; while to become a small farmer required more of both. Lacking these, the tenant remained content with usufruct rights in leasehold in exchange for his labor. Small farmers became fairly numerous as well, and held remote scattered homesteads in fee simple. Their risks and capital investments were relatively high. Renters could operate on a smaller outlay of capital, and their proximity to market and opportunities for earning supplementary income somewhat lessened for them the economic risks involved in subsistence farming. Nevertheless, with only leasehold privileges to land, they were subject to the conditions laid down by the landlord. Squatters holding land only on sufferance were also at the mercy of the landlord, and their capital investment was not negligible.

Not until 1953 did the threat of actual dispossession become immediate and widespread, through enactment of the federal land reform law. The agrarian reform was intended to effect marked changes in patterns of land tenure and use throughout the nation and served that purpose in parts of the Oriente.

Pre-Reform Land Tenure in Mojos and the Northeast

As is true of the rest of the Oriente, our understanding

of aboriginal land tenure patterns in Mojos and the Northeast
is fragmentary and inferential. Intensive agriculture seems
to have prevailed in Mojos during pre-Columbian times,
although it is now found nowhere in either region.

During the period of Jesuit dominance, Indian reservations
were generally held by the order and cultivated or grazed
collectively according to work assignments made periodically
by priest administrators (Tormo, 1966). Land reverted to
the Crown when the Jesuits were expelled, and their Franciscan successors never succeeded in reestablishing many of
the cooperative communities. With the formation of the
Republic, little changed in these areas except the name of
the government, which remained remote. The few ranchers
who claimed vast areas of Mojos had only to drive off the
Indians; there were few competitors for land in an area where
effective control is even today tantamount to ownership, and
fences and titles are still exceptional.

In the Northeast, unlike highland Bolivia, land seems
never to have been a focus of concern. Population is so
sparse that aboriginal cultures of many nomadic hunting and
gathering tribes are still little affected. Collectors of
rubber and brazil nuts live in isolated homesteads scattered
along the rivers, which are the routes of transportation, and
rarely cultivate more than a tiny kitchen-garden for their
own families. The trees occur at random in the jungle, and
the significant unit of measure is the estrada (200 trees),
which had no direct relation to actual land area. Immense
blocks of land were granted or sold by the Bolivian government to commercial enterprises during the nineteenth
century, and individual estradas were assigned as concessions
to workers who contracted to work for a particular company.

From the latter part of the nineteenth century, virtually
all of Mojos and the Northeast came under control of the
firm of Sáurez Brothers, headed by the hardy Cruceño,
Nícolas Suárez. They owned "uncounted millions of
hectares of land, and uncounted millions of cattle." Their
control over land and people varied locally, but in many
areas "don Nícolas ruled like a king." The collapse of the
rubber boom made the Northeast suddenly almost worthless;
the price of leather plummeted after World War I, so that
wild cattle of Mojos had no value on the world market; the

dynamic leader of the firm died. "The Suárez Empire" was collapsing when the threat of expropriation and political persecution at the hands of the MNR led to its complete dissolution.

LAND REFORM AND SOCIAL REVOLUTION

Although our research concern was much broader than land reform, it is not surprising that this event (or, more appropriately, this process) was considered crucial by Bolivians of all statuses, and it naturally became focal in our understanding of patterns and problems of land tenure and use.

In 1957, I was not at all sanguine about the extent or variety of effects achieved by the agrarian reform; now I am struck by several large-scale changes which affect residence patterns, labor relations, marketing practices, and several other aspects of culture in the Oriente.

The Agrarian Reform Decree

It is perhaps ironic that one of the few comprehensive agrarian reforms in world history should have been enacted in a nation as large as Spain and France combined, where more than one half of the total area is virtually uninhabited. The sparsely populated Oriente might seem a singularly improbable site for wholesale expropriation and reallocation of land, but in 1953 just such a program was initiated. At the same time, the northern Santa Cruz area was suddenly exposed to a number of diverse intrusive influences, many of them organized to effect rapid cultural change, especially in land tenure and use. The national agrarian reform described in more detail in Chapter 2, had among its explicit fundamental objectives the abolition of latifundia, commercialization of agriculture, and integration of the Oriente with the rest of the country.

It should not be surprising that actual outcomes of agrarian reform did not in all respects conform with its avowed aims. Furthermore, a number of changes in land tenure patterns have taken place which cannot be attributed directly to the law but which result from a variety of

simultaneous economic, political, and social innovations.
Nevertheless, it is both convenient and meaningful to discuss
actual changes in the Oriente in terms of the fundamental
objectives outlined in the decree.

Changing Patterns Since the Reform

Reallocation of Land

First among the aims of the agrarian reform was "to
allot arable land to the campesinos, who do not have it, or
have very little..." (Preamble). Although finqueros in the
Oriente were not in physical danger as were their counterparts
in the highlands, they perceived the threat of dispossession
from the state lands which they held under sufferance. One
of the earliest outcomes of the agrarian reform in this region
was, therefore, a change in the traditional laissez-faire
attitude toward land and a new concern with the formalization
of rights to land. Where physical possession had long been
the sole basis for "ownership," finqueros realized that their
undocumented claims would be indefensible if challenged. A
convenient expedient was devised in the period of anxious
uncertainty immediately after the enactment of the reform.
Some were proud of their ingenuity when they explained, for
example,

> The majority of us never had legal titles before
> the reform. Then we were afraid of losing our
> properties all of a sudden. What was there to do?
> Simple--secure titles. So we talked with the
> politicians--the judge, the notary, the tax
> collector--and we arranged it so that we could
> buy official titles, with full legal appearances...
> with previous dates. So we bought forged docu-
> ments showing our titles from ten, twenty,
> sometimes forty years previous. And they
> weren't too dear. The politicians had plenty
> of business so they charged only some Bs. 1,000
> /less than $.20/ per hectare. That was cheap
> enough for security at the time, and we didn't
> know what was going to happen in those days.

The ruling against retention of "absolutely" rented land
(Preamble) has been generally interpreted as a blanket

ruling that a landlord should forfeit to tenants the plots which
they had previously worked for their own families (Article 78),
as well as losing by expropriation those areas which had been
leased to renters. Although this has given land to many
peasants throughout much of the country, it has had the
opposite effect in the Oriente where many finqueros no longer
allow their tenants to cultivate small plots for their own use,
or lease to renters, or even tolerate squatters, for fear that
a campesino might claim right to title of the land on grounds
of having worked it personally. Leasehold and sufferance,
which in pre-reform days were the predominant forms of
tenancy in the Santa Cruz region, have, therefore, been displaced by fee simple, which suddenly gained importance.

One of the most liberal of the finqueros put it this way:

I would like to let my tenants have their own land.
I used to give /the use of/ land to anyone who
wanted it--as much as he could cultivate. It was
good for them and it was good for me. They could
have extra food for their families or for sale.
They cleared the land, and sometimes would sell
to me, at wholesale. One man seeded plantain--
two hectares--more than I had myself. And I used
to buy plantain from him to use right here on the
finca. Others would sell their products in town; I
would let them use the oxcart and team on Sundays
and holidays. But I can't do that anymore. I
wouldn't dare! If I let a campesino have a plot of
land for this year, next year he would certainly
go to the Agrarian Reform Judge in Montero and
claim it as his own. Things have come to a
pretty pass regarding land! We /finqueros/
want to help our people, but it's dangerous. They
used to be humble and nice, and some of them
still are. Not like the kollas. But with this /MNR/
government, the campesino is always right, and
some of them sense this new power, become drunk
with it, and are abusive. It's a curious thing that
anyone should have to be afraid to help his
employees, but in many respects we just don't
dare.... It's the same with renters and squatters;
we can no longer let them use our land, or we'd
lose it.

During the early years of the reform most of the
campesinos resented this withdrawal of land from use for
rent or tenancy. Since 1958, however, improved roads and
newly opened areas on the northern frontier have encouraged
campesinos to secure plots of their own through the reform,
from SNRA or CBF, and most of the former tenants have
become independent small farmers.

The specifications of efficient land use and of excess
holdings are not clearly spelled out in the decree, although
they are crucial in determining the eligibility of land for
expropriation. Efficiency is only partial basis of the key
distinction between agricultural enterprises which are
favored by the law and latifundia which the state declines to
recognize. Virtually every finca in the Santa Cruz area
lacked at least one of the criteria of the favored agricultural
enterprise, until rapid and widespread commercialization of
agriculture in the mid-1950's.

All of the northern Santa Cruz area lies within the zones
where maximum allowable extensions are largest. For
example, with reference to small property, this region lies
within the "Santa Cruz Subzone" of the "Subtropical Zone,"
where the maximum is fifty hectares (Article 15). The
zoning is the same for the medium property, which here has
a maximum extension of 500 hectares (Article 16); whereas
the agricultural enterprise is within the "Tropical and Subtropical Zones" of the "Eastern Region," where 2,000
hectares are allowable (Article 17).

As described in Chapter 2, the slow mechanics of
expropriation are set into motion only in response to the
filing of a specific brief by individuals who hope to be awarded
the land in question. Poor and uneducated campesinos were
never in a position to make any such formal bid for land, so
representatives of the MNR early organized them into
syndicates, and won land in the names of these corporate
bodies for distribution to members.

Partisan favoritism is plainly evident in the administration of the law, as indicated earlier. The implementation of
the agrarian reform decree was long in the hands of local
and regional agrarian reform judges who were appointed by
the MNR, and membership in the CNRA, which is at once a

planning and administrative body and the highest court of
appeal in land cases, is also appointive. In a country where
government has traditionally been strongly partisan, it is
not surprising that this affects the application of the law. We
have already noted that syndicates rarely petitioned for land
from estates belonging to MNR supporters, even when these
had vast expanses of land not in use. Until the 1964 revolution, expropriation had been almost exclusively from
supposed "enemies of the party," while partisan sympathizers
had been generally protected. Perhaps the most striking
example of this favoritism which I encountered was near
Montero, where one finquero lost almost one third of his 750
hectares to a syndicate, even though he lived there and had
invested heavily in making it a truly mechanized agricultural
enterprise. On the other hand, when a few individuals
independently applied for portions of Providencia, an underdeveloped 6,500-hectare latifundium to the north, their
petitions were refused by CNRA and the agrarian judge in
Montero was berated by the Minister of Interior (among others)
for having forwarded the briefs, and was exhorted to provide
the owner "full guarantees." In discussing these cases, I
asked the local agrarian judge about the clear statement in
the decree that "Whatever difficulty may arise in the application of the present Law will be resolved taking into account
primarily the interest of the landless peasants and of small
property owners; and subsequently, with consideration for
production, that of the medium property and of the agricultural enterprise" (Article 174). He explained in great detail
how political affiliation of landowners, not infrequently
supported by bribes, was the most important consideration
in applying the expropriative phase of the law.

In many instances, politicians in the city of Santa Cruz
have misused the land reform to their own ends. During the
early months after enactment, choice house lots were often
expropriated and awarded to relatives or friends of politicians, although they immediately proceeded to build rather
than to farm. Abuses were so numerous and so flagrant and
objections were so strenuous that the President felt obliged
to censure the violators as follows: "I have been informed
that indiscriminate reallotments of land have been made
with no consideration for legal norms, and of a special
ambitious rivalry among those who have undertaken this
without authorization.... The processes of affectation must

necessarily be undertaken by competent authorities and not by demagogues who seek only self-aggrandizement.... All those who have assumed the allotting of land, as well as those who receive it, without due process, will be prosecuted" (Consejo Nacional de Reforma Agraria, 1954). Such abuses have, in fact, not occurred since then, but the previous offenses have not been righted.

In stating the primary objective of the agrarian reform as the allocation of land to landless campesinos, the qualifying phrase is added: "...on the condition that they work it" (Preamble), with the further specification that the new owner is to forfeit land if he has not begun agricultural work "within two years" (Article 77). Grants of land under the reform are awarded, therefore, in fee limited tenure. However, it is not made clear when this period of grace commences. Even members of the legal staff of SNRA did not agree whether the deadline should be computed from the time when the local agrarian judge awards provisional possession to campesinos, pending settlement of the appeal (Article 59), or from the time of the granting of final titles to new owners.

In the northern Santa Cruz area, where allotments are fairly large (normally fifty hectares), merchants, mechanics, and other citydwellers have applied for plots which are to be cleared and cultivated by hired labor. Near Montero less than half of the jungle land awarded to the Monterico Campesino Syndicate was divided among members; union leaders are using the larger portion only as a source of readily salable lumber and firewood. Even among the fourteen recipients of land, only three had begun cultivation six years later.

In summary, the outcome of the reallocation of land in the Santa Cruz region reflects the fact that the MNR party used differential application of the law to serve its own ends. Increasingly since the late 1950's, campesinos have been benefited by grants of land until only a few remain tenants on large fincas, and the majority have become small farmers on their own land. Individual campesinos have usually applied for land through local syndicates.

Development of Indian Communities

The second aim of the reform is irrelevant here because there are no indigenous communities in the Oriente.

Revision of Agricultural Labor Relations

Another fundamental objective of the land reform decree was "to free rural laborers from their condition as serfs, proscribing gratuitous personal services and obligations..." (Preamble). This part of the law has far less significance in the Oriente than in the rest of the nation. The Santa Cruz area and scattered towns in the northern Oriente are unusual in Bolivia for the degree to which mestization has progressed, and for the relative homogeneity of finquero and campesino subcultures. For several years, most campesinos in the Oriente have been free of the quasi-feudal oppression to which their Quechua and Aymara counterparts in the western portion of the country were subjected. It has already been noted that tenants in this area were not bound to a finca, except occasionally by debt, and that they always enjoyed great freedom of movement within the northern Santa Cruz zone. Absentee landlords were rare and numbers of tenants small among the Camba; thus finquero-tenant relations tended to be personal even if they were not always warm. The practice of paying wages in cash to agricultural employees is not new here either, even though the "real income" consisted more of other perquisites. Among the fringe benefits which usually constituted a value greater than the wages were food for the tenant and his family on days when he worked (or during illness), as well as housing throughout his employment. Wives and children of tenants were also paid in cash for whatever work they might do for the finquero, such as helping to harvest rice or coffee, doing housework or laundry, and so forth. Most finqueros provided minor medical care for their tenants, and supported employees who were ill or too old to work, and a few let their workers cut firewood and sell it in town. All of these features stand in marked contrast with the pre-reform situation in the highlands; and the achievement of similar agricultural labor relations there was a major plank in the MNR's program of democratization.

The Camba have distinct and explicit conceptions of

ideal agricultural labor relations. We have already noted
that the ideal of campesinos has long been to attain the
independence of the small farmer, but that few tenants ever
ventured to start out on their own until the mid-1950's. For
them, the security of "resources in people" was more important than security in property resources, following Wolf's
phraseology (1957:10). Such dependent men looked for
benevolent paternalism in an employer, and held that "...a
good patrón is one who cares for his tenants in all respects.
Not only in respect to work, but in other things too. If an
employee is sick, he will cure him; if an employee has
trouble with the police, he will advise him; if an employee
needs money, he will lend some. A good patrón takes an
interest in the families of his tenants and helps them in any
way he can." Few finqueros met these specifications, but
those who valued their reputation as "good" employers and
who appreciated having tenants stay for any length of time
often approached the ideal. Good will between employer and
employees is important in an area of chronic shortage of
labor and only finqueros who had bad reputations among local
campesinos were obliged to resort to hiring a different group
of savages each year.

After losing their tenants, finqueros had to look elsewhere for a labor supply. It is in some respects a fortunate
coincidence that a new pool of unemployed sugar cane cutters
was forming at the same time elsewhere in the country.
Large numbers of kolla campesinos from Tarija and southern
Potosí had for many years gone to northern Argentina to work
in the cane harvest, but new restrictions in the mid-1950's
cut down on this "wet-back" style of transhumance. Labor
contractors now supply large numbers of skilled workers
who earn double the pay of the former Camba tenants but
who work at double their pace; and the finquero has no
year-round responsibility to these migrant laborers.

The division of labor recognizes differential skills. Although the migrant workers excel at cane cutting, "there is
nothing in the world like a Camba campesino for landclearing and weeding." For this reason many former
tenants who are now small farmers during most of the year,
return to the fincas of their former employers as day-laborers (or on a job-contract basis) to clear and burn new farmland and to weed young crops. In this way, they earn

much-needed cash and the finquero gets good work at reasonable rates.

The kollas who are brought by labor contractors to work in the sugar cane harvest stay only six months, after which they return to their homes in the remote southern highlands. They work hard and fast to cut, trim, and load about two tons of cane daily (twice what the Camba peons used to accomplish) for Bs. 10,000 per ton--about twice the pay of Cambas at 10,000 per tarea. By so doing, they earn nearly three times as much as the few Camba campesinos who have stayed on fincas and who are paid about Bs. 200,000 monthly for weeding, clearing land, cutting firewood, and so forth.

Now that the Camba are mostly small farmers rather than tenants, the cost of labor has soared for other jobs as well as harvesting sugar cane. For example, weeding now costs Bs. 10,000 per tarea, although just five years ago that was a day's work at a wage of Bs. 2,000 plus meals. The cutting of firewood is no longer commercially feasible except for those who have transportation, because labor costs Bs. 8,000 per tarea, and freight is at least Bs. 2,000 per ton from a finca to the sugar mill which pays only Bs. 20,000 per ton.

Relationships between the finquero and both kinds of employees (kolla migrant workers, and Camba part-time laborers) are generally impersonal and businesslike, with few vestiges of the former paternalism. Increased cash wages have superseded all perquisites; workers are neither resident throughout the year, nor dependent on the finquero for medical, legal, educational, or other services. Even the classic gesture of respect--the peon's doffing his hat when replying to the patrón--is fast disappearing.

Just as tenants rated employers with respect to specific criteria, finqueros also used to evaluate employees on the basis of certain preferences. "A tenant should work hard enough and know how to do things. He should be strong, and amiable. The worst thing you have to watch is stealing..." according to most finqueros. Cleanliness and humility were also highly valued. Such criteria no longer apply and kollas are hired who are said to "...work hard, but are dirty and

live like beasts. " The majority of Camba campesinos who
used to serve as tenants were competent in the traditional
agricultural methods and worked slowly but steadily at
whatever they were assigned. The kolla migrant harvesters,
by contrast, work hard and fast in order to accumulate money
to take home with them for the other half of the year.

Throughout other rural areas of Bolivia where armed
campesino syndicates were long under the leadership of
MNR organizers, agrarian reform even more drastically
upset the traditional social structure, and anarchy set the
stage for demagogy. Camba campesinos are less militant
than many of the kollas , in large part because they have
less reason to rebel against the oppression of abusive landlords. There are a few of the lower class who sometimes
become bold because they only recently achieved any voice
in political affairs and felt confident of MNR support. The
uneasiness expressed by a finquero who said he was so
afraid of the new power of his employees that he did not
dare to rent them land illustrates a dilemma which never
interfered with more than the small nonpartisan portion of
the upper class.

In brief, the movement for reform in agricultural labor
relations was slow in starting in the Santa Cruz area, but
has rapidly gained momentum. Tenants in this region had
long enjoyed the benefits of supposedly revolutionary reforms
in the legal status of agricultural employees; the peculiar
early colonial history of the area may in large part account
for the fact that quasi-feudal relationships did not occur
there, and local campesinos did not share the enthusiasm of
their kolla counterparts who found in the agrarian reform a
measure of liberation from traditional servile oppression.
The exodus from tenantry was not an antagonistic reaction,
and the new and different social system is already functioning
effectively.

Stimulation of Agricultural Development

The agrarian reform decree was also intended "to
stimulate greater productivity and commercialization of
the agricultural industry..." (Preamble). It is unfortunate
that data are so inadequate, but most qualified observers
believe that only after a decade of severe decline did national

agricultural production approach pre-reform levels. In the
Oriente especially, agricultural development--except for the
increased production of rice and sugar cane--continues to lag
behind official hopes and expectations.

The reform movement proposed to facilitate the investment of new capital, but capital investment does not flourish
in a climate of nationalization and expropriation. In the
Oriente, where fincas were run by the resident owner with
hired labor, liquid capital was scarce. The level terrain
lends itself to the use of agricultural machines which Point
Four rented at infinitesimal rates, and many owners there
chose to stay on the land and to transform their farms into
"agricultural enterprises" in order to defend their title to
large areas, but this incentive to stimulate capital investment soon failed because of inefficient and biased administration of the law (cf. Chapter 14). The campesinos who
were awarded land had no liquid assets to invest.

Where private enterprise was lacking, projects aimed at
increasing domestic food production were financed by national
and even international organizations. These ventures enjoyed
only limited success. The rice-hulling mill near Montero and
a yuca-flour mill near Santa Cruz, both established and supported by CBF, operated at increasing deficits until abandoned
around 1959. Enormous sums have been invested by the United
States to stimulate agricultural development within the region,
but results have been negligible, except with rice cultivation
throughout the north, including some large mechanized fincas
around Portachuelo, and with sugar cane production especially
around Montero.

Small and medium properties are explicitly exempted from
expropriation, but such farms are hardly likely "to stimulate
greater productivity and commercialization of agriculture,"
because of their limited scope as defined by the law. The
finqueros argue "...what can the campesino in his little plot
contribute to the national deficit in food production? The
majority cultivate just enough for their families. Then, if
they're lucky, maybe a little more for market. But not
enough to help the country. For that, you have to use large
fincas." Also, the guarantees for medium properties have
not always been adhered to. Around Cotoca, for example,
a large project administered by the United Nations for

resettlement of Quechua Indians was established on land
which had been expropriated from farmers who were
cultivating medium properties and who still resent having
been given remote jungle lands in exchange.

Another means proposed for stimulating agriculture is
"...developing agricultural cooperativism." Within the
northern Santa Cruz region, few cooperatives have been
attempted except by Italian and Japanese immigrants. These
ventures enjoyed marked success, in contrast to the many
experimental cooperatives established among Bolivian
campesinos throughout the valleys and altiplano. There
has been little effort, to date, to organize cooperatives
among local finqueros or campesinos, and once established
they have not been successful. In some instances cooperatives exist in name only and have the organization and
function of a syndicate. In a few other instances, cooperatives have become a variant of the old "protection racket."

In view of the support of cooperatives by the Bolivian
government and AID programs as a basic means of
stimulating economic development, it is perhaps unfortunate that the scepticism of Bolivian campesinos is so
well-founded in sad experience. An example of disillusionment with cooperatives occurred during the period of
research. According to the people of Santa Cruz--in all
socio-economic levels--the AID-sponsored rice cooperative
CONCA (Cooperativa Nacional para Comercialización de
Arroz, National Cooperative for Commercialization of
Rice) had promised to pay Bs. 15,000 per arroba for rice.
In June, 1963, the organization was in debt for Bs. 150 million
and declined to buy rice. Farmers who had planted large
quantities in anticipation of high supported prices resented
that the sale of their rice in the glutted market did not even
reimburse their costs. U. S. administrators denied any
significant disappearance of funds, or any promise to pay
the set price except for a limited quantity of rice. Furthermore, they took pains to point out that the shortage of funds
for CONCA was caused by budgetary revisions enforced from
Washington, rather than by miscalculation on their part.
These defenses enjoyed no acceptance among Bolivians,
however, and "the CONCA fiasco" continued to be a focus
of anti-U. S. sentiment, even after debts were paid. It
is also cited by Bolivians as an example of the supposedly

inevitable failure of cooperatives as contrasted with private enterprise.

"Lending technical aid" is also suggested in the decree, to stimulate agricultural development. Responsibility for this has been assigned to SAI under the Bolivian Ministry of Agriculture and Point Four. Apparent lack of interest in the needs or desires of campesinos have caused the program to have little effect on subsistence farming. Most commercial farmers have realized little more benefit apart from their belief and unsatisfactory ventures into mechanized land-clearing. Personnel at an agricultural experiment station maintained by SAI near Saavedra claim to be hampered by lack of funds. In general, they have concentrated their efforts to date on growing seed of a strain of maize which is too hard for customary use, and testing various strains of forage although they have no livestock with which to experiment. The model finca which had been under construction for several years near Montero was finally abandoned under Congressional fire (see United States Senate, 1960), and was given to the Salesian Fathers. In 1957, none of the staff of Point Four spoke Spanish, so they avoided contact with local people; during 1963, a Spanish-speaker arrived, the first North American SAI representative since the large-scale withdrawal from the area in 1958. This man unfortunately knew nothing about tropical agriculture and specifically declined to work with campesino syndicates, although these are the groups most interested in the information and advice that agricultural extension agents presumably have to offer.

Although credit programs were administered by Point Four until July, 1963, campesinos feel that class distinction has denied them credit at reasonable rates for farming. This is invariably the first lack mentioned by campesinos; and a program of small-scale credit could not only ease the incredibly difficult first year of the small farmer, but would probably also bring many more of them into fuller participation in the market. In contrast, many finqueros used to take Point Four agricultural loans and use the money for other purposes, exclaiming that "The supervised credit of Point Four makes gifts of money--not loans. They don't even know that with inflation as it is /in 1956/, to take a loan is good speculation without having to do anything. It costs nothing; in fact, what you pay back, including interest, is worth less than the initial loan." This is no longer the case, and more loans are actually being used to stimulate agricultural production now, but the delinquency rate remains high.

Conservation of Natural Resources

Although in the decree all unoccupied land beyond municipal boundaries, as well as all forests, are declared property of the state (Article 9), people in the Santa Cruz area do not respect eminent domain and continue to usurp unclaimed areas as their own. The continual northward expansion of the frontier, as well as the way in which finqueros bought predated titles during the early days of agrarian reform, are evidence of this attitude. In some instances, however, claims to state lands are processed in the same manner as are other claims.

The only natural resources which are afforded specific mention in the law are rubber and brazil nut trees, all of which reverted to public domain (Article 70). These are not sufficiently numerous in the Santa Cruz or Mojos regions for commercial exploitation, but they are of cardinal economic importance in the Northeast. Regulations of the relevant portions of the law have not been enforced.

Promotion of Migration

The authors of the agrarian reform envisioned among its revolutionary outcomes a major demographic realignment within the nation, which might break down the traditional isolation of the Oriente and thereby lessen the secessionist sentiment which had long characterized that region. Several projects for mass relocation of landless campesinos from the densely populated altiplano and valleys have been short-lived and unsuccessful. Offers of land were not sufficient incentive, as demonstrated in the fact that few soldiers ever took advantage of the homestead laws which were liberally phrased in the hope of attracting kolla campesinos as colonists to the Oriente where manpower is lacking. Under the agrarian reform, even more generous conditions are offered: "... any campesino laborer from the region of the altiplano or valleys will be given fifty hectares in the eastern area on request, and on his pledge to begin work within two years" (Article 91). This offer, like the previous ones failed to attract many kollas to the Oriente until the early 1960's. Reasons for the reluctance of kollas to go east are not difficult to find. In the first place there are traditional emotional and religious bonds between the Indians and the land. Furthermore, most of them had a fairly distinct, if only partially accurate, picture of the Oriente as a steaming, disease-ridden, tropical jungle infested with wild animals and hostile savages.

When it became clear that the promise of land was not enough to send kollas east on their own initiative, CBF and the United Nations set about trying to encourage them in other ways. One ambitious project for bringing kollas to the Oriente was the institution, in 1955, of a Colonial Regiment within the Bolivian Army, at the suggestion of CBF officials. Nineteen-year old conscriptees from the highlands who volunteered for the regiment were given only three months of standard military training before being moved to a camp near Montero for the remaining nine months of their term of service. These soldiers who traded their weapons for tools have been used to clear land and make roads for CBF, and have occasionally been hired out as day-laborers to local finqueros. At the end of a year's service, each is offered a grant of fifty hectares; the largest settlement of these veterans is Cuatro Ojitos on the northern frontier of the Santa Cruz area. The regiment has grown until it is now a division which supplies cheap labor for many CBF projects, although fewer than 12 per cent of the draftees have chosen to remain as colonists. Their "precolonization" work includes building roads, clearing narrow strips of land along them, and planting yuca and plantain there, constructing some houses, and so forth. It is evident in the recent growth of Cuatro Ojitos, Huaytú, and Colonia Yapacaní that some draftees have returned to the Oriente as colonists after briefly going home to the highlands; presumably the long-range success of the Colonial Division will be greater than is evidenced in the behavior of young unmarried men immediately after discharge.

The Army and CBF are justly proud of the "precolonization" accomplishments of the Colonial Division, and of their significant contribution through Civic Action (Acción Cívica) in old established communities such as Montero. For example, working together with local volunteers, they built the first water system for that town; subsequently, they did the same for Portachuelo. In some rural areas, soldiers conduct adult-education classes in basic literacy for eager campesinos. A feature of this organization which may be unique is the use of retired military officers; they are familiar with the Army's organization and operation, but are not involved in the machinations for advancement that often create tension in attempted liaisions between civilian and military administrators.

I shall not reiterate here the excellent historical and statistical summaries on colonization already available in Crossley (1961) and Ferragut (1961), the questionnaire-studies of Patch and his colleagues (1962), or the detailed survey by Monheim (1965). It does seem in order, however, to discuss briefly some of the dynamic factors involved, and in summary to update their evaluations of the situation.

Among the colonies administered by CBF and made up predominantly of veterans, Cuatro Ojitos is especially rent with dissension, because the administrator is accused of mismanagement and misappropriation of funds. At Huaytí and Caimanes, colonists are progressing fairly well, although they unanimously resent having "been abandoned by CBF after the first year or two." One of the oldest colonies, Aroma, founded in 1954, is losing its vitality as a few strong leaders are usurping wealth and power. Provision of credit, maintenance of roads, agricultural extension assistance, schools, and medical facilities are the lacks most often cited by colonists.

One of the most ambitious operations for the resettlement of highland Indians in the region was also begun in 1955 and has resulted in even fewer permanent placements than the Army-CBF project. Representatives of the Andean Mission of United Nations chose Cotoca, just east of Santa Cruz, as the site for a colony of Quechua migrants. CBF denounced the choice, and local farmers who were dispossessed resented being given poorer lands in exchange for their medium-size agricultural properties, which were

unexpropriable under the law. The migrants themselves were
disappointed at not finding, on arrival in the Oriente, the
houses, wells, and agricultural equipment which they had
been promised. Throughout the abrupt and continuing decline
of the colony, little has been done to improve living conditions or public relations, and fewer than 20 per cent of the
migrants have stayed. The usual prejudice of Camba
against kollas is understandably more intense around Cotoca,
although there have been no open demonstrations of animosity.
In 1963, the colony could at best be described as moribund.

The fact that few kollas had come to live permanently in
the Oriente despite offers of land on subsidized relocation
projects has been variously interpreted as reflecting their
"bondage to tradition," "hereditary love of the mountains,"
susceptibility to heat and disease of the tropics, physiological inability to adjust to a 12,000 foot drop in altitude, and
so forth. Other no less relevant considerations are the
problems of social adjustment in an area where the language
and customs of the native people are wholly different, and
where maladministration has served to intensify traditional
intersocietal prejudice. Drastic cultural adjustments also
have to be made by kollas who choose to settle in the
Oriente: crops and agricultural methods are different from
those in the altiplano or valleys; dress and diet must be
adjusted to altered local requirements and facilities. Under
such difficult conditions, it is noteworthy that a rising tide
of campesinos has begun during the 1960's to leave their
homes in the altiplano and valleys to be pioneer homesteaders
on the frontiers of the eastern lowlands.

Perhaps the most striking development in domestic
migration is the beginning, in the mid-1950's, of this
"spontaneous migration," the coming of migrants with no
aid whatsoever. Campesinos who came independently seem
to have made at least as good an adjustment as those who
enjoyed some benefits from CBF or the UN. The new road
from Río Yapacani to Puerto Grether is fast filling up with
such people; Río Hondo and Pueblo Nuevo, just west of
Cuatro Ojitos, were settled just recently. Somehow these
hardy pioneers survive their first year with almost nothing
at all, and then begin to look forward, realistically or not,
to producing for the market.

Seasonal migrations of kollas who work in the CBF sugar mill, on sugar cane fincas, and on the cotton plantation in the Santa Cruz region have already been mentioned, but they serve neither to alleviate population pressure in the highlands nor to expand settlement in the Oriente. They do, however, reflect partial accomplishments of another end envisioned by the authors of the agrarian reform, that of integrating the eastern portion of the nation economically with the western. The role of the new Cochabamba-Santa Cruz highway in breaking down the traditional isolation of the Oriente has already been discussed.

Resentment against the kollas will probably mount as the more thrifty and industrious people from the highlands get ahead at the cost of lowlanders. This is already happening in the municipal market at Santa Cruz, where kolla women sleep on the sidewalk and serve the first shoppers in the morning before the market building is even opened; Camba vendors complain that "No one even bothers to come inside to our stalls anymore. The kollas keep all the business on the street."

Although it was not specifically mentioned in the decree, immigration from abroad has been one of the most striking features of the post-reform period in Santa Cruz, and has had a considerable effect on the agrarian system. These movements, also summarized by Ferragut (1961) and Crossley (1961), have in many respects been more important than internal migration. The Japanese colony, San Juan Yapacaní, in the northwest of the Santa Cruz area, and the three Okinawan colonies on the east stand as striking examples of the success of producing and marketing cooperatives, when such ventures are amply funded and tightly administered. They also indicate how new ideas, with small capital and abundant effort, can produce similar crops in a similar environment but with two or three times the yield of local farmers.   The use of a simple manual rice-planter lets one man do the work of three; insecticides and some fertilizers appear to be a good investment. The Okinawans have even achieved the singular distinction of having their rice (larger and cleaner than most) recognized as "a name brand" which commands premium prices. With the rice market glutted in recent years, the Okinawans speak of turning to the production of vegetable oils, and the Japanese

plan to diversify with jute and a bag factory. Economic
success may eventually aggravate smouldering prejudices,
but some local laborers are learning new ideas and techniques
while they work for the colonists. The colonies themselves
are enclaves with traditional dress, language, and other
aspects of Old World culture persisting. Each colony is a
large block of land, and contacts with native Bolivians are
infrequent and generally brief.

The Japanese colony has grown into a young, self-contained community of nearly 2,000, with its own schools,
hospital, agricultural experiment station, rice mill, sawmills,
and internal facilities for credit. Not all of the 35,000
hectares have yet been allotted (on the basis of fifty hectares
per household), but few new immigrants are expected.
Fractionation of family plots has already started, as sons
marry and prefer to build on their parents' land rather than
move to the frontier, as much as thirty kilometers north.

The Mennonite colony northeast of Santa Cruz is even
more isolated from local culture; nearly every family has a
tractor, and they hire no Bolivian labor. They retain their
German language and dress after having lived successively
in Canada and Paraguay before coming to this area in 1958,
where they enjoy productive agriculture. A small colony of
Italian farmers is faring well, just south of Montero;
three families of Taiwanese settled just west of the city of
Santa Cruz in 1963. During the mid-1960's, there is little
discernible impact on the local culture by any of these
groups but the likelihood of eventual reciprocal acculturation
remains.

Agrarian Reform in Mojos and the Northeast

Our findings concerning the impact of agrarian reform
in Mojos and the Northeast are of special importance for
several reasons. Neither is an area where agriculture
figures significantly in the economy, but the land reform law
attempted to deal with all kinds of man-land relationships
rather than only agrarian ones. To be sure, the nature of
land tenure and use in these areas was virtually unknown to
those who drafted the law, and still remains unknown to all
but the few who have worked there. The demographic
aspect of property relations is thrown into sharp relief by

the distinctive ways in which specifications of the law, originally devised for areas of heavy population pressure, have
been adapted in these regions of extremely sparse population.

Reallocation of Land

What people used to say of Santa Cruz is still true of
Mojos and the Northeast--there is so much land and there
are so few people that no one need be without land.   But it
is true here, as everywhere else, that not all land is equally
valued.   There are some inhabitants of the northern Oriente
who would like to live nearer a town, others who would like
to be nearer a river, and so forth.   There is, at present, a
small-scale land rush as speculators vie for plots along the
projected trajectory of the Riberalta-Guayaramerín highway.
But there is probably no one there who yearns just for a
plot of land to call his; certainly there is no one who actually
needs it as a means of subsistence.   There are marked dis-
parities in holdings, such that some ranchers measure their
claims in terms of estancias (areas twenty-five kilometers
square), while many individuals lay no claim to land at all.
But even landless campesinos need not serve as feudal serfs
in order to get a piece of land on which to raise their livelihood, nor do the landlords drive squatters off their holdings.

Development of Indian Communities

There are no self-governing comunidades indígenas in
the Oriente, and there has been virtually nothing done by the
government for the tribal Indians who are still scattered
throughout the area.

Revision of Agricultural Labor Relations

Since agriculture was never an important economic
activity in either of these regions, let us interpret this aim
of the reform as reflecting a concern for the liberalization
of land-based employer-employee relationships in general.
Again, the contrast with the highlands is extreme; there was
no quasi-feudalism here and wages, however small, were
part of a very different kind of social order.   Ranchers often
share the hardships of a cattle drive with their cowboys in
Mojos; rubber and brazil nut wholesalers in the Northeast
are often viewed by the individual collectors as their agents,

rather than the opposite. The lurid accounts of slavery and
wholesale atrocities during the rubber boom* may have had
some foundation of truth a few hundred miles north, where
a different kind of tree produces a lower grade of latex for
only a few months, but in this region, a skilled collector is
valuable because he cares for the trees. Even the Suárez
Brothers are said not to have been abusive; although they
may have treated most of the region as their private fief,
they are generally characterized as benevolent autocrats.

Stimulation of Agricultural Development

Let us also generalize this fourth objective, to refer to
other economic activities dealing with the land. Farming,
even on a subsistence basis, is feasible only on the narrow
well-watered strips on either side of rivers in the Mojos
region. At most, these are 500 feet wide, and usually they
are considerably narrower. The soil is usable only for a
year, so that farmers tend to move to new areas, even in
those instances when the river returns to its old banks at
the end of the rainy season; nearly as often, the river
changes its course. In such a situation, farming is not
a sedentary occupation; there is no investment in fences,
permanent buildings, machinery, or other capital improvements; and geographic mobility is an advantage rather than
a handicap. For this kind of agriculture, there would be a
positive danger in being bound to a specific area of land,
and the few farmers in this region generally want nothing
to do with titles, and have no need for or interest in advanced
techniques.

Among the means suggested for stimulating development,
capital investment seems to have had little impact. On the
contrary, there has been some flight of capital from both
Mojos and the Northeast in recent years as a few people
with liquid assets seek a higher standard of living which is
available only in the cities.

With respect to technical aid, some beginnings toward
long-range programs have been made. SAI maintains cattle

---

*Tambs is amplifying his documentary history of the rubber
  boom (1966), with collection of oral history in 1968.

stations at Magdalena and Trinidad, which have as yet had
little impact on local stockraising practices, and they have
projected a base for artificial insemination in Santa Ana de
Yacuma. The excellent SAI experimental station at Riberalta
is a unique showcase of what tropical agriculture may sometime become in the Northeast, but the research on rubber,
brazil nuts, cocoa, and other native crops there has done
little to stimulate cultivation which could supplement or
supplant the present pattern of random collection.

Provision of credit, another potentially important way of
stimulating local development, has been neglected here as
throughout the rest of the nation. Cattlemen in Mojos claim
that they can't build fences or corrals, or improve their
stock or pasturage without credit, but none is available.
The wholesalers in the Northeast have funds enough for
their own operations and extend credit to their employees,
but this is a seasonal necessity and does not result in any
significant expansion of production. One exception is Blanca
Flor in the Northeast, where large loans from Point Four
have helped establish a profitable multipurpose cooperative
based on the brazil nut industry, under the administration
of Maryknoll missionaries.

Conservation of Natural Resources

The fifth fundamental objective is the only one which is
immediately relevant in the northern Oriente. The decree
emphasizes rubber and brazil nut trees, and the only part
of the nation where these occur in significant numbers is
the Northeast, where they are the basis of the economy.
The manner in which forest products are collected presents
no threat to these trees, since people there have no intention
of killing the proverbial "goose that lays golden eggs." The
government's concern may have been almost as much with
their getting a foothold in the wholesaling industry which is
now monopolized by a few private corporations. Whatever
the intention, there has been no discernible effect, although
the experimental station at Riberalta is developing a backlog
of knowledge that may sometime be the invaluable basis for
a shift from collecting in the forest to producing on plantations.

Promotion of Migration

This final objective has as yet had no impact on either Mojos or the Northeast. Eventually, it seems likely that the frontier of settlement of the northern Santa Cruz zone may meet the southern boundary of Mojos, and river traffic may markedly increase as improvements are made in the road from La Paz which recently reached the Río Beni at Santa Ana de Huachi, on the western edge of the Northeast. * In the mid-1960's, however, few people are coming into the area, and enough are leaving to produce something rare in Latin America--a slightly declining population.

It is clear that there were other objectives in the decree, perhaps less "fundamental" than those listed in the preamble. For example, one such was commercialization of the livestock industry. Ranchers in Mojos complain, however, that "the law should distinguish between those who use rational care, and those who just let their stock run wild." They say there should be no ceiling on a man's herds; the specified maximum of five hectares per head would, in effect, "freeze" a man's herd at the number he had at the time he applied for a land grant. In Trinidad, they tell of a rancher whose herd doubled during the years it took for his claim to be processed through SNRA, so that his ranch was far too small before he even got title to it. This is a problem even for ranchers who don't approach the absolute allowable maximum of 10,000 head. These problems now remain academic, since there is no cattle census and there is little concern with restriction of grazing lands; they could become problems of immense importance in the future.

Another unstated objective was that all land in the country should at last be registered and enter the tax rolls. It seemed reasonable to expect that, since titles

---

*A cattle trail has been opened between San Borja in the Mojos region and Santa Ana de Huachi in the Alto Beni, but overland transportation between highland cities and the lowlands is not yet economically feasible. Large-scale improvement and extension of roads is planned, and would be important if accomplished, although costs may be prohibitive.

issued by CNRA are now the only legal ones, any piece of
land that was not expropriated (afectado) would soon be
claimed for confirmation of title (inafectabilidad) by its
owner. This has not happened in Mojos or the Northeast.
Until there is a threat to the traditional ownership which
is based on nothing more than occupation of the land, people
there clearly want to avoid getting involved with filing claims
and paying legal costs for titles which would only subject them
to the obligation of paying taxes; all this for land which they
already treat as their own, without challenge. Even dis-
counting apathy, another problem is the disproportionate
cost of transportation, quite apart from whatever legal
fees might be involved. In the rare instances when an
inhabitant of the northern Oriente does choose to secure
legal title, it is often impracticable to file a claim for land
remote from administrative centers. Because the claimant
must pay costs of transportation and food for the agrarian
judge and topographer to inspect the site, expenses readily
add up to more than the value of the land, especially where
it is often more than a week by horse and canoe from the
provincial capital, and where land has no foreseeable
market value. The physical difficulties of mapping in dense
jungle, in swamps, across open prairie without landmarks,
and so forth, add to the costs of following the rules. These
are undoubtedly some of the reasons why there has not yet
been a single land claim awarded through the SNRA office
in Cobija, capital of the state of Pando;* there are certainly
other reasons for this decade of inactivity.

Even if there are few new landowners in the northern
Oriente, there has been one historic shift which may have
affected almost as much land area in total as the thousands
of tiny claims in the altiplano and valleys. A tantalizing
reference occurs in the judgment (sentencia) of dossier 3925-B
to "the latifundist firm Suárez Hnos. Ltda. which was owner
of various latifundia in the departments of Beni and Pando
which total various millions of hectares, having voluntarily
forfeited them (habiendose auto-afectado) before the agrarian
judge of Trinidad, as recorded in a memorandum of 17 January
1955..." Unfortunately, there is no trace of such a memo-

---

*The two properties in Pando which have been reallocated
  were processed through the office in Riberalta, Beni.

randum in Trinidad or in SNRA archives, but it is clear that
the Suárez domination did not long survive the MNR revolution.

It is difficult for the majority, including Bolivians, who
think of this as a nation of land-hungry campesinos under
heavy population pressure, to comprehend that there should
even now be areas with no competition for land. Perhaps
an extreme example will illustrate the relevance of demographic factors to property relations. I have spoken so far
about lands which no one claimed, but which the present
"owner" could claim at any time. What happens when one
does claim such land? Anywhere else we would expect him
to muster evidence to support his claim of ownership--per-
haps a forged and predated title, some tax receipts, and
other supporting documents. But in Mojos, these would be
an unnecessary expense and, according to local belief,
would delay the processing of the claim. Rather than make
an effort to demonstrate that he had in fact been in possession
of this land for a certain length of time, the claimant in
Mojos generally insists that it is unused fiscal land (tierra
baldía), and that he is asking for dotation (dotación) of
government property rather than confirmation of his own.
Not only does this relieve him of the bother of providing
documentation and the expense of paying delinquent taxes,
but Mojeños believe that claims for dotation are processed
faster by CNRA than those for confirmation. This expedient
of willfully denying ownership to a piece of land is unthinkable
to people of the altiplano or valleys, again illustrating
vividly the regional diversity that is the keynote in Bolivian
life.

CHAPTER **16** LESSONS FROM
THE ORIENTE

—Dwight B. Heath

Despite the opinion of administrators in both Bolivia and
United States governmental agencies that nothing of interest
to agrarian and social systems had occurred in the Oriente,
land reform and social revolution are dramatic realities in
the 1960's; and this area will probably become increasingly
a focus of economic development and cultural change in the
future.

SUMMARY AND CONCLUSIONS

The northern Santa Cruz area is enjoying a boom. This
is manifest in a great deal more traffic of people and goods,
and a pervasive sense of optimism. There is appreciably
more wealth than there was a few years ago; in the capital
city, a few stores sell phonograph records, office supplies,
high-quality clothing, and other luxury-items that simply
were not available during the mid-1950's. There is more
or less regular bus service along the highway, jeep-taxis
are numerous in the city, and some people have even fore-
gone the leisurely pace of life that was cherished there for
centuries.

Part of this is due to oil; part of it is the result of
tenuous speculation; but much of it is due to agriculture.
Because of the variety of things which happened at the
same time as agrarian reform, it would be facile to
attribute so much economic development specifically to
the decree. The expansion of sugar milling facilities,
the offering of supervised credit, the development of
roads in the area, and the expansion of the market all
combined during the late 1950's and early 1960's to produce visible progress and an optimism that may be
creative if it is coupled with the means for further

357

development.   Crossley's excellent study appropriately
concludes on the note that

> Though the spirit guiding the progress of the
> Santa Cruz area over the last decade has
> been Bolivian, the means and much of the
> driving force required to achieve the objects
> sought have been provided as the tangible
> products of international good will. . .   In
> the final analysis the future of the Santa
> Cruz area will depend on the attitudes of
> the people (old and new) of Bolivia and
> their leaders, on their awareness and under-
> standing of the problems, on their knowledge
> of the solutions needed and on their will and
> ability to apply that knowledge (Crossley, 1961:240).

The same will undoubtedly apply to Mojos and the Northeast,
whenever they begin to move from isolation and stability
toward expansion of their social and economic horizons.

   With the exception of the northern Santa Cruz region,
there seems to be lessening demographic pressure throughout the Oriente.   Like many backwater areas throughout the
world, Mojos and the Northeast are losing their ambitious
young men, who see very limited opportunities there.   A
few of the wealthier people have also been attracted to La
Paz by the physical conveniences and other attractions of
city life.   Even more striking than the slight decline in
human population is the enormous drop in numbers of
livestock in Mojos during the past few decades; these factors
combine to produce the unusual situation of considerably
less pressure on the land than was the case earlier.

   It is important to point out that Santa Cruz, like the
altiplano and valleys, reflects the more typical Latin
American pattern of an exploding population. It differs,
however, in that a major portion of the increase is caused
by immigration rather than normal population growth.
Sound statistical support for these generalizations is not
available, but estimates of immigration to the area during
the first half of the 1960's range from 7,000 to 40,000, and
even if we accept a likely figure of about 10,000, this is an
impressive increase for an area which probably had not
more than 120,000 inhabitants in 1957.

With respect to the specific matter of land reallocation
under the agrarian reform law, the entire Oriente is in
striking contrast with any part of the western highlands.
In the altiplano and highlands, grants are often measured
in areas (tenths of a hectare); in the Oriente, few are for
less than fifty hectares, and some ranchers in Mojos have
secured title to 120,000 hectares (of which 20 per cent is
said to be worthless because of swamps, lakes, anthills,
and other natural features).   Buechler and Erasmus have
indicated the gravity of the problem of minifundio in the
areas where they worked; I am tempted to speak of
"maxifundio" in the Oriente. With slash-and-burn methods
of cultivation, a hard-working man is doing well to manage
three hectares per year.   Allowing for rotation and fallowing,
the maximum manageable is about twenty hectares.   Few
campesinos can realistically expect to employ machinery
or hired help; perhaps two hardy sons could double a man's
working capacity, until they marry and want land of their
own.   In brief, there seems little prospect that many
campesinos will ever utilize more than 80 per cent of the
land allotted to them; nearly one fifth of the land allotted
under the reform will probably remain uncultivated for at
least a generation.   This, too, is unthinkable to highlanders,
although subdivision of land among heirs may eventually
lead to comparable problems.   The national Constitution
of 1961 disallowed division of small properties, but it was
doubtful that such a law could be enforced--even before the
Constitution was rescinded in November, 1964.

Later in this volume, I will also deal with the implications
of the perspectives which this study, together with those of
my colleagues, affords on the national scence.   But another
useful way of looking at these data is as a case history in
economic development and cultural change.   The following
is a discussion of some general principles as exemplified in
this local instance.

PROCESSES OF CULTURAL CHANGE

In effect, this entire volume constitutes a study in cultural
change, so that a recapitulation of even a representative
sample of the innumerable instances of innovation which have

occurred in local history would be too cumbersome. Fairly
detailed consideration of a single instance of change, the
introduction of mechanized agricultural techniques, can,
however, go far in illustrating an approach to larger problems.

During recent years anthropologists have been increasingly
concerned with problems of cultural change in general, and
especially with situations of acculturation or culture contact
and culture transfer, where intrusive forces from beyond a
single socio-cultural tradition are operative. Descriptions of
instances of such change are numerous and diverse, but a
coherent body of theory has not yet emerged. Members of
the Social Science Research Council's Summer Seminar on
Differential Culture Change did agree, however, that "The
distinction which Linton saw between directed and nondirected
situations in culture contact remains basic in any attempt to
develop generalizations in the field of acculturation" (Spicer,
1961:519). The difference between these types of situations is
phrased in terms of power relationships: directed contact,
they say, "... involves interaction in specific roles between
members of two different societies and effective control of
some type and degree by members of one society over the
members of the other." Nondirected contact situations, by
contrast, are described as those in which "Contacts between
members of societies with different cultures... occur without the establishment of one society in a superordinate position over the other... Hence the effective influence of the
interests, sanctions, and values of each culture is confined
to a single society" (Spicer, 1961:520). Our example represents another type of contact situation not noted by the
members of the seminar: a situation in which determinants
of change were derived from more than two cultural systems,
and one in which the effective model for change lay outside
the dominant-subordinate power relationship.

With agrarian reform, large landholders throughout
Bolivia were faced with the new alternative of developing
their fincas into "agricultural enterprises" through capital
investment and mechanization or of losing their land as
"latifundia." Nearly all of the fincas in the northern Santa
Cruz area were undeveloped latifundia; although agriculture
was the principal economic activity, it had never become an
important commercial undertaking. Nevertheless, most of
the finqueros wanted to retain the large tracts of land on

which their traditional prestige was based, but they commanded little liquid capital with which to make the investments that would be necessary in order to develop their
fincas as agricultural enterprises.

The Bolivian national government decreed major changes
in farm management and threatened expropriation as a
penalty for those who failed to adopt the innovation; and it
had sufficient power to enforce the threat. In terms of
power relationships, then, the contact situation which was
to precipitate a revision of agricultural methods was of
the "directed" type--the government had effective control
over the subordinate finqueros. However, the several
agencies of the government (individually and collectively)
lacked both the machinery and the capital which might have
allowed realization of such a change. In other words, a
change in the culture of one group was ordered by authori-
tative fiat from another, but means of effecting the change
were not available to either group.

It is more than mere coincidence that a few months
later, Bolivia's President invited the U. S. to undertake a
program of "Point Four" activities aimed at stimulating
agricultural development in the Oriente. The invitation
was accepted and it was not long before Point Four had
established a program of supervised credit whereby
finqueros could take loans, using their land and future
crops as collateral. Low interest rates combined with
runaway inflation to produce a situation in which all were
eager to take credit because repayment, including interest,
was invariably cheaper (in terms of buying power) than the
original loan had been. Point Four also rented modern
agricultural machinery with skilled operators at rates
lower than operating costs. Finqueros with loans were
glad to rent bulldozers for clearing jungle land, as well
as plows and harrows which allowed their properties to
qualify for the favored status of agricultural enterprise
with a minimum of effort and expense on their part.

The source of cultural transfer in this instance was
North American society--or, more precisely, a few Point
Four agents representing the culture of the United States.
Those who provided the model and the means for effecting
the prescribed change themselves enjoyed neither power

nor prestige in relations with the people of the Oriente. In
the region under sufferance of the dominant Bolivian government, this third social group lay wholly outside of the power
relationship between the other two.

What we have here is an example of cultural transfer in
a situation of clearly directed contact. And yet in this case
the group with power did not direct that members of the
subject group adopt their way of doing things. On the
contrary, the model for change was still another group,
who had no part in directing those to whom their cultural
traits were transferred.

In brief, it is fruitful to differentiate, in situations of
intersocietal contact, between sources of pressure favoring
cultural change, and feasible sources of the means of
effecting such change. That these two, which may be
characterized briefly as "the power" and "the model,"
need not be congruent has been amply illustrated, and it
would appear doubtful that such differentiation is unique
to this situation. It is rarely recognized that the power
relationship which obtains between societies does not
necessarily determine the direction of flow of cultural
transfer. To say that a decree of change by fiat may be
meaningless unless accompanied by effective means of
enforcement is a banal statement, but the implications
of the equally obvious fact that means of compliance must
also be available are seldom appreciated. To be sure, in
many such situations members of the subordinate group
already have access to means of compliance. In others--
and this is perhaps most often the case--they are obliged
to adopt innovations from the dominant group. The case
of finqueros in the Bolivian Oriente illustrates a third
possibility which has hitherto been unrecognized or ignored:
that in which means of compliance with decrees does not
exist in the cultural repertory of either the dominant or
subordinate society and recourse must be had to another
cultural tradition.

Moreover, there seems little reason to doubt that even
more than three social groupings and their ways of life must
sometimes be considered where extraneous cultural influences are even more numerous and varied. In sum, just
as the distinction between directed and nondirected situations

of culture contact is important, different types and degrees
of directedness must be recognized and analyzed.   The
social structural model of cultural transfer must sometimes be expanded from the relatively simple dyadic
paradigm which is now generally accepted, in order to
take into account the multiplicity of other social groupings.

PART V

CONCLUSIONS

CHAPTER **17** CONCLUSIONS AND
IMPLICATIONS FOR
ACTION

—Dwight B. Heath

The foregoing portions of this study constitute the first comparative study of agricultural and social systems in some of the major areas of Bolivia. They are the most detailed descriptions and analyses yet available concerning Bolivia's land reform and social revolution, and include the first substantive social science data on some of the regions. The following discussion is intended to deal more broadly, with Bolivia as a whole, and includes summary statements concerning some of the major revolutionary institutions, evaluation of successes and shortcomings, prospects and problems for further research, and some of the possible applications of our findings.

It seems appropriate here to voice a brief caveat concerning prospects for development in general, and also to offer a few comments which may be of interest and use to administrators and planners who address themselves to the fuller development of Bolivia's enormous potentialities, which the Bolivian government and people claim is their cardinal aim. The discussion is organized in terms of some categories which should be of particular interest to persons in such positions, namely: land reform, law and reality; the social revolution; agricultural production and marketing; syndicates; cooperatives; colonization; and opportunities for international aid.

It would be presumptuous, on the one hand, for a North American to offer ready solutions to the many complex problems of Bolivia's agrarian reform program, even after systematic study of a variety of situations. It would be inappropriate, on the other hand, for a research worker of any nationality to neglect to point out what he takes to be

some of the principal implications of his findings. The data
reported above are important as a baseline for any further
investigations; they also suggest some necessities and
possible fruitful avenues of action.

CAVEAT

It is important at the outset to emphasize the fact that
some of our findings are inconsistent with widely held beliefs.
Because our conclusions are based on substantive data
gathered through close and detailed work in the field, however,
I believe that their implications for action are likely to be
relatively more sound than those of hearsay, armchair social
philosophy, or myth.

At the same time, I do not mean to depreciate the work
of others who have also made appropriate recommendations
based on realistic evaluations of the national situation. Many
advisers have at various times prepared incisive and practical reports on various aspects of Bolivia, under the auspices
of United Nations, Point Four, or other international
agencies.* It is no fault of theirs that their recommendations
have been almost universally ignored. Unfortunately, such

---

*The number and variety of such reports belies the popular
  assertion that Bolivia is "unknown" to outsiders. A few of
  the more important studies which included sound recommendations for action are the following. "The Keenleyside
  Report" (United Nations, 1951) included a realistic diagnosis
  of the fundamental social and economic problems of Bolivia.
  and, except for changes effected by the agrarian reform
  applies almost as well to the contemporary situation. Much
  the same could be said of the earlier "Bohan Report"
  (Bohan, 1937).
  Specific aspects of the national situation are dealt with
  in considerably more detail in other reports. Among the
  best are studies and recommendations concerning: the
  mining industry (Ford, Bacon and Davis, 1956); public
  administration (Richards, 1961); agriculture (U.S. Department of Agriculture, 1962); colonization (Ferragut, 1961);
  agrarian reform (Ferragut, 1963); and economic development
  (Goodrich, 1955; Walinsky, 1962; Zondag, 1966).

recommendations are meaningful only in terms of a set of premises which differ markedly from those of the advisers, what Gillin calls "ethos components in modern Latin American culture" (1955).

Facile oversimplification of some important anthropological concepts in recent years has probably done more to hinder international understanding than to help it. It has become intellectually fashionable to minimize the importance of intercultural differences, for example, under the rationale that "basically, human beings are all very much alike." There is an important element of truth to this proposition, and anthropologists have championed its acceptance for many years. But there is another side to the coin, and even the most enthusiastic proponent of the recognition of the many fundamental similarities that do exist among the peoples of the world should recognize that there are deep-seated, pervasive, and fundamentally important differences among peoples as well. Among these differences are values, attitudes, and conceptions of man and the world that are the rationale for very different conceptions of right and wrong. Such basic differences cannot be ignored without obscuring understanding.

Another well-intentioned but misleading perspective is a naive conception of "cultural relativism," which holds that any customary pattern of thought or action must be accepted at face value, however inappropriate it may seem to outsiders. It is true that exotic and even contradictory beliefs and behaviors can accomplish similar ends, and that customs invariably "make sense" in the cultural context in which they have emerged. It is also true that the various parts of any way of life are interrelated, so that changing any single item will have repercussions in remote and some-times unexpected aspects of the culture. But few anthropologists expect to see the cultures of the world left intact as a sort of ethnographical zoo, and increasingly we turn our attention to attempting to predict necessities of change and to minimize the consequent strains. For example, there are some fundamental aspects of the Bolivian world view and culture pattern that are incompatible with economic development, and it would be pointless and mis-leading to underestimate their importance. Bolivia's social revolution has done much to alter the distribution of wealth

and power, and has had a fundamental and irreversible impact
on the social order. Without a major intellectual revolution,
however, changes of the order that most Bolivians say they
want can never be achieved.

This may sound like an overstatement, but I say it from
sincere conviction with no sense of melodrama. For example,
it is a truism that law, order, and stability are fundamental
to development, but it is no exaggeration to say that illegality,
disorder, and instability are characteristic of Bolivia now,
as they have been throughout most of her history. A pervasive egoism and opportunism characterizes the middle-
and upper-class Whites and Mestizos who are most active in
political and economic affairs. The ideal of personalismo
(personalism) probably accounts for widespread lack of
equity in the applications of laws and opportunistic manipulation of what North Americans might expect to be inflexible
bureaucratic routine. Coima, or graft, is an accepted way
of doing things, so that corruption and inefficiency are the
rule in government offices. There is even a different attitude
toward "truth," such that most Latins would prefer to tell a
person what they think he would like to hear rather than risk
injuring his pride (dignidad).

Hard work is scorned rather than esteemed, and the
ideal male is one who can best "get away with things" (cf.
Simmons, 1955). Public administration is often blatantly
corrupt, and there is little to inspire confidence in business,
government, or even personal relations. Such a value
system is viable, and even rewarding, among those who
understand and exploit it. But it does not provide a sound
basis for industrialization, democratization, economic
development, or other goals which official spokesmen and
many other Bolivians claim they want to achieve.

The beauty of Bolivia and the warmth of her people have
drawn me back time after time, so that I have spent nearly
one half of my professional career there. Nevertheless, I
recognize the correctness, from an international perspective,
of Arguedas's (1937) characterization of his countrymen as
"a sick people." In the simplest terms, nothing short of a
large-scale change of values will have any pervasive or
lasting effect on Bolivia's potential for development. A
genuine educational effort, combined with a number of

simultaneous and difficult corrective actions on the part of
the government, would be necessary in order to minimize
corruption, strengthen law and order, improve public administration, and, in general, to create an ambiance of confidence. Even these indispensable prerequisites could be
achieved only under strong leadership of a sort that the
nation has enjoyed only rarely and briefly in its history.

The following implications for action are stated simply
and straightforwardly--too much so to serve alone as pres-
criptions or recommendations for programs, but enough so
to provide a realistic basis for planning. My comments are
directed to Bolivians (in CBF, CNRA, Ministry of Agriculture,
Ministry of Economy, SAI, SNRA, and other agencies) to
personnel of the United States (AID, State, Peace Corps,
Army, and others), to representatives of other nations in
Bolivia, and to international organizations (such as United
Nations, Inter-American Development Bank, Organization of
American States, and others) which are active or interested
in developments there. Bolivia's experiments in land reform
and social revolution are among the first and most far-
reaching in the world; their enormous potential historic
importance, combined with the urgent human necessity for
action there, should evoke deep concern and, hopefully, a
commitment to action, on the part of people in all of the
above categories.

LAND REFORM: LAW AND REALITY

My conclusions concerning agrarian reform are based
on the premise that land cannot be considered as an isolated
entity, but has meaning only in the context of general
economic and social development.

In summary, the idea of Bolivia's land reform as having
been the product of grass roots action on the part of the
illiterate Indian majority is not supported, but claims by the
MNR that they instituted it as part of a deliberate program of
social revolution must be honored in the light of historical

evidence. *

Furthermore, it is clear that the evaluation of the
accomplishments of any land reform program must include
multiple perspectives--at least distinguishing between
psychological and economic aspects. Having learned what
local people feel and believe, I am convinced that, in the
opinion of the rural majority, Bolivia's experiment in land
reform and social revolution has been enormously success-
ful--at least in psychological terms. Increased morale and
active political involvement among campesinos are only two
of many indications of this. By contrast, an articulate but
powerless minority dismisses the whole program as a
culturally and economically disastrous triumph for a few
unscrupulous demagogues. Each of these extreme views
contains some truth; the advantage of an anthropological perspective is that it allows us to gain an awareness of both,
and to weigh them against other more objective bases for
evaluation. Some of the more important successes and
shortcomings, after a decade's attempt to achieve the objectives set forth in the decree, follow.

Reallocation of Land

Officials of SNRA pride themselves on having completed
what they call "the first stage of the reform," breaking up
latifundia and granting land to campesinos, at least on the
altiplano in the western provinces of La Paz department,
throughout most of the temperate valleys in the department
of Cochabamba, and in the small populated portion of Santa
Cruz in the tropical lowlands of the east. There remain large
areas in the rest of the country where there has been little
reallocation of land to date (see Table 25). The widespread
impact of land reallocation under the agrarian reform is
vividly demonstrated in Table 26, also.

Such tabulations provide some indication of the scope of

---

*As this book went to press, a Bolivian scholar requested
my evaluation of his recently completed manuscript on the
history of the campesino syndicate at Ucureña (Albó, 1968).
It convincingly documents the complementarity of Patch's
view and my own.

Table 25

LAND AREA REALLOCATED UNDER BOLIVIA'S AGRARIAN REFORM*

Department	Total area[a]	Area affected by agrarian reform[b]	
Beni	21,356,400 hectares	909,060 hectares	2¹/₁ ···
Chuquisaca	5,152,400	1,064,129	⁵/₁
Cochabamba	5,563,100	1,209,350	⁶/₁
La Paz	13,398,500	1,563,723	⁶/₁
Oruro	5,358,800	454,985	¹⁰/₁
Pando	6,382,700	5,034	12?2/₁ .
Potosí	11,821,800	1,154,113	12/₁
Santa Cruz	37,062,100	1,194,027	37/₁ ··
Tarija	3,762,300	351,862	12/₁
Totals:	109,858,100 hectares	7,906,283 hectares	

*through August 31, 1967

[a]Source: René Camacho Lara, <u>Atlas de Bolivia.</u>
Instituto Geografico de Agostini, Novara, 1958.

[b]Adapted from a summary tabulation prepared on request
by Servicio Nacional de Reforma Agraria, September 8,
1967.

labor of SNRA, but deserves some additional comment. A
marked feature of Table 25 is the enormous regional disparity in application of the reform, not all of which is
attributable to differential importance of agriculture in
economies of the areas. In Table 26, it is apparent that
some beneficiaries have received more than a single land-
grant; nevertheless, if we assume an average of only 5
members in each family that received a new title to land, it
is noteworthy that nearly one third of the total population of
the country appears to have benefited from the agrarian reform
in the immediate sense of land reallocation. It is also clear,
from Table 26, that the administrative machinery for
expropriation and reallocation started very slowly, and has
continued effectively even since the ouster of MNR.

Table 26

RATE OF LAND REALLOCATION UNDER BOLIVIA'S
AGRARIAN REFORM[a]

Year	Number of new titles distributed	Number of families receiving titles	Land areas allocated in titles
1955	3,400	2,809	51,811 hectares
1956	4,463	3,963	47,183
1957	11,400	8,028	276,396
1958	9,193	5,709	201,998
1959	18,380	12,097	320,502
1960	38,897	22,410	852,771
1961	45,511	28,210	1,167,821
1962	50,227	28,843	1,280,742
1963	47,461	40,641	1,363,591
1964	18,317	11,295	565,443
1965	15,600	9,652	388,282
1966	16,892	10,498	928,757
1967*	12,082	7,404	460,986
	291,823	191,459	7,906,283 hectares

*through August 31, 1967

[a]Adapted from a summary tabulation prepared on request by
Servicio Nacional de Reforma Agraria, September 8, 1967.

Application of the law has been colored by political considerations, so that partisans of the MNR did not lose even
excess land, whereas members of the opposition often lost
land even when they have less than legally allowable. Elaborate conditions for indemnification were spelled out too,
but no one has received or expects to receive any payment
for expropriated land. The net effect has been the granting
of token plots to an enormous number of campesinos; the
symbolic value of even a sub-subsistence fraction-of-an acre
has evoked grass roots support among campesinos who were
also given the vote.

Development of Indian Communities

A second major objective, development of the indigenous comunidades, autonomous traditional communities, has received almost no attention.

Revision of Agricultural Labor Relations

This third objective reflects the lawmakers' concern with effecting a thoroughgoing social revolution as well as revising land tenure patterns. In effect, the traditional social system has been crushed; cash wages have become commonplace; and many campesinos enjoy a heady sense of having been "liberated" from feudal oppression. The very denomination "campesino" is important, replacing the odious term "indio" which has become taboo.

Stimulation of Agricultural Development

The fourth "fundamental objective" of the agrarian reform was "to stimulate greater productivity and commercialization of the agricultural industry." Although detailed data are not available, it appears that there was an abrupt and general drop in agricultural production in the early years after enactment of the reform. In the eastern lowlands, there has recently been a marked increase in rice and sugar cane, the two large-scale cash crops. In most of the highlands, those enthusiasts who claim substantially increased production have no more data on which to base their stand than do the critics who claim that pre-reform levels have never yet been regained. Certainly the breakup of land into minifundia, coupled with the "cannibalization" and sale of what little machinery there was would suggest that many ex-haciendas might for a time have produced less. In Chapter 6, however, Erasmus reports a variety of crops spoiling in the southern valleys because of a glutted local market and no means of transportation, and provides convincing evidence that production has not suffered in that area. The loss of guidance and organization for campesinos unaccustomed to working without supervision probably was not an important problem for long anywhere. Although the highland situation is not one to encourage the investment of capital, that around Santa Cruz is. Unfortunately, cooperatives have almost universally failed, largely because of mismanagement and

misappropriation of funds, and technical assistance and
inexpensive credit have been loudly touted, but are little in
evidence.

Conservation of Natural Resources

A fifth fundamental objective emphasized conservation
of rubber and brazil nut trees, which provide the bulk of
income in the Northeast. Nothing has been done along these
lines, nor is there yet any feasible plan for action.

Promotion of Migration

Last among the stated objectives of the reform is promotion of domestic migration, in the hope of relieving
demographic pressure in the valley and altiplano regions,
and opening the frontier of the tropical east, where the Chaco
merges with the southern fringe of the Amazon basin. This
has been a dream for centuries, but after several false starts
with subsidized projects, the past couple of years have seen
the beginning of significant "spontaneous" (i. e., unsponsored
and unplanned) internal migration. Continued migration at
the present rate might conceivably keep pace with the high
birth rate, but could probably never alleviate the traditional
land-hunger of Quechua and Aymara inhabitants of the
densely populated highlands. The motivations of migrants,
the adjustments necessary in their new setting, their relations with surrounding groups, and so forth, all deserve
fuller study--this is an exciting frontier for research just as
it is for settlement.

Implications for Action

In brief, then, the land reform must be viewed as a
success if we speak in terms of "social justice"--the back
of the old quasi-feudal order has been broken and campesinos
are, in their own terms, "becoming human beings." Clearly
this has been achieved at no little cost to some other human
beings, but history shows little sympathy for dethroned
oligarchs. In cold economic terms, by contrast, the reform
is a mixed bag of a few dramatic successes and several dis-
mal failures, with very little information at all on far too
many crucial subjects. A basic need is for more intensive
and extensive research on all aspects of land tenure and use

throughout the nation. Far more information must be
collected before we can talk with any conviction of what has
occurred, much less how and why it happened, and how other
ends can be achieved. *

In the simplest terms, just administration of the law has
been hampered by the equivocal wording of the law itself.
For example, the basis for the crucial distinction between
"latifundium" and "agricultural enterprise" is not at all
clear-cut, although the former is subject to total expropriation and the latter is encouraged with large allowances of
land. By the same token, the inalienable "medium property"
is not clearly defined, and, in practice, we find an immense
range of variation in the size and administration of such lands.
A proposed revision to the law would in large part correct
these deficiencies, although it is not clear when (or even
whether) this will be enacted.

Another fundamental problem is that of public apathy in
some regions. Although the agrarian reform has been one
of the principal factors in engaging the kolla campesinos in
political awareness and activity, it has hardly been noticed
in portions of the Oriente. In Beni and Pando, where land is
abundant and population pressure low, informal traditional
usages continue with respect to the land, and, for most
practical purposes, the law might as well not exist. One way
to extend the rule of law would be to publicize the necessity
of securing land-titles from SNRA; these are the only titles
officially recognized now, but pre-reform titles are widely
accepted for various purposes, and no titles at all exist for
enormous regions in the Oriente. A deadline could be set
(within three or five years of promulgation perhaps), beyond
which any land which had not been specified in a title (or in
a pending claim) would revert to eminent domain. Landlords
who claim large areas are usually literate and accessible
through mass media or political channels, however remote
their homes from centers of population; scattered illiterate
holders of small plots could enjoy a special exemption, since

---

*A variety of intensive and extensive studies on various
 aspects of Bolivia's agrarian reform are being conducted
 under the auspices of Land Tenure Center and Comité Inter-
 Americano de Desarrollo Agrícola.

there would generally be little competition for their land.
Further details would have to be specified, but this seems a
feasible general approach to the problem of widespread dis-
regard for the law on the part of landlords.

A related problem is the supposed inertia of custom,
whereby traditional ways of thinking and acting persist among
the rural population. The immense changes that have come
about during the last decade indicate that this is far from an
insuperable obstacle to economic development and cultural
change. The success of the MNR in overcoming apparent
inertia in other realms (such as organizing campesinos into
syndicates, evoking political awareness and activity among
them, and so forth) suggests that sufficient sanctions can
accomplish much. Sanctions can be positive (rewards for
approved behavior) or negative (punishments for disapproved
behavior): discount coupons for staple foods and the
availability of land served to reward campesinos for joining
syndicates and taking part in politics; a variety of punishments
for the suppression of opposition political movements has
lessened in recent years. Fines or partial expropriation
could prompt landlords to register their holdings.

Physical features of the country present another obstacle
to prompt and just administration of the law. Sheer distance
can be prejudicial to a well-meaning claimant who may find
the cost of transportation and food for the judge and topographer
to be greater than the value of the land he would secure, even
assuming eventual approval of his claim. Distance is
meaningful only in relation to terrain and means of transportation, but both of these latter are serious handicaps throughout the nation. In parts of the Oriente, it would be a two-week
trek by canoe, ox, horse, and/or foot to arrive at outlying
homesteads, where swamps and dense undergrowth make
mapping both dangerous and difficult. There is no ready
solution to this problem ; helicopters, hovercraft, and
swamp-buggies would be useful but expensive.

Even in the best terrain, where distances are not
enormous, SNRA personnel are hampered by the virtual
lack of maps, and even of datum points from which accurate
and coordinated maps could be prepared. The Bolivian
Military Geographical Institute, in collaboration with U.S.
Army advisors is currently preparing large-scale

physiographic maps; ten years would seem an optimistic estimate of the minimum time required to complete the job. It is gratifying that work is proceeding cautiously on the basis of complete areophotogrammetric coverage, so that these will be the first maps in the public domain which have a basis more accurate than a compilation of the accumulated errors of previous efforts. This ambitious effort will be especially fruitful because it includes the first placing of permanent benchmarks at strategic locations throughout the nation. The difficulty and expense of such an undertaking is considerable, but it will undoubtedly be a worthwhile investment. The United Nations is collaborating in an ambitious geological and mineralogical survey of the highlands, which also yields useful maps.

As soon as adequate photogrammetric coverage is available, a detailed cadastral survey and registration of land should be undertaken. The experience of Australia and a number of former British colonies in Africa indicates that this need not be delayed until reliable base-maps have been prepared. I do not underestimate the size and difficulty of the task, but consider it a necessary step in order to minimize legal problems in future years. The Bolivian government has begun such a survey (through Oficina de Catastro Rústico, Administración de la Renta, within the Ministerio de Hacienda) but it is of limited value because each property is mapped according to the specifications of the supposed owner, with no reference to universal datum points, and no effort to reconcile differences between overlapping claims. This results in a situation where "the official survey" often records a given piece of land as belonging to two owners, and conflicting claims are perpetuated rather than resolved. Representatives of the British Mission for the Study of Tropical Agriculture, working jointly with Bolivia's Ministry of Economy, have already expressed concern about this need, and have the appropriate experience to direct such a project, although it is not planned as part of their current mission.

The inadequate budget of SNRA also imposes unrealistic hardships in the completion of a job which would be difficult under even ideal working conditions. The lack of basic equipment, supplies, and other facilities is a constant harassment, and grossly inadequate salaries provide little incentive for skilled and knowledgeable employees. It is a tribute to the intellectual and emotional dedication of a large portion of the staff that they have accomplished as much as they have, in the face of constant minor frustrations. A substantial increase in the budget of SNRA would undoubtedly result in a marked increase in efficiency, morale, and both the quality and quantity of work accomplished.

One important source of funds could be those benefited by the services of the organization; their contribution need not gross large, but would have symbolic value as well as a compelling logic. The imposition of a nominal tax on land awarded (perhaps assessed on a graduated scale according to area involved) would afford recipients a sense of participation in the administration and costs of the reform, and would provide some more funds for further work. Recognizing the special economic difficulties of the first few years for new landholders, payment might be deferred until the third or fifth year. The idea of enforcing the annual land-tax (which already exists "on the books") has aroused resentment among campesinos in some areas, but has been acclaimed in others as providing a sense of security and "validation" of titles. A "validating" seal on the original title, or the issuance of a special supplementary title after payment of the assessment, could be established as prestigeful, and valuable as well as requisite, without either negating the value of the original title or converting the award of land into a sale. This program would be no more burdensome to the beneficiaries of the reform than was the proposed payment, through bonds, to former owners, as is specified by law but completely ignored. Such funds could fruitfully be earmarked for use by SNRA.

Another means of supplementary subsidy for SNRA could be the inexpensive sale, by other nations and organizations, of surplus supplies and equipment in whatever usable or reparable condition.

The shortage of skilled personnel is another major problem in the effective administration of agrarian reform. In part, this is related to the overall poverty of SNRA, which has been discussed above as resulting in frustrating working conditions and a very low pay-scale. Other relevant factors must be considered, however, including the fact of an absolute shortage of skilled administrators and technicians throughout the entire nation, such that even organizations offering the best working conditions also have difficulties in staffing. At base, this is a problem in education and training; like underdeveloped countries everywhere, Bolivia has much to do in developing her own human resources. The tiny core of effective administrators and technical personnel must be supplemented by a manifold increase. It is important that the training which they receive should equip them to work effectively in the context in which they can reasonably expect to be assigned, since it is deceptively easy and tempting to "overtrain" people, preparing them to work under ideal conditions which cannot realistically be expected. In this respect, the Bolivian government could do more than it has; at the very least, agrarian judges should be given a brief training course in which the conditions of the law and their own responsibilities and limitations should be spelled out in some detail. Hopefully, appropriate training could eventually be made available to all personnel in positions of responsibility. There is no evident reason why such training could not be helped by representatives of other interested nations or international organizations. An early start in this direction was the School of Public Administration project of the University of Tennessee and the University Mayor de San Andrés, under the auspices of United States Operations Mission, which aborted after a few promising years; a more appropriate model for the training of field personnel might be the recent Programa Interamericano de Adiestramiento de Desarrollo de Comunidades Indígenas, ("Project 208"), sponsored by the Organization of American States and Instituto Indigenista Interamericano.

Training is a necessary, but not sufficient, means to developing the requisite technical personnel. Bolivia, like other developing nations, often loses those few persons who have developed valuable skills. Drastic action would be required in order to stem the exodus of trained people, that is harmful to the nation. Better facilities and working conditions would presumably do much to keep skilled nationals at home; realistic salaries should also help. Since the revolution of November, 1964, partisan political pressures have lessened in the workaday life of most Bolivians; this might encourage some competent people who were not supporters of MNR to stay in the country or even to return

from abroad--in re cent years their employment and personal
safety have been so precarious that most preferred to leave.
Needless to say, all of this would be totally meaningless
without a major shift toward responsibility, honesty, discipline, and equity in government service.

Problems built into the administrative process for land
claims have already been incisively analyzed by Ferragut,
who also made realistic recommendations (1936). It seems
appropriate here to reiterate briefly his main points and to
add a few. The time-lag in the processing of claims is both
costly and frustrating. Many of the steps now involved could
fruitfully be consolidated or dispensed with: the technical
and legal reviews could be done jointly rather than independently by CNRA and MAC; the President of the Republic need
not review each claim and sign each title; reversing the
present overcentralization of authority and decision-making,
far more responsibility for routine matters could be delegated
to local (or departmental) offices, so that the central office
could devote its attention to problematic cases; adequate pay
and strict policing of personnel would probably lessen the
frequency of graft and abuses. Perhaps the initial step
should be a codification of date concerning all those dossiers
which have already been processed, in order that we may
know what has been accomplished and what remains to be
done. Not only would this provide accurate statistics on the
work of SNRA, but it would also lessen the likelihood of
making duplicate grants involving the same property, of
granting different parcels of land to the same beneficiary,
and similar problems which have occurred.

Land reform does appear to be an indispensable adjunct
to social revolution in a quasi-feudal society based on
agriculture. It is not in itself, however, a sufficient basis
for restructuring the social order, and must be accompanied
by reforms in the distribution of other kinds of wealth and
power, technical operations, and so forth.

THE SOCIAL REVOLUTION

No one can deny that Bolivia has undergone a profound
transformation since the Nationalist Revolutionary Movement
came to power in 1952. On the contrary, it is difficult to

comprehend the breadth and depth of changes which have
revolutionized the social order.   Methods used by the party
in effecting change were controversial, but there is no longer
any doubt about the pervasiveness of change, and the durability
of many innovations seems assured.   Whatever new directions
may emerge, it is unthinkable that there might be a return to
the previous system. *

No social revolution can be unqualifiedly good--or bad--
although the Bolivian experiment has been characterized in
both ways.   Eager protagonists of the revolution proclaim
that "It has liberated an enormous potentially constructive
force.   The Indian population was a sleeping giant that only
now has awakened and cast off its chains." Opponents lament
that, "In order to gain the votes of ignorant Indians, the MNR
utterly destroyed the economy of the nation.   They offered
demagogy, without principles or planning, and the revolution
is a total calamity." There is some truth in each of these
stands, and, as is so often the case, the fuller truth may lie
somewhere between the extremes.

If we speak in terms of "social justice" for the masses,
we must credit MNR with having utterly destroyed the old
quasi-feudal order in most areas, by emancipating many
campesinos from traditional economic and social bondage.
It is difficult to overestimate the impact of the revolution,
even recognizing the fact that a campesino used to spend as
much as two thirds of his time doing unpaid and often
demeaning work for a landlord, and now has no such obligations.
It is equally true, and perhaps more dramatically impressive,
that campesinos who had been legally forbidden to bear arms
until 1952, were then given rifles, machine-guns, and mortars
so that they soon constituted a force stronger than the Army.
They who had had no voice in even local administration were
given the vote and became the major bloc in national politics.
They who had been required to get police permission to walk
on the streets of La Paz could roam through the city at will,
and even use the sidewalks.   Bolivia's campesinos were not

---

*Even the military "Revolution of Restoration" in 1964 did
 not rescind land reform, universal suffrage, or other
 populist innovations of the MNR's 1952 revolution.

merely admitted to citizenship in 1952; that marked virtually
their induction into the status of human beings, and many
have phrased it in just such terms (cf. Heath, 1966a, e).
Campesinos are generally proud to have the vote and their
own parcel of land, however tiny; even more important
appears to be a cherished intangible, dignidad de la persona
(individual dignity).

It goes without saying that such striking improvement in
the status of one portion of the population adversely affected
that of the other. The "liberation" of the campesino majority
could be achieved only at great cost to the landed gentry who
had enjoyed the leisure afforded by control over the peasantry.
In some instances, long-suppressed resentment broke out in
physical aggression, murder, rape, and looting. More often,
landlords merely abandoned their properties. In either
case, the life-style of the small, formerly dominant, group
suffered in greater proportion as that of the larger, formerly
subordinate, group improved.

Among the most readily visible outcomes of Bolivia's
social revolution is the drastic redistribution of wealth. It
is general knowledge that the major mines, notably the
holdings of Hochschild, Patiño, and Aramayo, were nationalized early in MNR control. The complex of falling production, "featherbedding," disguised subsidies, and other
problems which have made the mines a sort of white elephant
have already been analyzed in detail by Ford, Bacon and
Davis (1956) and by Zondag (1956); the symbolic value of the
nationalization cannot be overestimated, nevertheless.

It is largely MNR sympathizers who constitute the conspicuous class of nouveaux riches in the 1960's. Political
turmoil and galloping inflation created a context in which
there were abundant accusations of graft, and embezzlement
of public funds on a grand scale. Rumors about whole planeloads of gold being shipped to banks in Switzerland and the
United States, to personal accounts of high public officials,
defy documentation. Many people in lesser positions did,
however, clearly profit greatly from the differential
exchange-rates during the early 1950's. Those who could
secure permits were able to buy dollars at the official rate
of Bs. 190; imported goods were sold at the free rate, which
exceeded Bs. 16,000 before abolition of the official rate as

part of a thoroughgoing program of economic stabilization
late in 1956.

Although there is a common saying in Bolivia "The law
belongs to the rich," individuals do not always command
power and wealth in direct proportion. A system of government in which the incumbent party exercises complete control sharply limits the power of whatever opposition may
persist. Universal suffrage, instituted early by MNR,
shifted electoral power from the literate and landed elite to
the masses of campesinos, and MNR cultivated their interests
and continues to enjoy their support. Some new leaders are
emerging, not only from the urban middle class but also
from small towns and rural areas. The political organization
is one of the few which offers virtually unlimited possibilities
for advancement to dynamic and intelligent young men who
lack the formal education required for "the professions," law
and medicine. It is likely that some campesinos may
eventually assume positions of more responsibility, after
proving their political acumen in syndicate activities.

In sum, the locus of power shifted from the rosca* early
in the 1952 revolution, and new types of proudly "self-made"
leaders are emerging. The political complexion of Bolivia
is still changing, especially since the MNR was unseated in
the 1964 revolution. The Army, which had been emasculated
early in the MNR revolution, was revitalized and equipped
with new weapons, and the armed forces eventually assumed
control in the "Revolution of Restoration." The military
appear to remain in full control of the government even
since the president of the junta has been constitutionally
elected. Although there may be some competition among the
officers, there seems little likelihood of their being deposed.

Just as the power of the rosca has been virtually
neutralized, much of their wealth is gone also. In fact, most
of those who used to dominate the political and economic
spheres, have long since left the country. But not all could
afford to. In those few areas of militant campesino uprisings,

---

*Rosca is the opprobrious term used for the pre-1952
 oligarchy. It derives from "thread" (as of a screw or pipe),
 and presumably refers to their "grasping" and "biting" quality.

many were fortunate to escape with their lives, and lost
everything that had been on their haciendas. Others who
salvaged goods or money found these reserves quickly dis-
sipated by the rampant inflation of the early 1950's. Some
have made difficult adjustments in merchandising and other
service enterprises; a few continue directing agricultural
enterprises; but most have left Bolivia, with no intention of
returning.

The redistribution of wealth has been more pervasive in
Bolivia than many had expected. The nation still ranks with
Haiti among the lowest per-capita incomes in the New World,
but most campesinos are relatively much more affluent now
than a decade ago. On the altiplano, this is readily apparent
in the prevalence of consumer goods such as bicycles, radios,
and accordians, which were virtually unknown before, and in
the increase in Western dress, metal roofing, and two-story
houses. In some other areas it is apparent in better tools,
utensils, dress, and other improvements. For many
campesinos, personal participation in the market and money
economy is a new experience, but it has become general in
recent years. Furthermore, most campesinos appear to be
eating more of the produce which they cultivate, even if
their diet is no more varied than before.

In all of these respects, it is understandable why
campesinos are generally pleased with the 1952 revolution,
and still are outspoken in their support of the MNR. They
are actively concerned with education, and sometimes even
say "With schooling will come the real revolution!" Increased educational facilities are an urgent necessity
throughout the nation, although the most pressing immediate
demand is for teachers to staff the primary schools which
campesinos are building on their own initiative. Army
cooperation in education could fruitfully be expanded, and
the recent dissolution of SCIDE (Servicio Cooperativo
Interamericano de Educacion, Interamerican Cooperative
Education Service) is difficult to comprehend in terms of the
professed goals of AID.

In sum, we have a situation in which the former elite
has been virtually stripped of power and wealth. In part,
these have been distributed among the rural masses, but the
emergence of a new elite demonstrates the unevenness of

this redistribution.   The institution of a new social structure
is epitomized in the MNR's semantic victory over the negative
connotations of the word "indio," which has been replaced
by "campesino."* Although demagogy is still a powerful
force in the countryside, one of the most striking (and, to me,
frankly surprising) features of Bolivia's land reform and
social revolution is the degree to which campesinos have
begun to assume the roles of citizens and to participate in
social systems that were not only closed, but virtually
unknown, to them a decade ago.   These achievements appear
to be irreversible, so that the social revolution will probably
survive subsequent changes in national administration.   The
emphasis on developing human capital seems appropriate in
terms of long range economic and social progress.

AGRICULTURAL PRODUCTION AND MARKETING

The MNR's pervasive and profound restructuring of the
country's social order was intended not only to have important
psychological and sociological repercussions, but also to
strengthen the economic system through increased production and diversification.   Development of the agricultural
sector must, therefore, be viewed as part of a broader
pattern of economic and cultural development.

Many critics of Bolivia's agrarian reform pointed to the
apparent drop in agricultural production as a dangerous
economic failure of the reform.   Although adequate data are
not available to support or refute this supposed abrupt and
drastic decline, it is clear that at least some crops are now
in superproduction.   Sugar produced in Santa Cruz already
meets the demands of national consumption, and although the

_____

*In a similar vein, the term comunidad indígena was judged
to lend itself to invidious interpretation.   While this book
was in preparation, the "indigenous communities" were re-
designated comunidades campesinos de orígen (original
campesino communities).   It is somewhat ironic that
August 2, the date of the promulgation of the land reform
law, has been designated Día del Indio (Indian Day), com-
memorating the nation's rich folk heritage.

mills there could not utilize all the cane grown in 1963
another larger mill is planned for Bermejo, in southern
Tarija. If this is to be successful, efforts must be directed
toward increasing domestic consumption of sugar and/or
developing export markets. In a similar manner, rice and
maize have already glutted the local market in Santa Cruz and
meet present national consumption requirements. It is conceivable that, with the appropriate promotional campaign,
rice could come to constitute an important supplement to the
diet of highlanders, who now use hardly any. Maize could be
used fruitfully in the initiation of systematic feeding for
poultry and livestock, which is virtually neglected now.
Buechler mentions the surplus of fruits in yungas, as does
Erasmus in the southern valleys; they could be dried, or
preserved with surplus sugar from the Oriente, to provide
a valuable supplement to the local diet, and, with adequate
quality-control, might even become a valuable export commodity.

Simultaneously with plans for increased production of
some crops and full utilization of others, it appears
appropriate to develop a more diversified base for agriculture. Edible oils are in short supply in Bolivia, although
the Oriente appears well suited to the cultivation of soy,
safflower, peanut, and other oleaginous vegetables. Only
the Okinawan colony is making a modest start in this direction. Vegetable fibers and bags are in great demand
domestically and in nearby Brazil and Argentina. It has
been demonstrated that the Bolivian Oriente could produce
high yields of jute and kenaf; presumably hennequin would
also thrive there. Japanese colonists are beginning to
investigate such prospects.

Intensive research on production should be expanded to
provide ample detailed information on such basic questions
as inputs (including labor as well as other kinds of capital)
and outputs (including losses to disease and pests, and
domestically consumed produce as well as that which is
marketed). Such data are available for few crops and few
regions; intelligent planning would require fuller information
on virtually all crops in all areas, including various methods
of cultivation where they are pertinent.

Agricultural experiment stations could fruitfully concern

themselves more with the immediate problems and interests of farmers in the region, while also experimenting with prospects for diversification of production, rather than remaining preoccupied with pure research. They could also publicize their findings and offerings more effectively than they now do with only an annual barbecue and field day. It might also be appropriate to maintain demonstration plots, conspicuously identified, throughout the region. It also seems important that most extension demonstrations should involve only a single difference from prevailing methods; that is, campesinos would appear more ready to accept recommendations if they felt they were capable of achieving similar results by doing so. As it is, the use of mechanization, fertilizers, and insecticides at the experiment station disallows ready comparison with the situation of the campesino who might adopt one innovation at a time but can hardly be expected to emulate the ideal situation of the government installation. Emphasis should be placed on working from a baseline of what the campesinos have and do, before aiming at an ideal which is far beyond their capabilities with present resources.

Extension agents might also be more effective if they spent more time in the field. Their instruction should be directed to groups, such as the campesino syndicates, rather than individuals.

Credit facilities at reasonable cost are still unavailable except to the wealthy. A flexible program allowing small loans at low interest rates with minimum collateral would certainly be welcomed and might do much to increase agricultural production, although it would have to be strictly administered and should be integrated with the agricultural extension program.

There has been no systematic attempt to develop and expand herding, which predominates in parts of the Oriente, or rubber and brazil nut collecting which are important in the Northeast. There is no apparent reason why special consideration could not be given to the commercially feasible cattle ranch, in a manner similar to that afforded the agricultural enterprise. Objective and quantifiable criteria could be established (such as ratio of one-year-olds to live births, median weight of three-year-olds, and so forth), and stockmen who demonstrate a concern for improved production could be favored with allowance for larger herds and more land than those whose ranches are of the latifundium type.

Improved means of transportation seem to be of primary importance for any large-scale economic development. The projected extension of the existing road network toward the west of the northern Santa Cruz area could provide another valuable link with Cochabamba and with the rich developing Chapare area; and extension of roads to the east would connect with rich cattle country around Concepción and San Javier. Further development of the river network would facilitate transportation in Mojos and the Northeast. The projected road to Riberalta from Guayaramerín would provide the first overland link with the rest of the world, as well as relatively easy connection to Amazonian shipping.

The colorful markets which figure so importantly in Bolivian life, even in the major cities, are complex economic institutions about which we know very little. Other forms of brokerage, buying, and selling are similarly linked to problems of development in ways which cannot be fully understood without intensive research. The recent emergence of transportation as a large-scale industry relates to the degree of participation in the market by campesinos, and also affects the value of land in outlying areas. Determining the feasibility of colonization and roadbuilding in specific regions are only two problems of immediate practical importance which require the kinds of information that could be secured through such studies. The establishment of processing and storage facilities for products, and the promotion of nutritional campaigns should be similarly coordinated with data on production and distribution.

The occasional establishment of price supports and production quotas seems always to have created misunderstanding and ill will. It also opens the way for personal favoritism and patronage which could fruitfully be minimized, at least in international projects.

With the emergence of new entrepreneurial groups, it appears that very different economic attitudes must be rapidly developing. Landlords who previously considered any kind of commercial involvement as inherently demeaning have found themselves increasingly active in such enterprises, whether in the city as means of livelihood after expropriation, or on the farm as agriculture becomes increasingly market-oriented. Campesinos are taking a newly active part in the market, in terms of both selling and buying. We have little information on the ways in which individuals define "economic success," or on the ways in which they become involved in the national economy, although these questions are both crucial to economic development in any nation.

CAMPESINO SYNDICATES

Among the institutions which have emerged to assume an influential role in the new social system of Bolivia, the campesino syndicates are undoubtedly the most widespread and involve the largest membership. We have discussed the fact that some existed before the revolution of 1952, but it seems to have been MNR organizers who carried the idea and organized new ones throughout the countryside.

Syndicates today appear to be almost as variable in meaning and function as are the personalities of their leaders. Probably the most common are those which serve many of the functions specified for the "campesino community" in the agrarian reform law. It is interesting to note that these are designated as the functions for syndicates in the projected revision of the law. Having served as corporate entities in securing land-claims, many continue to provide services for the communities of new freeholder campesinos. Often, for example, syndicate members collectively build a school; syndical leaders can provide support and counsel for members in case of litigation; many campesino syndicates even constitute meaningful reference groups and act as a bloc politically. On some occasions, they also constitute an effective armed militia which provides militant support for local leaders or for the MNR.

There are some cases in which they fight among themselves in support of leaders who are vying for domination of a region; the sporadic civil war between the syndicates of Ucureña and Cliza in Cochabamba is a dramatic example. Another type of syndicate serves as a "gang" in support of their leader who shares some of the spoils got by illegal and extralegal means, such as stealing timber, smuggling, extorting "protection money," collecting unauthorized tolls along highways, and so forth. A few "phantom syndicates" exist on paper only, and the self-appointed secretary general has solicited and sometimes obtained land in the names of nonexistent members. More common are those which were formed in order to secure land for members, but which have been virtually dissolved since then and serve no further purpose.

Although Buechler offers detailed information concerning the formal structure of syndicates, and each investigator includes abundant anecdotal material illustrating the range of their activities, we could presumably still learn much from intensive study of a few cases. The information which we lack and which would be useful in terms of evaluating the actual and potential role of syndicates in cultural change includes, for example, the actual basis for leadership, the number of man-hours involved in various kinds of activities, the specifics of interrelations among syndicates themselves and between them and regional and national federations, and so forth. A fuller understanding of the realities of syndical organization and operation might suggest ways in which they could be helpful as channels for education, dissemination of extension supplies and counsel, establishment of credit unions, or other public services.

On balance, it appears that the economic cost of syndicates to the members, in terms of monthly dues plus occasional special assessments, is often not much greater than the economic benefits they derive from them. The socio-psychological value of syndicate membership seems appreciable from the point of view of the campesinos, and usually far outweighs the costs. When we shift our perspective to that of the regional or national economy, it seems that occasional abuses on the part of leaders are unfortunate but relatively unimportant obstacles to development. It may even be that such syndicate leaders are serving an effective apprenticeship for political action on a broader scale, where there are few other opportunities for training. Except in rare instances of virtual anarchy, which have remained strictly localized, the syndicates have been important means of distributing land, enlisting and sustaining political commitment on the part of campesinos, and bringing them into more meaningful relations with the party and the nation. It remains to be seen to what degree they also have potential value for fostering other kinds of economic development and cultural change.

COOPERATIVES

Cooperatives have become a by-word among planners in Bolivia, but sad experience and popular opinion indicate that they are not a panacea. There is a belief prevalent among the literati of Latin America that the predominant social institutions throughout the Andean area in pre-Columbian times were collectivistic or cooperative; in this connection, they refer to institutions for landholding, as well as production, distribution, and consumption. Although there is little historical support for such a view, it is generally believed that this supposedly collectivistic orientation has survived among the contemporary Quechua and Aymara, as a deep-seated aspect of their ethnic character. Each of the authors of this volume has illustrated the failure of cooperatives within his area; only a few successes were reported, none of which involved highland Indians. Reasons for failure have also been discussed, but bear repeating in this summary context.

There appears to have been little systematic attempt to teach the general principles of cooperativism. A widespread misunderstanding is that of a sort of "get-rich-quick" scheme, with an expectation of huge early profits, and no conception of plowing back capital for long-term investment. Inadequate accounting coupled with maladministration of funds have often profited a few at the expense of the majority. Most existing cooperatives in Bolivia are that in name only, and in actuality are identical with syndicates.

The few successful ventures in cooperativism should be investigated, and standard procedures for organization, administration, and accounting might be tested. Adequate capitalization and sound accounting procedures are indispensible prerequisites; responsibility should be vested in a trusted and experienced person, even if he is not a member (missionaries and Peace Corps volunteers are sometimes selected by campesinos themselves).

COLONIZATION

The experience of the early 1960's demonstrates dramatically that people from the altiplano and valleys are willing, and often even eager, to come to the Oriente if suitable land is available. Contrary to the widely held opinion that Andean campesinos are irrationally devoted to the mountains, they often move to the lowland frontier even faster than roads are being built, settling along the trajectory of roads which are still only projected. Also contrary to general belief, such highlanders appear to be able to adjust to the lower altitude and greater heat of the Oriente. Problems of cultural adaptation seem to be far more common and intense than physiological ones.

In our discussion of the Oriente, we have already noted the apparently greater tendency for Bolivian colonists who came in "spontaneous" (unsponsored) migration to stay than for those who came under the auspices of national or international programs. Immigrant colonists have uniformly stayed and prospered more t han Bolivians, often with less institutionalized technical and economic assistance. An approximate computation of per-capita costs, per-capita income, and other economic indices could be made for each of the colonies without great difficulty, and comparison of them might suggest especially fruitful ways of fostering colonization. *

Other generalizations and suggestions for research on this subject are listed in Chapter 15. It is relevant here to note that two other subtropical regions previously inhabited only by small bands of Indians are becoming major areas of colonization. One is Alto Beni, where Aymara-speaking campesinos are settling along a new road cut through the rugged eastern portion of the department of La Paz toward the lowland department of Beni, that is, between Mojos (described by Heath) and the Yungas (described by Buechler). The other is Chapare, along the northwest of the Santa Cruz area, where virgin lands are being brought under intensive cultivation by Quechuas from around Cochabamba. Both areas have become foci of very different kinds of aid under

---

*A promising start was made in this direction by Monje Rada (1963).

a $9 million loan from Inter-American Development Bank.
In Alto Beni, planned settlements (núcleos) are being
established along the road, and in Chapare, small-scale
supervised credit is available, together with agricultural
extension. It is interesting to note that settlers who have
been in Santa Cruz for only three or four years begrudge the
fact that their "old colonization zones are being abandoned in
favor of these new experiments"; this is a part of their
intensely personal sense of being real pioneers.

The Colonial Division's role in Civic Action projects
could be expanded, not only for the immediate material
benefits that would accrue but for the salutory symbolic value
of seeing the Army contributing to public works, and having
kollas work with and for Cambas.

Many problems and even conflicts could be avoided if
there were coordination among land-granting institutions. We
have focused on the role of SNRA in this connection, but that
is not the only government agency empowered to grant public
lands. Institutions and individuals can also secure property,
under special conditions, through petition to the Ministry of
Agriculture (Division de Colonizacion, Ministerio de
Agricultura, Cria y Colonizacion), or to CBF. The former
channel is primarily for corporate entities which are
planning to establish organized colonies with groups of
people; the latter has jurisdiction over specific areas which
are divided into small parcels and assigned to individual
colonists, usually on an unplanned first-come-first-served
basis. Duplication of authority would be less problematic if
there were close and regular integration in the planning of
these organizations, together with consensus on the disposition of specific tracts. But the present situation is very
different, and there seems to be no awareness or concern on
the part of any one of these organizations about the activities
of the others. For example, within the Santa Cruz area, a
local agrarian judge was not notified that the Ministry of
Agriculture had granted a tract of 35,000 hectares within the
area of his jurisdiction for the establishment of a Japanese-
immigrant colony, and he in turn awarded much of the same
land to local campesinos. Friction was inevitable, and it
is a tribute to the individuals involved that open warfare was
avoided during the trying period before a special commission
from La Paz ruled in favor of the Japanese. An agency for

coordination among these groups has long existed in name
only (Consejo Nacional de Colonización, National Colonization
Council), and it remains to be seen whether it will serve the
purpose any better after recent reorganization (as Comision
Nacional para Coordinacion de Colonizacion, National Commission for the Coordination of Colonization).

We lack information on the emergence of leadership and
new social structures within the colonies. If we knew more
about how people find out about the possibilities of migration
or on what basis they decide to come east, it might be
possible to increase or be more selective in the flow of
colonists. "Successful" colonists, however specified, might
be effective recruiters if a brief return to their areas of
origin could be subsidized during a "slack season."

INTERNATIONAL AID

One of the ironies of our modern world is the fact that
international programs of economic and technical assistance
often result in the presence of a higher proportion of
specialized "experts" in underdeveloped areas than in the
traditional centers of training. But a combination of factors
too often combine to vitiate the effectiveness of even the
most competent persons in such situations. Personal and
family problems of cultural shock, administrative obstacles,
inadequate familiarity with the complex social and historical
background relevant to understanding local problems, and
inability to grasp the cultural implications of proposed
projects are a few of the most common shortcomings which
are difficult to avoid (Foster, 1962). I have already remarked
on the pitfalls of facile ignoring of important cultural
differences, and the necessity of basic changes in values and
attitudes if an ambiance suitable to economic development is
to be achieved.

The decision-makers often have very different percep-
tions of the needs and wants of campesinos than do
campesinos themselves. It is clear that budgetary and other
administrative considerations combine with the availability
of supplies and personnel to restrict the freedom of planners,
but even limited resources are often squandered on programs
which have little meaning to the masses of people, and little

foreseeable long-range economic impact in favor of the
nation as a whole. A preoccupation with political expediency
and the necessity of short-term budgeting make systematic
development difficult.

It appears that any program of economic development
must be evaluated from at least two points of view, that of
the national economy, and that of the individual. Too often
these are in considerable contrast. For example, in terms
of the national economy it is appropriate to stimulate commercial agriculture by large-scale farmers, although the
individual campesino may resent what he considers "favoritism
to the rich." By contrast, a program of short-term supervised
credit and other aid to campesinos would be warmly received
but would probably be prohibitively expensive to administer.
Roads, airports, and processing facilities are long-range
investments that can have a large and enduring impact on the
national economy, although local people may resent feeling
no immediate improvement in their own position despite the
enormous expenditure; small sums spent on a soccer field
or prizes for an agricultural exposition, by contrast, have a
psychological value out of all proportion to their economic
contribution.

In spite of all these problems, there remains widespread
interest in and concern for international aid, whether for
humanitarian or political purposes. A number of aid projects
have operated in Bolivia, and most of them continue to do so.
Among missionary groups, the New Tribes Missions and
Summer Institute of Linguistics (Wycliffe Bible Translators)
have been especially helpful to tribal Indians in the Oriente;
Methodist educational and medical facilities have long been
respected; Maryknoll priests have been active in community
development and the establishment of credit unions; U. S.
Franciscans run respected schools; and so forth. CARE
(Committee for American Remittances to Everywhere) provided great quantities of milk, butter, and cheese which
were an important food supplement to schoolchildren and
pregnant women during the early 1950's; Heifer, Inc. , sends
occasional livestock; lowlanders are thankful for the
Rockefeller Foundation's campaign against malaria in the
1930's; and there are many others.

Among international agencies, the United Nations long
maintained stations of its Andean Program in Pillapi and

Playa Verde in highland Bolivia, and at Cotoca in the Oriente.
The ostensible purpose of economic development and
cultural change was not achieved with the rapidity, breadth,
or depth that had been hoped (Lockwood, 1956; Leonard, 1966),
and these projects have been given over to the Bolivian Rural
Development Program. The UN's Food and Agricultural
Organization underwrote the excellent studies by Ferragut on
land reform (1963) and colonization (1961). UNICEF played
a major role in establishment of a dairy and milk-powdering
plant near Cochabamba, which is just beginning to produce a
surplus beyond local daily requirements.

The British Mission on Tropical Agriculture has begun
to provide the first realistic estimates of the potential of
the Oriente (Misión Británica, 1962). German participation
has heretofore focused on the mining industry, but will
undoubtedly be expanded. Japan's role in colonization and
economic diversification has already been discussed.

Without a doubt, the country which has aided Bolivia
longest and most lavishly is the United States; a program in
public health was begun in the mid-1940's, and a variety of
other projects have proliferated until U. S. funds constituted
over 30 per cent of the national budget in the early 1960's.
The joint Bolivian-American public health service was dissolved in 1963, but Peace Corps remains active in this area;
a similarly joint educational service was dissolved then. The
joint agricultural service is again expanding its activities
after having cut them short following Congressional criticism
in the mid-1950's. A joint highway service is still in operation; special missions are concerned with civil aeronautics,
police training, military training, mapping, mining, and a
variety of other activities.

An analysis of the psychological failure of extravagant
U. S. aid programs here would be a dreary repetition of an
old story already familiar from other areas--the fundamental
problem, from the point of view of the local people, seems
to be a total lack of concern for (or even awareness of) their
wants and needs. It is only fair to point out, however, that
several large-scale AID projects have been immensely
beneficial in economic terms. Anthropologists have often
been hypercritical of such programs, because of faults

which loom large in the minds of the host people. This "inside" view is important, but should not obscure our broader understanding. For example, it is clear that, whatever the abuses and shortcomings of U. S. technical and economic assistance at the local level throughout Bolivia, the program has not only provided important machinery, public works, and sources of credit which have stimulated economic development, but, in a larger sense, has provided the funds without which the national government could not have achieved its unusual degree of stability, and the thoroughgoing revolution might long ago have been "nipped in the bud. "

Opportunities for constructive international aid have been implied throughout this volume, but a few recurrent points deserve special mention. If one wishes to have an intelligent basis for planning, a variety of basic research projects should be undertaken as indicated above. If one wishes to assure the continued growth of the national economy, more and better routes of communication have a high priority, as does the development of safeguards to assure that industrious and imaginative individuals not be hampered by arbitrary and inappropriate limitations on their enterprise. If one wishes to provide immediate and appreciated aid to a large number of individuals, a program of small-scale credit and rural education should have top priority.

In this final chapter, I have spoken perhaps more about the weaknesses of Bolivia's present situation than I have about her strengths. This is not academic objectivity, but reflects my particular concern with needs and opportunities for further research, and implications for action. Criticism seems somehow weightier in print than does praise, and I fear that the overall picture may seem far gloomier to many readers than it would if I did not have such concerns. The Bolivia of today is vastly different from that of 1952; in many ways it is a stronger country in which many people enjoy a better life. The Bolivia of tomorrow will undoubtedly be vastly different from that of today; I point out present problems in the hope that some of them may be lessened, and it may become an even stronger country in which more people enjoy an even better life.

Land reform and social revolution continue to be an exciting adventure for Bolivia and Bolivians. They have demonstrated that the dominance by a powerful minority over a disenfranchized majority can be broken, without physical annihilation of the oligarchy. They have further shown that campesinos can be integrated into economic and political systems at the national level within less than a generation. This may be taking a little longer than social philosophers or economic planners would wish, but it is taking far less time than most social scientists would have predicted. During the decade and a half of Bolivia's land reform and social revolution, campesinos have developed an awareness and demonstrated activity in these realms that outstripped any temperate expectation.

In different ways, people in many different countries want to share parts of this adventure. The problems of Bolivia are world-wide ones. We hope that other peopies may learn, as we have, and profit from this experience.

APPENDIX PARAPHRASE OF
BOLIVIA'S AGRARIAN
REFORM LAW OF
AUGUST 2, 1953

—Dwight B. Heath*

SECTION I: ON AGRARIAN PROPERTY

Part I: Original Right of the Nation

Article 1
  The soil, subsoil, and water belong by original right to the Bolivian nation.

Article 2
  The State recognizes and guarantees private agrarian property when it fills a useful function for the society.

Part II: Forms of Agrarian Property

Article 3
  Public domain comprises all roads, lakes, ponds, and rivers.

Article 4
  Patrimonial domain of the State comprises all unused land beyond town limits, lands belonging to government institutions, and public forests.

———————————

*Paraphrase and annotations are by Heath. The Spanish is included in those instances where shades of meaning may be crucial; quotation marks enclose direct translations. The full text of the decree, together with a number of amendments and supplementary related documents, is available in del Castillo (1955).

Article 5
Private agrarian property is that which is given to persons (individual or corporate) in order that they may exercise their rights according to civil law, including this decree. The State recognizes only the following types.

Article 6
The campesino homestead (solar campesino) is a rural residence, insufficient for the subsistence requirements of a family.

Article 7
The small property (pequeña propiedad) is worked by the campesino and his family for their own needs. Other workers may occasionally be used for specific jobs.

Article 8
The medium property (propiedad mediana) is larger than the small, but lacks the characteristics of the agricultural enterprise. Salaried laborers or machines are employed, and the major portion of production is for market.

Article 9
The property of the indigenous community (propiedad de comunidad indígena) belongs to specific indigenous social groups.

Article 10
The cooperative agrarian property (propiedad agraria cooperativa) is that owned, individually or collectively, by members of an agricultural cooperative.

Article 11
The agricultural enterprise (empresa agrícola) has large-scale investment of capital, salaried labor, and modern technology (except where irregular topography disallows it).

Article 12
The State does not recognize the latifundium (latifundio), the large, rural holding which is minimally exploited by

antiquated labor-intensive methods, and which perpetuates
a system of feudal oppression in the altiplano. [1]

Part III: Maximum Extensions of Agrarian Properties

Article 13
Only the economically cultivable area is counted in
determining the maximum extension of a private property. [2]

Article 14
Unusable lands (described in Article 100 d, e) may be
included, but their area not counted, in the property which
surrounds them.

Article 15
The maximum extension of the small property is listed
for various geographic zones: altiplano and puna (4 subzones,

---

[1] The distinguishing features of the latifundium are extremely
vague, especially in view of the fact that this sort of property
is subject to total expropriation whereas the agricultural
enterprise (distinguished only by imprecise features) may
retain large extensions of land. Cf. Articles 11, 17, 34, 35,
36.

[2] There is a compelling logic to counting only "economically
cultivable areas" in determining the extension of land which
may be given to an individual. SNRA does not have agronomists
in the field, however, and it is the local topographer who
determines which areas should be so classified. There is no
question that the rugged terrain and other natural features often
negate the agricultural value of a large portion of many
holdings. Among such impediments are salt flats in the southern
altiplano, rocky outcroppings and steep hillsides in the valleys
and yungas, craggy and snowcapped puna throughout the
mountains, swamps and deserts in the lowlands. Even
recognizing these problems, it still seems doubtful that any
property should be as much as 90 per cent useless, so that one
is tempted to suspect that some graft may be involved in those
situations where grants involve thousands of hectares of
"uncultivable" land surrounding a "medium property" of 150
hectares or less.

ranging from 10 to 35 hectares[3]); valleys (3 subzones, two of which are further subdivided among dry, irrigated, and viticultural lands, ranging from 3 to 20 hras.); subtropical zone (3 subzones, ranging from 10 to 80 hras.).

Article 16
        The maximum extension of the medium property varies in geographic zones as follows: altiplano zone (4 subzones, ranging from 80 to 350 hectares); valleys (several specified open valleys around Cochabamba, subdivided to distinguish among irrigated and very moist, dry, and viticultural lands, ranging from 24 to 100 hras.[4]; other open valleys, similarly subdivided, ranging from 24 to 150 hras.; closed valleys, 80 hras., of which not more than 40 may be in bottomlands); subtropical zone (3 subzones, ranging from 150 to 600 hras.); tropical agricultural zone, 500 hras.

Article 17
        The maximum extension of the agricultural enterprise is: zone influenced by Lake Titicaca, 400 hectares; Andean, altiplano, and puna zone, 800 hras.; open valleys neither adjacent to the city of Cochabamba nor affected by the Angostura irrigation system, 600 hras.; closed valleys, 230 hras., of which not more than 80 may be bottomlands; tropical and subtropical zone, 2,000 hras.[5]
        Such grants can only be made where the land is available and where there is bona fide capital investment, or intention of it.

----

[3] Land areas are given in hectares (hras.); one hectare equals 10,000 square meters, or 2.471 acres.

[4] This was subsequently reduced to 6 to 40 hectares, by DS 03960, February 17, 1955.

[5] It is noteworthy that the "zones" and "subzones" in which different maximum extensions apply are very different in Articles 15-17. There is thus no comparability of regions when one speaks of the various types of agrarian properties, or vice versa. Nor is any of the regions strictly delimited in geographic terms; the local topographer assigns a property to a given zone and subzone when he prepares his maps and technical report (informe).

Article 18
    National Agrarian Reform Service (Servicio Nacional de
Reforma Agraria, SNRA) will determine where such enterprises may be established.

Article 19
    The maximum extension of an agricultural cooperative
depends on the number of associates. When small and
medium holdings are both included, the latter may comprise
no more than 25 per cent of the total.

Article 20
    A cooperative of medium landholders may not hold more
than twice the area allowable to an agricultural enterprise in
that zone.

Part IV: Maximum Extensions of Livestock Properties

Article 21
    A livestock property (propiedad ganadera) in the tropical
or subtropical zone may be small (pequeña, to 500 hectares);
medium (mediana, to 2,500 hras.), or a large enterprise
(gran empresa, with 5 hras. per head of adult stock, to a
maximum of 50,000 hras.). [6]

Article 22
    Livestock enterprises have a year in which to dispose of
surplus stock or land.

Article 23
    Waterholes and hillocks which do not become flooded are
for common use.

Article 24
    Campesino communities (comunidades campesinos, see
Article 124-8) should have pastureland in common.

Article 25
    Stock remains the property of the present owner, and any
reallocation will be limited to land.

---

[6] Allotting land to stockraisers on a per capita basis obviously
sets a ceiling on their herds.

Article 26
    Natural pastures in the altiplano and valleys should be
divided among employees and owners, in proportion to the
number of livestock they own, with certain maximum limitations on the landlord. [7]

Article 27
    Improvements made for the cattle industry (such as
cultivated pasturage) remain the property of whoever made
them.

Article 28
    SNRA will regulate further expansion of livestock opera-
tions.

SECTION II: THE EXPROPRIATION (AFECTACIÓN)
                    OF PROPERTY

Part I: The Concentration of Land

Article 29
    This decree establishes the bases for political and
economic democracy in the rural area, through its specifications for reallocation of land.

Article 30
    The latifundium is completely abolished.

Article 31
    Although industrial capitalization is beneficial, monopo-
lization of land is prejudicial.

Part II: The Non-Expropriability (Inafectabilidad) of
                Small and Medium Properties

Article 32
    The small property cannot be expropriated.

---

[7] In order to encourage commercial dairying in the valleys
around Cochabamba, the grazing land of enterprises with
select stock, wages, and other capitalistic features was subsequently declared inalienable, DL 03817, August 26, 1954.

Article 33
      Neither can the medium, except that plots worked by
tenants (such as sayañas, pequjales, etc.) should be made
theirs.   Eligibility for such plots should not interfere with
tenants' right to obtain grants of small properties elsewhere;
plots abandoned by tenants who do so may revert to the owner,
if he reimburses the tenant for improvements.

            Part III: The Expropriation (Afectación) of the
                       Latifundium

Article 34
      All lands characterized as latifundio (see Article 12) are
expropriated in full.

Article 35
      Investment of capital or use of machinery exempt large
landholdings from the status of latifundium, as does work on
the land by the owner or his immediate family. If only the
last of these criteria for exemption obtains, however, the
holding should be reduced to medium size.

            Part IV: The Expropriation (Afectación) of the
                      Agricultural Enterprise

Article 36
      The agricultural enterprise is not subject to expropria-
tion, if unsalaried tenancy is combined with wage labor,
modern techniques are employed, and at least twice the
initial capital is invested.

Article 37
      Unsalaried tenants (colonos) on agricultural enterprises
should be given land as follows: if the property exceeds the
maximum the surplus should be given to them collectively;
if the property does not exceed the maximum, as much as 33
per cent may be divided evenly among the tenants, so long as
no tenant would thus have less than before.

Article 38
The authorities in charge of redistribution should determine the form of regrouping of individual plots, so that the landlord and campesinos have continuous rather than scattered holdings. [8]

Part V: The Expropriation of Agricultural Properties in the Tropical and Subtropical Zones

Article 39
Medium properties in these areas may not be expropriated.

Article 40
On properties of more than 1,200 hectares, 100 hras. should be set aside for the establishment of settlements (caserios), whose occupants should be given plots of not more than 1 hectare per family.

Article 41
The owner of any partially expropriated property may select the areas he chooses to keep, within a quadrilateral outline if possible, with the major axis perpendicular to the nearest state road.

Part VI: The Restitution of Land

Article 42
Lands usurped from indigenous communities should be restored to them.

Article 43
Lands thus claimed may be occupied provisionally by the members of a community while their claim is pending.

---

[8] This attempt to consolidate the scattered holdings of each individual into a larger single parcel has some rationale in terms of mechanical efficiency, both in cultivation by the campesino and in surveying by the topographer. Campesinos have often resisted, however, not so much because of sentimental attachment to specific plots as because dispersed holdings often support very different crops in different ecological areas.

Article 44

An area equal to that of medium property should be provisionally reserved for the owner; resident campesinos are eligible for claims as specified in Articles 77-91; non-residents who can prove that they are members of the community may get portions of unused land.

Article 45

If the judgment favors the community's claims, the area which was provisionally occupied by the landlord reverts, without indemnization, to the community.

Article 46

The land referred to in the previous article should be for collective use; plots held individually by campesinos may be made theirs.

Article 47

Plots belonging to members who die without heirs revert to the community, for collective use or for school-fields.

Article 48

Members who have a right to a claim in either of two communities may claim a plot only in one.

Article 49

The indigenous communities, as corporate entities, may claim restitution of usurped lands.

Part VII: Properties of the State and of Corporate Entities

Article 50

Agrarian properties belonging to agencies (órganos) of the State, universities, and self-governing institutions are unencumberable as long as they are used for appropriate purposes. Unsalaried tenants of these properties should be given land.

Article 51

Such institutions may acquire areas beyond the fixed maxima, as long as such lands fulfill a useful function for society at large.

Article 52
Properties held as undivided legacies (en lo proindiviso) should be divided into as many properties as there are co-owners.

Part VIII: Municipal Properties

Article 53
Municipal properties where there is no public service are all expropriated.

Part IX: Properties of Religious Institutions

Article 54
Religious institutions of whatever creed may retain as much as a medium property, subject to the usual conditions except that members of contemplative religious orders need not work the land personally.

Article 55
Concessions of unused land requested by missionaries for purposes of colonization may exceed the limits of individual properties only when they are to be divided into small properties comprising a cooperative.

Part X: Properties of Social Welfare Institutions

Article 56
Institutions of social welfare which maintain schools, asylums, and shelters (albergues), using rent from agricultural properties, may have as much as three times the area allowable for a medium property in that zone. Non-salaried tenants there should be given land, and feudal systems of exploitation must be discontinued.

Part XI: Lands of Indigenous Communities

Article 57
Indigenous communities are owners of the lands which they possess in common. Apportionment among families may follow custom.

Article 58
The properties of indigenous communities are inalienable, except by special regulation. Communities have all the rights and obligations of private and cooperative landholders.

Article 59
Members should plan, with the counsel of State technicians, for the efficient redistribution of plots.

Article 60
Members have no obligations in labor or cash; politicians, soldiers, or clerics who solicit payment are criminally abusing their authority.

Article 61
Non-member campesinos who live and work in an indigenous community may solicit land in the uncultivated area, of not more than the average size owned by members.

Article 62
Unsalaried tenants of feudal fincas owned by indigenous communities have the same rights of claim to land as do those of private properties.

SECTION III: SURPLUS AND REVERTED EXPROPRIATED
              LANDS

Part I: Populated Zones

Article 63
There are three categories of encumbered lands: those expropriated for immediate adjudication, surplus lands, and uninhabited expropriated lands.

Article 64
Lands expropriated for immediate adjudication are those which are transferred directly from a medium property-holder or latifundista to campesinos so that the land belongs immediately to him who works it or who lives on it.

Article 65

Surplus lands are those which remain after the reallocation of latifundium land among local campesinos. They remain
property of the community, for future allocation to new
families or to neighboring campesinos. Where a latifundium
extends beyond the frontier of settlement, the community may
claim as surplus three times the total area occupied by them;
the rest reverts to the State.

Article 66

Uninhabited expropriated lands are those which revert
to public domain when expropriated from a latifundium, because no eligible campesinos live there to claim portions.
The State will endeavor to reallocate them to individuals and
institutions which will make them productive, without
developing a rural monopoly.

Part II: The Reversion of Vacant Fiscal Lands
(Tierras Baldías)

Article 67

All concessions of fiscal lands which do not comply with
previously specified conditions revert to the State without
indemnization. Those which have complied with specifications also revert, with indemnization, if required for the
establishment of settlements, colonies, defense posts, or
other collective necessities.

Article 68

Concessions which have been settled and cultivated, as
specified, may be kept to the same maximum extension as
private properties in the area.

Article 69

Such reverted lands constitute the Fiscal Reserve of the
Nation. SNRA will plan distribution, immigration, and
colonization for national benefit.

SECTION IV: RUBBER AND BRAZIL NUT FORESTS

Part I: Encumberability and Concession

Article 70
All rubber and brazil nut trees revert to public domain.
Concessions for their exploitation will be subject to the
following conditions:
(a) each worker who collects the sap or nuts is granted a
concession of the trees which he presently exploits, to a
maximum of 400 (dos estradas). He may also have a small
property in a place suitable for farming.
(b) workers may form cooperatives for production and
marketing.
(c) the State, in collaboration with private enterprise, will
form companies for exploitation of forest products, but only
in areas currently unworked.[9]

Article 71
Land in the rubber-producing area is subject to the same
conditions specified for agricultural and stockraising properties in tropical and subtropical zones. Surplus lands
revert to the State without indemnization.

Article 72
Brazil nut trees are for common use, except where they
occur on private property or in rubber concessions.

Part II: Formation of Urban Centers in the Outposts
(Barracas)[10]

---

[9]Revision of this article increases individual concessions to
600 trees (three estradas), but disallows that any foreigners hold concessions within 50 kilometers of the
national border (DS 03615, January 28, 1954). Not only
does the revision purport to defend the national territory
against supposed incursions of Brazilians along the still
undemarcated boundary in the Northeast, but it also provides some defense for the individual collectors against
abuses of wholesalers, by requiring that prices of goods
with which they barter be approved by national labor
inspectors.

[10]The barracas grew as collecting points for rubber or nuts;
each developed as a tiny "company town," around a ware-
house set on a riverbank. Many have been abandoned by the
wholesalers, but the settlers have stayed on.

Article 73
All outposts (barracas) are centers of free access. In those which have more than fifteen houses, the homesteads (solares) should belong to the owners of the buildings, without indemnization.

Article 74
The municipal administration of the state capital should determine the boundaries (radio urbano) of the outposts, with sufficient space to give a homestead to each worker, to install public services and parks, and to reserve an area for grazing livestock.

Article 75
The area within a radius of 5 kilometers around any outpost is reserved for lots of not more than 50 hectares each, following a specific plan which should be prepared for each case.

Article 76
All roads, ports, and paths are for common use, so are water and trees, to the extent that they are needed for domestic purposes.

SECTION V: DOTATION

Part I: Priorities in the Right to Dotation

Article 77
All Bolivians, above 18 years, of either sex, "who dedicate or want to dedicate themselves to agricultural labors will be given lands where they are available in accordance with the plans of the Government, on the condition that they initiate agricultural work within two years."[11]

------

[11] These are noble, if difficult, provisions. In this instance, political expediency clearly outweighed economic feasibility. Among the inexperienced farmers who have applied for land grants are undoubtedly many sincere individuals for whom such "homesteading" has been a real challenge. Many others have misrepresented their intentions, however, in order to get land for speculative purposes. There

Article 78
    Campesinos over 18 who have been subject to feudal ex-
ploitation, married men over 14, and widows with minor sons
are hereby declared owners of the plots which they now occupy
and work, until SNRA grants them a small property or access
to enough collectively worked land to allow them sufficient
family income.

Article 79
    All previously stated exceptions to the granting of small
properties apply in the above instance as well.

Article 80
    Foreigners have the same rights specified in Article 77,
on condition that they comply with specifications for immigration and colonization. [12]

Article 81
    The priority (derecho de preferencia) of an individual for
a land grant in an area is based on his permanently residing
in the place and having the occupation of farmer. Degree of
priority (grado de preferencia) should be determined for each
zone and type of property.

Article 82
    In a feudal latifundium, the colonos and agricultural
laborers with two years or more of residence to date, have
priority. At the time of the initial dotation, an area of not
less than 10 per cent of the total individual plots should be
set aside for collective use. A school-field should be set
aside, of an area at least as large as each of the individual plots.

----

is no official check on whether land is in fact farmed by
the claimant within two years, and neither of these types
of new landowners is likely to contribute significantly to
agricultural production.

[12] Generous conditions for immigration were intended to
bring foreigners to expand and develop the frontier areas
of the eastern tropical lowlands. "Colonies" of Japanese,
Ryukyuans, Italians, and others have done just that, and
contribute significantly to the national economy.

Article 83
        Rights to adjudicable lands in such case should be
decided as follows:
(a) if there is enough land, each family should get a unit of
dotation (unidad de dotación, see Article 92). If surplus
cultivable land remains, it should be given to campesinos
from medium and small properties within the same or a
neighboring canton, within a radius of 6 kilometers. If a
surplus still remains, the community should extend its
collectively cultivated land.
(b) if there is not enough to provide a unit of dotation to each
family, the grants (extensiones adjudicables) should be
reduced proportionately so that each who has priority may
have some land. Campesinos who get too little may solicit
new grants in areas where land is available.

Article 84
        Campesinos of medium properties have priority to
surplus lands on latifundia within a radius of 6 kilometers.

Article 85
        Colonos who already have private property should be
granted only enough more to make their total holding the
same size as grants to other campesinos on the same property.

Article 86
        In first class colonizable areas (see Article 100a),
people who solicit plots no larger than the small property
should have priority.

Article 87
        In the tropical and subtropical area, where workers get
wages, they should have priority to the uncultivated lands
nearest their residence.

Article 88
        In the regions of Nor and Sud Yungas, in the department
of La Paz, and in other similar areas where the same agricultural labor system obtains, tenants should have priority
to the usufruct plots (sayañas y arriendos) which they now
occupy.

Article 89
        Graduates of departments of agronomy and agricultural

schools should enjoy the same priority accorded to campesinos of medium properties, in colonizable areas or in surplus ex-latifundium lands in the rural area nearest their homes.

Article 90
      The expropriated surplus in the yungas area of La Paz and Cochabamba is reserved for preferential concession, in small properties, to the wounded and survivors of those killed in the National Revolution, to all middle-class Bolivians, rail and transport workers, factory and construction workers, and miners who wish to settle there.

Article 91
      Aside from the land grants discussed in this part, any campesino from the altiplano and valleys may solicit 50 hectares in the Oriente, on the condition that he begin work within two years.

Part II: The Unit of Dotation (Unidad de Dotación)

Article 92
      Where there is land enough, the unit of dotation per family[13] is equal to the small property. Where there is not enough, the area per family should be reduced proportionately to give space to all who have claim.[14]

----

[13] This article is the first which speaks of the beneficiary as a "family" rather than an individual. According to Article 77, any adult may solicit land; most judges interpret this and Article 92 as meaning that only a head of household should do so. The problem of subsequent subdivision of land through inheritance is nowhere treated in the decree.

[14] The political expedient of providing at least token satisfaction for the land-hunger of a maximum number of campesinos in a minimum length of time has aggravated one of the key problems that agrarian reform might have solved. Minifundismo, the excessive fractionation of land into plots too small even for subsistence farming, has become even more widespread in densely populated areas where it was long recognized as a major obstacle to increased agricultural production and living standards in pre-reform

Article 93
    SNRA should effect the reductions where necessary.

Article 94
    Cooperatives of minifundistas should have priority to
land nearest to transportation routes in colonization zones.

Part III: Procedures for Dotation

Article 95
    Campesinos or the landlord, separately or together, may
solicit determination of the encumberable area. [15]   Special

---

times. The authors of the reform were well aware of the
economic fallacy of this provision, but were correct in
considering it of extreme importance in symbolic terms for
assuming that campesinos would support the administration.
Article 83(b) provides an alternative, but only in very
recent years have any appreciable number of campesinos
begun to move to frontier areas where ample land is
available, and, even at the present rate, it is doubtful
that internal migration can ever actually relieve population
pressure in the altiplano and valleys; it seems barely to
keep pace with normal population growth.

[15]The initiator may be a proprietor, requesting a judgment of
non-expropriability (inafectabilidad); or he may be a
claimant (demandante) requesting that land be given (dotado)
to him through expropriation (afectación) of a specific
property which is not appropriately used by its present
owner, or which is in the public domain, either municipal
(tierras municipales) or rural and federally owned
(tierras baldías, or tierras fiscales). Such a claimant may
be an individual, acting on his own behalf, or the secretary
general of a campesino syndicate, acting on behalf of the
members. Such syndicates seem, in most instances, to
have been formed for the sole or primary purpose of serving
as a corporate entity for the filing of such a claim. The
syndicate is, in essence, a sort of cooperative land company,
since campesinos share the legal fees, costs of mapping,
and related expenses, and yet expect to receive individual
titles to specified plots after their consolidated claim has
been processed.

regulations will apply. [16]

Article 96

When properties have fewer than 25 campesinos, they may form a campesino community (as specified in Article 121).

Part IV: Redistribution of Land

Article 97
Once they have determined that a latifundium is to be expropriated, SNRA should plan its redistribution.

Article 98
Lands for collective farming should constitute not less than 10 per cent of the total assigned to individual families.

Article 99
An evaluative typology of land will serve in determining compensation as follows.

Article 100
Until adequate agronomic studies are made, [17] the following classification of soils provides guidelines for differential compensation, and so forth:
(a) first-class soils are those which, because of composition, irrigation or normal moisture, and good climate, can produce on a commercial basis the two agricultural products which are grown in the most fertile lands of that zone, without much fertilizer and without more than a year's fallowing between crops;
(b) second-class soils are those which are adequate for crops

---

[16]The procedures for processing land claims under the agrarian reform are described in the section on "Administration of the Law," in Chapter 2.

[17]"Adequate agronomic studies" had nowhere been initiated by mid-1965, and it seems doubtful that they ever will be conducted on any meaningful scale. It is patent that the classificatory categories listed here are neither clear-cut nor exhaustive. This matters little, however, since there seems no prospect of anyone's ever being compensated for expropriated land.

other than the two which are grown in the best lands in the zone. Except in the yungas, all lands with a slope of 7 per cent or more, and all flatlands too rocky for mechanized agriculture, are second-class even if they support those prime crops;
(c) high-class pasture (pastizales de buena clase) and timber-yielding forests are those which are suitable for grazing or for lumbering but not for systematic cultivation, whether because of a steep slope or the quality of the soil;
(d) unfertile lands (terrenos de escasa fertilidad) are those which have poor pasture, or vegetation usable only as fuel;
(e) wasteland (terreno inaprovechable) is that which is barren and useless to man.

SECTION VI: RURAL SETTLEMENTS (POBLADOS)

Part I: Forms of Rural Population Establishments

Article 101
    Three forms of establishments are distinguished in rural areas:
(a) towns or villages (pueblos o aldeas);
(b) hamlets (villorios o rancherías);
(c) dispersed homesteads (establecimientos diseminados en el campo).

Article 102
    Towns or villages tend to have houses ranged forming streets and blocks. The municipal administration of the state capital should recognize as such any center with more than fifty inhabited houses. Such legally recognized villages (aldeas) may petition the municipality for the establishment of boundaries (radio urbano), and means for the development of a water system. The area within the boundaries then become subject to planning.

Article 103
    The lots (or homesteads, solares) occupied by houses, together with an enclosed patio and a yard (canchón) of at least 500 square meters should be confirmed to each house-owner.

Article 104

In cases where the town lies wholly or partly within a medium property or other legal large holding, and the landlord also owns the house, adjudication should be in favor of the colonos who have lived there at least two years. In such case, the houselot (solar) is in addition to the individual dotation of land; recipients should indemnize the owner for buildings at a just price set by SNRA, under the same conditions as indemnization for land.

Article 105

Exceptions to the above are general-use buildings such as the manor house (casa de hacienda), warehouses, industrial installations, servants' quarters, and other outbuildings occupied by colonos.

Article 106

Hamlets (villorios o rancherías) are groups of campesino houses in a line or in a random cluster concentrated so that there is no more than an average distance of twenty meters between them.

Article 107

On medium properties and agricultural enterprises, a campesino may continue living in his present house until the landlord builds, at his expense, a similar house on the campesino's own land. Indemnization may be arranged as they see fit.

Article 108

Water sources are for common use for domestic purposes, whether or not the settlement is incorporated (constituida).

Part II: The Founding of Towns and Hamlets
(Pueblos y Caseríos)

Article 109

The municipal administration of each department capital may determine areas for the founding of new towns, independently or at the request of at least fifty families.

Article 110

Such founding should take place preferably on municipal lands or in private lands expropriated for that purpose; each

family should be given a houselot (solar) on which to build a
house.

Article 111
Areas sufficient for the founding of new urban centers
should be reserved near railway stations, important highway
intersections, and on the shores of navigable rivers.

Article 112
In the tropical and subtropical plains, hamlets should be
founded on portions of large private landholdings, as specified
in Article 40.

Article 113
Lands on which they have built should be confirmed to
inhabitants of all provincial capitals, sections (secciones),
and cantons; land for streets, parks, official buildings,
athletic fields, and other public uses should become public
domain after indemnization.

SECTION VII: COLONIZABLE AREAS

Part I

Article 114
Concessions of first-class lands up to the size of a medium
property should be provided to stimulate colonization by
citizens and immigrants.[18] SNRA will determine whether,
in not more than one third of the colonizable area, agricultural enterprises may be established.

Article 115
First-class colonization zones are:
(a) a strip 25 kilometers wide on either side along railways,
national highways (present and future), and navigable rivers,
where there are fiscal lands (tierras baldías) or others
reverted to public domain;
(b) a radius of 5 kilometers around settlements of more than
1,000 population, in the tropical and subtropical plains;
(c) any region so designated by the government.

---

[18]See note 12 and Article 83(b) above.

Article 116
    In such zones, priority for dotation is allowed to landless
campesinos, unemployed laborers, returning Bolivian emi-
grants, veterans of the Chaco War, and survivors of those
killed in the National Revolution.

SECTION VIII: EXCESSIVELY FRAGMENTED AREAS

    Part I: Types

Article 117
    Rural areas in which holdings (predios) are excessively
fragmented are: rural residential areas, and areas of
predominant minifundio.

    Part II: Rural Residential Areas

Article 118
    Rural residential areas are those in which the population
is concentrated and holdings are progressively subdivided
principally because of each family's preference for keeping
their own homestead with their own lot, with more concern
for the area of residence than for agricultural lands.

Article 119
    Such an area may have one or more of the following
characteristics: near urban or industrial centers; location
favorable for rural trade and communication; near good
areas for hunting, fishing, forests, or vegetable or animal
resources; climate, topography, water, and means for the
subsistence of a social group.

    Part III: Areas of Predominant Minifundio

Article 120
    Areas of predominant minifundio are those in which the
great majority of properties are too small to assure the
subsistence of the owners, whose principal occupation is
agriculture.[19]

---

[19]See note 14 above.

Article 121
   In such area, where the scarcity of workable land is
aggravated by the fragmentation of each property into
scattered parcels, a policy of regrouping of holdings
should be applied. [20]

SECTION IX: CAMPESINO ORGANIZATION

Part I: The Campesino Community

Article 122
   The campesino community (comunidad campesino)is the
social group based on proximity of residence and common
interests, and whose members more often interact among
themselves than among others for the satisfaction of the
needs of social living (necesidades de convivencia social).
The State recognizes and guarantees the existence of such
groups. Their recognition as corporate entities will be
regulated by law. [21]

---

[20]See note 8 above.

[21]There is no doubt that the campesino community does
   exist as a sort of "natural community," but it was not
   recognized in this usage--as a corporate legal entity--
   by any of the Bolivians consulted in the course of this
   investigation, including CNRA officials as well as syndicate
   leaders, campesinos, agrarian judges, and others. The
   concerns of the community spelled out in Article 124 are
   generally those attributed to the syndicate (the concerns
   appropriate to the syndicate are nowhere specified in the
   law), and most informants assumed that investigators had
   confused the terms "sindicato campesino"and "comunidad
   indígena" in "inventing" the unheard-of term, "comunidad
   campesino." It appears that Articles 125 and 126 have been
   generally disregarded, and the comunidad campesino is
   almost everywhere indistinguishable from the sindicato
   campesino (or, in a few instances, the cooperativa
   campesina, which differed in name only from nearby
   sindicatos).

Article 123
     Three types of campesino communities are recognized,
depending on their origin:
(a) an hacienda community is composed of at least fifty
families who, under a latifundium system, were subject
to the same patronal dependence, whether on a single
finca or on several fincas belonging to the same landlords.
Such a community has its basis in having been a productive
unit, with discipline of joint labor, and families considering
themselves members of the group. Such a community may
maintain the cooperative system of production, for their
own benefit, on lands assigned to the community;
(b) a grouped campesino community (comunidad campesino
agrupada) is composed of at least fifty families from various
medium and small properties who join together voluntarily
in order to be recognized as a corporate entity;
(c) an indigenous community is composed of the families of
campesinos who, under the name of originarios and agregados,
are owners of an area legally recognized as an indigenous
community by virtue of titles granted by the colonial or
republican governments, or traditional occupation. Such
a community is self-governing in internal affairs.

Part II: Functions of the Campesino Community

Article 124
     The campesino community has the following functions:
(a) to represent the interests of its members in legal affairs;
(b) to promote the general welfare of the population, with
special attention to education, in school and out; improvement of housing and living standards; care and protection of
health; improvement of productive techniques and social and
economic relations; promotion of cooperativism. [22]

Article 125
     The campesino community as such is independent and
may not form part of any association, federation, con-
federation, or other group. [23]

---

[22]See note 21 above.

[23]See note 21 above.

Article 126
   The campesino community differs from the agrarian
syndicate as follows: the former is not involved in the
class-struggle beyond the locality; nor can it form part
of provincial, departmental, or national organization.[24]

Article 127
   Although distinct from them, the campesino community
need not exclude agrarian syndicates and other cultural,
political, or economic organizations.

Article 128
   The economic resources of a campesino community
should be applied only to local benefits. Any contribution
to outside organizations is a punishable malversion of funds.

Part III: Jungle Indian Reservations (Reducciones
Selvicolas)

Article 129
   The jungle-dwelling groups of the tropical and
subtropical plain "which are in a savage state and have
a primitive organization" are protected by the State.

Article 130
   Field schools (núcleos escolares campesinos) and
authorized private institutions charged with incorporating
such people into national life should have sufficient land
to settle each family and convert them to independent
farmers. The collective and private property of such
people is inalienable. All reservations (instituciones
de reducción selvícola) are always under government
control.

Article 131
   Cooperative work should be stimulated, without
prejudicing the establishment of family properties there.

---

[24]See note 21 above.

Part IV: Campesino Syndicates

Article 132

The campesino syndical organization is recognized as a means of defending members' rights and conserving social conquests. "Campesino syndicates should intervene in the execution of the Agrarian Reform." They may be independent or affiliated. [25]

Part V: Agricultural Cooperatives

Article 133

The social utility of agricultural and stockraising cooperatives comprising members of communities, colonists, or medium or small propertyholders, is recognized. The State will promote their organization and development through a forthcoming law. [26]

Article 134

Agricultural cooperativism is founded on the following basic principles: voluntary membership; equal rights and obligations among members; democratic control and independent personal voting in proportion to the capital subscribed by each; voluntary group work (ejecución libre de las actividades sociales) and distribution of income in proportion to the quality and quantity of work contributed or the sum of business conducted (monto de las operaciones realizadas).

---

[25]It is striking that the campesino syndicate, which has been one of the key institutions in both land reform and social revolution, is not discussed in more detail. Compare notes 15 and 21 above.

[26] This was done in 1958, and a Bolivian National Cooperative Service was established within MAC. The widespread assumption that campesinos find cooperativism especially congenial seems unfounded. Furthermore, the high rate of failure among experimental cooperatives (due to misunderstandings, inept management, and embezzlement) has done little to inspire confidence.

Article 135
   The lands of such cooperatives are unencumbrable,
within limits fixed in Articles 19 and 20.

Part VI: Exploitation of Collective Lands

Article 136
   Collective lands of the campesino community are used
by all members. Agents (personeros) of the community
should direct work.

Article 137
   Income should be devoted to:
(a) paying costs of production;
(b) amortization of the price of the expropriated land;
(c) costs of general welfare for the community;
(d) distribution of profits (utilidades) among members.

Article 138
   The community has a responsibility, with necessary
technical assistance, to "achieve lasting changes in methods
of cultivation, and improve its collectivist experience. "[27]

Article 139
   The community may extend its collective landholdings
and capital "to introduce the division of labor through new
methods of exploitation, and lay the basis for collectivist
agriculture to benefit the nation. "

Part VII: School Organization

Article 140
   Campesino communities should found schools,
controlling them through school boards (Juntos Escolares)
composed of community members.

Article 141
   Such communities should maintain schools which
ex-landlords heretofore maintained.

----

[27]The collectivist emphasis of this and related articles
   has been virtually ignored in practice.

Article 142
The community is responsible for cultivating and
exploiting the schoolfield   to provide produce for student
breakfasts and luncheons; such land may be used for no
other purpose.

Part VIII: Community Power (Disposiciones Comunes)
of Campesino Organizations

Article 143
The agents (personeros) of a campesino community,
cooperative, school board, or other local organization
must be members and residents of the community.   Offices
in campesino organizations are unpaid.

SECTION X: REGIMEN OF CAMPESINO WORK

Part I

Article 144
The system of unpaid tenantry (colonato) is abolished,
as are all forms of unpaid servitude.   The campesino is
incorporated into the juridico-social regimen of the nation,
with full legal rights. [28]

Article 145
The system of wages is established as the norm of
remuneration in all individual or collective contracts. All
debts stemming from the feudal system (provenientes de
obligaciones personales) are cancelled in favor of the
workers.

---

[28]The truly revolutionary intention of the decree is clear
   in this article which had clear and immediate implications for the entire social order of the nation.
   Land reform was obviously conceived as only part
   of the intended social revolution, much of which has
   subsequently been accomplished.

SECTION XI: CONSERVATION AND DEFENSE OF NATIONAL RESOURCES

Part I: Forest and Animal Resources

Article 146
    Vegetable resources (such as cinchona, fine woods, and
so forth) and animal resources (with fine hides or plumage
or otherwise usable for industrial purposes) which are
nearing extinction are under national protection. The State
will control their exploitation.

Article 147
    Woods and pasturage may not be destroyed on any land
with a slope of over 15 per cent; except that in the yungas
and in regions of dense rural population with little cultivable
land, such land may be worked in horizontal furrows or
terraces.

Article 148
    The Government will defend renewable natural resources
by issuing:
(a) a forestry law;
(b) a hunting and fishing law, and regulations;
(c) a law for soil conservation and national parks. [29]

Part II: Livestock Exploitation

Article 149
    The exploitation of livestock will be regulated by the
State, in the following aspects:
(a) the size and labor regulation on livestock ranches;
(b) registration, number, care, sanitation, industry, and
commerce of cattle, horses, mules, sheep, pigs, goats,
and auchenia;
(c) development and protection of animal husbandry.

---

[29] The Directorate of Forestry, Hunting, and Soil Conser-
    vation was created within the Ministry of Agriculture,
    Stockraising, and Colonization, to serve this purpose
    (DL 03612, January 22, 1954).

SECTION XII: TERRITORIAL AND URBAN PLANNING

Part I

Article 150

A General Office of Territorial and Urban Planning will be created within the National Commission on Coordination and Planning.

SECTION XIII: WATER REGULATION

Part I

Article 151

Settlements (poblaciones) have a right to the use of sources of potable water for domestic purposes; agricultural or livestock properties have equal right to necessary quantities for their use, irrigation, or stockwatering (explotaciones, regadío o abrevaderos).

Article 152

Irrigation systems should still be maintained by the system of mitas or turnos (periodic labor draft, or taking turns), on all lands, encumbrable or not.

Article 153

Without affecting the system of mitas or turnos, the general rule is that the water which enters a property may be used within it, in the quantity required.

Article 154

The sale of water is forbidden, and the surplus from one property should pass freely to others which may need it.

Article 155

Special regulations will apply to the above, and regulate the activities of organizations charged with overseeing water use and irrigation.

SECTION XIV: PAYMENT FOR EXPROPRIATIONS AND
AMORTIZATION OF AGRARIAN DEBTS

Part I

Article 156
    Expropriations effected in accordance with Article 34
will be paid for, at their present cadastral value, prorated
in terms of area expropriated, with agrarian reform bonds,
which will earn 2 per cent non-capitalizable interest
annually, over 25 years. [30]

Article 157
    In amortization (redención) of the bonds, preference is
given to the Bolivian Agricultural Bank and to small-scale
rather than large-scale creditors. Collateral includes
mortgage on the campesino's land, harvests, livestock, and
industrial installations, and, furthermore, the guarantee of
the State.

Article 158
    Bonds can serve to cancel mortgages owed to the
Bolivian Agricultural Bank, or to taxes owed on encumbered
lands. They may also be used for the acquisition of national
lands in colonizable areas.

Article 159
    Special regulations will apply to these bonds. [31]

_____

[30] It is of academic but not practical interest to note that
galloping inflation of the time would have made even
prompt payments at cadastral value little more than
tokens. No one has received any reimbursement for
expropriated land, nor is there any longer the expectation
that they might.

[31] Conditions for payment of the bonds were spelled out in
considerable detail in DL 03525, October 15, 1953, but
have been completely ignored.

Article 160
    Campesinos benefited by the dotation of land should pay
for them at cadastral value, within 25 years of the date of
possession. SNRA will indicate how to determine costs for
each parcel. [32]

SECTION XV: EXECUTION OF THE AGRARIAN REFORM

        Part I: Agencies (Órganos)

Article 161
    The National Agrarian Reform Service (SNRA) is
created as the principal agency for the execution of this law
and of subsequent related provisions.

Article 162
    SNRA is composed of the following:
(a) President of the Republic;
(b) National Agrarian Reform Council (CNRA)[33] under the
Ministry of Rural Affairs (MAC);
(c) agrarian judges;[34]
(d) rural agrarian reform juntas;[35]
(e) rural inspectors.

---

[32] See notes 30 and 31 above. In the proposed revision of the
agrarian reform law which was approved by the Cabinet in
mid-1962 but remains in congressional committee, the fic-
tion of campesino payment for dotation would be removed.
The State, however, would be supposed to reimburse owners
for expropriated land, on similar terms.

[33] CNRA is the administrative board of SNRA. Its functions are
described in the section on "Administration of the Law," in
Chapter 2. See also note 36 and Article 165.

[34] Virtually every province has an agrarian judge whose job is
to administer the reform within the area of his jurisdiction.
See "Administration of the Law," note 36 and Article 166.

[35] These rural juntas were soon disbanded when it became
clear that the campesinos charged with local enforcement of
the reform often abused their authority and persecuted individuals in "kangaroo courts." See note 36 and Article 167.

Article 163
    Special laws will regulate the constitution, designation, eligibility, territorial jurisdiction, and procedures of these agencies. [36]

Part II: Their Functions (Atribuciones)

Article 164
    The President of the Republic is the supreme authority and evaluator (fiscalizadora) of SNRA. He will definitively resolve any questions emerging from the application of the law and subsequent provisions.

Article 165
    CNRA has the following functions:
(a) complete (integral y superior) planning in agrarian and campesino matters;
(b) subsequent regulation (elaboración reglamentaria) of the Agrarian Reform Law;
(c) hearing appealed suits (conocimiento, en grado de apelacion de las acciones) concerning petitions for land;
(d) issuance of titles to new landholders;
(e) organization of systems of development, cooperativism, and credit, in agriculture and stockraising;
(f) organization of systems of colonization.

Article 166
    Agrarian judges have the following functions:
(a) receiving litigious petitions for land, and reviewing (conocer en revision) the judgments of the rural junta;
(b) hearing these claims and making provisional judgments (resolverlas en primera instancia);
(c) hearing, on appeal, claims of Water Judges, as will be provided in a subsequent law.

----

[36] SNRA was established and CNRA's functions were spelled out by DL 03471, August 27, 1953. The job of agrarian judges was described there and in DS 03558, November 20, 1953, and DL 03803, August 12, 1954. The last decree also dealt with rural juntas, as did DL 03771, June 24, 1954.

Article 167
      The rural juntas have the following functions:
(a) applying the conditions of the present law and subsequent
regulations, within the area of their jurisdiction, through
discussion (en procedimiento conciliatorio), when asked by
a party or by rural inspectors;
(b) administering possession to new landholders, laying out
their boundaries as specified in the judgment (fallo).

SECTION XVI: FINAL AND TRANSITORY DISPOSITIONS

Part I: Leading and Usufruct (Arrendamientos y
           Permisos de Ocupación)

Article 168
      A special law will regulate those exceptional cases in
which leasing, tenancy (?, compania), and sharecropping
(aparcería) are permitted.

Article 169
      All contracts for concessions of fiscal land for rent or
usufruct (simple permiso de ocupación), for purposes of
agriculture, stockraising, lumbering, or collecting of forest
products, are subject to revision by agencies of agrarian
reform.

Article 170
      Leases of fiscal lands and permissions for the above
types of exploitation may not exceed the area of an agricultural enterprise.

Part II: The Double Property

Article 171
      The owner of two or more minifundios or small pro-
perties situated in different locations may keep them if
their total area does not exceed the maximum for a small
and medium property.

Article 172
      The owner of two or more plots in different locations
which total more than a medium property may choose one
or more to retain, totaling not more than a medium property.

Article 173
    Sharecroppers (aparceros) who have the use of a small
individual plot (pegujal o sayaña) as well may retain it and
cancel their sharecropping contract.

Article 174
    Whatever difficulty may occur in the application of this
law should be resolved in favor, first, of landless campesinos
and small property owners, and incidentally with attention to
production, the medium property, and the agricultural enterprise. [37]

Article 175
    "A didactically summarized and simplified translation
of the law shall be published in the Aymara, Quechua, and
Guaraní languages so that the campesino masses of all rural
districts may have a deep awareness of the new rights which
they have."

Article 176
    All laws, decrees, and resolutions contrary to the
present decree are revoked.

Article 177
    "From today, August 2, 1953, the unpaid servile system
of labor which prevailed in agriculture is abolished, and the
right to dotation of land, with title, is declared for all
Bolivian campesinos."

---

[37] This article again illustrates the primacy of political
expediency over economic feasibility in the phrasing of
the law. Giving small claims priority over agricultural
production gained widespread campesino support for the
MNR, but has been costly to the national economy where
a major portion of foodstuffs still must be imported.

GLOSSARY

Each of the authors has attempted to use a minimum of foreign and technical terms; by and large, we have preferred to define critical terms where they first appear in the text, and then to use English glosses, or quasi-synonyms. It has been necessary, nevertheless, to introduce a few specialized terms because they are important within the local context. Many such terms are specific to regions; for this reason, each definition is followed by the author's initials, in parentheses, and by the region to which it applies.

afectación	- encumbrance, almost always in the sense of full expropriation (general).
ahijadero	- pastureland to which the patrón has exclusive access (HCB - altiplano).
AID	- U.S. Agency for International Development, "Point Four" (general).
aini	- reciprocal labor (HCB - altiplano, yungas).
alcalde	- 1) second to the jilakata in the hierarchy among colonos. Functions are to make peons work and help the jilakata; Syn.: alcalde de campo (HCB - altiplano); 2) mayor of a town (general).
alcalde de agua	- colono who distributes water in haciendas with irrigation (HCB - altiplano).
alcalde de campo	- see alcalde (1).

alcalde de quezo
- colono charged with cheese-making (HCB - altiplano).

alcalde escolar
- colono who helps the teacher (HCB - altiplano).

aljeria
- hacienda store in the city (HCB - altiplano).

aljiri
- colono who sells hacienda produce in the capital (HCB - altiplano).

anaka
- small hut and enclosure for pasturing sheep on a fallow aynoka (HCB - Province of Aroma, La Paz).

apiri
- colono who brings produce of the hacienda to La Paz, using his own animals (HCB - Province of Los Andes, La Paz).

arrendero
- 1) campesino who rents land, usually paying in labor; cf. colono (HCB - yungas);
2) colono (CJE - valleys).

arrienda
- like sayaña (CJE - valleys).

arrimante
- 1) colono who has recently received land (HCB - altiplano);
2) arrendero of an arrendero (CJE - valleys).

audiencia
- hearing; as used here, the hearing between claimant and proprietor, before an agrarian judge, concerning a land claim (general).

auto de vista
- recommendation; as used here, the review of entire land claim case and recommendation for action, prepared by CNRA (general).

awatiri   - colono who herds sheep and llamas
                             (HCB - altiplano).

aynoka   - large section of land, cultivated in a
                             rotational pattern which includes one
                             or more years of fallowing. Every
                             colono has one or more plots in each
                             of several aynokas (HCB - altiplano).

azul   - literally: "blue," used by putatively
                             "blue-blooded Whites" (CJE -
                             valleys).

blanco   - literally: "White," used as designa-
                             tion of social race.

Bs. - bolivianos   - the monetary unit (during the 1960's
                             the exchange rate has been fairly
                             constant at Bs. 11,000-12,000 per
                             dollar) (general).

camana   - colono who watches over fields and
                             makes fires as defense against hail
                             (HCB - altiplano).

camani   - colono who dries coca (HCB - yungas).

campesino   - 1(peasant; rural-dweller; small-
                             scale farmer (general);
                             2) affectively neutral innovation for
                             "indio" (Indian) which was formerly
                             an epithet (DBH - altiplano, valleys,
                             yungas);
                             3) person of low socio-economic
                             status (DBH - Oriente).

campo   - messenger of the jilakata (HCB -
                             altiplano).

cargo   - periodic office or obligation of
                             limited duration (HCB - altiplano,
                             yungas).

catastro   - sharecropping (CJE - valleys).

CBF   - Corporacion Boliviano de Fomentos
                               (Bolivian Development Corporation),
                               a cabinet-level agency charged with
                               economic development (general).

chuño   - frozen and dried potato (HCB -
                               altiplano).

chuño camana   - colono who prepares chuño (HCB -
                               altiplano).

CNRA   - Consejo Nacional de Reforma Agraria
                               (National Agrarian Reform Council),
                               executive board of SNRA (general).

COB   - Central Obrera Boliviana
                               Labor Central), the federation of all
                               labor unions (general).

cocal   - coca planting (HCB - yungas).

colono   - tenant farmer, or serf on quasi-feudal
                               hacienda (general).

comando   - regional cell of MNR (general).

comunario   - member of a comunidad (HCB -
                               altiplano, yungas; CJE - valleys).

comunidad,   - free community, i.e., group
comunidad indigena   of campesinos with pre-reform
                               corporate title to land (not a commune
                               or cooperative) (general).

consolidación   - consolidation; as used here, confirma-
                               tion by CNRA to the proprietor, of a
                               portion of his land remaining after
                               other portions have been expropriated
                               (general).

demanda   - initial claim (especially for land,
                               under agrarian reform) (general).

diezma   share-herding (CJE - valleys).

estancia	- 1) ranch (DBH - Santa Cruz); 2) area of land 25 kilometers square (DBH - Mojos); 3) outlying hamlet within an hacienda (HCB - altiplano); 4) hacienda above well-watered valley (CJE - valleys).
estrada	- a group of 200 rubber trees, regardless of land-area covered (DBH - Northeast).
expediente	- dossier; as used here, all papers relating to an individual land claim processed through SNRA (general).
haba	- broad bean (HCB - altiplano)
habilitado	- colono who is paid wages (HCB - Province of Nor Yungas, La Paz).
inafectabilidad	- inexpropriability; confirmation, by CNRA to the proprietor, that his land is not subject to expropriation (general).
indio	- Indian (general).
informe	- report; especially the technical report submitted by SNRA topographer concerning data relevant to a land claim (general).
inquilino	- renter (general).
jilakata	- top of the hierarchy of campesino officers; directs work, usually is also a judge, appointed by the patrón or his administrator (HCB - altiplano).
jornal	- daily wage (HCB - yungas; DBH - Oriente).

jornalero   - resident laborer on a finca DBH -
                               Santa Cruz).

kallpa   - individual plot within an aynoka; Syn. :
                               ligua, ligua kallpa. (HCB - altiplano).

kolla   - any inhabitant of the altiplano or
                               valleys (DBH - Oriente).

konuri   - a peon who had land only in the aynokas
                               (HCB - Province of Manko Kapac, La
                               Paz).

ligua, ligua kallpa   - see kallpa (HCB - altiplano).

MAC   - Ministerio de Asuntos Campesinos
                               (Ministry of Rural Affairs) (DBH -
                               general).

mayordomo   - 1) paid foreman (general);
                               2) more rarely, the top of the colono
                               hierarchy of offices (HCB - altiplano,
                               yungas).

media persona   - a person who has less land than a
                               full colono; Syn. : segundo persona
                               (HCB - altiplano).

mediana   - medium-size landholding (as
                               designated by SNRA) (general).

mejoras   - improvements made on land (general).

Mestizo   - culturally and racially hybrid of
                               Indian and European heritage (general).

militante   - a colono who has recently
                               received land; Syn. : arrimante.
                               (HCB - altiplano).

minga   - 1) labor paid either in produce or in
                               money (HCB - altiplano);
                               2) a large labor gang, as used for
                               harvesting coca (HCB - yungas).

minifundium	- a plot too small to be economically feasible for family subsistence farming (general).
MNR	- Movimiento Nacionalista Revolucionario (Nationalist Revolutionary Movement), the incumbent political party from April, 1952 , to November, 1964 (general).
parcela	- plot of land (general).
patrón	- "boss," usually implying a paternalistic relationship with the employee (peon) (general).
peón efectivo	- colono skilled in viticulture and paid wages as well as usufruct privilege (CJE - valleys).
pequeña propiedad	- small landholding (as designated by SNRA) (general).
persona mayor	- colono with maximum usufruct privileges.
PIR	- Partido de la Izquierda Revolucionario (Revolutionary Leftist Party) (general).
pongo	- colono who works as house servant for the landowner (HCB - altiplano, yungas).
POR	- Partido Obrero Revolucionario (Revolutionary Labor Party) (general).
preste	- sponsor of a fiesta (HCB - altiplano, yungas; CJE - valleys).
propiedad agricola	- hacienda classified by the SNRA as predominantly agricultural (HCB - general).
reducción	- Indian reservation (DBH - Oriente).

rescatador   - middle man who buys from producers
                        and sells to wholesalers or retailers
                        (general).

SAI   - Servicio Agricola Interamericano
                        (Interamerican Agricultural Service),
                        a joint U. S. -AID and Bolivian Ministry
                        of Agriculture agency (general).

sayaña   - plot on which colono has usufruct
                        privileges (HCB - altiplano, yungas).

secretario   - secretary; as used here, member of
                        the board of a campesino syndicate
                        (HCB - general).

segunda persona   - a campesino with less land and fewer
                        obligations than a persona mayor
                        (HCB - altiplano, valleys).

sentencia   - sentence, i. e., interim judgment by
                        agrarian judge on the basis of an
                        audiencia, which is binding until the
                        case is reviewed by CNRA (DBH -
                        general).

sindicato   - 1) syndicate; as used here, union or
                        league of campesinos (general);
                        2) directive board governing an
                        ex-hacienda after reform (HCB -
                        altiplano, yungas);
                        3) sometimes, secretary general of
                        such group (general).

SNRA   - Servicio Nacional de Reforma Agraria
                        (National Agrarian Reform Service),
                        the organization charged with
                        administering agrarian reform (DBH -
                        general).

sutta   - similar to jilakata (HCB - yungas).

tercera persona   - a campesino with less land and fewer
                        obligations than a segunda persona
                        (HCB - altiplano, yungas).

tolerado — squatter (HCB - altiplano, yungas).

tunta — potatoes laid in cold water, then frozen and dried (HCB - altiplano).

utawawa — landless person living and working with a colono, usually adopted in childhood (HCB - altiplano, yungas).

yerbajero — share-herder (CJE - valleys).

BIBLIOGRAPHY

Adams, Richard N.

    1962   The community in Latin America: a changing myth. <u>Centenniel Review</u> 6:409-34.

Alba, Victor

    1961   The Latin American style and the new social forces. In A. O. Hirschman (ed.), <u>Latin American Issues: Essays and Comments.</u> New York, Twentieth Century Fund.

Albó, Xavier

    1968   Ucurena en el contexto de la revolución nacional de Bolivia: 1935-1952-1967, (mimeographed).

Alexander, Robert N.

    1958   <u>The Bolivian National Revolution.</u> New Brunswick, Rutgers University Press.

Arguedas, Alcides

    1937   Pueblo enfermo (3rd revised edition). Santiago de Chile, Ercilla.

Arnade, Charles W.

    1957   <u>The Emergence of the Republic of Bolivia.</u> Gainesville, University of Florida Press.

447

————.

1962   The historiography of colonial and
                       modern Bolivia. Hispanic American
                       Historical Review   42:333-84.

Bandelier, Adolphe F.

1910   The Islands of Titicaca and Koati .
                       New York, American Geographical
                       Society.

Bennett, Wendell C. and Junius B. Bird

1960   Andean Culture History (2nd revised
                       edition). Garden City, Natural History
                       Press.

Bergmann, Barbara R.

1966   The Cochabamba-Santa Cruz highway
                       in Bolivia. In G. W. Wilson et al. ,
                       The Impact of Highway Investment on
                       Development. Washington, Brookings
                       Institution.

Blasier, Cole

1967   Studies of social revolution: origins
                       in Mexico, Bolivia, and Cuba. Latin
                       American Research Review 2, 3:28-64.

Bohan, Merwin L.

1937   Commercial and industrial survey of
                       Bolivia. Washington, Department of
                       Commerce, Special Circular 388.

Bolivia, Republica de

1950   Censo agropecuario: 1950. La Paz,
                       Ministerio de Hacienda (mimeographed).

1953   Decreto ley 03464, Reforma agraria
                       en Bolivia.

————.

1954   Economic development of the Republic
               of Bolivia. La Paz, Ministry of Foreign
               Affairs Memorandum 2 (multilithed).

Bowman, Isaiah

1931   The Pioneer Fringe. New York,
               American Geographical Society.

Bresson, André

1886   Bolivia: sept années d'explorations,
               de voyages, et des séjours dans
               l'Amérique australe. Paris,
               Challamel Aîné.

Buechler, Hans C.

1966   Agrarian reform and migration on the
               Bolivian altiplano. Ph. D. dissertation,
               Columbia University.

Burela, J. Benjamín

1912   Contribución al estudio de la etnografía
               boliviana: distribución geográfica de
               los indígenas actuales del Departamento
               de Santa Cruz. Actas del 17e Congreso
               Internacional de Americanistas: 447-58.

Burges, Franfois

1781   État des missions des pères jésuites
               de la province du Paraguay, parmi
               les Indiens de l'Amérique méridionale...
               Lettres edifiantes et curieuses écrites
               par les missionaires de la compagnie
               de Jésus 8:337-73.

Carballo, Manuel

1963   Agrarian reform in Bolivia.   A. B. thesis,
                       Princeton University.

Cardozo, Armando

1962   Contribución al conocimiento de la
                       bibliografía de la reforma agraria en
                       Bolivia.   La Paz, Sociedad de Ingenieros
                       Agrónomos de Bolivia, Boletín Biblio-
                       gráfico No. 1.

Cardús, José

1886   Las misiones franciscanas entre los
                       infieles de Bolivia.   Barcelona,
                       Libería de la Inmaculada Concepción.

Carroll, Thomas F.

1965   Land Tenure and Land Reform in Latin
                       America: A Selective Annotated
                       Bibliography (2nd revised edition).
                       Washington, Inter-American Develop-
                       ment Bank.

Carter, William C.

1963   The ambiguity of reform: highland
                       Bolivian peasants and their land.
                       Ph. D. dissertation, Columbia Uni-
                       versity.

1965   Aymara communities and agrarian
                       reform in Bolivia.   Gainesville,
                       University of Florida Monograph in
                       Social Science 24.

Consejo Nacional de Reforma Agraria (de Bolivia)

1954   Circular 16.

1963   Informe de labores del 10 de julio de
                       1951 /sic/ al 30 de junio de 1962.

Crossley, J. Colin

1961   Santa Cruz at the crossroads: a study
                        of development in eastern Bolivia.
                        Tijdschrift voor Economische en
                        Sociale Geografie 52:197-206, 230-41.

Dandler-Hanhart, Jorge

1967   Local group, community, and nation:
                        a study of changing structure in
                        Ucureña, Bolivia (1935-52).
                        M. A. thesis, University of Wisconsin.

Debray, Régis

1967   Revolution in the Revolution? New York,
                        Monthly Review Press.

del Castillo Avendaño, Walter

1955   Compilación legal de la reforma
                        agraria en Bolivia. La Paz, Editorial
                        Fénix.

Denevan, William N.

1963   Cattle ranching in the Mojos savannas
                        of northeastern Bolivia. American
                        Association of Pacific Coast Geographers
                        Yearbook 25:37-44.

1966   The aboriginal cultural geography of the
                        Llanos de Mojos of Bolivia.
                        Ibero-Americana 48.

Erasmus, Charles J.

1961   Man Takes Control: Cultural Develop-
                        ment and American Aid. Minneapolis,
                        University of Minnesota Press.

Ferragut, Casto

    1961   Principales características de las
                                 colonias agrícolas de Bolivia y
                                 surgerencias para una política de
                                 colonización. La Paz, F.A.O.
                                 (mimeographed).

    1963   La reforma agraria boliviana: Sus
                                 antecedentes, fundamentos, aplicación
                                 y resultados. Revista Interamericana
                                 de Ciencias Sociales 2, 1:78-151.

Flores, Edmundo

    1954   Land reform in Bolivia. Land Economics
                                 30:112-24.

    1961   Tratado de economía agrícola. Mexico,
                                 Fondo de Cultura Económica.

Ford, Thomas R.

    1962   Man and Land in Peru. Gainesville,
                                 University of Florida Press.

Foreign Operations Administration (of U. S. A.)

    1954   Report of the Santa Cruz Area Develop-
                                 ment Mission. Washington, Foreign
                                 Operations Administration.

Foster, George M.

    1962   Traditional Cultures: and the Impact
                                 of Technological Change. New York
                                 and Evanston, Harper and Row.

Gandía, Enrique de

    1935   Historia de Santa Cruz de la Sierra:
                                 una nueva república en Sud América.
                                 Buenos Aires, L. J. Rosso.

Gillin, John

1955   Ethos components in modern Latin
                        American culture. American
                        Anthropologist 57:488-500.

Goldschmidt, Walter

1950   Social class in America--a critical
                        review. American Anthropologist
                        52:483-98.

Guevara, Che

1961   Guerrilla Warfare. New York,
                        Monthly Review Press.

Hallowell, A. I.

1943   The nature and function of property as
                        a social institution. Journal of Legal
                        and Political Sociology 1:115-38.

Heath, Dwight B.

1958   Drinking patterns of the Bolivian
                        Camba. Quarterly Journal of Studies
                        on Alcohol 19:491-508.

1959a   Land reform in Bolivia. Inter-American
                        Economic Affairs 12, 4:3-27.

1959b   Commercial agriculture and land reform
                        in the Bolivian Oriente. Inter-American
                        Economic Affairs 13, 2:35-45.

1959c   Boribia no nochi kaikaku. Kokusai
                        Shokuryo Nogyo Kyokai 8, 11.

1959d   Camba: a study of land and society in
                        eastern Bolivia. Ph.D. dissertation,
                        Yale University.

_____.

1960a   Land tenure and social organization:
               an ethnohistorical study from the
               Bolivian Oriente. Inter-American
               Economic Affairs 13, 4:46-66.

1960b   Boribia no Oriente chiho no tochi
               kaikaku to shogyoteki-nogyo. Kokusai
               Shokuryo Nogyo Kyokai 9, 8.

1961a   Agricultura comercial y reforma agraria
               en el Oriente boliviano. Revista de la
               Universidad Autónoma "Gabriel René
               Moreno" 8, 16:94-102.

1961b   Los Cambas: un pueblo emergente.
               In Antonio Velasco F. (ed.), Album
               conmemorativo del IV Centenario de
               Santa Cruz de la Sierra. Buenos
               Aires, Talleres Gráficos Lúmen.

1963   Successes and shortcomings of agrarian
               reform in Bolivia. Land Tenure Center
               Discussion Paper 2:16-23.

1964a   Ethnogenesis and ethnohistory:
               sociocultural emergence in the Bolivian
               Oriente. Actas y Memorias del
               XXXV Congreso Internacional de
               Americanistas 2:149-53.

1964b   Reforma agraria en Bolivia. Revista
               del Instituto de Sociología Boliviana
               21, 6:192-214.

1965a   Kamba: ethnograficheskiy finomin
               Bolivii. Nauka i Zhizn 9:124-28.

1965b   Profiles of acculturation. Rocky
               Mountain Review 2:29-33.

1965c   Revolution and stability in Bolivia.
               Current History 49, 292:328ff.

_____.

1965d   Comments on David Mandelbaum's
                 "Alcohol and culture." Current
                 Anthropology 6:289-90.

1966a   Comentarios a William Mangin.
                 In Las comunidades alteñas en
                 América Latina, Instituto Indigenista
                 Interamericano Serie Antropología
                 Social 5.

1966b   The sequence of culture history in the
                 Bolivian Oriente. Revista de Historia
                 de América (in press).

1966c   La sucesión de la historia de la cultura
                 en el Oriente de Bolivia. Suplemento
                 Antropológico de la Revista del Ateneo
                 Paraguayo 2, 1:161-66.

1966d   A preliminary bibliography on land
                 tenure in Bolivia. Boletin Bibliográfico
                 de Antropología Americana 26-28,
                 1:77-88.

1966e   The Aymara Indians and Bolivia's
                 revolutions. Inter-American Economic
                 Affairs 19, 4:31-40.

1967   Bolivia under Barrientos. Current
                 History 53, 315:275ff.

Holmberg, Allan R.

1950   Nomads of the long bow: the Siriono
                 of eastern Bolivia. Smithsonian
                 Institution, Institute of Social
                 Anthropology Publication 10.

Irmay, Hernando de

1956   Bosques de la Quebrada Espejos.
                 Appended to Servicio Boliviano
                 Forestal y de Caza Boletín Forestal 2.

Kelly, Isabel

 1959   La antropología, la cultura y la salud
                        pública. La Paz, United States
                        Operations Mission to Bolivia,
                        Institute of Inter-American Affairs
                        (mimeographed).

Kirkpatrick, F. A.

 1939   Repartimiento-encomienda. Hispanic
                        American Historical Review 19:372-79.

 1942   The landless encomienda. Hispanic
                        American Historical Review 22:765-74.

Land Tenure Center

 1963   The progress of land reform in Bolivia.
                        Madison, Land Tenure Center,
                        Discussion Paper 2.

 1964   Frontier settlement of Japanese from
                        overseas, /and/ Indians from the
                        highlands. 16mm. color/sound film.

León Pinelos, Antonio de

 1650   El Paraíso en el Nuevo Mundo (2 volumes).
                        R. Porras P. (ed.), (1943), Lima,
                        Comité del 4 Centenario del Descubri-
                        miento del Amazonas.

Leonard, Olen E.

 1948   Santa Cruz: a socio-economic study of
                        an area in Bolivia. Washington,
                        U. S. Department of Agriculture
                        Foreign Agricultural Report 31.

 1952   Bolivia: Land, People, and Institutions.
                        Washington, Scarecrow Press.

————.

1966   El cambio económico y social en cuatro
                comunidades del altiplano de Bolivia.
                Mexico, Instituto Indigenista Inter-
                americano, Serie: Antropología Social 3.

Leons, M. Barbara

1966   Changing patterns of stratification in
                an emergent Bolivian community.
                Ph. D. dissertation, University of
                California, Los Angeles.

Lockwood, Agnese N.

1956   Indians of the Andes. International
                Conciliation 508:353-431.

Marsh, Margaret A.

1928   The Bankers in Bolivia: Studies in
                American Imperialism. New York,
                Vanguard Press.

Marshall, C. E.

1939   The birth of the Mestizo in New Spain.
                Hispanic American Historical Review
                19:161-84.

Means, Philip A.

1917   A note on the Guaraní invasions of
                the Inca Empire. Geographical
                Review 4:482-84.

Métraux, Alfred

1930   Études sur la civilisation des Indiens
                Chiriguano. Revista del Instituto de
                Etnología de la Universidad Nacional
                de Tucumán 1:295-495.

————.

1942   The native tribes of eastern Bolivia
                and the western Matto Grosso.
                Washington, Bureau of American
                Ethnology Bulletin 134.

1948   Tribes of eastern Bolivia and the
                Madeira headwaters. In Steward,
                1948: 381-454.

Misión Británica (en Bolivia)

1962   La agricultura tropical en Bolivia.
                La Paz, Ministerio de Economía
                (mimeographed).

Monheim, Felix

1965   Junge Indianerkolonisation in den
                Tiefländern Ostboliviens. Braun-
                schweig, Georg Westermann.

Monje Rada, José

1963   Estudio de costos de colonización.
                La Paz, United States Aid Mission to
                Bolivia (mimeographed).

Moore, Sally F.

1958   Power and Property in Inca Peru.
                New York, Columbia University Press.

Morales, Juan

1929   Monografía de las Provincias of Nor
                y Sud Yungas (Departamento de La
                Paz) Bolivia. La Paz, Imprenta
                Artística.

Mujía, Ricardo

1914   Bolivia-Paraguay: Anexos 1, Época
                colonial. La Paz, El Tiempo.

New York Times, The

           New York, daily newspaper.

Orbigny, Alcides d'

   1835-47   Voyage dans l'Amérique Méridionale
           (18 volumes). Strasbourg, Ve. Levrault.

Osborne, Harold

   1964   Bolivia: A Land Divided (3rd revised
           edition). London, Royal Institute of
           International Affairs.

Ostría G., Alberto

   1958   The Tragedy of Bolivia: A People
           Crucified. New York, Devon-Adair.

Ots Capdequi, J. M.

   1959   España en América: el régimen de
           tierras en la época colonial. Mexico,
           Fondo de Cultura Económica.

País, El

           Cochabamba, daily newspaper.

Patch, Richard W.

   1956   Social implications of the Bolivian
           agrarian reform. Ph.D. dissertation,
           Cornell University.

   1960   Bolivia: United States assistance in a
           revolutionary setting. In R. Adams
           et al., Social Change in Latin America
           Today. New York, Harper and Brothers.

_____.   John S. Marus, and José Monje Rada

1962   Estudios de colonización en Bolivia
                                  (2 volumes).   La Paz   /U.S. Agency
                                  for International Development/
                                  (mimeographed).

Paz Estenssoro, Victor and Walter Guevara Arze

1944   Proyecto de reformas constitucionales
                                  del régimen agrario y campesino. In
                                  A. Sanjines G. , La reforma agraria
                                  en Bolivia (2nd revised edition. La
                                  Paz, Universo (1945).

Prensa, La

                                  Sucre, daily newspaper.

Rattray, R. S.

    1929   Ashanti Law and Constitution.   London,
                                  Oxford University Press.

Renne, Ronald R.

    1947   Land Economics.   New York, Harper
                                  and Brothers.

Revista Jurídica

    1953   La reforma agraria en Bolivia.
                                  Edición especial, 17, 63-66.

Saavedra, Carlos

    1946   El problema integral del indio.   La
                                  Paz /privately printed/.

Sanabria-Fernandez, Hernando

1949   Los Chanés: apuntes para el estudio de
                       una incipiente cultura aborígen prehispánica
                       en el oriente boliviano. Boletín de la
                       Sociedad de Geografía y Historia, Santa
                       Cruz 29-30.

1958   En busca de Eldorado: la colonización
                       del oriente boliviano por los Cruceños.
                       Santa Cruz, Publications de la
                       Universidad "Gabriel René Moreno."

Sanjines G., Alfredo

1945   La reforma agraria en Bolivia (2nd
                       edition). La Paz, Universo.

Sariola, Sakari

1960   A colonization experiment in Bolivia.
                       Rural Sociology 25:76-90.

Simmons, Ozzie

1955   The criollo outlook in the Mestizo
                       culture of coastal Peru. American
                       Anthropologist 57:107-17.

Social Science Research Council, Summer Seminar on
Acculturation

1954   Acculturation: an exploratory formula-
                       tion. American Anthropologist 56:973-
                       1002.

Special Operations Research Office

1963   U.S. Army Area Handbook for Bolivia.
                       Washington, Special Operations
                       Research Office.

Spicer, Edward H. (ed.)

1961   Perspectives in American Indian
                         Culture Change. Chicago, University
                         of Chicago Press.

Steward, Julian H. (ed.)

1946   Handbook of South American Indians 1.
                         Washington, Bureau of American
                         Ethnology Bulletin 143.

1948   Handbook of South American Indians 3.
                         Washington, Bureau of American
                         Ethnology Bulletin 143.

Tambs, Lewis A.

1966   Rubber, rebels, and the Río Branco:
                         the contest for the Acre. Hispanic
                         American Historical Review 46:254-73.

Téllez D. , Diego

n. d.   Relación a S. M. , Quoted in Blas
                         Garay (ed.), Colección de documentos
                         relativos a la historia de América.
                         Asunción /privately printed/ (1899-
                         1901).

Thompson, Stephen I.

1968   San Juan Yapacaní: a Japanese colony
                         in eastern Bolivia. Ph. D. dissertation,
                         University of Illinois.

Tigner, James L.

1963   The Ryukyuans in Bolivia. Hispanic
                         American Historical Review 43:206-29.

Tormo, Leandro

1966   El sistema comunalista indiano en la
        región comunera de Mojos-Chiquitos.
        Comunidades 1:96-140, 2:89-117.

Torrico Arze, Armando M.

1956   The colonization of tropical Bolivia.
        A.B. thesis, Wadham College, Oxford.

United Nations, Technical Assistance Administration

1951   Report of the United Nations Mission
        of Technical Assistance to Bolivia.
        New York, United Nations.

United States Senate

1960   Administration of United States foreign
        aid programs in Bolivia. 86th Congress,
        2nd Session, Report 1030.

Viedma, Franciso de

/1787/   Descripción de la Provincia de Santa
        Cruz de la Sierra. In Pedro de Ángelis
        (ed.), Colección de obras y documentos
        relativos a la historia antigua y moderna
        de las Provincias del Río de La Plata,
        3. Buenos Aires, Imprenta del Estado
        (1836-37).

Walinsky, Louis J.

1963   Economic and Policy Implications of
        Bolivia's Ten-Year Plan. La Paz,
        USAID-Bolivia.

Webster's Third New International Dictionary of the
English Language

1961   Springfield, Mass., G and C. Merriam.

Weeks, David

    1947a   European antecedents of land tenure and
                    agrarian organization of Hispanic America.
                    Journal of Land and Public Utility Economics
                    13:60-75.

    1947b   Land tenure and agrarian organization in
                    the Spanish colonies of America. Journal
                    of Land and Public Utility Economics
                    13:153-68.

Wolf, Eric R.

    1955   Types of Latin American peasantry: a
                    preliminary discussion. American
                    Anthropologist 57:452-71.

    1957   Closed corporate peasant communities
                    in Mesoamerica and Central Java.
                    Southwestern Journal of Anthropology
                    13:1-18.

    1959   Sons of the Shaking Earth. Chicago,
                    University of Chicago Press.

    1966   Peasants. Englewood Cliffs, Prentice-
                    Hall.

Zondag, Cornelius H.

    1966   The Bolivian Economy, 1962-1965.
                    New York, Frederick A. Praeger.

ABOUT THE AUTHORS

Dwight B. Heath is Associate Professor of Anthropology at Brown University. He has done extensive ethnographic field work among tribal and peasant peoples in Bolivia, Costa Rica, Guatemala, Mexico, and the southwestern United States. He has published widely on contemporary social and economic aspects of Bolivia, as well as on alcoholism, the history of the Pilgrims, and a variety of other subjects. He holds a Ph. D. degree from Yale University.

Charles J. Erasmus is Professor of Anthropology at the University of California, Santa Barbara. He was awarded a Ph. D. from the University of California at Berkeley and has done extensive ethnographic field work in Chile, Bolivia, Colombia, Ecuador, Haiti, Mexico, and Venezuela, and has published widely on several aspects of theoretical and applied anthropology, with special attention to cultural change.

Hans C. Buechler is Assistant Professor of Anthropology at the Université de Montreal. During his graduate study at the Sorbonne and Columbia University (where he earned his Ph. D.), he conducted a variety of ethnographic research projects in his native Bolivia and in Ecuador.